THE ORTHODOX CHURCH IN UKRAINE

The ORTHODOX CHURCH *in* UKRAINE

A CENTURY OF SEPARATION

NICHOLAS E. DENYSENKO

NIU Press / DeKalb, IL

978-0-87580-789-8 (paper)
978-1-60909-244-3 (e-book)

Book and cover design by Yuni Dorr

Excerpts from the Tymofii Minenko archive at the University of Alberta in Edmonton
used with permission.
Excerpts from Мартирологія Українських Церков, vol. 1: Українська Православна
Церква [Martyrology of the Ukrainian Churches, vol. 1: The Ukrainian Orthodox
Church], edited by Osyp Zinkewich and Oleksander Voronyn (Baltimore, MD:
Smoloskyp Publishers, 1987), used with permission.
Excerpts from documents gathered by Mr. Yaroslaw Lozowchuk used with permission.

Library of Congress Cataloging-in-Publication Data is available online at
http://catalog.loc.gov

Dedicated to the memory of my grandparents,

PROTOPRESBYTER NICHOLAS METULYNSKY (2011)

and

MATUSHKA MARGARITA METULYNSKY (2015)

Вічна їм пам'ять!

Contents

Illustrations

Acknowledgments

When I was an eighteen-year-old freshman at the University of Minnesota in 1990–1991, the world around me was changing. For the entirety of my young life, the possibility that the Soviet Union might collapse and that independent nations would emerge from the imperial wreckage amounted to a "fool's hope." By the end of 1991, it was hard for me to believe that Ukraine was independent. As a child, I attended the Ukrainian Orthodox parishes of my family, and our parish was always the one shepherded by my grandfather, the archpriest (and later protopresbyter) Nicholas Metulynsky. It was upon enrolling at the university and joining the Orthodox Christian Fellowship that I discovered that we were "uncanonical" and "self-consecrated" as adherents of the Ukrainian Autocephalous Orthodox Church. The passions of youth prevented me from reflecting patiently on my encounters with my Orthodox Christian peers, so I took my frustrations to my grandfather. The next several years constituted a domestic crash course in the history of the Orthodox Church in Ukraine. I would visit my grandparents' home and immerse myself in his fascinating library of books and periodicals, trying to understand the perspective of my fellow Orthodox.

The experiences of my youth functioned as an introduction to a world that is even more complex than I had imagined it to be. My musical skills brought me to non-Ukrainian Orthodox parishes where I learned the unique histories of other traditions. Inspired by the legacy of Alexander Schmemann, I pledged myself to the cause of establishing an authentically local Orthodox Church in America, rooted in mission, by joining the Orthodox Church in America and attending its renowned St. Vladimir's Seminary. Eventually, I immersed myself in liturgical studies, and have been blessed to land my first appointment, and tenure, at Loyola Marymount University in Los Angeles. My path continues to be blessed, as I begin a new chapter as Jochum Professor and chair at Valparaiso University in Indiana.

As I continued my work in liturgical studies, I never forgot my crash course in Ukrainian church history. I exchanged hundreds of e-mails on the chaotic church situation in Ukraine, and discovered that many of my peers had no knowledge of the Church in Ukraine. I wrote a handful of articles and essays in an attempt to explain the intra-Orthodox tensions in Ukraine for English-speakers These initial presentations evolved into a series of conference papers, and before I knew it, I already had collected much of the material needed for this book. My objective is the same as it was originally: to explain the situation of the Orthodox Church in Ukraine as clearly as possible. The primary purpose of the book is to illustrate how aspirations for autocephaly and church renewal caused the Orthodox Church in Ukraine to splinter over the span of one hundred years. The features and objectives of autocephaly developed a stigma of ecclesial illegitimacy, and the inability of church leaders to shed this stigma has deepened the divisions and sharpened intrachurch polemics. I hope I have achieved this objective with this book: let the reader decide.

Every study is the result of dialogue with others, and dozens of people have helped me think through the issues featured in this book. Amy Farranto has been a patient and devoted editor, gently guiding me through the publication process and encouraging me to make the changes needed to improve the text and its arguments. I'm very grateful to Amy for her devotion to publishing this book! Sincere thanks to Dr. Antoine Arjakovsky, Dr. Paul Gavrilyuk, Dr. Roy Robson, and Dr. Christine Worobec, who read multiple drafts and provided me with the critical insight needed to strengthen the manuscript and clarify its arguments. I extend my thanks to numerous people who have engaged me in discussion, especially Dr. Michael Andrec, Nataliya Bezborodova, George Demacopoulos, Fr. Andrii Dudchenko, Daniel Galadza, Fr. Peter Galadza, Brandon Gallaher, Jacob Grekhovetsky, Fr. Dellas Oliver Herbel, Archimandrite Cyril Hovorun, Fr. Paul Koroluk, Fr. Heorhii Kovalenko, Yaroslav Lozowchuk, Petro Melnyk, Aristotle Papanikolaou, Fr. Michael Plekon, Dr. Constantine Sigov, Frank Sysyn, Halyna Teslyuk, and Fr. Roman Zaviyskyy. I have received encouragement from bishops of the churches who have answered questions and provided me with guidance on sources. Special thanks to Metropolitan Oleksandr (Drabinko) of the UOC-MP, who ensured that I received posthumously published works of the ever-memorable Metropolitan Volodymyr (Sabodan), and Archbishop Yevstratiy (Zoria) of the UOC-KP, who answered my questions patiently. Metropolitan Yurii (Kalishchuk) of the UOCC, and Metropolitan Antony (Scharba) and Archbishop Daniel (Zelinsky) of the UOC-USA have also supported my efforts. Ms. Larissa Bulya of the UOC-USA library in South Bound Brook, New Jersey, sent me several hand-picked issues of the *Ukrainian Orthodox Word* for two projects.

This book would have been impossible without the gracious assistance of the Canadian Institute of Ukrainian Studies at the University of Alberta in Edmonton. I made two trips to Edmonton, one to deliver the Bohdan Bociurkiw memorial lecture in February 2015, and the other to immerse myself in the Tymofii Minenko archives and the Bohdan Bociurkiw Memorial Library. My second trip was made possible by the Anna and Nikander Bukowsky research grant I received from the Canadian Institute of Ukrainian Studies. Dr. Volodymyr Kravchenko and Ms. Iryna Fedoriw were terrific hosts, and Mr. James Franks made research in the archive a pleasant experience. I am especially grateful to Dr. Heather Coleman for numerous engaging discussions about Ukrainian and Russian history, and for her friendship.

In closing, I return to the beginning, the intense discussions about the Ukrainian Orthodox Church that occurred in my youth. As a young adult, I was entranced by the beautiful music of Kyrylo Stetsenko, priest and musician of the 1921 UAOC (1882–1922). His niece, Mrs. Kira Tsarehradsky, carried on the Ukrainian musical heritage in the Twin Cities area with skill and grace, and she shared many stories of family reminiscences of the UAOC with me, for which I am very grateful. Thanks to my parents, Eugene (d. 2005) and Olga (d. 2017), who encouraged us to learn about our heritage. My brother Greg and I learned more from our grandparents, Fr. Nicholas and Matushka Margarita, than we could have learned from books, so I dedicate this work to them. In 2016, my wife Tresja and daughter Sophia traveled to Kyiv and L'viv with me. They tolerated my passion and wonder with the unconditional love of family, and I thank them.

Abbreviations and Conventions

I am employing abbreviations and conventions in this book to assist the reader in making distinctions between church movements and their periodization. The following short glossary briefly defines each convention.

EP   Ecumenical Patriarchate

KP   Kyivan Patriarchate

MP   Moscow Patriarchate

PV   *Православний вісник* [Pravoslavnyi visnyk (Orthodox herald)], periodical of the Orthodox Church in Ukraine under the jurisdiction of Moscow

UAOC   Ukrainian Autocephalous Orthodox Church

UGCC   Ukrainian Greek-Catholic Church

UOC-USA   Ukrainian Orthodox Church of the USA (returned to communion with the Ecumenical Patriarchate in 1995)

UOW   *Ukrainian Orthodox Word* (periodical of the Ukrainian Orthodox Church in the USA)

ZMP   *Журнал Московской Патриархии* [Zhurnal Moskovskoi Patriarkhii (Journal of the Moscow Patriarchate)], periodical of the Russian Orthodox Church

AUOCC. All-Ukrainian Orthodox Church Council. The AUOCC was created by the Kyiv eparchy in 1917 to prepare for the All-Ukrainian Church Council scheduled for 1918. The council consisted primarily of Church progressives who favored ecclesial autocephaly for the Church in Ukraine. The AUOCC was briefly disbanded in 1918 after the Kyivan eparchial assembly elected Antony Khrapovitsky as metropolitan of Kyiv and the Church in Ukraine began to prepare for the second session of the All-Ukrainian Council. The AUOCC reassembled in 1919 and aggressively pursued a program of Ukrainization within the Church in Ukraine, working with the local Soviet authorities to acquire permission to use temples for Ukrainian-language liturgical services. The AUOCC came into open conflict with the bishops of the Moscow Patriarchate in Ukraine and became the primary group seeking the creation of a Ukrainian Church

liberated from Russian control and completely independent. The AUOCC's efforts resulted in the creation and promulgation of the Ukrainian Autocephalous Orthodox
Church in 1921. The AUOCC was the chief administrative organ of the 1921 UAOC
until its liquidation by the Soviet state in 1930.

1921 UAOC. Refers to the Ukrainian Autocephalous Orthodox Church established in
October 1921. The 1921 UAOC came into being in October 1921 when a council consisting of laity and clergy, most of whom were suspended or deposed, gathered and created their own episcopate by an innovative conciliar rite of ordination. No bishops participated in the council. The 1921 UAOC fiercely promoted liberation from the Moscow
Patriarchate, Ukrainization of all aspects of church life, democratic and egalitarian principles of governance within the church, and the promotion of innovative canons that
permitted bishops to be married. The 1921 UAOC grew rather rapidly until the Soviet
state began to persecute it in 1926–1927; no Orthodox church in the world recognized
the 1921 UAOC as legitimate. Several pejorative terms caricatured the 1921 UAOC, including uncanonical, *samosviati* (self-consecrated), *bezblahodatni* (without grace), and
Lypkivtsi (disciples of Vasyl Lypkivs'kyi, the charismatic leader of the UAOC from 1921
to 1927). An extraordinary council assembled in 1930 to proclaim the self-liquidation
of the 1921 UAOC; this council was orchestrated by the Soviet authorities.

1942 UAOC. Often referred to as the second rebirth of the Ukrainian Autocephalous
Orthodox Church, the 1942 UAOC was created in German-occupied Ukraine in 1942
when the head of the Orthodox Church in Poland, Metropolitan Dionysii (Valedynsky),
appointed Archbishop Policarp (Sikorsky) as the temporary administrator of the
Autocephalous Church in Ukraine in late 1941. The 1942 the UAOC attained autocephaly when several bishops were consecrated to form an episcopate in February of
that year. The church was de facto autocephalous, although its bishops officially designated Metropolitan Dionysii as their head. The 1942 UAOC was essentially a new
church in Ukraine because they disavowed the canons and ecclesiology of the 1921
UAOC while retaining the first church's program of Ukrainization and opposition to
the Moscow Patriarchate. The 1942 UAOC rejected the pledge of loyalty made to the
Soviet Union by Moscow metropolitan Sergei (Stragorodsky) in 1927, and maintained
a consistent anti-Soviet, anti-Bolshevik platform. The bishops of the 1942 UAOC welcomed the Germans as liberators when they defeated the Soviets in 1941; this stance put
the bishops of the 1942 UAOC (along with many other bishops in Ukraine and Russia)
at odds with the leaders of the Moscow Patriarchate, who were nominally loyal to the
Soviet state. The 1942 UAOC came into conflict with a cohort of bishops that reverted to the autonomous canonical status of the Church in Ukraine under the Moscow
Patriarchate in 1941. This church became known as the Autonomous Church, and they
favored the use of Church Slavonic in the liturgy. The conflict between the 1942 UAOC
and the Autonomous Church became permanent when the 1942 UAOC received surviving clergy of the 1921 UAOC through a special rite of reception as opposed to a new

ordination. The bishops of the 1942 UAOC left Ukraine and immigrated to Western Europe and North America beginning in 1945, following World War II.

1989 UAOC. Also known as the third rebirth of the Ukrainian Autocephalous Orthodox Church, the 1989 UAOC came into existence when parishes in L'viv and other cities in Western Ukraine defected from the Moscow Patriarchate to reconstitute the UAOC. The 1989 UAOC kept the primary principles of the 1942 UAOC, but in a new development, assigned itself patriarchal status. In June 1990, the 1989 UAOC elected Metropolitan Mstyslav (Skrypnyk) as its patriarch, strengthening its connection to the 1942 UAOC, as Mstyslav was one of the bishops ordained to the episcopate in German-occupied Ukraine. In June 1992, the UAOC held a council at which a merger was announced with the Ukrainian Orthodox Church under the leadership of Metropolitan Filaret (Denysenko). At this time, the united churches changed the official name to Ukrainian Orthodox Church-Kyivan Patriarchate. In reality, three churches resulted from the merger, as a minority of bishops and parishes, including Patriarch Mstyslav, rejected the council and the merger, and remained within the UAOC. Furthermore, the vast majority of the bishops and parishes of the Ukrainian Orthodox Church under Moscow rejected the merger and remained under the leadership of Metropolitan Volodymyr (Sabodan), who was elected in a controversial bishops' council held in Kharkiv in May 1992. For the purposes of this study, the 1989 UAOC refers to the church that existed up until the June 1992 council in Kyiv. After the June council, I refer to three distinct churches: UAOC (the small minority that rejected the June council), the UOC-KP (the church emerging from the council members who accepted its resolutions), and the UOC-MP (the church remaining under the jurisdiction of the Moscow Patriarchate). KP and UOC-KP are equivalent. UGCC refers to the Ukrainian Greek-Catholic Church, the large Byzantine-rite church that claims to be the legitimate heir of the Kyivan Metropolia, asserts patriarchal status, and that restored communion with the Roman Catholic Church at the Union of Brest in 1596. Most of the Orthodox laity rejected the union, and the patriarchate of Jerusalem restored the Orthodox hierarchy of the Kyivan Metropolia in 1620. The UGCC was coerced by Soviet officials to return to the Orthodox Church at a council in L'viv in 1946. The UGCC returned to Ukraine in 1989 and has often come into conflict with Orthodox churches, especially the Moscow Patriarchate.

EP. The book often refers to the EP, or Ecumenical Patriarchate: this is the ancient church of Constantinople, which is considered to be the "first among equals" within the family of Orthodox churches.

MP. Moscow Patriarchate.

Sobornopravnist'. Refers to the notion of church government by council. Similar to *sobornost'* in nomenclature, *sobornopravnist'* was actually democratic and egalitarian. The 1921 UAOC implemented *sobornopravnist'* as the governing principle for the church, a system that significantly reduced the authority of synods and bishops within the church.

Ukrainians debated the proper place of *sobornopravnist'* within the life of the church throughout the twentieth century.

UAA Accession No. 2011–27. This accession number refers to specific materials taken from the Tymofii Minenko Collection at the archives of the University of Alberta Library in Edmonton. "2011–27" is the official accession number for this collection. As I cite sources from the collection throughout the study, I am using the following convention: 2011-27-Box #-File #, so the third number refers to the box and the fourth number refers to the file within the box.

Lozowchuk Archive. Refers to materials collected by Mr. Yaroslaw Lozowchuk via his extensive contacts with Orthodox leaders in Ukraine. I am deeply indebted to Mr. Lozowchuk for granting me permission to use the sources he provided.

THE ORTHODOX CHURCH IN UKRAINE

Introduction

LIKE ITS NEIGHBORS IN CENTRAL Europe, Ukraine is a country of religious pluralism. Greek Catholics, Roman Catholics, Protestants, Jews, Muslims, and other churches and religious organizations have historical roots in Ukraine and remain active in the present day. Most Ukrainians identify themselves as Orthodox Christians, and among Ukraine's Orthodox Churches a state of confusion prevails.[1] The Orthodox Church is the dominant religious organization in Ukraine, as it is in other East Slavic nations such as Russia, Belarus, Bulgaria, and Serbia. However, unlike the Orthodox populations in most of these other countries, Ukraine has three Orthodox churches that claim to be the legitimate heirs of the medieval Kyivan see (or metropolia), a church born from the legendary baptism of Kyiv by Grand Prince Volodymyr in 988. Today's three Orthodox churches in Ukraine do not coexist peacefully. They are stuck in the cycle of an intrachurch polemical war, and each church appeals to political and ecclesial entities in and outside of Ukraine for endorsement of its legitimacy.

Within the global Orthodox church community, there is a dominant narrative referring to an episode in the early 1990s that catalyzed the disruption of church unity and led to Orthodox plurality in Ukraine. According to this version of events, Metropolitan Filaret (Denysenko), who presided over the Orthodox Church in Ukraine from 1966 to 1992, fomented schism in the Kyivan Church when he voluntarily left the Moscow Patriarchate (MP) and merged with most of the Ukrainian Autocephalous Orthodox Church (UAOC) to form the Kyivan Patriarchate (KP) in June of 1992. This prevailing narrative asserts that Filaret was angered by the lack of support for Ukrainian autocephaly in Moscow and among a few of the bishops on the Kyivan Church's synod. At the Bishops'Council of the Russian Orthodox Church held in March–April 1992, he was asked to submit his resignation, and agreed to do so, but then he rescinded and led those who followed him into schism. Filaret, for his part, claims that his promise to resign was extracted under pressure and that he acted responsibly when he returned to Kyiv to resume his church's move towards autocephaly.

The turmoil among the Orthodox in Ukraine has implications beyond determining the truth between competing versions of events. For the Orthodox people of Ukraine, the current divorce among the Orthodox raises questions about the legitimacy of clerical ordinations, baptisms, and marriages, especially those performed in the Kyivan Patriarchate (KP) and Ukrainian Autocephalous Orthodox Church (UAOC). Orthodox people belonging to these churches may be required to be rebaptized or remarried if they attend a Moscow Patriarchate (MP) parish. The sister Orthodox churches of the world need to know with whom they can pray and worship, and how to receive clerical and lay delegations representing the three churches. The Ecumenical Patriarchate (EP) and the MP disagree on who possesses the authority to adjudicate and mediate the Ukrainian problem, as they both claim to be the mother church of the Kyivan Metropolia. Their dispute compromises the authority of the EP within the global communion of Orthodox churches, as the MP's history of granting autocephaly to churches in the twentieth century places it on an equal footing with the EP. The EP and MP continue to disagree on the mechanism for granting autocephaly to an Orthodox church, an issue related to their divergent interpretations of canon 28 of the Council of Chalcedon (451).[2] The dispute concerns primacy within the Orthodox Church, as the EP refers to canon 28 from the Council of Chalcedon as the authoritative text recognizing the primacy of the EP among the Orthodox Churches, an authority that would grant the EP the right to grant autocephaly to the Church in Ukraine, not the MP.[3] The MP would stand to lose millions of people and thousands of parishes were the Church in Ukraine to become completely and permanently autocephalous. Ukraine has a great deal at stake. After the bloodshed from the wars of the twentieth century and the persecutions of the Soviet regime, Ukraine has struggled to attain stability and internal unity in the post-Soviet period. The Orange Revolution (2004), Maidan crisis (2013), annexation of Crimea (2014), and war in Eastern Ukraine (2014 to the present) are the results of Russian aggression and divisions among the Ukrainian people. The intense disputes among the Orthodox churches in Ukraine constitute a microcosm of the current political crisis, which is why President Petro Poroshenko and Ukraine's parliament have repeatedly appealed to the EP and the Holy and Great Council in Crete to end the church war by granting the Ukrainian Church autocephaly and contributing to the liberation of Ukraine from Russian colonialism.

The Problem: Nationalism, Autocephaly, and Ukrainization

The rationale for Ukrainian autocephaly and its Ukrainianizing agenda are the central issues of dispute among the Orthodox churches in Ukraine. The relationship between national sovereignty and ecclesial autocephaly belongs to modernity, as the movement for church autocephaly coincided with the struggle to establish a Ukrainian republic in the early twentieth century.[4] At the global level, the Orthodox Church has felt the impact of the emergence of the nation-state. In the nineteenth and twentieth centuries, the patriarchate of Constantinople recognized the autocephaly of the churches in Serbia, Greece, Bulgaria, Albania, and Poland. This action of establishing canonical territories in the Orthodox ecclesiological structural system responded to the changes caused by political reconfiguration. In 1872, the Synod of the Church of Constantinople protected the integrity of local churches' ecclesial autocephaly from the heresy of ethnophyletism, in which a local church's identity is exclusively national. The specter of ethnophyletism has hampered the movement for autocephaly in Ukraine for nearly a century as the chief ideologues of the Ukrainian autocephalous movement often had experience in serving as public officers or publicly declared themselves to be patriots. In all the phases of its modern history, aspirations for liberation from the oppressor (tsarist, Soviet, Nazi, and Russian) and the process of nation-building coincided with passionate pleas for ecclesial autocephaly. The national element of the Ukrainian Church movement has perhaps been the greatest obstacle to achieving recognition of ecclesial autocephaly.

Despite the coincidence of nation-building and the movement for autocephaly, the role of nationalism in the movement for Ukrainian Church independence is not easily settled. The rationale for Ukrainian autocephaly followed the modern template of Orthodoxy, which recognized the local church in the modern nation-state, as the larger regional structures corresponding to old imperial borders diminished. Furthermore, the autocephalous movement envisioned the restoration of the Kyivan Church and the return of its native traditions. The precedents established by the recognition of autocephaly of churches in neighboring states would thus apply to the Kyivan Church; it would be natural for this church to be autocephalous in an independent Ukrainian republic. The proposals for autocephaly included petitions for Ukrainization, especially the introduction of vernacular Ukrainian to the liturgy. Ukrainization proved to be the primary symbol of the uneasy relationship between autocephaly and Ukrainian nationalism, as Orthodox leaders and believers viewed it as either a legitimate organic development of Church traditions, or a Trojan horse for the promotion of nationalism.

This study aims to show how the failure of Orthodox Church leaders to reach a consensus on autocephaly and Ukrainization resulted in the splintering of the Church and a pattern of dispute that evolved from 1917 to 2016. I show how the separated churches developed public religious identities that were based primarily on their respective positions on autocephaly, Ukrainization, and the stigma of illegitimacy. One hundred years of polemical exchanges, statements, appeals, letters, and decrees by leaders of the separated Orthodox churches in Ukraine have contributed to the formation of these distinct identities. Each church's public identity is shaped by the definitions articulated by its leaders, and those assigned to it by its opponents. My study also elaborates the development of a series of political theologies within the historical contexts of the churches. These theologies are based on liberation from external aggressors (especially the tsar), the compatibility of *sobornopravnist'* with Western values of democracy, and the *Russkii mir* ideology that sought to restore an idealized image of medieval Rus' on the basis of contemporary Russian nationalism.[5]

Historical Events That Shaped the Movement for Autocephaly and Ukrainization

Shifts in political boundaries, imperial allegiances, and church affiliations necessitated adjustment on the part of Ukrainians in the Kyivan Metropolia and created the conditions for autocephaly and Ukrainization at the dawn of the twentieth century. The first separation occurred when the episcopate of the Kyivan Metropolia ratified the Council of Florence and renewed communion with the Roman Catholic Church at the Union of Brest in 1596.[6] Most of the laity rejected the union, and the Kyivan Metropolia was without an episcopate until Patriarch Theophanes of Jerusalem renewed it in 1620. The metropolia existed in a Polish orbit, and its Westernization resulted in the emergence of educational systems based on the Jesuit model, advocated by the laity and fully established by Metropolitan Petro Mohyla.[7] In the sixteenth and seventeenth centuries, the laity assumed leadership of the Church, an important episode in the history of the metropolia that the ideologues of the twentieth century sought to renew in their dream of the restoration of the Kyivan Metropolia.

The seventeenth and eighteenth centuries required another adjustment on the part of the metropolia, as the Treaty of Pereiaslav in 1654 brought Kyiv and the Church into the Muscovite orbit.[8] The subjugation of the metropolia to the MP in 1686 completed the process of union. Ukrainians exercised considerable influence in the upper echelons of the Russian Church during this period, but there were also episodes of friction between Russians and Ukrainians, especially concerning the legitimacy of Kyivan Church traditions.[9] The friction between peoples also had a political component, as Russian rulers attempted to quell Cossack rebellions, culminating in Ivan Mazepa's alliance with the Swedes against the Russians in 1709. Empress Catherine II established firm control over the Zaporozhian Cossacks by abolishing their status of political autonomy and Russifying their elites.[10] In the mid-nineteenth century Tsar Nicholas I punished the poet Taras

Shevchenko, who dreamed of an independent Ukraine.[11] Decades of Russification followed in the late nineteenth century.

The imperial regime's punishment of Ivan Mazepa in the eighteenth century and Taras Shevchenko in the nineteenth, as well as its Russification policies, transformed the figure of the tsar into an antagonist for Ukrainians in the twentieth century. When the twentieth-century movement for church renewal in the Russian empire introduced models for modernization of church life, such as the creation of conciliar structures strengthening the role of the laity, the creation of lay preachers, and the introduction of vernacular in the liturgy, and the tsarist regime collapsed, adjustments to new political and ecclesial conditions gained speed and resulted in the creation of a republic of Ukraine (June 1917) and eventual independence (January 1918), as well as the splintering of the churches in Ukraine.[12] The convergence of church renewal and political chaos created a perfect storm. In Russia, the Moscow Council of 1917–1918 restored the patriarchate (which had been abolished in the early eighteenth century), but had to defer many of the proposals that would introduce renewal because of a lack of funding and the fierce persecution of the Church by the Bolsheviks. The tsar was not the only public leader whose authority was rejected during the revolution: Orthodox bishops were unable to satisfy everyone who wanted church reform, and this was especially true in Ukraine. Ukraine provided an environment in which an alternative church could arise to challenge the authority of the MP, and a contingent of leaders that formed the All-Ukrainian Orthodox Church Council (AUOCC) could sustain the movement for church renewal that they envisioned would be incarnate in a restored, renewed, and independent Kyivan Metropolia.

Autocephaly and Ukrainization at the Councils of 1918 and 1921

The literary corpus of two formative councils, the first in 1918, the second in 1921, provide the primary sources that inform us about the initial separation of Ukrainians from the MP and their disputes on autocephaly and Ukrainization. The 1918 All-Ukrainian Council was convoked in January 1918 at the request of the Church in Ukraine. The Moscow Council, which was still in session, blessed the convocation of the Ukrainian council, which met in three sessions. Until recently, most of the literature on this council could be found only in memoirs, historical monographs, and in information about the Moscow Council. In 2010, Andryi Starodub published the proceedings of the 1918 All-Ukrainian Council, which included a section that assessed the evidence.[13] As Starodub mentions, the 1918 council was rejected by many Ukrainians, and there were many figures that remained in the patriarchate who viewed it as an inconsequential gathering.

However, the 1918 All-Ukrainian Council is regarded as a canonical gathering and thus has implications for two of the most important features of this study.[14] The council's decisions to seek autonomy within the MP instead of autocephaly, and to reject the liturgical use of vernacular Ukrainian in favor of Church Slavonic became the first primary degree of separation between the Ukrainians and the synod in Ukraine.

The rejection of autocephaly and Ukrainization by the 1918 council catalyzed the initial separation of Orthodox Ukrainians from the Kyivan Metropolia of the MP. For the trajectory of Ukrainian Orthodox history in the twentieth century, the 1918 council was definitive. While the autocephalists rejected its authority, the Ukrainian Orthodox who remained within the Moscow Patriarchate viewed the 1918 council as the most recent ecclesial gathering establishing canonical structures in Ukraine. The 1918 council became pivotal when the Germans liberated Western Ukraine from Soviet rule in 1941, as one cohort of bishops in Volyn' met at the Pochaiv Monastery and returned to the jurisdiction of Moscow in accordance with the resolutions of the 1918 council in Kyiv. Thus, loyalty to Moscow was not based solely on ideological positions, but also on the reception of the most recent councils of the Church.

The 1918 council brings us to the October 1921 council in Kyiv that resulted in the birth of the 1921 UAOC. These conciliar documents include both the proceedings and the conciliar declarations.[15] I engage the conciliar documents and the correspondence between the 1921 UAOC and the MP as the primary sources for presenting the causes of separation within the Orthodox Church in Ukraine and the promotion of the objectives of the autocephalists. I also consult Iryna Prelovs'ka's detailed account of the sources for the history of the Church and memoirs of the council published by the émigré Ukrainian Orthodox community, along with Tetiana Ievsieieva's analysis of Orthodox Church groups during this period.[16]

The first part of this study shows how the 1921 UAOC relentlessly pursued the progressive objectives of the church renewal movement while also seeking the restoration of the Kyivan Metropolia. The establishment of a married episcopate through a renovated rite of episcopal consecration caused the stigma of ecclesial illegitimacy to become a permanent scar on the 1921 UAOC and its sympathizers, as traditional Orthodox who were sympathetic to autocephaly could not accept the UAOC because of its disregard for apostolic succession. All other components of modernization hailed by the UAOC, including Ukrainization and a conciliar-oriented ecclesiology, became attached to the stigma of illegitimacy and established a pattern of suspicion of Ukrainian autocephaly in the following decades. Therefore, the initial period of study establishes the features of public religious identities that formed rapidly during the Nazi occupation of Ukraine. The 1921

UAOC defined its identity through a desire for liberation from the tsar and the bishops loyal to him, its promotion of Ukrainization, and its reception of modernization. The exarchate defined itself by fidelity to canonical norms and traditions, such as the preservation of a monastic episcopate and the official use of Church Slavonic for the liturgy.

Autocephaly, Ukrainization, and Canonicity: World War II

The methods employed for achieving autocephaly and Ukrainization developed differently among Ukrainians who belonged to the Orthodox Church of Poland. I analyze the evolution of autocephalist aspirations and the resilience of the stigma of ecclesial illegitimacy through the second UAOC, which was established in German-occupied Ukraine in 1942 through the patronage of the autocephalous Orthodox Church in Poland. I discuss how autocephalists hailed the legitimacy of an independent Kyivan Metropolia through the *tomos* of autocephaly granted by the EP to the Church in Poland in 1924, a document that defined the subjugation of Kyiv to Moscow as uncanonical.[17] Documents detailing synodal meetings and correspondence between bishops serve as the primary sources for narrating the emergence of the 1942 UAOC and the creation of the Autonomous Church in Ukraine, with their bishops meeting at the Pochaiv Monastery.[18] I analyze these documents to show how Orthodox Ukrainians could not agree on the event that had binding authority for church organization in Ukraine (the 1924 *tomos* or the 1918 All-Ukrainian Council). I also show how attempts to implement liturgical Ukrainization complicated relations among Orthodox, while the UAOC's decision to receive clergy ordained by the 1921 UAOC proved to be an insurmountable stumbling block. Chapter 2 also illuminates how alleged collaboration of UAOC leaders with Nazi officials enhanced the perception of illegitimacy associated with the movement for autocephaly. I discuss how these new developments contributed to the evolution of the public ecclesial identities of the Church in Ukraine, as illegitimacy continued to stigmatize the 1942 UAOC, while the autonomist preference for Church Slavonic and fidelity to the 1918 council and traditional liturgical practices was in continuity with the feature of canonicity.

Migration of Autocephaly and Ukrainization and the Political Theology of Democracy

Chapter 3 examines the Church in North America, which carried the banner in the émigré community for both Ukrainian national sovereignty and ecclesial independence. Two Ukrainian churches are profiled: the one in Canada, which was the largest Church numerically, and the one in the United States, which became the new center for the diaspora church on account of its first bishop, Archbishop

Mstyslav (Skrypnyk), who later became metropolitan and then patriarch upon his return to Ukraine. This section demonstrates how the aspirations for autocephaly and the problem of ecclesial illegitimacy evolved in conditions outside of Ukraine. I analyze the persistent Ukrainian attempts to overcome the reputation of illegitimacy with three major actions. The UOC-USA corrected the ordination of Archbishop John (Teodorovych) in 1949 by celebrating the rite of monastic tonsure and the rite of ordination with the laying on of hands by two canonical bishops, ritual elements absent from his original ordination in 1921. I also examine the decision of the Canadian (and American) churches to renew communion with the EP in 1990 (Canada) and 1995 (USA), respectively. I discuss how efforts to attain canonical legitimacy were regarded by some people and parishes in Canada as threats to Ukrainian aspirations for autocephaly. Chapter 3 explores the development of a political theology anchored in democracy and freedom, as the UOC-USA exploited American political positions on religious rights in the Soviet Union to delegitimize the MP and attempt to liberate Ukraine's Orthodox from their new captor, the USSR. These developments demonstrate the evolution of public religious identity in the context of immigration. The émigré churches' sustained attempts to normalize relations with the EP and correct the ordination of Archbishop John illustrate their desire to legitimize Ukrainian autocephaly and gather all faithful into one united Church.

In chapter 4, I profile the patriarchal exarchate's activity during the Cold War through the celebration of the millennium.[19] This section profiles the life of the Orthodox Church in Ukraine with reference to the 1946 synod in L'viv that liquidated the Greek-Catholic Church. I discuss the material published in the exarchate's Ukrainian-language periodical, *Православний вісник*, to demonstrate how the new narrative coalesced around the notion that all peoples of Rus' were again gathered together in one church under Moscow. The promotion of a political theology sponsored by the MP is presented here as a justification of the USSR's liquidation of the Greek-Catholic Church to eradicate the vestiges of Nazi fascism from the Unia.[20] Last, I illustrate the complexity of the multiple identities borne by Orthodox Ukrainians during the Cold War by drawing from the scholarship of Natalia Shlikhta on the subaltern strategies of resistance to the state employed by faithful, clergy, and hierarchs within the Church.

Post-Soviet Identities in Conflict: Ukrainian Autocephaly and Russian Nationalism

Chapter 5 examines post-Soviet developments in the public religious identity of the Orthodox churches in Ukraine. The primary topics are the dismissal of the 1989

UAOC on the basis of ecclesial illegitimacy,[21] the emergence of a new crisis involving dispute about the methods for obtaining autocephaly within the UOC-MP, the creation of the UOC-KP and the rise of Patriarch Filaret (Denysenko), and the responses of the Church to the Russian nationalism espoused by Patriarch Kirill (Gundiaev)'s *Russkii mir* strategy.[22] The chapter examines how Church leaders attempted to gain both state and popular support during epic events affecting Ukraine, including the 2004 Orange Revolution, the Maidan crisis, and the annexation of Crimea and war in Eastern Ukraine. It also shows how the legacy of narratives of illegitimacy both defined the identities of the respective churches and imposed identities on their competitors. The UAOC's election of Patriarch Mstyslav and promotion of Ukrainization retained the legacy of the diaspora churches, but were construed as illegitimate because of their connection to the 1921 UAOC. The KP also followed the path of the UAOC through its campaign for autocephaly and Ukrainization, but its appointment of Patriarch Filaret raised the question of legitimacy because of the MP's deposition of Filaret from holy orders and anathematization from the Church. Change in the public religious identity of the UOC-MP was the most intriguing development of this period. The UOC-MP maintained its identity as the only officially canonical Church in Ukraine, but it also pursued modest Ukrainization during the tenure of Metropolitan Volodymyr. This church encountered a new dilemma when it found its post-Soviet destiny challenged by the introduction of the *Russkii mir* initiative, as it sought to balance its emerging Ukrainian identity with the demands of Russian nationalism promulgated by the MP.

The Orthodox churches in Ukraine continue to struggle through a crisis of separation and polemics that has steadily gained momentum since 1917. The instability of the Ukrainian state and the many wars that ravaged Ukraine left church leaders without the calm needed to systematically work through their disputes. Autocephaly, Ukrainization, and fierce competition for recognition of legitimacy have deepened the divisions among Orthodox people, and these fissures are detrimental to efforts toward unity. The remainder of this book narrates the separation of the churches in Ukraine, and the problems of the autocephaly agenda and the stigma of ecclesial illegitimacy. I hope that the rest of this story clarifies the problems of autocephaly and Ukrainization, their origins, development, and contributions to the public religious identities of the Orthodox churches in Ukraine, so that readers understand the complex layers of this story and become familiar with its details.

1

The First Autocephalist Movement and the Creation of the UAOC (1917–1930)

THIS CHAPTER NARRATES THE STORY of the attempt to establish autoceph-aly in a renewed Kyivan Metropolia in the early twentieth century. The Ukrainian Autocephalous Orthodox Church of 1921–1930 (1921 UAOC) took bold steps by recreating the Kyivan Metropolia on the foundational principles of liberation, Ukrainization, and modernization.[1] The main events leading up to the formation of the 1921 UAOC include the eparchial assemblies of 1917, the 1918 All-Ukrainian Council, and a series of confrontations between the All-Ukrainian Orthodox Church Council (AUOCC) and the synod of bishops of the Ukrainian Exarchate (under the Moscow Patriarchate). This resulted in the restoration of a distinct public identity featuring liberation, newness, and a flattened ecclesiology. Plurality in Orthodox religious identity also emerged, as evidenced by Ukrainization within the patriarchal exarchate.

The Origins of the Ukrainian Autocephalist Movement

In the nineteenth century, a sense of national consciousness began to develop among Ukrainians. Churchmen were included among the intellectuals who sought the creation of an independent church alongside a sovereign state. The Ukrainian intellectuals who adhered to the national dream were aware of the for-mation of autocephalous churches in Serbia, Greece, and Bulgaria. The Bulgarian example was a cautionary tale, since the movement for autocephaly introduced the unfortunate tendency for churches to exclude anyone who was not ethnically Bulgarian from membership and participation. The Constantinopolitan synod of 1872 condemned this policy as ethnophyletism, the heresy of limiting participa-tion in ecclesial life to people of an exclusive national identity.[2] The Ukrainians who dreamed of an autocephalous church sought to excise their notion of a unique religious identity from the amalgamation of identities that had formed during the period of Kyiv's annexation to the Russian empire.

The aspirations for an autocephalous church in Ukraine began in the late nineteenth century as a component of national awakening and the objective of liberating the people from impoverished living conditions. Arsen Zinchenko characterizes the program for autocephaly as originating with larger political, community, educational, and cultural movements tinged with nationalism.[3] According to Zinchenko, the entire prerevolutionary national movement emphasized the villages and the peasants who constituted the backbone of Ukraine's agricultural output. Political ideologues implicated the institutional synodal church as one of the worst offenders in failing to elevate the lives of the people in the village. Progressive clergy and political thinkers caricatured the seminaries as places where clergy were discouraged from reading the daily news and becoming aware of the state of affairs throughout the empire. Some rank-and-file clergy were among those who were not only interested in peoples' ordinary lives, but also proposed programs of church reform which that strengthen the bonds between the people and the Church. Teachers such as Volodymyr Chekhivsky and S. M. Ivanitsky advocated for Ukrainianizing the curriculum of the Podil' Seminary by pressuring parents of seminarians to demand the creation of a chair of Ukrainian language, literature, and history.[4]

Zinchenko introduces multiple examples of attempts to promote Ukrainization, particularly through education, from the period of 1890 to 1917. For example, a symbol of emergent Ukrainization was the publication in 1906 of the Gospel of St. Matthew in vernacular Ukrainian, the fruit of a collaborative process shepherded by Archbishop Parfenii (Levitsky).[5] Archbishop Parfenii also supported the publication of the Paschal Gospel reading and celebrated the first public proclamation of the Gospel lection for Pascha (Easter) in Ukrainian on April 2, 1906, in Kamjanci.[6]

The outcomes of Ukrainization attempts during this period prefigure the struggle for control of the Kyivan Church that erupted in 1917–1921. Division among the clergy was one of the reasons for the conflict. While bishops such as Archbishop Parfenii advocated for Ukrainization, other hierarchs and clergy opposed it. Zinchenko discusses the fate of Archimandrite Feodosii (Oltarzhevsky), who was appointed as rector of the Kyivan seminary and academy in 1908 and was sympathetic to Ukrainization. Archbishop Antony (Khrapovitsky) of Volyn' oversaw an examination of the Kyivan academy in 1908, and recommended revisions while accusing several professors of plagiarism, incompetence, liberalism, atheism, and having sympathy for revolution, which constituted an "adversarial stance toward the Orthodox Church."[7] In 1908 several professors were removed from their posts, and Archimandrite Feodosii was likewise removed from his post as rector. While this episode suggests that Ukrainization was connected to the larger revolutionary movement sweeping through the empire, a closer look suggests that the Ukrainian movement envisioned reforms that would strengthen the relationship between the Church and the people, and that would encourage the clergy to serve the people beyond the administration of the sacraments. Zinchenko refers to the program for church renewal proposed by M. Mikhnovsky of the Ukrainian National Party in 1902, which was published in 1906.[8] The program called for the election of rectors by parishes, the prohibition of appointing parish rectors against the will of the parish, the provision by the parish of financial support for clergy, and periodical local councils to handle all church affairs in Ukraine.[9]

The primary ideologues of the national movement sought to reform the Church so that the clergy would become active advocates on behalf of the people and attend to their needs and concerns, as opposed to serving a state that exploited them.[10] Zinchenko notes that appeals for the "renewal [and] the democratization of the Church through her return to national sources" were published on the pages of Ukrainian periodicals.[11] The appeals shed light on the divided loyalties of the clergy, including those who refused to support monarchists and those who belonged to the "Union of the Russian people," a right-wing party espousing autocracy and Russian nationalism.[12] Perhaps the most telling testimony from Zinchenko's review of this period is his summary of the August 1906 edition of *Громадська думка* (Community thought), especially its report on the reaction of clergy to the revolutionary episodes of 1905–1906:

> The events of the last two years stirred up this "dead strength," requiring it to listen around itself. Priests began to discuss the events, to claim that the All-Russian Church Council was to be convened, to reform church schools . . . the Ukrainian village clergy must place the interests of the Ukrainian people first.[13]

Zinchenko's review of this period demonstrates that there was a general sentiment in favor of church reform in imperial Ukraine: many politicians and clergy supported the restoration of democratic mechanisms in the life of the Church, the use of vernacular Ukrainian in the liturgy, the updating of schools, and especially attention to the needs of the local people. To be sure, there were also appeals for some form of local Ukrainian Church independence, but these were not uniform. Some envisioned autonomous metropolitanates forming in parallel with autonomous republics, some called for an increase in democratization, especially with reference to the appointment of clergy to parishes, while some called for autocephaly. Alongside the reformers in Kyiv were conservatives who sought no change in church structures and depicted Ukrainianizers as radical revolutionaries. These prerevolutionary divisions would come to a head when the empire fell in 1917 and Ukraine embarked on a road with several paths potentially leading to some form of national and ecclesial sovereignty, but ultimately resulting in the deepening of divisions within society.

The Eparchial Assemblies in 1917

The movement for autocephaly among Ukrainians gained traction and momentum during the course of the 1917 revolution. Ivan Vlasovs'kyi cites Anton Kartashev, who described the political environment of the former Russian empire as one of "the liquidation of the previous governors and police rulers."[14] Kartashev goes on to describe the arrest of bishops who were well known for their connections with the tsarist regime or with Grigorii Rasputin. In the spring and summer of 1917, a series of eparchial assemblies occurred throughout Ukraine.[15] Vlasovs'kyi states that the assemblies occurred with the participation of laity, a new development that began during the the revolution of 1905.[16] The delegates at the assemblies took up the question of how the Church was to reclaim moral and spiritual authority in society with the fall of the tsarist regime and the status of the autonomy of the Kyivan Metropolia within the Moscow Patriarchate.[17] At the eparchial assembly of Poltava, several questions concerning the potential Ukrainization of the Church were raised.[18] The Kyivan eparchial assembly elected a commission on the convocation of an All-Ukrainian Church Council that would consist of clergy and laity from all eparchies in Ukraine. In his memoirs on the rebirth of the Ukrainian Church, Metropolitan Vasyl Lypkivs'kyi also attributed the movement for Church rebirth to the eparchial assemblies that had gathered throughout Ukraine.[19] Lypkivs'kyi referred to the influence on the Church of Ukraine's gradual separation from Russia, noting the formation of Ukrainian armed forces in September and October.[20] He added that many clergy ministering to the military engaged one another in active discussion on how the create a distinctly Ukrainian church. Thus, the origins of the creation of a Ukrainian Church in late 1917 occurred in concert with the formation of the Ukrainian state.

Many of the clergy working for a Ukrainian Church formed the core group of the newly formed All-Ukrainian Orthodox Church Council (AUOCC), which petitioned Patriarch Tikhon for the convocation of a council.[21] The composition of the leaders of the AUOCC was decidedly pro-Ukrainian, and they encountered opposition in Kyiv, especially among the bishops.[22] First, Metropolitan Volodymyr (Bogoiavlensky) of Kyiv was initially opposed to the eparchial assemblies, but eventually assented.[23] The council asked Metropolitan Volodymyr to abandon his see in Kyiv.[24] In his historical assessment of these eparchial assemblies, Metropolitan Feodosii (Protsiuk) concludes that the assemblies considered canonical autocephaly but voted in favor of autonomy.[25] The evidence shows that the eparchies desired independence and even Ukrainization, but did not agree on whether its canonical form should be autonomy or autocephaly.

Kartashev argues that the extraordinary eparchial assemblies were necessitated by a process of destruction and reconstruction of national and religious structures throughout the entirety of the empire. One of the potential outcomes of this process was the reconfiguration of Ukrainian eparchies connected to an All-Ukrainian church center.[26] Such a reorganization of the eparchies seemed possible when a chorus of voices called for the All-Ukrainian Council of clergy and laity to determine the next phase of ecclesial life in Ukraine. Vlasovs'kyi notes that the restoration of ecclesial autonomy was the original goal of those who supported such a gathering. He quotes a priest, P. Korsunovsky, who said "there were no thoughts about autocephaly at that time, just as there was no thinking about the complete independence of Ukraine at the time. There were thoughts that following the collapse of the monarchy, the Ukrainian and Russian nations would live in brotherly concord in a free Russia."[27] During the revolution, as the Ukrainian church movement gained momentum, Metropolitan Volodymyr issued an archpastoral epistle published in the church periodical *Kyivan Eparchial News*.[28] He suggested that Orthodox Ukrainians and Russians should build "one great Orthodox Russian Church" together.[29] Iryna Prelovs'ka summarized Metropolitan Volodymyr's letter as a "testimony of the reasons . . . that explain the impossibility of separating the Russian and Ukrainian Churches."[30]

The Moscow Council of 1917–1918

The entire church was adjusting to the new situation in the former empire. The collapse of the monarchy and its replacement by the provisional government headed by Alexander Kerensky simultaneously challenged the Orthodox Church and provided it with an unanticipated freedom. The Orthodox Church in Russia had paved a path toward reform and renewal since the early twentieth century, when the bishops began the process of convoking a council to address several matters affecting the life of the Church in Russia. Many of the issues also pertained to the establishment of Ukrainian distinctiveness in the Kyivan Metropolia, and these issues included the question of introducing vernacular Russian and Ukrainian into the liturgy, the involvement of the laity in the life of the Church at all of its levels, greater participation of women in the life of the Church, deliberations on the possibilities of reducing the disciplinary measures directed toward divorced or deposed clergy, and an increase in the visible conciliarity of the Church. But the most pressing issue taken up by the Russian bishops was the matter of restoring the Moscow Patriarchate.[31] The restoration of the patriarchate would restore an identifiable leader who would be responsible for implementing the measures of renewal in the life of the Church, and would also liberate the Church from the decay caused by its fixed attachment to the state as a result of Peter I's Spiritual Regulation.[32]

The Moscow Council took place in 1917–1918. In November of 1917, the council elected Metropolitan Tikhon (Bellavin) of Moscow as the new patriarch of the Russian Church.[33] Metropolitan Volodymyr of Kyiv, who presided over the opening of the council until Metropolitan Tikhon was elected as chair of the presidium, was the senior bishop during the course of much of the council.[34] The council, which met somewhat sporadically on account of the political turbulence, approved the convocation of the All-Ukrainian Council in 1918 and ultimately accepted the Ukrainian council's declarations of autonomy.[35] At least one other matter taken up by the Moscow Council had a profound effect on the future trajectory of church life in Ukraine: the matter of translating church services from Slavonic into Ukrainian. The conciliar liturgical commission had submitted numerous proposals and redactions for the translation of the liturgy into Russian and Ukrainian, and blessings to read the lessons in Slavonic and Russian, or Slavonic and Ukrainian. Metropolitan Evlogy (Georgievsky), who served on the liturgical commission, reported (in his memoirs) that the proposals for translations were turned down, and that "the Ukrainians were furious."[36] Evlogy noted the enormous corpus of work taken on by prestigious scholars of the liturgical commission, and the reluctance of Metropolitan Tikhon to accept the proposals, "for fear of objections, mostly from the Old Believers."[37] But the larger objective of the Moscow Council, to restore the Old Believers to the communion of the patriarchate, did not deter the Ukrainians from seeking episcopal blessings to celebrate the liturgy in the vernacular.

Nikolai Balashov's detailed report on the work of the liturgical commission presents the evolution of the proposals over the course of several months.[38] Balashov notes that the proposals were largely produced by Archbishop Evlogy, and in each model promoting either partial or complete use of the vernacular, Russian and Ukrainian are the two languages mentioned. An important revision occurred following the meeting of the liturgical commission on August 12, 1917. The revisions concerned the ten theses of translation for liturgy, and in each case, the word "Ukrainian" ("Украинский") is replaced by "Little Russian" ("Малороссийский").[39] Balashov suggests that the redaction was executed in response to "the emergence of Ukrainian nationalism and ecclesial separatism."[40] This episode of redaction did not appear to have any bearing on the decision to continue to privilege Church Slavonic as the only approved liturgical language. Balashov's assessment of the situation following the Moscow Council is perhaps the most accurate of the accounts of the fate of vernacular languages. He states that there is limited evidence of authoritative declarations on liturgical language in the liturgy; the Moscow Council had referred the matter for ultimate resolution to the Holy Synod of Bishops and the Superior Church Council. Balashov notes that the first hard evidence available on the matter occurred with the hearing of the report of Bishop Nazarii (Blinov) in June 1919, who was serving as the vicar of Kyiv eparchy at the time and requested a decision on a petition to use vernacular Ukrainian as a liturgical language.[41] The report of tendencies toward Ukrainian separatism at the Moscow Council and the angst surrounding the reluctance to adopt proposals for the use of vernacular in the liturgy amounted to a shift in the strategy of Ukrainians who desired an authentically Ukrainian Church. The absence of permission to use vernacular Ukrainian in the liturgy did not deter the cohort of Ukrainians in Kyiv from celebrating the liturgy in Ukrainian, and therefore the debate about language became the first of several topics of disagreement between Ukrainian cohorts and the council of bishops in Ukraine that led to schism and the development of a distinct public religious identity among autocephalist Ukrainians.

The Ukrainian council convened in January of 1918 and continued its work through three sessions, with the second occurring in June 1918, and the third from October through December of the same year.[42] The political turbulence impacted its proceedings. In Ukraine, a central committee consisting of several disparate political parties ruled a fledgling Ukrainian national republic in early 1918, only to be temporarily replaced by the Hetmanate of Pavlo Skoropadsky in April of 1918.[43] A Ukrainian Church Committee consisting of elected members from the Kyivan eparchial assemblies was created to begin the process of planning the All-Ukrainian Church Council.[44] The church situation mirrored the political one. Hyacinthe Destivelle's depiction is accurate: "parallel to this political evolution, there were two tendencies within the Ukrainian Church—one in favor of a status of autonomy for the Ukrainian Church within the context of the All-Russian Church, the other in favor of autocephaly."[45] Tensions between Russian and Ukrainian cohorts in Kyiv were high, as evidenced by the memorandum written by Archpriest K. Titov and other clergy in Kyiv on the "chauvinistic politics of a group of Ukrainian clergy."[46] The Moscow Council blessed the convocation of the All-Ukrainian Council that opened on January 7 of 1918 and adopted a draft of its statute on July 9, 1918.[47] To place the situation in context, an epic and tragic event affected the environment of the Ukrainian council, which was already complicated by its surrounding political climate. The entire church was shaken by the murder of Metropolitan Volodymyr in January of 1918, an episode that further distanced proponents of Ukrainian ecclesial separatism on account of Metropolitan Volodymyr's resistance to appeals to Ukrainian nationalism.[48] Following Volodymyr's martyrdom, Metropolitan Antony (Khrapovitsky) was elected as the new metropolitan of Kyiv by a special eparchial council in May 1918.[49] Metropolitan Antony was familiar with the Ukrainian situation from his lengthy tenure as archbishop of Volyn' and Zhitomir, and archbishop of Kharkiv, yet he was also an avowed monarchist and church conservative.[50]

The 1918 All-Ukrainian Council

It has been difficult to assess the 1918 All-Ukrainian Church Council without access to its proceedings, which until recently were concealed by archives. The publication of the council's proceedings by Andryi Starodub in 2010 has made it possible to obtain the declarations of the council, although in terms of its reception and significance, opinions vary. In his memoirs, Metropolitan Evlogy viewed the Ukrainian council negatively in comparison with the potential contributions of the Moscow Council, and he participated in its planning as the bishop of Volyn'. Evlogy highlighted the tensions among the parties in Ukraine, referring to "a mob of bitter Ukrainians aroused by political passions."[51] Angry Ukrainian clergy also tried to influence Metropolitan Platon (Rozhdestvenskii), who was doing the preparatory work for the council.[52] Evlogy described the council as having a powerful anti-Moscow sentiment, with delegates shouting "away with Moscow!"[53] It was during this period that the Bolsheviks temporarily seized Kyiv and murdered Metropolitan Volodymyr. Soon afterward, Pavlo Skoropadsky assumed leadership of Ukraine in its brief period as a hetmanate.[54] Evlogy presided over the May Kyivan eparchial assembly to elect Metropolitan Volodymyr's successor, Metropolitan Antony. In July 1918, the All-Ukrainian Council assembled for its second session with Antony as the chair of the presidium, and Evlogy described the council as a "struggle between the Ukrainian and Russian parties" with the desire for autocephaly "relentless."[55] Evlogy's memoirs mention the presence and activity of the minister of cults under the Hetmanate, Vasyl Zinkivs'kyi who was replaced by Oleksander Lotocky. Evlogy concludes his brief treatment of the council by stating that "we were victorious," with Lotocky and the struggle for autocephaly defeated. Evlogy also said that "the Ukrainians were fit to be tied."[56]

Vlasovs'kyi's account of the council of 1918 is consistent with Evlogy's, and Vlasovs'kyi cites Evlogy repeatedly in his account of the proceedings.[57] Vlasovs'kyi also refers to the Ukrainian majority at the council, manifested perhaps most powerfully by a lecture given by Ivan (Ohienko) on the work of the council, which ended with the singing of the Ukrainian national anthem, "Ще не вмерла Україна" ("Ukraine has not died yet").[58] Given the principle of conciliarity adopted by the Moscow Council and the Ukrainian council's general favoring of autocephaly, it is difficult to understand how the council adopted the more conservative course of autonomy and the rejection of Ukrainization, since there seemed to be a pro-Ukrainian majority among the delegates. Vlasovs'kyi casts doubt on the legitimacy of the election of Metropolitan Antony in his analysis of the council, stating that the council violated the Moscow Council's rule that a candidate required two-thirds of the vote for the election to be valid.[59] Vlasovs'kyi's exploration of the sources available to him led him to conclude that a certain cohort within the 1918 council attempted to steer the assembly away from the inevitable path of autocephaly. Vlasovs'kyi refers to the memoirs of the priest Korsunowsky, who stated that the preparatory commission had instructed high-ranking clergy to purify the Ukrainian council by removing the "Mazepa element," a reference to the early eighteenth-century hetman Ivan Mazepa, who was disavowed in Russian history and Orthodox Church circles for joining an alliance with the Swedish king to defeat Russia.[60] Vlasovs'kyi cites as an example a group of fifty-two people from Kherson who were not elected as delegates to the council but instead appointed by the eparchial leadership, which was justified by a lack of time to hold elections for a proper eparchial delegation.[61] In other words, Vlasovs'kyi asserted that this was an instance of assuring sufficient representation to support the pro-Russian coalition within the council.[62] Vlasovs'kyi claimed that the pro-Ukrainian coalition protested the exclusion of members of the Ukrainian Church Committee, who had pushed for the convocation of the All-Ukrainian council, and that Bishop Pimen (as the council chair) refused to bring their proposition to include the pro-Ukrainian council members to the entire assembly, claiming that the Ukrainian church council itself refused representation at the Ukrainian council.[63] The perception of an agenda by a pro-Russian minority to remove Ukrainian representation from the council led Vlasovs'kyi to conclude that this was an event "similar to the usurpation by the Catholic political leadership of the Ukrainian Orthodox Council in Brest in 1596."[64] Vlasovs'kyi's perspective differs from that of Metropolitan Feodosii (Protsiuk), who described the act of removing the former members of the preparatory council as a way of honoring the laity. Feodosii justified this act on the grounds that the members of the preparatory council would indeed become the separatists who were "self-consecrated," an explicit reference to the autocephalist church that was born in 1921.[65]

An episode that occurred in 1918 between conciliar sessions illustrates the pressure the Ukrainians placed on the Orthodox bishops to honor Ukrainization. On June 27, 1918, in memory of Ivan Mazepa's defeat in Poltava, the Ukrainian Church leaders petitioned Metropolitan Antony to serve a *panakhyda* (brief liturgical office for the dead) on the plaza of St. Sophia Cathedral.[66] Metropolitan Antony formally requested that Patriarch Tikhon remove the anathema placed on Mazepa, and the patriarch consented, although Antony declined the invitation to preside at the *panakhyda*. Instead, Bishop Nazarii of Cherkassk presided, and the *panakhyda* was served at St. Sophia with the first Ukrainian national choir singing the responses under the direction of Kyrylo Stetsenko. The report indicates that ten thousand people participated, but the service had a distinctly anti-Russian theme as well. The priest Kramarenko addressed the people prior to the *panakhyda*, and he referred to the anniversary of the defeat at Poltava as the victory of Tsar Peter I over Mazepa.[67] The *panakhyda* served in his memory ritualized the symbolic battle between Ukraine and Russia, and became a symbol of Ukrainian national and ecclesial independence.[68]

Two significant perceptions emerge from this brief consideration of Vlasovs'kyi's perspective. First, Vlasovs'kyi attended to the particular political situation of Ukraine with great detail. For example, he mentions the efforts of Minister of Cults Zinkinvs'kyi to obtain canonical autonomy for the Church in Ukraine: "thus the government regards it as necessary that the organization of the administration of the Ukrainian Church should be translated into autonomous structures" to prevent the influence of adversarial elements.[69] Evlogy praised Zinkivs'kyi for his centrist approach to resolving the political divisions of the council.[70] Skoropadsky's cautious approach to the Ukrainian situation resulted in Ukraine seeking a cooperative federation with Russia. Since the July session of the 1918 council had defeated the movement for autocephaly, the pro-Ukrainian cohort temporarily lost interest in the work of the council, which was set to continue in late October under the leadership of Metropolitan Antony.

While the Ukrainian Church Council eventually adopted the autonomous path, which was accepted by the Moscow Council, the ongoing political turbulence in Ukraine disrupted both civic and church life. Zinkivs'kyi was replaced as minister of cults by Oleksander Lotocky, an advocate for canonical autocephaly. Lotocky delivered a speech at the third session of the 1918 council on behalf of the government, advocating for ecclesial autocephaly, which he believed was a necessary component not only for the Church, but also for the country.[71] Lotocky's speech did not have any binding authority on the work of the council, which opted for autonomy, a position parallel to Skoropadsky's conciliatory political approach.[72] However, the Hetmanate itself was weak and Skoropadsky himself resigned on December 14, to be replaced briefly by the Directory of the Ukrainian National Republic, a government led by Symon Petliura.[73] Thus, Lotocky's advocacy for canonical autocephaly was short-lived in his capacity as minister of cults under the Hetmanate. However, as Vlasovs'kyi notes, the arguments of the 1918 council resulted in a second significant perception that ultimately sustained the autocephalist movement: the Russian bishops were blamed by the pro-Ukrainian cohort for usurping the council and manipulating its proceedings to further a political agenda.

Vlasovs'kyi referred to an example from the appearance of Metropolitan Antony at a public event, the festivities surrounding the opening of the Ukrainian University in Kyiv. Metropolitan Antony delivered a speech at this event (in Russian), and used "Малороссия" and "малороссийский" in place of "Ukraine" and "Ukrainian," which caused students at the assembly to mock him and call for him to leave. This example of the collision of languages brings us full circle to the matter of liturgical language deliberated at the Moscow Council. Balashov mentioned that the only extant evidence of an authoritative decision prohibiting the use of the vernacular in the liturgy came from the 1918 Ukrainian council. The council resolved to retain Church Slavonic as the only language permissible for liturgy.[74] Politics defined the arena of battle between the pro-Russian and pro-Ukrainian cohorts at the 1918 council. As the history of the Ukrainian Church evolved in 1919 and beyond, liturgical language would come to symbolize the separation between the Ukrainian cohort and the synod of patriarchal bishops in Ukraine. Vlasovs'kyi disagreed with Metropolitan Vasyl Lypkivs'kyi's assessment of the situation. Lypkivs'kyi wrote that the rebirth of the Ukrainian Church needed to come from the lower ranks, the laity, and not the upper ranks; Vlasovs'kyi argued that the creation of an authentically Ukrainian national hierarchy would have resolved the problem.[75] Regardless of one's position on this matter, it is clear that the role of the bishops was crucial in the changes in the ecclesial landscape that unfolded in Ukraine, and the attempt to redefine the role of the bishops in the administration of the Church would become the most complex feature of Ukrainian Orthodox religious identity and remain so to this day.

Liturgical Language and the First Degree of Separation

The fissures between the Ukrainian and Russian cohorts in Ukraine's Orthodox Church deepened following the collapse of the Hetmanate and the establishment of Directory rule under Petliura in Ukraine. The Directory's church agenda was established from the outset, as Metropolitan Antony and Archbishop Evlogy were arrested in December 1918 and sent to a Greek-Catholic monastery.[76] The Directory also established a law on the superior administration of the Ukrainian Autocephalous Orthodox Church, which decreed that the Orthodox Church in Ukraine was autocephalous.[77] The new decree maintained the traditional relationship between church and state familiar to Orthodox Christians in Ukraine. The law featured new elements representing the progressive cohorts in the Orthodox Church, including the creation of a synod consisting of two bishops, one archpriest, a priest, one deacon, three lay people, and one priest serving the military; the government appointment of one delegate who would participate in synodal meetings; the support of the synod through the government's treasury; the independence of the Ukrainian Church from the patriarch of Moscow; and government confirmation of synodal decisions and proceedings. This illustration of a church that is essentially an organ of the Ukrainian state coheres with the political environment of the first years following the revolution. Vlasovs'kyi notes that the close relationship between church and state formulated by the Directory should not have been alarming since the Orthodox Church in Ukraine always had a formal relationship with the state.[78] Furthermore, a similar situation occurred in Russia, as the preconciliar preparations involved cooperative planning between church and state agents, and the Moscow Council itself enjoyed the support of the provisional government in Russia.[79] The Directory understood the need for the Church to navigate the canonical process of legitimization among the other global Orthodox churches, so the government established a special mission to Istanbul led by Lotocky to obtain canonical autocephaly.[80] The mission's failure was partially attributable to the vacancy in the patriarchal cathedral of Constantinople, but was also influenced by the bewildering political scene in Ukraine.

The Directory was in rapid decline, so the officials had to move their headquarters from Kyiv to Vinnytsia by February 2. From the December 1918 to December 1919, the Directory, the White Army, the Bolsheviks, the French entente, and the military serving the West Ukrainian Republic all had a hand in taking and evacuating Kyiv. Orest Subtelny describes the political scene as a series of military defeats, diplomatic disappointments, and ideological conflict among Ukrainians.[81] Subtelny's terse summary of the war for political hegemony in Ukraine is instructive for its analysis of Ukraine's autocephalist movement: "by fall 1919, the situation of the Ukrainians was truly tragic . . . in Ukraine alone, the fighting, executions, and epidemics associated with the upheaval, especially the Civil War, took about 1.5 million lives."[82] The next phase of the development of Ukrainian public religious identity occurred under Soviet rule, where the rules of the relationship changed drastically due to the legislation of separation of church from state and the state's assumption of control of Church property. The debate about language came to a head in this milieu, and the pro-Ukrainian cohort discovered new power in asserting its claim to ecclesial legitimacy.

Following the disappointment and anger resulting from the 1918 conciliar decision to continue the privileging of Church Slavonic, the Ukrainians in 1919 cautiously reopened the matter of using the vernacular in liturgy. In March 1919, the reconstituted AUOCC appealed to Bishop Nazarii, the vicar of Kyiv eparchy in the absence of Metropolitan Antony, to permit the reading of the Gospel in vernacular Ukrainian for the Passion services and for Easter in the lesser church of Saint Sophia's Cathedral in Kyiv. Bishop Nazarii denied the council's request, and the council decided to register a Ukrainian parish with the Soviet government, a decision that hastened the process of separation between the Ukrainian cohort and the bishops.[83] The Ukrainians' ability to manipulate the Soviet policy of separation of church from state was the result of the transfer of power from the synod to the local parish, a process that had started before the revolution with the demands for ecclesial decentralization, democratization, and opportunities for parish clergy to receive more power within the Church.[84] In the early Soviet period, the state essentially rendered eparchial bishops impotent in parish administration.[85] Gregory Freeze observes that power transferred "from prelate to parishioner."[86] The bishops had no real power to resist the Soviet transfer of a parish to the Ukrainian cohort, and this move would contribute to the destabilization of the episcopate itself.

The decision to register a Ukrainian parish with the Soviet authorities led to the Ukrainian cohort receiving St. Nicholas Cathedral in the Pechersk district as their parish. The council again requested Bishop Nazarii's blessing to serve the liturgy in Ukrainian, and he responded by permitting them to read the Gospel in Ukrainian with the rest of the service sung in Slavonic.[87] On May 9, 1919, the Ukrainians celebrated the first ever liturgy with select elements in Ukrainian, with the music composed by the renowned Mykola Leontovich who directed the choir himself.[88] This inaugural Ukrainian-language liturgy resulted in a domino effect, with Ukrainians in Kyiv receiving permission to use churches for worship from the Soviet government. Ukrainian-language parishes were organized outside of Kyiv as well. Soon afterward, on July 10, the entire liturgy was celebrated in vernacular Ukrainian at St. Sophia's Cathedral; the cohort invited Bishop Nazarii to celebrate the liturgy, but he declined.

A brief reflection on the process employed by the Ukrainian cohort to accomplish their objectives is worthwhile. Vlasovs'kyi's historical review is apologetic, as he depicts the Ukrainian council as desiring to maintain a relationship with the episcopacy. He also mentions that Bishop Nazarii was irritated by the invitation and repeated petitions for Ukrainian-language services. The bishop's consternation is understandable.[89] The Ukrainian cohort had gained the upper hand in its battle with the synod by exercising the new and temporary freedom to register parishes that were no longer controlled by the Church. While the cohort petitioned Bishop Nazarii, they had also formed communities gathered around a common cause, the use of Ukrainian in the liturgy, on their own. The process was irregular, as the bishop was petitioned to bless gatherings that were already affirmed by the state. Furthermore, the bishop was challenged by a situation in which he had very little power, given that the state's attempt to render bishops impotent resulted in the transfer of power from the bishops to the laity. The bishop's initial blessing for some Ukrainian to be used at the first liturgy was reluctant, and represented a coerced adjustment to an increasingly impotent episcopacy that had no official place as an organ of the state. This episode also betrays a deeper and irreconcilable collision of ideologies. The bishop viewed the use of vernacular Ukrainian as a violation of the decree of the 1918 council. The Ukrainian cohort viewed the prohibition of vernacular Ukrainian as a violation of Orthodox tradition traceable to Saints Cyril and Methodius, whose translation of the liturgical Gospels and texts from Greek to Slavonic affirmed the evangelical value of the primacy of local language.[90]

The matter of liturgical language and the new separation of church and state resulted in an unprecedented conflict that gave the Ukrainian cohort temporary power. As the Ukrainians continued to form communities in and around Kyiv that used Ukrainian for the liturgy, the conflict with the bishops deepened on the ideological lines of ecclesial authority and the legitimacy of ethnic language. The political situation resulted in the temporary return of Metropolitan Antony to Kyiv in the late summer of 1919, facilitated by the brief occupation of the city by the White Army.[91] During his brief return to the city, Antony suspended all of the clergy of the Ukrainian cohort who had promoted the celebration of the liturgy in Ukrainian from liturgical ministry. By the time the Soviets had established power, Antony had fled Ukraine, and Patriarch Tikhon replaced him with Metropolitan Michael (Ermakov). The suspended pro-Ukrainian clergy were deposed from the ranks of the clergy altogether in 1921.[92] Thus, the matter was not merely one of liturgical language. The debate over liturgical language between the Ukrainian and Russian cohorts increased in vitriol, with each side employing the power at its disposal. The Ukrainian cohorts continued to establish Ukrainian-language parishes, whereas the Russian bishops canonically disposed of the primary clerical figures of the Ukrainian cohort. The power struggle over liturgical language continued, but a new issue rose to prominence alongside language: the limits of episcopal power in the Orthodox Church.

Several related episodes demonstrate how the use of vernacular Ukrainian for the liturgy became one of the primary features of public religious identity for the Ukrainian cohort. Their disagreement with the bishops on language became so intense that the Ukrainians used their advocacy of the vernacular to seek ecclesial autocephaly instead of autonomy. In addition to the seminal events surveyed above, episodes and documents from the October Council of 1921 testify to the increasing prominence the Ukrainian language attained in the autocephaly movement of the Ukrainian cohort.

The Ukrainian Language at the October Council of 1921

Language and the Liturgy, 1919–1921

The October 1921 council was a permanent turning point in the history of Ukrainian Orthodox religious identity because it marked a determined separation from the Moscow Patriarchate and established a new course for Orthodoxy in Ukraine that is one of the sources of the current divisions within the Church. The residual divisions within the Orthodox Church serve as a reminder that not all bishops, clergy, and laity joined the movement for an autocephalous Orthodox Church that was distinctly Ukrainian.

In order to assess the October 1921 council, a review of crucial events in the interim period is necessary. Returning to 1919, during the heat of the battles between the pro-Ukrainian cohort and the episcopate in Kyiv, a second manifestation of the AUOCC convened.[93] This council was similar to the original gathering that was interrupted by the war, but it had a slightly different trajectory. The group originated from the pro-Ukrainian cohort itself, the one that was organizing Ukrainian parishes distinct from the synod in Kyiv. The group consisted of thirty people and took on the name of the AUOCC with a new purpose, to be the superior governing organ for the organization of Ukrainian parishes.[94] The AUOCC elected Michael Moroz as its chair, a close friend to Lypkivs'kyi. Vlasovs'kyi raises the relevant problem of representation; how could the group call itself "all-Ukrainian" when it was a tight-knit cohort of Ukrainianizing clergy and laity who sought separation from Moscow?[95] Vlasovs'kyi paraphrases Lypkivs'kyi's analysis of the AUOCC's charter: "her ultimate goal is the creation of Ukrainian parishes, the rebirth of the Ukrainian Church throughout all Ukraine; she regards herself only as a temporary superior church organ of the Ukrainian Church up until the convocation of an authentic all-Ukrainian church council with representatives from Ukrainian parishes."[96] The AUOCC was the core group of leaders that pushed the agenda of establishing Ukrainian parishes in spite of episcopal resistance in Kyiv, and was the essential ecclesial cell that ultimately grew into the first autocephalous church of Ukraine. In other words, the AUOCC consisted of the people who promulgated the ideology that eventually resulted in the first autocephalous Ukrainian Church.

The AUOCC came into conflict with the Orthodox synod in Kyiv by creating parishes without episcopal blessing. Vlasovs'kyi writes of an episode concerning the delegation of rights to parishes in Kyiv that reveals the perception of an emerging religious identity in both the pro- and anti-Ukrainian delegations.[97] The context is the first Ukrainian-language liturgy celebrated on May 9, 1919, at St. Nicholas Cathedral in the Pechersk district.[98] According to Vlasovs'kyi, over one thousand Ukrainians registered for membership in the first Ukrainian parish. Many others sought to establish St. Andrew's Cathedral as another Ukrainian parish, an episode that led Bishop Nazarii and his clerical supporters to distinguish the "Ukrainians" from the "Orthodox."[99]

While this episode is consistent with the evidence presented on the matter of language, it exposes the beginnings of a public juxtaposition of religious identity on the part of the synod in Ukraine. The local clergy and laity were given the choice of remaining Orthodox or joining the Ukrainians. The inscription of non-Orthodox identity upon the people of the AUOCC was not merely a matter of language, but primarily a convenient way of distinguishing the proper, canonical manner of resolving disputes. In this scheme, the Orthodox way would approach the dispute within the church with the involvement of the bishop. The

AUOCC's establishment of Ukrainian-language parishes with direct appeal to the local authorities circumvented the canonical process. As polemics permeated the inscription of religious identity and deepened the separation between the cohorts, the legitimacy of praying in the vernacular was undermined.

Tetiana Ievsieieva explains the ideology of the Russian bishops in Ukraine during this period by stating that many Orthodox eparchies of the Russian empire were essentially polynational with non-Russian majorities.[100] Because of the fusion of the Orthodox Church and state established during the imperial period, the bishops represented both the Church and the state's elite. Ievsieieva asserts that the Church periodicals of the period aligned nationalism with the heresy of ethnophyletism, the capitulation to secularism, and a betrayal of the catholic nature of the Church.[101] She states that it was practically impossible for someone with nationalistic sympathies to become a candidate for the office of bishop.[102] Clergy and bishops who expressed any kind of patriotism other than the promotion of Great Russian identity were deemed "uncanonical."[103] Ievsieieva's observation on the ideology of multinational unity held together by the Russian church as an organ of the state explains how the Russian bishops came to dominate church leadership in Ukraine, and how they came into conflict with the AUOCC. The close alignment of the Church as a multinational constituency with Orthodox canonicity is also noteworthy for its early appearance as a staple feature of the religious identity of the patriarchal church in Ukraine.

The AUOCC, encouraged by the popular response, continued to establish Ukrainian parishes and broadened its reach outside of Kyiv.[104] The conflict between the two sides was exacerbated, leading to Bishop Nazarii's decision to suspend the Ukrainian clergy from the right to officiate at divine services on April 17, 1920.[105] At this point, the conflict between the AUOCC and the bishops was irreconcilable. In a letter to the Orthodox community of Ukraine of May 5, 1920, the AUOCC declared Bishop Nazarii's canonical suspension of the Ukrainian clergy to be immoral and uncanonical.[106] The AUOCC established a permanent path of separation by appealing for the creation of a Ukrainian episcopate for Ukrainian parishes.[107] It is also noteworthy that the AUOCC identified the new Ukrainian church as autocephalous and ruled by *sobornopravnist'* (conciliar governance).

As the process of separation continued and the AUOCC solidified its plans to create an autocephalous body in Ukraine, an important figure emerged: Archbishop Parfenii (Levitsky), who was overseeing the eparchy of Poltava. Archbishop Parfenii was sympathetic to the Ukrainian cause, and the AUOCC believed that he had agreed to be their new primate.[108] The Ukrainian cohort commemorated him as "archbishop of Ukraine" in the liturgy. But the AUOCC had mistaken Parfenii's sympathy for a full commitment to separation from the patriarchate. The synod of bishops in Ukraine admonished Parfenii for encouraging the autocephalists in a resolution from their meeting on March 3, 1921; the synod asserted that Parfenii was leading clergy and laity astray by permitting this commemoration and instructed him to communicate via letter his promise to cease interfering in the canonical affairs of other eparchies.[109] In a letter written to Patriarch Tikhon on December 31, 1920, Parfenii explained the Ukrainian cohort's frustration with the inconsistent application of the canonical permission to pray in Ukrainian granted in 1918 and admitted that they had commemorated him liturgically. Parfenii asked Patriarch Tikhon to bless him or another bishop to care for the Ukrainians for the sake of peace in the Church. In his letter, Parfenii also testified to the Ukrainian cohort's search for an episcopal supporter outside of Ukraine, which included trips to Istanbul and Georgia.[110]

Parfenii eventually acquiesced to the demands of the synod in Ukraine that he cease association with the AUOCC, and the fissures between the two groups deepened, especially after the synod deposed all of the Ukrainian clergy from holy orders in February 1921. Parfenii ultimately declined the Ukrainian cohort's invitation to preside at their council on account of poor health and travel time. The Ukrainian cohort was reluctant to invite other bishops on account of their refusal to grant or proclaim autocephaly, and had already experienced the disappointment of a lack of action on the part of the Ecumenical Patriarchate.

This series of events led up to the AUOCC's first council held on May 22–26, 1921, in Kyiv.[111] This was a council of the Ukrainian churches of Kyiv and was essentially a preparatory meeting for the October Council.[112] The May Council's declarations functioned as foundations for the October Council and thus represented the Ukrainian cohort's distinct ideology. Among the most significant decisions of the May gathering was its election of Archbishop Parfenii as metropolitan of Kyiv and its strong disavowal of the existing synod in Ukraine.[113] Parfenii, however, did not attend the council and ceased his association with the AUOCC, which left it and its rapidly increasing roster of parishes without an episcopal patron. Vlasovs'kyi concluded that Parfenii was not to blame for his failure to appear at the council and preside over it, given his patronage of the Ukrainian movement in general. Concerning the errors of the May gathering, Prelovs'ka is likely correct in stating that the error of the leaders of the AUOCC was in appointing bishops who had "communicated their support for the rebirth of the Church in Ukraine in correspondence, but did not offer any guarantees."[114]

The remainder of this section will analyze the October 1921 council of the Ukrainian Church since this marks the establishment of a new hierarchy and the final separation of the Ukrainian Church from the standing Orthodox synod and the MP. The proceedings of the council and its acts and resolutions are the primary texts expressing its identity. In some instances, the resolutions from the May 1921 meeting in Kyiv also amplify points of religious identity.

The May 1921 Preparatory Council

The series of events that resulted in the establishment of Ukrainian-language parishes in Kyiv and other select regions of Ukraine influenced the work of the council and its final attempts to reconcile with the Orthodox episcopate in Ukraine. The appeal of Patriarch Tikhon to the faithful in Ukraine (July 23, 1921) to preserve the unity of the Church coalesces around the problem of liturgical language.[115] The patriarch identified the cause of division among Orthodox in Ukraine at the very beginning of his letter:

> Enemies of the long-standing unity of Orthodox Ukrainians with the entire Russian Church have produced discord and enmity among members of the Orthodox Church in Ukraine, and are said to be in violation of Church discipline, and have voluntarily introduced services in the Ukrainian language in several parishes with aggression.[116]

The patriarch referred to a concession made by the Ukrainian synod in its meeting on February 12–15 of 1921, which permitted the possibility of celebrating the services in Ukrainian parishes with Ukrainian pronunciation of Church Slavonic, the reading of the Gospel in Ukrainian (following the Church Slavonic reading), and the preaching of the homily in Ukrainian, as long as the faithful indicate their desire for the vernacular.[117] The patriarch argued that the synod responded affirmatively to the desire of the Ukrainian cohort for increased Ukrainization of church life. He asserted that bishops would protect beloved Ukrainian traditions from falling into decay and promised to create a special committee to translate the Bible and liturgical books from Church Slavonic into vernacular Ukrainian.[118] Furthermore, the patriarchal church would permit parishes to celebrate liturgy in Ukrainian if two-thirds of the parish membership voted for it.[119]

It is notable that the patriarch appointed Archbishop Michael (Ermakov) to the seat of metropolitan of Kyiv in the same letter, referring to the request of the synod of bishops from their meeting on May 19–20, 1921, and the Kyivan union of parish churches.[120] The patriarch asked the Ukrainian faithful to accept Metropolitan Michael with love, and expressed hope that these decisions would end the internal enmity and division among the faithful.

The patriarch's letter was quite conciliatory in tone and suggested that the patriarchate was ready to respond affirmatively to the Ukrainian cohort's desire for ecclesial Ukrainization. The patriarch's letter, though, was issued only nine days following a stern rebuke issued by the synod of bishops in Kyiv to the Ukrainian faithful. In their letter of July 14, 1921, the bishops attempted to delegitimize the meeting held by the Ukrainian cohort in May of 1921.[121] The bishops depicted the activity of the Ukrainian cohort as canonically dubious, arguing that a gathering of laity, deacons and presbyters, without the knowledge and blessing of the synod of bishops, was a violation of Apostolic Canon 29, which prohibits clergy and laity from doing anything without the permission of the bishop.[122] The synod instructed the faithful to use the proper liturgical commemorations at divine services, including an admonition to include a commemoration of "His Holiness Our Father Patriarch Tikhon."[123] The letter also referred implicitly to the deposition from sacred orders of priests and deacons who belonged to the Ukrainian cohort and had participated in the May gathering in Kyiv, reminding the faithful that "those who are deposed from orders and priests who are suspended from liturgical service are not permitted to perform any church services or sacraments, and that celebrating them does not yield any gracious power."[124]

The messages communicated by the synod of Ukrainian bishops and Patriarch Tikhon to the faithful in Ukraine were mixed. On the one hand, they depicted the activity of the Ukrainian cohort as illegitimate, in violation of ancient canons and recent conciliar directives. Any association with clergy who were under ecclesiastical interdict on account of their canonical violations would deprive faithful of access to divine grace. On the other hand, the tone is conciliatory. The patriarch wanted to avoid the spread of discord and schism, and was willing to permit the Ukrainization of the Church in accordance with the will of the local laity. The patriarch's primary concern was to avoid additional separation of Ukrainians from the Moscow Patriarchate. The messages of the bishops simultaneously honor the distinct character of Ukrainian religious identity while excising the very proponents of Ukrainization from positions of leadership within the Church. Furthermore, another objective of the July letters was to snuff out the convocation of an October gathering that had the potential for schism.

The October Council: The Birth of the 1921 UAOC

The October Council took place in spite of the episcopal directives instructing the faithful to ignore it. The leaders of the Ukrainian cohort invited the new patriarchal exarch, Metropolitan Michael, to participate in the council. The metropolitan responded politely on September 28, 1921, informing Michael Moroz (the chair of the AUOCC) that the All-Ukrainian Council did not have the canonical right to convene a council on the territory governed by the episcopate of the Church in Ukraine and without the blessing of the bishops.[125] Metropolitan Michael pleaded with Moroz to arrange for the Ukrainian cohort to bring their concerns to him as the exarch, and stated that "I will always be ready" to consider their appeals in consultation with his brother bishops. The metropolitan's letter followed one issued by the synod of bishops on August 18, 1921, in which they expressed deep sorrow about the impending church schism.

The synodal letter referred again to the discussion about liturgical language and communicated the synod's blessing for the Ukrainian cohort to celebrate the liturgy in vernacular Ukrainian. The letter also informed them that the previously promised translation committee was already working on a Ukrainian-language Bible and liturgical texts.[126] The synodal letter also unveils new developments that had come to the attention of the bishops. The bishops bless the general platform of Ukrainization of the Church in terms of permitting customs and celebrations. But the letter also addresses the desire of the Ukrainian cohort to establish an independent and completely free autocephalous church. The bishops underscored the fact that the entire Church had elected Tikhon as patriarch, including the Ukrainian delegates to the Moscow Council, and that the patriarch sought to serve all the people of the "Slavo-Russian Church" in prayer and wisdom, and not exercise dominion over them.[127]

The letters from Metropolitan Michael and the synod of bishops in Ukraine elucidate the position of the bishops in the aftermath of the events that commenced in 1917. Initially, the MP had refuted attempts by the Ukrainian cohort to seek a platform of Ukrainization and had also resisted attempts to seek assistance from the EP in obtaining autocephaly. When the Bolsheviks assumed power in Ukraine and the state assumed control of parish property, the Ukrainian cohort found a new avenue for pursuing their platform of Ukrainization. Historians sympathetic to the cause of the Ukrainian cohort depict them as constantly seeking to perform their work within the parameters of the Church by requesting the blessing of the bishops. The letters from the patriarch, synod, and metropolitan illustrate an episcopate gradually permitting increased Ukrainization within the Church, with the caveat that two-thirds of any given parish must indicate their desire to use Ukrainian liturgically. The evidence from this short course of events shows that all of the church leaders who had authority in Ukraine were amenable to permitting a course of ecclesial Ukrainization in liturgical language and aesthetics. The position of the Ukrainian Church leadership essentially ignored the decision of the 1918 council to retain only Church Slavonic as the Church's liturgical language. On the surface, this shift in policy appears to be conciliatory. The only concession the bishops were not willing to make was the granting of ecclesial autocephaly.

The bishops' acknowledgement of the legitimacy of vernacular Ukrainian and the restoration of Ukrainian customs and rites as belonging to Orthodox tradition was an attempt to reconcile with the Ukrainian cohort. From the bishops' perspective, it was not the Ukrainian cohort's objectives that were illegitimate, it was the process they adopted for pursuing those objectives because it violated Orthodox Church order. The sequence of correspondence is likewise telling: the bishops warn faithful to avoid ecclesially illegitimate gatherings and appeal to the Ukrainian cohort to pursue their objectives within the church simultaneously. The themes of proper canonical order and the sanctioning of Ukrainization appear in the letters written by the synod, Patriarch Tikhon, and Metropolitan Michael, and all of the letters were issued after the Ukrainian cohort gathering in May and prior to the October 1921 council.

The conciliatory appeals of the bishops and the Ukrainian cohort failed, and the October Council was convened as planned. The council convened on October 14, 1921, and endured significant disagreement among its participants on how to proceed with the construction of a Ukrainian Church separate from Moscow. Many of the conciliar delegates were prepared to disavow the bishops and build a church from scratch. Several delegates were discouraged by the absence of sympathy from the hierarchy for their objective of Ukrainization. One bishop in Ukraine had briefly adopted the Ukrainian cohort. Kyiv eparchy had experienced its own grave turmoil when Metropolitan Volodymyr (Bogoiavlensky) was murdered by the Bolsheviks in 1918. His successors, Metropolitan Antony (Khrapovitsky) and Bishop Nazarii, had very short tenures in Ukraine on account of the war.

The Ukrainian cohort interpreted the bishops' refusal to grant autocephaly as their desire to retain Ukraine as a vassal of the Russian empire. They acknowledged the turnover in the Kyivan See, but interpreted Metropolitan Antony's departure as an act of abandonment. In short, they used their identity as ecclesial orphans no father wanted to adopt as an opportunity to construct their own episcopate, an endeavor that would further pollute their identity within global Orthodoxy.

Such was the situation confronting patriarchal exarch Metropolitan Michael when he arrived at St. Sophia's Cathedral on the sixth day of the October Council in 1921. The council greeted him with the traditional singing of the hymn to the Mother of God, and he addressed the council.[128] The proceedings contain mostly the statements made by council delegates in response to brief words by Metropolitan Michael. For example, Volodymyr Chekhivsky's statement is an apology for the legitimacy of the gathering as an authentic and canonical council, based on historical precedents of ecumenical councils convoked by emperors. Chekhivsky stated that the Holy Spirit had convened a legitimate council of the faithful from parish churches; clearly, he responded to some reference to the canonical illegitimacy of their gathering. Ivan (John) Teodorovych asked the exarch if he would understand him when he spoke Ukrainian; the metropolitan responded that he understood everything that had taken place since his arrival. One of the most prestigious lay delegates, Mykola Levitsky, requested that the metropolitan arrange for the consecration of an episcopate for the Ukrainian Church.[129] Levitsky warned the exarch of the impending historical judgment of his decision:

"I would like to direct your attention, Vladyko,[130] to the fact that it is no boy who stands before you. I am seventy-nine years old and have worked only for the community for forty-three years. Before you stands a person who desires only truth and love, and for the forty-three years of my community labors I have the right to request that you think about these things, that this matter of the people, it is great, holy. In your love and goodness, you should think about this . . . that to oppose a living act means to oppose God. We ask you to help us. Help us to bring about the consecration of bishops, that this moment would be great, and that we would remember your name unto the ages of ages. And if this does not happen, then history will say that the entire people appealed to you with love, and you responded to them with a stone. We asked for fish, and you gave us a stone. I believe that you will not do this." [Metropolitan Michael responds:] "I wouldn't consecrate stones, so you should not worry." [Levitsky responds:] "This is just a comparison, I did not want to offend you. My ultimate request was this: we appeal to you with love. Help us on the matter of consecrating an episcopate. We believe that you will do this and may God help you!"[131]

Delegates offered several additional appeals and explanations to Metropolitan Michael. Toward the end of their discussion with him, Chekhivsky observed that the Ukrainian cohort no longer trusted the patriarchal episcopate in Ukraine, and wanted to know the steps the synod planned to take to restore trust.[132]

Moroz summarized the bishop's final appeal to the gathering: the metropolitan refused to acknowledge its legitimacy. Despite the repeated appeals for the construction of an episcopacy, the response was that all-Ukrainian, all-Russian, and ecumenical councils must gather first, and only afterward could any discussion of autocephaly occur.[133] The encounter between Metropolitan Michael and the delegates of the October Council was intense: one delegate referred to the open weeping of several delegates and the metropolitan himself.[134] After Metropolitan Michael left without conceding to the Ukrainian cohort's requests, the council embarked on a path of separation from the Moscow Patriarchate. Delegates consistently stressed that their objective was to establish themselves as equals in the family of Orthodox churches, to be siblings and not aliens. Most of the analysis of the steps taken by the Ukrainian cohort at this juncture in its history has focused on the canonical illegitimacy of consecrating bishops by presbyters and deacons at a council. However, a review of the history shows that liturgical language was the topic that originally generated the disagreement between the Ukrainian cohort and the synod in Ukraine.

Language was the primary identity marker for the Ukrainian cohort, and their decision to petition for the establishment of parishes by directly appealing to the state instead of working with the ecclesial apparatus intensified the animosity between the two groups. The bishops were initially annoyed by the persistent requests to use vernacular Ukrainian in the liturgy when the 1918 council had voted to use Church Slavonic exclusively. The Ukrainians viewed the synodal rejections of the petitions to use Ukrainian as a case of Russian bigotry employed to eradicate Ukrainian identity, a pattern that had gone on for too long. Historically, when the Soviet government in Ukraine assumed control of all church property and managed the process of granting it to communities, a door was opened for the Ukrainian cohort to achieve their objective of establishing their own church without encountering the same obstacle of denial from the Russian synod.

This historical episode yields problems of assessment that continue to permeate the contemporary Orthodox environment in Ukraine. The problems listed here represent the legacy of the language debate between the Ukrainian cohort and the synod that resulted in a permanent ecclesial separation. The first problem is the matter of finality in deciding the fate of vernacular Ukrainian in the liturgy. The evidence indicates that the preconciliar commission on liturgy had several different proposals for using liturgical Ukrainian in the liturgy, but the Moscow Council deferred the matter to the competence of the patriarch and the synod.[135] Clearly, the Ukrainian cohort expected that the Church would permit Ukrainian to be used in the liturgy, and the rejection of the petition was a surprise. This problem was complicated by the authority of the 1918 All-Ukrainian Council held in Kyiv, which adopted Church Slavonic as the only language of worship. The patriarch and bishops understood this council as authoritative, but Ukrainians viewed it as illegitimate because of the removal of delegates who were sympathetic to the Ukrainian cause. The later decision by the synod of bishops and Patriarch Tikhon to bless the use of Ukrainian in the liturgy seems to indicate that the decision of the 1918 council was not final and could be changed. However, the stipulation that two-thirds of a parish must vote for the use of liturgical language introduced another related problem. First, the stipulation would require parishes to create mechanisms for determining the will of the people at the local level. Second, it could serve as a precedent for other matters of debate within the Church. Furthermore, both the elusive finality on the language issue and the introduction of a vote for adopting the vernacular would become models for other issues of debate within the Ukrainian Church. Future generations of church leaders would defer decisions on canonical autocephaly either to a pan-Orthodox council or to the will of the people, or both. As a result, any discussion of autocephaly occurred only in juridical or democratic terms; there was no substantive evaluation of the veracity of the petition for canonical autocephaly.

The second major problem emerging from the language debate is the matter of accepting the ecclesial decisions made during the process of establishing Ukrainian-language parishes. The letters from the Ukrainian synod and Patriarch

Tikhon are telling in this regard, as they clearly warn laity and clergy to avoid priests and deacons who have either been suspended from ministry or canonically deposed. The Ukrainian cohort appointed bishops who were deposed from holy orders, and this was one of the primary markers of ecclesial illegitimacy from the synodal perspective. The Ukrainian leaders believed that their action was necessary because the Ukrainians had established parishes and an assembly with recurring meetings and obvious aspirations for autocephaly without either the blessing or the participation of bishops. In other words, the Ukrainian cohort consistently bypassed canonical order to achieve their objectives, which disrupted church life. From the Ukrainian perspective, the strategy of suspending and deposing the clerical figures leading the Ukrainian cause had two consequences: first, it removed the clergy who would have presided at Ukrainian services. Second, it would slowly dampen the repeated requests for using vernacular Ukrainian in the liturgy, and symbolically stifle the movement for Ukrainization of church life. The Ukrainian cohort noted the absurdity of such decisions given the legacy of the churches of Rus'; the people of Rus' became Orthodox through the mediation of Greeks who translated the Gospels and the liturgy into the vernacular. The denial of the petition to pray in Ukrainian was the rejection of a core principle held dear by Orthodox on a global scale; the local dimension of the Church was symbolized by communities praying in their own language. For the Ukrainian cohort, this was a point of no return: relinquishing the right to pray in the vernacular was tantamount to betraying Christ and the very Gospel he preached.

The above problems continue to contribute to the divisions within Ukrainian Orthodoxy in the twenty-first century, but it is essential to return to the matter of language as an identity marker. For the Ukrainian cohort, retaining Ukrainian and translating the services was a primary act of cultivating a native identity that distinguished them from the Russian Church in Ukraine. Of all the features emphasizing Ukrainian identity for the 1921 UAOC, language was the most significant in symbolizing the particularity of the local Ukrainian community. From a historical perspective, the conciliar resolution on the use of the native language in the church offers a final punctuating point for this section that requires no additional commentary.

Conciliar Resolution No. 7: Native Language in the Church

In the Ukrainian Autocephalous Orthodox Church the living Ukrainian language of the people is used, because Christ, the apostles, and their assistants preached in the native languages of the peoples, because only in one's native language can one pray best and present one's soul to God. Whoever mocks evangelization in the Ukrainian language sins against the Holy Spirit, which gave the gift of language for the evangelization of all peoples in fiery tongues; he [who mocks] must be cast out of the Church until he repents.[136]

The evidence indicates a softening in the synodal position on the Ukrainization of church life. In the correspondence, the bishops seem to approve of the restoration of rituals and customs that enhance a distinctly Ukrainian religious identity. There seems to be no solid rationale for the prohibition of expressing native religious identity outside of the circumvention of standard procedures within the Church's canonical order. Prelovs'ka suggests that Ukrainization itself introduced not only a religious distinction, but a juxtaposition of national identities that might have threatened the synod in Ukraine. She claims that the description of the Ukrainians as an unchurchly group was due to their open adulation for national poets and heroes in the liturgy, including the great poet Taras Shevchenko.[137] Apparently the Ukrainians had introduced the custom of singing Shevchenko's "Testament" to open meetings of the Kyivan eparchial gatherings as early as 1917.[138] This custom illuminates Ukrainian religious identity as ineluctably associated with the emergence of national consciousness, a trait that certainly contributed to tensions between the Ukrainian Church and the synod.

An Assessment of the Episcopacy as the Second Degree of Separation

This review of the separation of the Ukrainians from the patriarchal synod has established how the Ukrainians viewed the existing bishops negatively. The controversy surrounding language deepened the fissures between the episcopate and the Ukrainian cohort, but language was not the only issue. The Ukrainians were determined to restore the Kyivan Church, which had become part of the Moscow Patriarchate in 1686. As the Orthodox Church prepared for the Moscow Council and attempted to adjust to political and civil turbulence, Ukrainians with aspirations of autocephaly saw an opportunity for the restoration of a Kyivan Church that would be the equal of both the Moscow and Constantinopolitan patriarchates. The Ukrainian cohort appealed for the convocation of the 1918 All-Ukrainian Council, and more than one witness testified to the presence of a pro-autocephaly majority at the council. However, the sudden and tragic murder of Metropolitan Volodymyr altered the landscape and an anti-autocephaly majority somehow prevailed. Arguing that each nation should have its own autocephalous church, the Ukrainian cohort pursued autocephaly relentlessly. One of the main elements of its rationale for separation was its description of the existing episcopate.

The autocephalists named orphanage as their primary rationale for separating from the bishops in Ukraine. They interpreted the modern Ukrainian period of church history as a series of episcopal failures, beginning with the Union of Brest in 1596 and exacerbated by the annexation of the metropolia to Moscow in 1686. Most significant was their perception of the bishops' fidelity to the tsarist regime.

Professor Vasyl Danylevich described the bishops' loyalty to the tsar as an act resulting in the orphanage of the Ukrainian faithful in his address to the council on October 14, 1921.[139]

Danylevich proposed that the October 1921 council was on the verge of inaugurating the rebirth of the Church, and he situated this rebirth in theological terms, referring to the Gospel of John chapter 3, in which Jesus discusses birth from water and the Spirit with Nicodemus. Another delegate named H. Kolomiets argued that the current bishops in Ukraine "do not take the path of the Savior" and only wish to govern them, "despite the fact that the monarchy has fallen."[140] Kolomiets stated that "we are going on a revolutionary path. We, the All-Ukrainian Orthodox Church Council . . . have the right to elect a bishop who will bless us."[141] Kolomiets was among the first at the council to advocate for the construction of a native episcopate without seeking permission from the Orthodox synod.

When Metropolitan Michael left the council without a reconciliation between the episcopate and the Church, the council began the process of constructing its own episcopacy since their appeals to the Constantinopolitan and Georgian churches were unsuccessful. Volodymyr Chekhivsky was the chief proponent for constructing an episcopate without the participation of the bishops. Chekhivsky was a complex figure who had served as minister of external affairs in the upper levels of the cabinet of the Directory of the Ukrainian National Republic before the Bolsheviks resumed control in late 1919 and early 1920. Chekhivsky had a theological education from the Kyivan Theological Academy with a specialization in church history. Besides Lypkivs'kyi, Chekhivsky was the most influential ideologue of the 1921 Ukrainian Church.[142] He was a herald, or lay evangelizer, and he published essays that reflected on the liberation of the Church from the tsarist regime, an early variant of liberation theology circulating within the nascent Soviet milieu. Chekhivsky presented the case for the construction of an episcopate during multiple sessions that took place on October 20. The central part of his presentation concerns ecclesial participation in a sacrament: Chekhivsky asserts that each sacrament is an act of the whole church, together, and therefore not dependent on the sacerdotal power of the episcopate.[143]

Likewise, Chekhivsky asserts that the sacrament of ordination is performed by the entire Church gathered together, which is demonstrated in the liturgical rites that call for the whole Church to sing the responses. Chekhivsky insisted that each order within the Church has a responsibility to act as a guardian of the gifts of the Holy Spirit, and he provides numerous examples of bishops who abused the spiritual gift they had received. Chekhivsky refers to the argument between Eusebius and bishop Nestorius, and how Nestorius failed to uphold the highest duty of his office, correct teaching.[144] Chekhivsky also referred to Sophronius, the seventh-century monk and later patriarch of Jerusalem, who defended the Church's teaching on the divine and human wills of Christ against the heresy of monothelitism, which the majority of the bishops professed at the time. Chckhivsky utilized the examples of laity defending the faith to set the stage for the problem confronting the Ukrainians. He argued that the bishops were encouraging the people to worship the princes of darkness as a metaphor for using the Church as a vassal who is actually serving the tsarist regime.[145] Chekhivsky accused the episcopate in Ukraine of demanding the Ukrainians' loyalty to the tsarist regime; in return for their fidelity, the bishops would consider their demands. Chekhivsky was implying that the bishops of the MP hoped for the restoration of the tsar, despite the regime's collapse. The theological basis for the conciliar construction of an episcopate was that the grace of the Holy Spirit had been given to the entire church, so the Ukrainians had a responsibility to act since the bishops had abused the gifts they had received. Chekhivsky justified the rite of consecrating bishops by a council by referring to the historical precedents of defending the faith, and attempted to assure the people that the grace of the Spirit they had received would remain intact in the absence of a bishop from the process of electing and consecrating an episcopate.

Several delegates argued that the path adopted by the October Council was too much of a departure from global Orthodoxy, and that the October Council needed to retain its unity with the rest of the Church. Some delegates argued that delegations should approach other Orthodox churches to ask them for assistance. In fact, the October Council had approached both the Ecumenical Patriarchate and the Georgian Orthodox Church, but the conditions of war prevented them from responding. Requesting the intervention of another Orthodox Church for the establishment of an episcopate had a historical antecedent in Ukraine. After the entire synod of bishops agreed to the Union of Brest in 1596, the majority Orthodox population in Ukraine was left without a hierarchy. In 1620, Patriarch Theophanes of Jerusalem consecrated a new episcopate for the Kyivan Metropolia, making a stop in Kyiv during his travel to Moscow to participate in the enthronization of Patriarch Filaret (Romanov) In this instance, no foreign church representing global Orthodoxy responded to the council's petition for help, so they opted to construct their own episcopate with a council consisting of priests, deacons, and laity, but no bishops.

Those who were uncomfortable with this brazen proposal explained their position. Ksenofont Sokolowsky, a priest, predicted that the council's act would be interpreted as "a violation of the foundations of our Orthodox faith."[146] Sokolowsky affirmed Chekhivsky's emphasis on the contribution of the laity to the process of selecting, ordaining, and installing clergy, but he reserved the traditional privilege of fulfilling the selection through the laying on of hands to the bishops as the successors of the apostles, emphasizing that bishops, and not councils, enact the ritual of ordination.[147]

Sokolowsky offered a counterproposal to the council, arguing that they were impatient, especially since their ancestors waited ten years before Patriarch Theophanes renewed the Orthodox episcopate.[148] Sokolowsky presented a four-point proposal to the delegates: to issue an epistle to the Russian episcopate demanding that the Russians renew for their Kyivan mother an episcopate; to expend considerable energy in attracting bishops to the church from Ukraine and Russia[149] who support her movement, or to ask them to consecrate bishops for her; to send epistles to all of the Eastern churches requesting the consecration of a bishop; to continue to build up the Ukrainian Church while remembering that the process can be successful only with a standing episcopate.[150]

In a contribution offered later in the same day, a council delegate by the name of M. Homichevsky (from Zhytomyr') argued that absolute consensus was necessary for such a decision. He encouraged the council to seek consensus with global Orthodoxy on the matter since it lacked historical precedent, and expressed doubt about the oneness of mind among the delegates at the council who were on the verge of making this decision.[151] At the end of the day, the council voted on the question of constructing their own episcopate: 181 delegates voted "yes," 5 voted "no," and 5 abstained. The next day, 83 delegates (who had been absent) voted: 72 "yes," 4 "no," and 7 "abstained." Ultimately the council did not have a consensus, but had an overwhelming majority that favored the rite of consecration without a bishop, with 92 percent of the vote in favor. However, Sokolowsky's dissenting opinion prefigured the divisions among the Ukrainians who desired ecclesial autocephaly. Sokolowsky would become an influential bishop devoted to Ukrainization and autocephaly without radical changes to church tradition; his activities are summarized later in this chapter.

The conciliar decision to consecrate a bishop without a participating bishop in the council marked Ukrainian Orthodox religious identity in two ways. First, global Orthodoxy rejected the legitimacy of the new bishops, so the Ukrainian cohort became infected with the disease of ecclesial illegitimacy, a stigma that has afflicted pro-Ukrainian movements up until this day. Second, the Ukrainian cohort believed that they were acting in accordance with their own history on the basis of their orphanhood. They asserted that they were resuscitating a dead church and breathing life into it by making this move, and they also believed that it was their moral responsibility to take immediate action as opposed to waiting.

The conciliar decision to construct a new episcopacy established a new church and created a new problem for the Ukrainians. The new episcopate finalized its separation from the Moscow Patriarchate in Ukraine, even though most of the people remained within the patriarchate. The new episcopate also functioned as a condemnation of the old one.[152] The Ukrainian Church expressed this condemnation clearly in their conciliar resolutions from the initial council held in May

1921. Resolution 8 questioned the legitimacy of the 1918 All-Ukrainian Council because its delegates were not elected by the Ukrainian Orthodox faithful.[153]

The council in May 1921 also condemned Bishop Nazarii's deposition of Ukrainian clergy, affirmed its recognition of the canonical legitimacy of said clergy, and affirmed the right of Ukrainian clergy to refuse to commemorate Bishop Nazarii, other bishops, and the patriarch at divine services.[154] The May Council reserved the most condemnatory words for the synod of bishops in Ukraine in resolution 8, "On the Kyivan Episcopate," pejoratively referring to them as "spiritual government workers" who had forsaken their right to govern the Kyivan Church with the collapse of the tsarist regime.[155]

The May Council noted that Metropolitan Antony and his assistant Nikodim had abandoned Kyiv and the council refused to recognize the legitimacy of instructions issued by bishops who had left their flocks. The October Council adhered to the declarations of the one in May, and elaborated the objectives of the council in the first canon, claiming that the creation of a conciliar-governed church structure conformed to the spirit of Orthodoxy.[156]

Canon 10 of the October Council condemned both the 1917 Moscow Council and the 1918 All-Ukrainian Council as gatherings that did not observe the commandments of Christ. This particular canon appears to simply repeat earlier rejections of Russian Church leaders. But in fact, the canon disavowed the resolutions of both the 1917 and 1918 councils in an attempt to demonstrate the October Council's continuity with Orthodox tradition. The rationale for liberation from the Russian episcopate was its continued service to the tsarist regime. This canonical explanation concludes this section that establishes the Ukrainian cohort as liberated from Moscow. This instance is a variation from the pattern of decisions yielding multiple and conflicting problems. The Ukrainian identity marker was to be a church liberated from service to the state. The Ukrainian cohort, enjoying a brief period of favoritism from the ominous Bolshevik regime, capitalized on the new decree on the separation of church and state to distinguish itself from the politics of the Russian synod. One of the two identity markers for the Ukrainian cohort was inscribed upon the "old" Russian episcopate. This episcopate was unable to liberate itself from its previous affiliation with the tsarist regime and the Ukrainians defined this affiliation as inconsistent with the Gospel's commandments. The identity borne by the Russian episcopate was the opposite of the Ukrainian identity, which had no state affiliation. This argument was very convenient for the Ukrainians at the time; they issued their own decree on the relationship between the church and the state beginning with a canon stating that the "intermingling of church life with the state is a violation of the will of Christ and his commandments."[157] The canon also called for the casting out of any member of the Church who attempted to exploit it for political purposes, or for the "renewal of lordship over the lower classes of society."[158] This canon confirms Bociurkiw's assertion that the Ukrainian intelligentsia who were in the highest structures of the Church had socialist tendencies.[159]

Of all the arguments advanced by the Ukrainian cohort to support its case for separation, liberation, and autocephaly, the separation of church and state is the weakest. The benefit of this arrangement under the Soviets was short-lived for the Ukrainians, who came under close scrutiny and pressure by the Soviet regime as early as 1922, just one year after their council. The 1921 UAOC had many ideologues, the best known of them its first metropolitan, Vasil Lypkivs'kyi.[160] Lypkivs'kyi gladly took on the task of inscribing the Ukrainian identity as a new church in his pastoral work.

The 1921 UAOC as a New Church

In a homily on the second Sunday after Pentecost, Lypkivs'kyi raises the matter of grace and its presence in the Church. In the homily, Lypkivs'kyi refers to the polemical battle between the "old Russian Church" and the "new Ukrainian Church."[161] He discusses the dynamic of ecclesial legitimacy located in the sacramental life of the Church and paraphrases the "old Russian" bishops as grounding their ecclesial legitimacy in apostolic succession, baptism, marriage, and burial. He paraphrases the Russians as stating that only those who participate in legitimate sacraments will enter the kingdom of heaven, whereas those outside of sacramental grace are bound for hell. Lypkivs'kyi stated that the Ukrainian Church had followed the path indicated by Christ by abandoning the old ways and taking up the new.[162] Lypkivs'kyi interprets the historical event of Christ's resurrection as authorizing a new path, with the assembly of the entire Church (and not just the bishops) the only legitimate means toward receiving this grace. Essentially, the 1921 UAOC bore two concurrent identity markers: they were completely unlike the old regime represented by the Moscow Patriarchate in Ukraine, and their new identity was rooted in the creation of new governing structures representing the Ukrainian people. With their newness came the tinge of revolutionary tendencies. Throughout the process of deliberating their future, the 1921 UAOC championed *sobornopravnist'* and espoused egalitarianism in church life, sentiments that resonated with the socialist climate of the time. But by 1924, Lypkivs'kyi was under immense duress and prohibited from traveling, and by 1927, he was forced out of his office of metropolitan. The Soviet regime unveiled its animosity toward the Ukrainians as the Church's popularity spread rapidly, and Lypkivs'kyi was accused of being an enemy of the people. He vehemently defended his own position as a faithful citizen of the Soviet Union in a voluminous apology that was ultimately unsuccessful.[163] Lypkivs'kyi described himself as a church revolutionary whose attitude toward tsarism was consistent with the socialist values of the regime. To be fair, Lypkivs'kyi carefully professed his sole interest as building up the life of the church and sustained the absolute separation of church and state required by law. But his fate, and that of the entire Autocephalous Church, which was ultimately liquidated by the Soviet regime in 1930, shows that some identity markers for the 1921 UAOC proved to be quite short-lived. The two identity markers that proved to be permanent were the perception of the patriarchate as the undesirable opposite and the notion of the 1921 UAOC as the people's church, which is ruled by the very people who elected the episcopate.

A New Vision for Church Governance as the Third Degree of Separation

The establishment of the episcopate by the people of the Church connects the final degree of separation to the second degree, which disavowed the existing Orthodox bishops in Ukraine. The living cells for the new vision of governance of the Church were established by the revision of the rite of consecration of a bishop employed by the Ukrainians as they constructed their own episcopate on October 23, 1921.

The received Byzantine rite begins with an examination of faith on the eve of the consecration, with the bishop-elect presenting three confessions of faith demonstrating his fidelity to Orthodoxy and ability to teach the faith. The consecration occurs at the Divine Liturgy and the ordination requires the participation of a minimum of two bishops. The bishop-elect is ordained after the "Little Entrance" and before the Trisagion, prior to the proclamation of the Word. The rite includes his presentation to the altar: the deacon intones "command" to the presiding bishop, the presbyters and deacons, and the laity as the bishop-elect is escorted to the altar. After the bishop-elect kisses the four corners of the altar, participating bishops engage in the primary ritual act of opening the Gospel book and laying it upon the bishop-elect's head as the prayer of ordination is read. The position of the bishop's ordination indicates the duties of his office: the newly ordained bishop is consecrated before the proclamation of the Word because this is the primary aspect of his ministry.[164] The order and requirements for the rite of a bishop's consecration symbolize the ecclesiology of the Orthodox Church. The participation of a minimum of two bishops illustrates Orthodoxy's value of synodality; no bishop ministers in isolation, but in cooperation with the others on his synod. Furthermore, the bishop exercises apostolic succession in the church because he receives it, necessitating the presence of other bishops with whom he exercises apostolic ministry.

The October 1921 council altered the rite for a bishop's consecration by ordaining their own bishop without the participation of any other bishops. Protodeacon

Vasyl Potienko witnessed the ordination of Vasyl Lypkivs'kyi to the office of archbishop and metropolitan of Kyiv on October 23, 1921.[165] Here is a lengthy excerpt of his account of the rite:

> At that time the rite of examination of the one to be ordained occurred and his confession of faith and solemn oaths for the service to the UAOC were heard. The words of Archdeacon Sylvester, unheard of in the native [language] and moving, resounded: "The Archpriest Vasyl, beloved by God and elected by the All-Ukrainian Church Council is prevailed upon to receive the laying on of hands as metropolitan of Kyiv and all-Ukraine, the Ukrainian Autocephalous Orthodox Church.
>
> The liturgy began. Little entrance. Two of the clergy—Archpriest Yuri Mihnovsky and Archpriest Michael Malecha—escort Archpriest Vasyl Lypkivs'kyi. "Command, honorable Christian people!" "Command, holy Council." Singing: "Rejoice Isaiah," "Glory to You, Christ God"—"Holy Martyrs."
>
> The primary, most significant moment arrived. The one elected by the Council kneels at the right hand of the holy altar, they place a large Gospel book bound with gold on his head, they opened it [the Gospel], all priests place their hands on the Gospel, from the priests to the solea are two chains of the hands of the deacons, on the solea are two chains of the hands of the elders from the deacons to all of the delegates of the Council, among the elders the artisan father Mykola Levitsky, and then each delegate placed his right hand on the left shoulder of his neighbor. And everyone was one their knees, with heads bowed.
>
> The voice of Archpriest Nestor Sharaivsky was heard from the altar: "The divine grace, which always heals the infirm and completes the deficient, through the laying on of our hands ordains the honorable archpriest Vasyl to archbishop and metropolitan of Kyiv and all-Ukraine of the Ukrainian Autocephalous Orthodox Church. Let us pray for him, that the grace of the All-Holy Spirit would descend on him." The clergy sings "Lord, Have Mercy," and "Kyrie Eleison." Both choirs repeat the same. The Church is frozen. Then. "Axios." "He Is worthy!" sang the clergy, the choirs, the whole church.
>
> Then, at last, Archbishop Vasyl, metropolitan of Kyiv and all-Ukraine appears on the solea. He blesses the people with the *dikir* and *trikir* on all sides, and the people stand from kneeling. Tears are in all eyes. The people see before them their . . . first bishop of their Church, a sign of the fullness of Church life, a symbol of the unity of the Ukrainian nation, they see their spiritual leader. A great historical act occurred. Like a heavy stone that fell from their shoulders. . . . the entire time, to the last moment, each delegate of the Council feared that some unanticipated power would interfere with the realization of that which was intimated, that something would happen to harm the ordination. When they kneeled and placed their hands on the

shoulder of their neighbor, there was the sense of an electrical current going through everyone to the altar and to the one elected by the Church.[166]

An examination of the most significant revisions made to the rite of a bishop's consecration reveals the October Council's particular ecclesiology. The first hint occurs with the "commands" that begin the rite. The received tradition has the deacon requesting the command according to hierarchical protocol: first, the presiding bishop, followed by the clergy, and the people, in order. The 1921 October Council's rite revises the order, by requesting commands from the "honorable Christian people" and the "holy council." Thus, the opening portion of the rite establishes the ecclesiological tone. The commands do not occur hierarchically, even though there were numerous priests who concelebrated. The commands establish conciliarity as the ecclesiological foundation: the rite of ordination follows the proceedings from the election that occurred at the council. The acclamation of divine grace confirms the conciliar tone of the rite as it describes who performs the primary ritual act by referring to "the laying on of our hands." The most significant revision is in the laying on of hands itself, which is performed by the entire council through the chain created from the altar through the solea and to the nave with all of the participating delegates of the council placing his right hand on the left shoulder of his neighbor. Clearly, it was the October Council that ordained Lypkivs'kyi as its archbishop.

The revision of the traditional rite of consecration to permit a council to be the primary celebrant was designed to set the tone for the new ecclesiological principle to govern the new Ukrainian Church, namely *sobornopravnist'*, or governance of the people via the council. The ecclesiological principles originated from the rite of consecration: since the chief bishop (metropolitan) of the church was selected from a conciliar gathering, the metropolitan would never have external power to exercise over the church. The council was essentially the first order of the church and the metropolitan's power was limited to leading the council as a member.

The church's statute elaborated the regulations of its new governing structure.[167] The highest authority of the church was the council that was to be convened every five years. The governing structure during the interim period would be the All-Ukrainian Church Council consisting of the metropolitan, bishops, and representatives from parishes in Kyiv and other regions, with up to ten from many of those parishes. On the one hand, the new structure was not altogether radical, since all of the bishops of the church were members. The 1921 UAOC revised the episcopate; it did not eradicate it. On the other hand, the change was quite radical since the church was now governed by a council with popular representation; absent from the new structure was a synod of bishops with almost absolute power. In this vein, the structure created by the October Council was both new and radical. In addition to permanently linking the episcopate with the people in governance, the UAOC stipulated that upbringing and marital status could no longer be obstacles to otherwise qualified men receiving ordination to the church's orders.[168]

The 1921 UAOC established twenty-five as the minimum age for a bishop and decreed that monastics could not have any special privileges in advancement to the episcopate.[169] These canons finalized a process that was inaugurated at the May meeting; at that time, all of the same principles were reiterated.[170]

The new liturgical ecclesiology implemented by the rite of consecration was supported by lesser-known canonical decisions of the 1921 UAOC. Small revisions to the liturgy proposed by the council symbolized the new ecclesiology of popular governance adopted by the UAOC and the rejection of the old system. In the debates on the need for liturgical reform during the course of the council, the delegates considered two changes that would be of no consequence for the quantity of text but would have significant impact on the shift in religious identity. The council accepted the proposal of replacing the common request for a blessing invoked by the deacon and singers during the course of the liturgy—"Владико, благослови!" (Master, bless")—with "Найпошеснійший отче, благослови!" ("Most honorable father, bless!). The proceedings indicate that the council accepted this resolution, and there is supporting evidence despite the lack of a second appearance in the canons issued by the council. Levitsky offered a second proposal and a most intriguing representation of the church's newness in suggesting the eradication of the word "rab" (servant, slave, Slavonic for the Greek doulos) from the liturgy since the people of the church were free, and not slaves. Teodorovych suggested "child" as a more suitable word.[171]

The council did not adopt the resolution, but deferred it to the relevant commission. The deliberation of these terms punctuates our understanding of the public religious identity claimed and expressed by the Ukrainian cohort. Having established the existing synodal bishops as representatives of an old state regime, they cast themselves as new and free people who approached God of their own free will. The Ukrainians inscribed an identity of cruel overseers on the bishops in Ukraine and the patriarchate and established an ecclesiology of egalitarianism that reformed the episcopate and elevated the representation and ruling power of the people in the church through the principle of *sobornopravnist'*. The new Ukrainian Church was both a restoration of the old Kyivan Metropolia and its update, especially given the relaxation of marital impediments to episcopal consecration. The council made modest revisions to the liturgy to reflect its egalitarian ecclesiology; in turn, the liturgy would imprint that ecclesiology on the Orthodox faithful by employing vocabulary that excised elements of external lordship from the Church.

Despite the newness professed by the 1921 UAOC, its inner tensions were never completely resolved. While the Ukrainians attempted to restore a Kyivan Metropolia characterized by church renewal, their identity also bore the marks that global Orthodoxy ascribed to them, particularly that of ecclesial illegitimacy. The heated debate over whether or not to consecrate their own episcopate without episcopal participation foreshadowed a dire consequence: alienation from the Orthodox world. The Ukrainian cohort was certainly new, a group promoting evangelization, Ukrainization, and the dignity of the laity; but the world also perceived the Ukrainians as being without grace since their process of electing and consecrating a bishop excluded an order of the Church, that of the bishop itself. The Ukrainians themselves seemed to waver on this identity marker, since the deliberations on the process of constructing an episcopate were the most intense of the council, and the rite of consecration was used only for the first two bishops of the episcopate due to extraordinary circumstances. The Ukrainians reverted to the customary rite of consecrating bishops once they had the quota of two bishops, a decision that seemingly betrayed the underpinning of popular ecclesiology of the revised rite.

Ukrainization in the Ukrainian Exarchate of the Moscow Patriarchate

The 1921 UAOC is the most appropriate model for the formation of a distinct Ukrainian Orthodox religious identity in the twentieth century because of its commitment to permanent separation from the Moscow Patriarchate. It is crucial to note, however, that Ukrainization was both considered and implemented within the patriarchate, a series of events attributable to the continuation of discourse that originated before the 1921 UAOC firmly committed to the path of independence and separation. In 1922, the exarchate scheduled an All-Ukrainian Council to discuss the possibility of implementing reforms in the Church.[172] Bohdan Bociurkiw states that the purpose of the assembly was to prevent a "Renovationist takeover of the Ukrainian exarchate," with provisional autocephaly as the tactic.[173] Instead of an all-church council, an assembly was held with eighty-four delegates, which included twelve bishops.[174] The assembly adopted a resolution described by Bociurkiw as a concession to "the aspiration of the Ukrainian church movement."[175] Bociurkiw lists the primary components of the resolution:

> By an "overwhelming majority of votes" . . . the conference decided in favor of: (a) autocephaly for the Orthodox Church in the Ukraine, with the request that the Holy

Sobor [council] of Bishops of All Ukraine declare . . . that the Ukrainian church has, as of today, taken the road of autocephaly, and take measures for the realization of this autocephaly in a legal-canonical manner; (b) the introduction into the ecclesiastical life of a broad conciliar principle [*shirokaia sobornopravnost'*]; (c) Ukrainization of church services and ecclesiastical life, but without coercion.[176]

Bociurkiw notes that the gathering also created a commission to begin negotiations with the UAOC on healing the schism in the Church.[177]

Ultimately, the resolution of the 1922 gathering had no outcome because the bishops deferred action until the convocation of an all-Ukrainian council, and committed only to studying the possibilities of implementing the proposals. Negotiations with the UAOC also failed, which Bociurkiw attributed to an irreparable breach between the two churches.[178] Bociurkiw noted that Patriarch Tikhon dismissed Ukrainian autocephaly as a mere "provisional device" considered during his imprisonment.

The "Lubny" Schism

Ukrainization contributed to a new division within the MP in Ukraine, resulting in the so-called Lubny Schism of 1925. The leader of this schism was the controversial Bishop Feofil (Buldovsky), an important figure who bridges the divergent Ukrainian Orthodox Church movements from their genesis in 1917 until the end of World War II. Buldovsky was another example of an advocate for Ukrainization of the Church via canonical methods. Ordained and appointed as the vicar bishop for Lubny and Myrhorod in 1923—hence the name "Lubny" Schism—Buldovsky became the center of a controversy within the Ukrainian Exarchate due to a disputed account of Patriarch Tikhon's support, or lack thereof, for Ukrainian autocephaly.[179] Buldovsky openly called for the creation of a canonical Ukrainian autocephalous church in 1925 following Patriarch Tikhon's death, and he was joined by Archbishop Ioanikii (Sokolowsky), who presented the dissenting opinion on the conciliar ordination of an episcopate at the October 1921 UAOC council.[180] Bociurkiw states that four canonically ordained bishops met in May 1925 to establish an episcopate representing all of Ukraine that strongly advocated for ecclesial Ukrainization. Bociurkiw notes that the group was able to win over some patriarchal and renovationist parishes, but struggled to compete with the popular UAOC.

In response to this new schism the patriarchal exarchate in Ukraine deposed and excommunicated all of the bishops who belonged to the Lubny group, and Bociurkiw notes that the excommunication resulted in a loss of prestige among the local faithful.[181] The divisions among the Orthodox and state persecution of the Church prohibited the Lubny group from achieving its objectives.[182] Despite the disintegration of church life, Buldovsky endured, and reemerged anew as a proponent of Ukrainian autocephaly when he joined the reborn UAOC in 1942.[183]

These snapshots of developments within the Ukrainian Exarchate and the Lubny Schism reflect both the chaos reigning in church life during the Soviet period and the spread of aspirations for autocephaly and Ukrainization. While the 1921 UAOC carried the torch of autocephaly and Ukrainization, the sustained attempts to achieve autocephaly and implement Ukrainization among patriarchal bishops and communities demonstrates that these are identity markers transcending jurisdictional boundaries. Only the fierce Soviet persecution of church life, along with the destruction of Ukraine through Soviet occupation, collectivization, and dekulakization were able to pause the movement for Ukrainian autocephaly. A major difference between the 1921 UAOC and the Lubny Schism was the latter's commitment to obtaining autocephaly via canonical means. When the four bishops established an episcopate in 1925, claiming to represent the entire Ukrainian Church, they believed that they had succeeded where the 1921 UAOC had failed, as the UAOC had established a church without any participating bishops.

The methods used for implementing Ukrainization in church life are equally noteworthy. The UAOC translated texts and worshipped in Ukrainian, sometimes hurriedly. Buldovsky exemplifies a more gradual, nuanced approach to Ukrainization. While he was an ardent advocate for Ukrainization of the Church, he did not impose it. Bociurkiw adds that Buldovsky and his clergy used UAOC liturgical books, but that he refused to impose Ukrainian as a liturgical language, leaving the decision to the priests and their faithful, with a majority deciding to use Church Slavonic.[184]

The legacy of the Ukrainization movements within the patriarchal church is limited, but noteworthy for its distinguishing features of identity. First, the temporary endorsement of Ukrainization by the exarchate and its implementation by the Lubny group shows that autocephaly and Ukrainization were goals shared by numerous Orthodox Ukrainians. Thus, these initiatives were not exclusive to the 1921 UAOC. Second, the existence of these initiatives illuminates a cohort of Ukrainian Church leaders who were committed to remaining on a canonical path while carefully implementing Ukrainization without imposing it. In other words, changes to church life were possible and were not necessarily illegitimate innovations created by schismatics and heretics. The 1922 exarchate gathering and the Lubny Schism were driven by Orthodox Ukrainians who were committed to recreating a canonical Church in Ukraine that was independent from Moscow, but not separate from world Orthodoxy. The aspirations and activities of Ukrainian leaders within the Orthodox Church in Poland, treated in the next chapter, complete the story of the immediate post-revolutionary Orthodox Church in Ukraine.

A Sudden Ending: The Soviet Liquidation of the UAOC

In 1926, the UAOC prepared for its fifth anniversary. While the leaders of the UAOC had implemented an aggressive strategy of church reform that proved to be somewhat popular with the Ukrainian intelligentsia, the majority of the Orthodox population remained within the Moscow Patriarchate. The patriarchate's overtures to the UAOC for union demonstrate both the recognition that many people were drawn to the UAOC and an affirmation of the legitimacy of Ukrainization. The attempt of the exarchate to resolve their differences with the UAOC in 1922 ultimately failed, but the UAOC interpreted the exarchate's willingness to approach the UAOC positively. The AUOCC published a historical review of the life of the UAOC in 1925, which expressed satisfaction that the bishops of the exarchate "recognized the need to change their position" on the "renewal of the hierarchy" of the UAOC.[185] Metropolitan Vasyl Lypkivs'kyi noted that the bishops of the exarchate never attempted to anathematize the UAOC, even though it was disappointing that a joint commission for union never came to fruition.[186] Furthermore, the attempts of the Living Church to unite with the UAOC also affirmed its popularity.[187] These attempts at rapprochement by traditional church officials and newcomers all testify to the vitality and impact of the UAOC, despite the fact that the patriarchal churches still claimed about 90 percent of believers in Ukraine.[188]

If the UAOC's greatest success was the implementation of Ukrainization, its primary challenge was to permanently revise internal church culture by inscribing the principle of *sobornopravnist'* into all structures and internal church operations. In his reflection on the five-year anniversary of the UAOC, Lypkivs'kyi lamented the tendency of the laity to depend on official church structures for everything and predicted that the future of the UAOC would depend on the realization of *sobornopravnist'*, where everyone in the church would contribute to its ministry in some way.[189] But the aspirations of the UAOC were on the verge of catastrophe, as the political priorities of the USSR had shifted under Stalin.[190] Bociurkiw notes that the ascension of Stalin resulted in a decisive move away from appeasing nationalities and curbing Russian hegemony within the USSR by 1927.[191] The tepid state toleration of the UAOC coincided with the regime's authorization of Ukrainization and pitted an innovative church body against the patriarchate, which remained an ideological vestige of Russia's imperial past. The regime came to view Ukrainian nationalism as a serious threat to its economic and political objectives. The return of Muscovite tyranny over Ukraine would provide a centralizing and stabilizing power.[192]

For the churches, the commitment of patriarchal locum tenens Metropolitan Sergei (Stragorodsky) to supporting Soviet policies rendered the advocacy of anti-patriarchal church groups unnecessary, as the Church was under state con-trol.[193] The convergence of these political and ecclesial circumstances spelled the beginning of the end of the vitality of the UAOC in Ukraine. The UAOC's second All-Ukrainian Council in 1927 was a pseudo-council that forced Metropolitan Vasyl Lypkivs'kyi out of office.[194] By 1929, two additional bishops were arrested and Volodymyr Chekhivsky, the primary ideologue of the UAOC, was also imprisoned. The UAOC was implicated in a series of counterrevolutionary charges against the entire Ukrainian intelligentsia in a purge designed to bring Ukraine under centralized Soviet control.[195] The regime charged the UAOC with participating in the activities of the League for the Liberation of Ukraine (SVU), and used the state secret police (GPU) to execute the purge of Church officials. The penultimate act of liquidation occurred in 1930, as the GPU staged a pseu-do-council that voted to liquidate the UAOC.[196]

The state's purge of the UAOC occurred at a show trial lasting forty-one days (from March through April 1930) in the Kharkiv Opera House.[197] During the trial, the leaders of the UAOC were accused of attempting to revive national con-sciousness among the peasants in the countryside.[198] The impact of the purge on the life of the Church was devastating: a number of bishops, priests, and laity were deported, imprisoned, or put to death.[199] The state permitted the survival of the UAOC with a hastily organized conglomerate of a few hundred parishes that promised loyalty to the state and excised all counterrevolutionary precepts from the canons and statutes of the 1921 council in Kyiv.[200] From 1930 until the "revival" of the Orthodox Church in Ukraine during World War II, all of the churches were persecuted, with extremely limited ability to operate.

The hasty end to the brief but vital life of the 1921 UAOC illustrates salient features of its public religious identity. On the one hand, the 1921 UAOC's oppo-sition to the Moscow Patriarchate seemed to mirror the principles of the October Revolution itself. The UAOC openly valued and privileged a radical form of gov-ernance by all of the people while establishing its foundation on the political the-ology of liberation from the church structures of the tsarist period. On the surface, the UAOC's platform gives the appearance of a state-sponsored church designed to subvert the authority of the patriarchate in Ukraine. Also, there is no doubt that the UAOC's campaign of Ukrainization of the Church was fueled by state Ukrainization, at least in part. The presence of political activists among the intel-ligentsia of the UAOC, especially Chekhivsky, demonstrates a certain cross-pol-lination of political and church values with the emergence and rapid growth of the UAOC in Ukraine. In his memoirs, Metropolitan Vasyl Lypkivs'kyi attempted to address the accusations made by the Soviet authorities during the course of the pseudo-council ("extraordinary council") of 1930, when the UAOC voted to liquidate itself, that the UAOC was a nationalistic and chauvinistic organization:

> That the UAOC from the second All-Ukrainian Orthodox Council [up until 1926] was a political organization, this is truly a lie. On the contrary, at that time, the UAOC sincerely and carefully refrained from all politics . . . with all its strength. Nowhere—not in councils, not in conciliar meetings, not in speeches—were any political questions raised, and they were not discussed. And the traitor meetings of the year 1930 boldly lie when they implicate the UAOC in this. . . . Their Judases say that the UAOC was a "nationalistic-chauvinistic" organization. That the UAOC was built upon a nationalistic foundation, the UAOC had no enmity toward other faiths or peoples, and on the contrary preached the brotherhood of all nations.[201]

Lypkivs'kyi's claim about the UAOC's openness to other peoples has some support, primarily in the UAOC's open attitude to promoting Christian unity. The question of the UAOC's open and often harsh dismissals of Russian bishops is a more challenging matter. It is not easy to see the UAOC as a church welcoming people of Russian descent; however, the UAOC specifically implicated the tsar and his church policies as the agents who had enslaved the Ukrainian Church in this matter. The evidence favors a vision of the UAOC attempting to establish itself as the national Orthodox Church in Ukraine, following the pattern of autocephalous churches in sovereign republics emerging in modernity, while capturing the spirit of church reform ushered in by the twentieth century. The coincidence of the emergence of the UAOC with the aspirations for Ukrainian statehood suggest a strong connection between nation-building and church-building during this period in Ukrainian history.

Nevertheless, the UAOC was a decidedly Christian church. The accusation that is encouraged national consciousness was a response to the UAOC's prioritization of more engaged ministry by the clergy to Christianize the Ukrainian people, especially in the countryside. Ukrainization was designed to facilitate comprehension of the Church's liturgy and life among the people, and the UAOC's general platform for church renewal was both parallel to and partly inspired by the church renewal movement in the Orthodox Church of imperial Russia. Thus, one can conclude that the UAOC was influenced by the political environment of the time, but it agenda for active, engaged ministry was driven equally by the Christian values circulating among progressive Orthodox thinkers of the time.

As for the attempt to completely eradicate the UAOC, the state's initiative ultimately failed. First, the UAOC was not solely an inward-looking nationalistic cell: it dialogued with other Christians of the world and established roots outside of the USSR. Second, the state was unable to completely purge the ranks of clergy and laity who had belonged to the UAOC. The question of how to treat the legacy of the UAOC clergy who wished to return to active ministry in German-occupied Ukraine would prove to be significant for the Orthodox Church, which vied for power and influence during the temporary absence of the Soviet state. Finally, it is crucial to remember the power of memory. The violent and hostile acts of the Soviet state against the Church were not only viewed through the lens of church-state relations, but were also construed by Ukrainian advocates for autocephaly as acts perpetrated by Moscow against Kyiv. Many Ukrainians would resist any notion of agreement with Moscow, as long as it was governed by Bolsheviks. The perception of Moscow itself as Bolshevik, and of the Moscow Patriarchate as a servant of the Bolshevik state, would become an important feature of religious polemics in the next stage of the history of the Orthodox Church in Ukraine.

Not all Orthodox Ukrainians shared this perception of the Moscow Patriarchate as the handmaiden of the Soviet state. The laity continued to resist Stalin's anti-religious policies, with Soviet authorities expressing alarm about popular religiosity in parish life and lay people taking an active and often dangerous role in defending their legal right to keep parishes open and preventing local Soviet officers from dismantling churches and promoting anti-religious propaganda.[202] Furthermore, Roslof asserts that the faithful of patriarchal parishes in Russia vigorously resisted renovationism as a "heresy created by the Bolsheviks."[203] The renovationists had adopted a variety of policies of reform, including the new calendar, the reading of the Gospel in vernacular Russian, and permitting married clergy to advance to the ranks of the episcopate, characteristics rejected by the people, often fiercely and violently.[204] Despite the distinction that Bociurkiw sees between the 1921 UAOC and the Renovationist Church, there were parallels between the two groups manifest in candidacy for the episcopate and liturgical language, among other things. The 1921 UAOC and renovationist churches were decidedly new: one can see how an observant Orthodox Christian would view the new churches and their leaders dubiously, especially when the UAOC unashamedly promoted itself as the replacement of the patriarchal church. But from the perspective of the rank-and-file laity, there was one enemy: the Soviet state and its agents.[205]

Conclusion

The early twentieth century was a time of epic change for the Orthodox Church in Ukraine. The Russian empire's encounter with modernity and its gradual internal decline paved the way for Ukraine to establish national sovereignty and to recreate ecclesiastical independence from Moscow. In some ways, the situation of the Church mirrored that of the country. Ukraine's sovereignty occurred in fits and starts, and while the tsarist regime's disappearance was permanent, Ukraine became part of the Soviet Union. As a Soviet republic, Ukraine experienced a brief intensification of national identity in the early twenties. This period coincided with the emergence of an independent Ukrainian Orthodox Church. The leaders of the 1921 UAOC were members of the Ukrainian intelligentsia, and they sought to re-evangelize and Ukrainianize a populace that had been under Russian tyranny. To do so successfully, they had to literally separate from the Russian Church and elect leaders who would approve of a Ukrainianization campaign. It is ironic that their success occurred primarily during the Soviet period. Soviet favoritism toward the Ukrainians was strategically aimed at dividing the Church and weakening the patriarchate. Soviet support of the Ukrainians was very brief, but long enough to both energize the Ukrainian movement and establish a brief period where church and state tolerated one another. The state's assistance of the Ukrainians is one of the most significant aspects of this period in history because the Soviet determination to weaken the patriarchate unleashed an Orthodox Church movement grounded by the implementation of church renewal initiatives that has endured the many revolutions that have shaken Ukraine and Russia up until this day. Without the brief period of toleration by the state, the Ukrainization program that jump-started the autocephalous movement might never have gained ground among Ukrainians. Furthermore, the decree of separation of church and state justified the Ukrainians' rationale for separating from the patriarchate. The synod of bishops represented the legacy of servitude to the tsarist regime and lordship over ethnic groups. As a result, Ukrainian public religious identity includes the marks of orphanhood and its antidote, liberation and freedom. These identity markers carried weight in Ukraine on account of the conflict between the Ukrainianizers and the synod of bishops. Thus, this chapter has established the following markers of Ukrainian Orthodox public religious identity, which developed in this first stage of Soviet history: restoration of the Kyivan Church, equality, freedom and liberty, preference for the Gospel over the state, Ukrainization—especially linguistic—and popular governance. The political and social climate of the time inevitably permeated the theologies underpinning public religious identity, so it is not surprising to find socialistic elements in the egalitarianism of church structures and the absolute condemnation of the Russian monarchy. The socialistic elements were particularly manifest in the 1921 UAOC's attempt to establish itself as a significant ecumenical player in the international forum. Ievsieieva refers to the UAOC's theses presented to the Stockholm All-World Conference of Christian Communities in August 1925 as examples of the Christian socialism embedded in the UAOC's ideology.[206] The 1921 UAOC's political theology was communicated through egalitarianism in church structures, where the laity had considerable authority, and liturgical reforms, with a liturgy celebrated in modern Ukrainian. These structural and liturgical identity markers became permanent fixtures of the legacy of the 1921 UAOC.

It is much more challenging to describe the identity markers of the majority of believers who remained within the patriarchate. This chapter has reviewed the public religious identity the Ukrainians inscribed on the episcopate, but the correspondence between the bishops of the exarchate and the 1921 UAOC evidences a church struggling to adjust to the signs of the times. Certainly the exarchal synod viewed the Ukrainians as illegitimate because of their persistent circumvention of proper church order, but on several occasions the bishops indicated their approval of Ukrainization of the Church. Furthermore, the bishops referred to conciliar decisions, particularly the Moscow council of 1917 and the Ukrainian council of 1918, as having settled these matters definitively. Ievsieieva's profile of the patriarchal bishops as conservative churchmen who advocated for sustaining church unity and the canonical purity of Orthodoxy in Ukraine illuminates the sudden and violent removal of the Russian state from the scene.[207] The bishops sustained the ideology that had formed them, which permitted loyalty only to the Russian state.

The 1921 UAOC's claim that both the Moscow and Kyiv councils were illegitimate is difficult to sustain given that the majority of the people remained in the patriarchate. Little is known about the people's perceptions of the Ukrainian movement, but suffice it to say that the Ukrainians had enough in common with the Living Church that it enhanced their illegitimate appearance.[208] Furthermore, there is evidence indicating that clergy and laity approved of the possibility of autocephaly and the introduction of Ukrainization, as long as the means were canonical and the measures were not coercive. The immediate warm responses to the exarchate's consideration of autocephaly in 1922 and the separation of the Lubny group from the patriarchate attest to some people's preference for a canonical alternative to the admitted radicalism of the 1921 UAOC. It is also true that people are generally resistant to change. Just as many people opposed the political revolutionaries, many preferred to remain in their native ecclesial homes instead of joining the ecclesial revolution. Gregory Freeze's study of Soviet anti-religious policy in Ukraine shows that the clergy had limited power to resist change, but the Soviet strategy of weakening the Church by rendering the clergy impotent only emboldened and strengthened lay resolve to defend Orthodoxy against all threats.[209] The 1921 UAOC had openly declared its opposition to the patriarchal church: lay rejection of the UAOC was likely a result of its promotion of innovationist structures and traditions in its attempt to reform the Church and evangelize the populace. The accusation that the Ukrainians were innovators is true, as supported by the evidence. The synodal letter to the faithful instructing them to avoid deposed clergy and illegitimate gatherings of people of dubious canonical veracity likely mirrors the people's perception of the Ukrainians as a radical group, to a certain degree. Perhaps the most intriguing insight about the way other Orthodox viewed the Ukrainians comes from the internal debate on the course of action to be adopted by the October 1921 council. Many Ukrainians who supported autocephaly did not want to abandon tradition; one can surmise that Ukrainians who remained sympathetic to the autocephalous aspirations stayed in the patriarchate. It is also likely that these Ukrainians tended to trust the authority of the episcopate, which deposed and excommunicated leaders of both the UAOC and the Lubny cohort. Despite the Lubny group's fidelity to a canonical path, its prestige declined when the exarchate deposed its leaders. In other words, the authoritarian act of casting one out of a community was valid for the majority of believers.

This inner tension between support for autocephaly and tradition reveals a theological challenge: how does one assess the degree to which the Ukrainians and the patriarchate remained faithful to Orthodox tradition? The 1921 UAOC attempted to demonstrate its dependence on Orthodox tradition on the basis of separation and liberation; union with global Orthodoxy through the Moscow Patriarchate was the most important identity marker for the larger Orthodox population in Ukraine, one that was enhanced as autocephalous movements recurred in the twentieth century.

The Soviet regime liquidated the UAOC in 1930, but this brief episode in Ukrainian Church history was relevant for several reasons. First, this was the first of a series of attempts to restore and recreate the Kyivan Metropolia infused with the spirit of church renewal, and it proved to be formative by introducing the goal of liberation from Moscow and promoting popular governance of the Church. The fine differences between paths to autocephaly and implementation of Ukrainization adopted by the 1921 UAOC and the Lubny cohort show that Ukrainians themselves did not agree on the means to be employed for securing autocephaly and restoring their native church traditions. Each successive Ukrainian autocephalous church inherited all of the marks representing the legacy of the 1921 church, which causes problems in assessing subsequent movements. The 1921 UAOC also left a legacy of ecclesial subversion: the result of their church revolution was the casting out of the traditional leaders of the Church who were endowed with the divine grace of canonicity, the bishops. The absence of bishops from the May and October 1921 conciliar gatherings of the UAOC revealed a telling reality of their core constituency: their primary ideologues and disciples were rank-and-file clergy and laity. Furthermore, it was a married archpriest who became their first metropolitan of Kyiv, while ordinary laymen administered the proceedings (Michael Moroz) and articulated the ecclesiology underpinning the new Ukrainian Church (Volodymyr Chekhivsky). Eventually, the Soviet decision to eradicate the 1921 UAOC muted the influence of Moroz and Chekhivsky, but together with Lypkivs'kyi, they left a legacy of subversion that would challenge the Ukrainian Orthodox Church until the present day. The pattern of popular laity and married clergy becoming the ordained leaders of the Church would continue in successive generations when popular Ukrainian figures such as Ivan (Ohienko), Stepan (Skrypnyk), and Volodymyr (Romaniuk) would become the actual bishops leading the Church.

2

The Orthodox Church in Ukraine to the End of World War II (1939–1945)

THIS CHAPTER PRESENTS THE NEXT stage of the autocephalist movement and the deepening of division in the Orthodox Church in Ukraine by examining central events and figures. The chapter begins with a description of the autocephaly of the Orthodox Church in Poland, granted by Constantinople in 1924. It also explores Ukrainization efforts within the Church of Poland, and confrontations between Ukrainian and Russian cohorts in the eparchy of Volyn'. It discusses the emergence of a serious conflict between Ukrainian autocephalists and autonomists through their divergent approaches to reestablishing Orthodox church life in Ukraine.[1] It also illuminates striking similarities between the autocephalists and autonomists, especially the common anti-Soviet rhetoric used by the bishops and their expressions of hope for the restoration of the Church in a liberated Ukraine, which formed the basis for their political theologies. This analysis features the failed attempt to unify the churches at the Pochaiv Council of October 1942, which the leaders of the respective churches explained at great length in private correspondence. The chapter also discusses the problem of how to receive the clergy who were ordained in the 1921 UAOC, a canonical issue that divided the two camps.

Ukrainians in the Orthodox Church in Poland

With the reconfiguration of borders after the conclusion of World War I, the Orthodox Church in Poland consisted primarily of Eastern Slavs, approximately 2.5 million Ukrainians, one million Belarusians, and about twenty-five thousand Great Russians.[2] The vast majority of the Orthodox in Poland were people who had belonged to the Kyivan Metropolia: for the Orthodox population, the regions included West Volyn', Cholm, Pidlisha, and Polissia.[3] All of Galicia also belonged to Poland, where the vast majority of residents belonged to the Greek-Catholic Church. The Orthodox encounter with Latin and Greek Catholics had been a fixture since the fourteenth century, and in the early twentieth century, Orthodox in these regions were attempting to sustain their identity and distinguish it from the Greek-Catholic majority.

The Orthodox peoples in Poland were canonically dependent on the Moscow Patriarchate, a relationship that remained from the years prior to the revolution as the synodal church appointed bishops to shepherd the Orthodox sees in these regions. As early as 1921, the Orthodox in Poland began to request canonical autocephaly from Moscow, with the synod of bishops in Poland formally petitioning Patriarch Tikhon in 1922.[4] Oleksander Voronyn asserted that the Polish bishops began to establish a path for canonical autocephaly in 1923–1924, and that Metropolitan Yurii (Yaroshevsky) supported Ukrainization initiatives within the Ukrainian-dominated eparchies of the Polish Church.[5] Voronyn also mentions confrontations between Ukrainians and Russians within the Church, a problem that would occasionally plague the internal life of the Church well into World War II.[6] On July 8, 1923, a monk assassinated Metropolitan Yurii, and the Polish Church elected Archbishop Dionysii (Valedynsky) as the new Metropolitan.[7] Metropolitan Dionysii would prove to be one of the figures who contributed most prominently to the development of Ukrainian Orthodox identity from 1924 to the end of World War II, because he was an ethnic Russian who was fluent in Ukrainian, and was a vocal advocate for establishing an autocephalous Orthodox Church in a liberated Ukraine, as manifested by his ordination and his appointment of bishops who were avid Ukrainianizers.

Ukrainization in the Autocephalous Church in Poland

The Orthodox Church in Poland proved to be fertile ground for a canonical version of Ukrainization, an initiative that produced mixed results, especially in Western Volyn'.[8] Voronyn notes that the eparchial assembly of Volyn' in 1917 called for the pronunciation of Church Slavonic according to the Ukrainian style at liturgy, and for preaching in vernacular Ukrainian.[9] In October 1921, the eparchial assembly advocated a transition from Slavonic to vernacular Ukrainian as the primary liturgical language.[10] Essentially, the aspirations for Ukrainization that had percolated among Orthodox Ukrainians in 1917–1918 continued even as they found themselves under Polish rule. In this case, the Ukrainians formed an ethnic majority, so Ukrainization could be implemented in a canonical context with episcopal patronage. Throughout the history of the Church in Poland, Ukrainization proved to be both inconsistent and controversial in eparchial and parish life.

The synod of bishops of the Church in Poland seem to have adopted contradictory positions on Ukrainization. On some occasions, the bishops appear to support Ukrainization, but at other times, Ukrainian activists complain that the synod is ignoring them or failing to enforce their rules. It is likely that the Polish bishops were attempting to learn how to navigate church life with a multinational population. An early document from the synod of bishops seems to indicate support for Ukrainization, but also acknowledges the other ethnic groups belonging to the Church in Poland. On September 3, 1924, the synod of bishops issued resolutions pertaining to Ukrainization and treating liturgical language.[11] Resolution number 1 "permits the use of Ukrainian, Belarusian, Polish, and Czech languages in those liturgical rites in which the texts are ratified by the Supreme Church Council, and in those parishes where the parishioners desire it and where it is possible in local conditions."[12] The declaration also allowed clergy to preach in the "language of the local Orthodox population," and extended the use of local languages to local schools where the Law of God is taught and to spiritual schools as well. These resolutions authorize Ukrainization, but are even more intriguing in their pastoral sensitivity to the multinational composition of the Church.

Two examples from the interwar history of the Church in Poland illustrate the problems resulting from Ukrainization initiatives. Contemporaneous reports from a news periodical in Volyn' confirm the tension at the cathedral in Volodymyr-Volyn'. Metropolitan Dionysii had permitted Ukrainian language liturgies at the cathedral. A controversy erupted in March 1927 when the new rector, Father Heorhyi (Borishkevich), allegedly acquiesced to pressure by a Russian group to celebrate liturgy in Slavonic, and not Ukrainian.[13] The writer alleged that 1500 of the 1800 parishioners had voted in favor of vernacular Ukrainian, and sent a delegation to Warsaw to appeal to the minister of education and religious affairs about the dispute.[14] The church responded by attempting to compromise, with three liturgies scheduled for March 27: the early cathedral liturgy in Ukrainian, the second cathedral service in Slavonic, and another parish liturgy in St. Nicholas Church in Ukrainian. This situation continued into April, as the disagreement between the parties in the church intensified. On April 10, 1927, the cathedral offered two Divine Liturgies, one in Slavonic and one in Ukrainian, which the anonymous writer attributed to a temporary compromise on the part of Archbishop Theodosius, until the Holy Synod made a final determination.[15] The anonymous writer depicts the compromise as the attempt of a minority Russian political party to subvert the wishes of the Ukrainian majority at the cathedral. A view of this episode in light of the larger picture suggests that the Ukrainianizers within the Church of Poland pushed their agenda and encountered resistance among other Slavs.

The pastoral approach to implementing Ukrainization in the multinational Church of Poland was not easily resolved. The deliberations and resolutions of the Orthodox gathering in Lutsk in 1927 also addressed the question of liturgical language, yielding both defensive and occasionally profound resolutions. Following a gathering of Ukrainian cultural and educational organizations in Rivne in the winter of 1926, a Ukrainian Orthodox meeting of eight hundred delegates was held in Lutsk on June 5–6, 1927. The Lutsk gathering attempted to influence Metropolitan Dionysii and the synod of bishops to be more consistent in their support for Ukrainization.[16] The gathering expressed dismay over the lack of consultation with the entire Church in the spirit of conciliarity, referring as an example to the mistakes made by the hierarchy during the establishment of the UAOC in Ukraine.[17] The gathering called upon the hierarchy to appease each nationality within the Church, including the Ukrainians, to remove the problem of battles between the synod and the people in the Church.[18]

The gathering called upon the synod to restore all of the Ukrainian traditions and customs that had been prohibited by the Russian Church under the tsar, the most significant being a blessing to celebrate the liturgy in Ukrainian. Ukrainian liturgies should be blessed wherever they were requested by the Ukrainian population; the gathering recommended that one Slavonic liturgy be celebrated in places where a significant portion of the population requested it, but not in the cathedral church.[19] The gathering also stipulated that the Gospels, epistles, psalms, and homilies should all be proclaimed in Ukrainian during the Slavonic liturgies.

The synod of the Church in Poland was also asked to take specific measures to ensure the successful implementation of these reforms: "the congress categorically demands the appointment of Ukrainian bishops to three episcopal sees on the lands of predominantly Ukrainian people, with the rights of governing hierarchs and members of the Holy Synod."[20] The remainder of the assembly called for Ukrainianizing other areas of church life, and condemned the local Russian media for disseminating "Russian imperialism" in the Church, while also alleging that Orthodox clergy were attempting to create provocations in the church by intensifying antagonism between Ukrainians and Russians, and were even resorting to "Bolshevik propaganda."[21]

The eparchial assembly of Volyn' of June 16–17, 1927, protested against the Ukrainianizing proposals put forward earlier in the month by the Lutsk Ukrainian gathering. Metropolitan Dionysii himself participated in the eparchial gathering. The question of liturgical language was among the most contested issues. In its statement, the Volyn' eparchial assembly questioned Metropolitan Dionysii's approval of Ukrainianizing the liturgy and called upon him to "appeal to the entire people of Volyn'" to learn their opinion on the Ukrainianizing of divine offices.[22] The gathering expressed concern about the damage resulting from the removal of Slavonic, which had implications for "our thousand-year history" and "relations with other Orthodox Slavs."[23] The council also requested that the liturgy be celebrated in Slavonic at the cathedral of Volodymyr Volyn', and that "teaching of the prayers in the Law of God" in schools remain in the Slavonic text.[24] The official text of the liturgy throughout the eparchy was to be Church Slavonic, while the eparchy recognized the urgent need for publishing liturgical books and Bibles with Church Slavonic and vernacular Ukrainian in parallel, for use at school and home.[25] Perhaps even more telling was the assembly's explanation of the use of the Russian language for teaching the Divine Liturgy at church and the Law of God in schools, and for correspondence within church life: it stated that Russian should not be depicted as the language of a "foreign republic," but as a native language that is "equal to the Ukrainian language."[26] Another excerpt from the Volyn' gathering demonstrates that the interpretation of Ukrainization initiatives was similar to those that were hotly debated from 1917–1922 in Ukraine. The eparchial assembly declared that the Ukrainization of Church structures, namely the election and appointment of clergy—references to the creation of three Ukrainian sees—were "uncanonical mechanisms" that would doom the Orthodox Church in Poland to participation in a political battle.[27] These examples from the 1927 eparchial gathering in Volyn' demonstrate that Ukrainization within the Orthodox Church in Poland was a serious initiative, one that some construed as undermining both Slavonic and Russian, and that the cathedral in Volodymyr-Volyn' was one of the parishes where the Church was considering the implementation of Ukrainian liturgical services, at least as a possibility.

Our second example comes from the Cholm eparchy, a traditional Orthodox stronghold boasting over 250,000 Orthodox Ukrainians.[28] In 1940, Ivan (Ohienko) was elected and appointed as the bishop of Cholm. Ohienko was a prominent historian who taught at the university in Kyiv and delivered a lecture on Ukrainization at the All-Ukrainian Council of Kyiv in 1918.[29] Bishop-Elect Ilarion presented his pastoral agenda to the church in Cholm as part of his examination for the office of bishop, which occurred on the eve of his consecration. The appointment of Bishop Ilarion to the Cholm eparchy was fateful for the future of Ukrainian Orthodoxy, because he, perhaps more than any other Ukrainian hierarch, exemplified a vision for autocephaly and Ukrainization by canonical means, without employing the innovative tactics used by the 1921 UAOC. Furthermore, Ilarion falls into the pattern of an influential layperson who was elected to episcopal office in modern Ukrainian Orthodox history.

In his presentation of his pastoral agenda, Bishop-Elect Ilarion openly declared his advocacy for an autocephalous Ukrainian Church, and he also favored the governing principle of *sobornopravnist'* and Ukrainization. However, he insisted that Ukrainization could not be imposed upon the people, and that *sobornopravnist'* demanded consultation so that initiatives would be received.[30] As a bishop, Ilarion promised to consult laity and clergy who belonged to the eparchial council, and when they expressed their desire to retain Church Slavonic as the liturgical language, he honored their preference and stipulated the celebration of the liturgy in Slavonic with Ukrainian pronunciation. This decision was taken up in 1941 alongside several others, communicated from the eparchial council of Cholm on October 19–21, 1941.[31]

As a critic of the initiatives of the 1921 UAOC, especially their platform for Ukrainization, Ilarion's program can be described as both pro-Ukrainian and somewhat restrained. On the one hand, his prohibition of Russian pronunciation of Slavonic is notable. On the other hand, a pastoral reluctance to immediately eradicate Church Slavonic in favor of Ukrainian is detectable here. Ilarion's program of Ukrainization was assertive, but not aggressive. This distinction is particularly evident in the preservation of Slavonic at the Divine Liturgy, which more people attend, while introducing Ukrainian into more sparsely attended divine offices.

A final example of tension surrounding Ukrainization occurred during the celebration of the feast day of St. Job of Pochaiv at the Pochaiv monastery on September 10, 1933.[32] Several thousand people gathered for the feast, with Metropolitan Dionysii himself presiding over the festivities. The celebration was marked by a large gathering of Ukrainians bearing blue and yellow flags, who demonstrated in favor of Ukrainization and called for the eradication of pro-Moscow forces in with the church of Volyn'.[33] The primary leader of this gathering was Stepan Skrypnyk, a member of the Polish parliament and the nephew of Symon Petliura, the former president of the Ukrainian republic under the Directory. Skrypnyk was one of the most vocal and active ideologues in favor of ecclesial Ukrainization in Volyn' eparchy, and his notion of Ukrainization was oriented toward the de-Russification of the Orthodox Church in native Ukrainian lands.[34] Skrypnyk had experience as a participant in the church gatherings that periodically took place in Volyn', and Andrii Smyrnov refers to the demonstration at Pochaiv as a victory for Ukrainians largely attributable to Skrypnyk's advocacy.[35] Smyrnov depicts Bishop Oleksii (Hromadsky)'s appointment as bishop of Volyn' in 1934 as a Ukrainian victory because Skrypnyk had publicly appealed for the appointment of several Ukrainian bishops to eparchial sees within the Church of Poland as a way of facilitating Ukrainization, with Volyn' as the most important of these.[36] Skrypnyk's populist approach to ecclesial Ukrainization is noteworthy for another reason: he would be ordained to the episcopacy in May 1942, becoming yet another influential layman who would ascend to the ranks of the hierarchy in modern Ukrainian Orthodox history.

The debate on Ukrainization and language lingered within the Church of Poland until the Soviets took possession of most of Western Ukraine in 1939–1941, which led some of the eparchies to leave the Polish Church and return to the Moscow Patriarchate. It is clear that the Church of Poland blessed limited Ukrainization in some eparchies, and conflict resulted due to the multinational constituency. The occurrence of yet another dispute in Rivne occurred when Bishop Policarp (Sikorsky), the bishop of Lutsk in Rivne, served the Divine Liturgy at the Rivne cathedral in Ukrainian on July 17, 1934, in commemoration of the tenth anniversary of the municipal Ukrainian school.[37] An argument broke out among the people because the majority of the parishioners wanted to hear the Divine Liturgy in Slavonic, not Ukrainian.

These examples of debates on Ukrainization within the Church of Poland are illustrative for many reasons. First, the attempt to restore Ukrainian traditions that had been prohibited during the tsarist period was not limited to the 1921 UAOC, but continued as a vibrant movement among Orthodox Ukrainians in the Church of Poland. Second, the Ukrainian majority experienced friction with the Russian minority, and many people refused to accept Ukrainization. Third, the eparchial deliberations referred to themes from the earlier stage of the history of Ukrainian Orthodoxy: the error of bishops refusing to hear the people and the danger of resorting to uncanonical mechanisms to ensure implementation of one's preferred agenda. The Ukrainian and Russian sides accused one another of resorting to politics as well. Despite the gloomy view of constant polemical battles, one new development stands out: Ukrainization was blessed by hierarchs and was aligned with canonical church life, even though the outcomes of its implementation were inconsistent.

The influence and prestige of the Ukrainian cohort within the Polish Church was formidable, if controversial and frequently subject to dispute. The previous chapter reviewed the commemoration of the Battle of Poltava in 1708 as a significant identity marker for Orthodox Ukrainians, who rejected the anathematization of Ivan Mazepa by the Russian synod as a symbol of the Russian captivity of Ukraine and her church. Orthodox Ukrainians within the Polish Church made an emotional appeal to the Holy Synod to remove the anathema on Mazepa, and the Polish Church granted this request, as evidenced by Metropolitan Dionysii's letter to Archbishop Ilarion. Dionysii informed Ilarion that he "permitted and blessed prayer in Orthodox temples for the repose of the soul of the departed servant of God Hetman Ivan Mazepa."[38] This minor detail demonstrates the tolerance of the bishops for Ukrainization within the Church, and the influence wielded by a Ukrainianizing bishop, in this case, Bishop Ilarion.

The commitment to Ukrainization within the Church of Poland allowed for the possibility of restoring a canonical Church in Ukraine, which was much more feasible with the support of Constantinople and its *tomos* of autocephaly granted to Poland. There are numerous additional examples that support this point. The tolerance for Ukrainization was perhaps most evident in the appointment of Ukrainian bishops to prominent eparchial sees, including that of Ilarion to Cholm, and especially the ordination of Bishop Oleksii to the eparchy of Volyn'.[39] Ivan Vlasovs'kyi adds that a genuine Ukrainian school emerged within the Church of Poland, especially with the appointment of Ukrainianizing professors to the Orthodox theological school in Warsaw, such as Ivan (Ohienko) (who taught Slavonic and paleography) and Oleksander Lotocky (the history of the Slavic Orthodox churches).[40] Vlasovs'kyi also describes the publication of numerous liturgical books in vernacular Ukrainian and the publication of religious and theological journals featuring Ukrainian-language essays, along with works in Polish and Russian.[41] Clearly, the campaign for Ukrainization was permeating the fabric of Polish Church life, from the appointment of Ukrainian bishops to the publication of journals with Ukrainian essays.

Autocephaly for the Church in Poland

The canonical status of the Church in Poland followed the customary pattern of a local, autocephalous church existing in a sovereign republic. This pattern gained momentum within global Orthodoxy from the mid-nineteenth century, as empires collapsed and nation-states emerged. The nineteenth and twentieth centuries witnessed the establishment of autocephalous churches in Serbia, Greece, Bulgaria, Poland, the Czech Republic and Slovakia (Czechoslovakia prior to 1993), and America.[42] Orthodox people formed a sizable minority in predominantly Catholic Poland, and as mentioned earlier, the Church in Poland requested autocephaly from the Moscow Patriarchate, and the request was denied. The leaders of the Church in Poland sought autocephaly to be free of the influence of the Soviet regime and its strategy of dividing and conquering the Church, which included the promotion of the Living Church.[43] For his part, in a letter addressed to Metropolitan Dionysii on May 23, 1924, Patriarch Tikhon appealed to discussions he had inaugurated with the Polish government on the organization of the Orthodox Church in Poland, which would remain within the Moscow Patriarchate, an ongoing negotiation that was interrupted by the patriarch's arrest and imprisonment.[44] Patriarch Tikhon complained that it was impossible for him to grant autocephaly to the Polish Church on his own without the approbation of an all-Russian council.[45] He also appealed to reports he had received from bishops, clergy, and faithful protesting the possibility of autocephaly for the Church in Poland.[46] Referring to inconsistencies and disputes within the Church in Poland, Patriarch Tikhon denied Metropolitan Dionysii's request to bless autocephaly and stated that the topic would be taken up by the next all-Russian church council.[47]

Vlasovs'kyi asserts that the Polish government did not want the Orthodox Church in Poland to depend upon the Church in Russia, so it encouraged the Church to turn to "its first capital," Constantinople.[48] The Ecumenical Patriarchate issued a *tomos* granting autocephaly to the Church in Poland on November 13, 1924.[49] The autocephalous status of the Church in Poland was officially celebrated on September 16–19, 1925, in Warsaw.[50] The text of the *tomos* is particularly pertinent to the forthcoming analysis of the emergence of the Autocephalous Church in Ukraine under the canonical auspices of the Church in Poland, because the text rationalizes autocephaly on the basis of the historical patrimony of the Kyivan Metropolia. The following passage from the *tomos* pertains to the Kyivan Metropolia:

> Considering also the fact, which is not contradicted by history (for it is recorded that the first separation from our See of the Kyivan Metropolia and the Orthodox Metropolia of Lithuania and Poland, dependent upon it, as well as the incorporation within the Holy Muscovite Church was accomplished contrary to canon law, as also all that which was agreed upon regarding the full church autonomy of the Kyivan Metropolitan, who at the time had the title Exarch of the Ecumenical See), We . . . considered it our obligation to give ear to the request presented to us by the Holy Orthodox Church in Poland and to give our blessing and approval to its autocephalous and independent administration.[51]

Two aspects of the *tomos* of autocephaly stand out for our analysis. First, the immediate historical background of the Moscow Patriarchate's refusal to bless the Polish Church's autocephaly sets the stage for the text on the Kyivan Metropolia in the *tomos*. Here, the Ecumenical Patriarchate defines itself as the rightful mother church of Kyiv, and also assesses the transfer of jurisdiction to Moscow in 1686 as uncanonical. Second, the language of the *tomos* refers to blessing and approving autocephaly, not creating it. The first part of the *tomos* states that the Ecumenical Patriarchal See blesses and approves an existing autocephalous church. The nuances of this language are crucial, as it is clear that the Ecumenical Patriarchate did not create a new structure, but acknowledged the independent existence of a structure already in place. The Church in Poland was the continuation of the ancient Kyivan Metropolia, manifest in its current state in the sovereign republic of Poland, and presided over by the metropolitan of Warsaw—not Kyiv.[52]

For the majority Ukrainian population within the Orthodox Church in Poland, the acknowledgment of autocephaly in an official document, the *tomos* from the Ecumenical Patriarchate, established the possibility for the expansion of autocephaly to the liberated lands of Ukraine. For our purposes, the 1924 *tomos* was perhaps more important for pro-autocephaly Ukrainians and the Ecumenical Patriarchate than it was for the Church in Poland, as the rationale for autocephaly consistently iterated by its Ukrainian proponents in the period following the issuing of the *tomos* was verifiable and tangible within it. Furthermore, the *tomos* provided an official document defining the Ecumenical Patriarchate as the rightful patron of the Kyivan Church, and not Moscow. However, one could read this historical episode as the Church of Poland essentially replacing the Kyivan Metropolia, with Warsaw becoming the new Kyiv. As for the Church in Poland, it marked its autocephaly with a solemn celebration in the Warsaw cathedral from September 16–19, 1925.[53] The Polish Church later revoked its autocephaly from the Ecumenical Patriarchate and received it anew from Moscow in 1948.

Ukrainian Interpretation of the *Tomos* of Autocephaly for Poland

The reception and interpretation of Polish autocephaly among Orthodox Ukrainians is not univocal. The 1924 *tomos* of autocephaly was significant for the majority of Ukrainian Orthodox who desired autocephaly on a canonical basis. The 1921 UAOC officially protested the *tomos* of autocephaly granted to the Polish Church in an open letter to Ecumenical Patriarch Basil III, issued by the UAOC's most authoritative organ, the AUOCC, on February 13, 1926.[54] The AUOCC described its letter as an official protest, alleging that the recognition of Polish autocephaly was anticanonical and antichurch, and also "detrimental for the Orthodox Ukrainian people."[55] The protest states that "the Orthodox Church in Poland was never subject to the Constantinopolitan patriarchal throne," but actually belonged to the autonomous Kyivan metropolitan.[56] The UAOC also argued that monarchs, patriarchs, and other leaders had no right to grant autocephaly, but that autocephaly was a church right for each nation. The UAOC interpreted Polish autocephaly as a political gesture designed to appease the Catholic Polish government, which would subject the people of the Church to the government's will. The tenor of the UAOC appeal is evident: having departed from the customary mechanisms of seeking legitimacy from temporal and ecclesial powers, the UAOC viewed this decision as a negative instance of subjecting Orthodox people—of whom Ukrainians were the majority—to a foreign and malevolent Catholic regime. Besides the accusation of placing their fellow Ukrainians in harm's way, the UAOC criticized the ecumenical patriarch for "not recognizing and calling upon the Ukrainian Church community in the Polish state to construct its own authentic autocephaly . . . upon the freedom to which Christ called all nations."[57] The UAOC referred to itself as the preferable model for autocephaly: "the Ukrainian Church has already proclaimed this kind of autocephaly. It was not proclaimed in Warsaw or by some other enemy within the life of the Ukrainian nation . . . but in the city of Kyiv . . . not by patriarchs or princes, but by the Ukrainian people itself, which gathered for its All-Ukrainian Church Council in the year 1921."[58]

The fierce opposition of the UAOC in Ukraine to the autocephaly of the Church in Poland marks a division among Orthodox Ukrainians for autocephaly. The Orthodox Ukrainians who refer to the 1924 *tomos* as a canonical basis for autocephaly essentially identify the Ecumenical Patriarchate as their patron. Fidelity to the Ecumenical See's historical protection of the Ukrainians grants all of the power to the Ecumenical Throne. The Ukrainians who insist on this path view it as the only canonical mechanism for having their own autocephalous church. This position stands in contrast to that of the 1921 UAOC, which defined the power of independence as belonging to the people, and not patriarchs or temporal rulers. The UAOC's position would also prove to be a foreshadowing of the future, as many Orthodox Ukrainians would proclaim autocephaly without requesting permission or a blessing from a ruling body. This tendency to take autocephaly was attributable, in part, to the spirit of the first UAOC, which resisted the temptation to appease authoritative bodies within global Orthodoxy.

The Genesis of an Autocephalous Ukrainian Church: 1939–1941

The material of this chapter treats the majority community of Ukrainians within the Orthodox Church of Poland, and the significance of the historical legacy of the Kyivan Metropolia in the proclamation and acknowledgment of Polish autocephaly. The Church scene began to change in Ukraine when the drums of war began to beat, beginning with the annexation of Western Ukraine to the Soviet Union in 1939. This annexation was a direct result of the Nazi-Soviet Pact of August 23, 1939, at which "almost all the West Ukrainian lands were allotted to the Soviet Union."[59] This annexation is a truly epic event for Ukraine because of its significant impact on the history of the country and the future fate of the churches in Ukraine. The narratives treating the absorption of Western Ukraine into the Soviet Union vary.[60] For the Soviet leaders, their taking of Western Ukraine marked the reunion of Ukraine, an act that made the country whole again, and a more complete republic within the Soviet Union. The entrance of Western Ukraine into the Soviet Union also had immediate consequences for the churches. The Greek-Catholic Church would be temporarily liquidated and become illegal in the Soviet Union as a result of the 1946 "Council" in L'viv; these Greek Catholics were coerced into becoming Orthodox, and a crucial portion of the exarchate's pastoral strategy was to celebrate the healing of a schism. But the change in political borders and sovereign masters also had serious repercussions for the Orthodox Church, especially the large and influential eparchy of Volyn'. These territories had belonged to the Orthodox Church of Poland, but Volyn' was now in a country where the only functioning Orthodox Church was the Moscow Patriarchate, which had officially made peace with the Soviet regime through Metropolitan Sergei's declaration of loyalty in 1927.

The immediate future of the Orthodox Church in Ukraine became quite uncertain when the eparchy of Volyn' resolved to become an autonomous part of the Moscow Patriarchate at a council at Pochaiv Monastery in 1941. Essentially, the decision to return to Moscow was pragmatic, since the sovereign territory of the Church had changed. However, the decision to return to the Moscow Patriarchate entailed separation from the autocephalous Church of Poland, a move fiercely protested by the primate of the Polish Church, Metropolitan Dionysii, who was concerned about the Moscow Patriarchate's precarious situation in an anti-religious republic. When the Nazi regime waged war against the Soviet Union, the Orthodox leaders viewed it as an opportunity to liberate Orthodoxy from the clutches of the Soviet Union once and for all. The Nazi invasion of the Soviet Union began on June 22, 1941, and the Germans occupied most of Ukraine by October 1941.[61] So Metropolitan Dionysii supported and encouraged his Ukrainian bishops to establish a provisional Church in Nazi-ruled Ukraine, while envisioning the eventual establishment of an autocephalous church under the patronage of the Church of Poland. In the early stages of this process, most of the bishops involved appeared to hope for the creation of a canonical and autocephalous Church in Ukraine that would be free of both Bolshevism and the Moscow Patriarchate. However, the leading figures constantly disagreed on the process for autocephaly along with the necessary actions. This section reviews the enormously complex history of the Orthodox churches in Ukraine during World War II by studying the Pochaiv Council and the temporary return to the Moscow Patriarchate, the failed attempt to elect and enthrone Archbishop Ilarion (Ohienko) as the metropolitan of Kyiv, the Polish Church's creation of the Ukrainian Autocephalous Orthodox Church (1942 UAOC), the collapse of the Pochaiv Unification Council of 1942, and the complications caused by constant Nazi interference in church affairs.

The Pochaiv Council of 1941 and the Decision to Return to the Moscow Patriarchate

Most of the eparchies of Western Ukraine found themselves under Soviet rule from late 1939 to the late summer of 1941, while the Germans were in the process of invading the Soviet Union. At the time, the ruling hierarch of the Moscow Patriarchate in Ukraine was Metropolitan Nikolai (Yarushevich).[62] A council of bishops gathered at Pochaiv Monastery on August 5, 1941, to discuss a number of issues, including the future of the Orthodox Church in Ukraine.[63] The evolving political context significantly impacted the bishops' deliberations, as they clearly anticipated the permanent defeat of the Soviet Union and hailed the arrival of Hitler with his army.[64] Excerpts from the Bishops' council at Pochaiv demonstrate their attitude toward both Hitler and the Soviet Union, and their plans for the restoration of church life in Ukraine.

The council drafted a resolution, which included a greeting to Hitler via telegram, recorded in act 3 of the council.[65] The council's resolution was formulated following an introduction by the president of the council, who spoke about the liberation of Ukraine and the Ukrainian Orthodox Church from the clutches of Bolshevism and the godless regime.[66] In addition to the warm greetings extended to Hitler, the Pochaiv Council also addressed the situation of the Orthodox Church in Ukraine and declared that autocephaly could not be determined by the hierarchy, but only by an all-church council.[67]

In addition to returning to the canonical status of the Orthodox Church in Ukraine established by the 1918 All-Ukrainian Council in Kyiv and confirmed by the Moscow Council and Patriarch Tikhon in 1922, the August 1941 Pochaiv Council called for the liturgical commemoration of all of those who were murdered by the Soviet regime (act. 10), appointed Archbishop Oleksii (Hromadsky) as locum tenens of the Kyivan metropolitan throne (act 17), and identified Church Slavonic as the official liturgical language while blessing the use of liturgical Ukrainian (act 16).[68]

Daniela Kalkandjieva notes that the Pochaiv Council essentially dismissed Metropolitan Nikolai as the ruling hierarch of Kyiv, a situation necessitated by his absence from the city.[69] The Pochaiv conciliar discussion on liturgical language was quite lengthy, constituting a thorough review of the history of liturgical language in Volyn' when the eparchy belonged to the Church in Poland. The review establishes that many parishes elected to pray in vernacular Ukrainian and used the translations by Archbishop Ilarion (Ohienko) and the Ukrainian Institute in Warsaw, noting that these translations were adopted without the review and approbation of the Holy Synod.[70] It observes that almost all of the parishes that elected to pray in Ukrainian reverted to Church Slavonic when the eparchy fell under Soviet rule, on account of priests and cantors fearing a Russian regime, and especially because "the most active elements in the parishes that defended Ukrainization went to serve in the Soviet government."[71] The report states that the situation had now changed drastically, presumably because of the retreat of the Soviet regime, and the movement for Ukrainization had returned in full force. It recommends that the bishops move gradually and slowly in consultation with the people, following the example of Archbishop Ilarion himself, who had recommended that his clergy retain Slavonic with Ukrainian pronunciation without coercing parishes to serve in Ukrainian. The synodal resolution chose a conservative route by adopting the practice of the synod of the Polish Church from February 27, 1937, which blessed the use of Ukrainian in parishes where a majority voted for it, while also blessing the singing of the hymn praying for Ukraine ("Боже Великий," or "Great God") following the conclusion of the Divine Liturgy.

The bishops met in Pochaiv again on November 25, 1941, to continue their discussion on the construction of church life in Ukraine. The synodal meeting included a report by Archbishop Oleksii on his visit to Kyiv, and his reflections on the situation there.[72] The report referred to the problems caused by the survivors of the 1921 UAOC, accusing them of occupying the "upper ranks" of church life in Ukraine.[73]

Archbishop Oleksii's report indicates that the proper method for electing the metropolitan of Kyiv is to convoke an all-Ukrainian council, and he also states that the election requires the participation of the republic's government as well. Furthermore, Ilarion's election would be possible only with the blessing and release of Metropolitan Dionysii, the primate of the Orthodox Church in Poland.[74]

The council resolved to declare Archbishop Ilarion as an "honorable candidate for the vacant throne of the archbishop of Kyiv and Pereiaslav," and called upon Archbishop Oleksii to call Archbishop Ilarion to assume the primatial office, and to request Metropolitan Dionysii's blessing for Ilarion to become the archbishop of Kyiv. The November meeting of the council of bishops at Pochaiv also declared the beginning of canonical autocephaly for the Orthodox Church in Ukraine, with a formal request that the recognition of autocephaly be sent to Moscow and all the other Orthodox churches. The conciliar deliberation on this matter referred to Patriarch Tikhon's blessing to begin the process of canonical auto-cephaly bestowed on November 20, 1920, and to the decision of the gathering of the exarchate in Kyiv in 1922 that called upon the bishops to declare autocephaly. Archbishop Ilarion responded affirmatively to the conciliar invitation to become the new archbishop of Kyiv in a letter addressed to Archbishop Oleksii and dated December 26, 1941.[75]

At the end of his letter, Archbishop Ilarion pledges to visit the bishops to begin the process of organizing church life. Archbishop Ilarion's election is confirmed by a letter sent by Archpriest F. Kovalsky, member of the Volyn' Consistory, to the deans of Volyn' eparchy, communicating Archbishop Ilarion's official response to the synodal invitation verbatim.[76] Archbishop Ilarion was never able to travel to Ukraine to respond to the invitation in person on account of an absolute prohibition of his travel by the Germans, though the evidence certainly suggests that the invitation was extended, he accepted it, and the news was communicated to clergy of Volyn' eparchy.[77] The evidence establishes two facts: the Pochaiv Council invited Archbishop Ilarion to become archbishop of Kyiv, and this invitation was with the hope of appeasing the nationalist element in the Ukrainian Church while pursuing a canonical path to autocephaly. The synod of bishops declared Archbishop Oleksii "Metropolitan of Volyn' and Zhytomyr, and Exarch of all Ukraine" at their meeting on December 9, 1941. Oleksii would remain the leader of the autonomist group until his untimely and tragic death in 1943.

These initial decisions of the Orthodox bishops who gathered for two meetings in the summer and late fall of 1941 at Pochaiv are crucial to the complex developments that followed. First, the bishops who assembled for the eparchial gatherings had broken away from the Orthodox Church in Poland. The political changes gave them an opportunity to reconsider their ecclesial status, and the bishops in 1941 opted to return to the Moscow Patriarchate. When Metropolitan Dionysii severely reprimanded Archbishop Oleksii for making an uncanonical change in jurisdiction, he also began the process of inaugurating an autocephalous Church in Ukraine under the leadership of Archbishop Policarp (Sikorsky). In fact, a schism among the Ukrainian bishops was already in progress during the August conciliar meeting at Pochaiv, when Bishop Policarp (Sikorsky) disagreed with the path adopted by the Pochaiv Council. Immediately following the council, Archbishop Oleksii openly accused Bishop Policarp of violating the canons in a letter sent to the clergy of the Volyn' provinces of Lutsk, Kovelsky, Volodymyr, and Liubolmsk.[78] In the letter, Archbishop Oleksii states that Bishop Policarp claims to be functioning as the "eparchial hierarch of Lutsk eparchy, separated from Volyn' eparchy," actions he depicts as illegitimate.[79]

Oleksii's letter to the Volyn clergy makes two powerful statements. First, Oleksii views Policarp as having betrayed his eparchy and brother bishops, who made the decision to return to the Moscow Patriarchate. Second, Oleksii's letter implicitly rejects the notion that he and his fellow bishops were guilty of leaving the autocephalous Church in Poland. The Pochaiv opposition to Dionysii and Policarp would prove to be fateful for the immediate future of the Orthodox Church in Ukraine, as Policarp would become the primary episcopal figure in orchestrating the birth of the second UAOC. The situation became even more complicated for Policarp when the Moscow Patriarchate deposed him on March 28, 1942, for leading the Church into schism.[80] The rationale for the deposition of Policarp by Moscow was saturated with the political ideology of the Soviet Union, as Metropolitan Sergei (Stragorodsky) accused Policarp of creating an alliance with the fascists and betraying the interests of the people.[81]

The synodal resolutions of the Pochaiv councils depict a complicated identity on the part of the bishops. First, the move to return to the Moscow Patriarchate appears to have been an attempt to restore the ecclesial status of the Church in Ukraine established by the All-Ukrainian Council of 1918. The conciliar references to the 1922 exarchal gathering that strongly encouraged canonical autocephaly suggests that the bishops wanted to resume the path of the Church from 1918–1922; autonomy was thus provisional for the bishops who gathered at Pochaiv in 1922. Autocephaly was also possible because the apparent eradication of the Soviet regime by the Germans made the creation of an independent Ukrainian republic conceivable.

The bishops were also attentive to the fissures within the Ukrainian Orthodox community. The path adopted by the 1921 UAOC was the one to be avoided at all costs, evidenced by the report of Archbishop Oleksii following his visit to Kyiv. The 1921 UAOC had implemented Ukrainization without compromise, and the bishops in Pochaiv favored the more cautious approach of permitting Ukrainization in parishes that clearly requested it without imposing it on the entire eparchy. The synodal decision to invite Archbishop Ilarion to become the primate of the Church in Ukraine is one of the most notable developments: the synod seems to have viewed Archbishop Ilarion as the leader most able to construct an autocephalous Church in Ukraine on a canonical basis.

The election of Archbishop Ilarion was strategic: he was a fierce public critic of the path of the 1921 UAOC and rejected their particular definitions of church reform as distortions. In an essay published in 1948, Ilarion argued that the UAOC's conciliar rite of ordination was uncanonical and Protestant, despite the historical precedent of presbyters ordaining a bishop in the first and second centuries.[82] Ilarion also argued that the UAOC's version of *sobornopravnist'* was not actually conciliar, but consisted of the laity ruling the church, or *myrianopravnist'*.[83] Ilarion implied that the 1921 UAOC misinterpreted the correct notion of *sobornopravnist'* and turned it into *narodocezarysmu*.[84] Ilarion was a bridge figure because he wanted to establish a Kyivan Church in which everyone could find a home: it would be distinctly Ukrainian and would bless Ukrainization, but it would respect parishes and clergy that wanted to retain Church Slavonic.[85] Ilarion also belonged to the cohort of Ukrainian Church leaders who disavowed the 1921 UAOC, along with its ecclesiology and canons. The election of Ilarion by the Pochaiv Council of bishops marks a point of separation among Orthodox in Ukraine: the Pochaiv bishops wanted to pursue canonical autocephaly and wanted to seek it in a way that would result in confirmation by world Orthodoxy. The staunch anti-UAOC approach of the Pochaiv Council would result in the failure to achieve union with the second UAOC, which emerged in Ukraine in 1942, as the 1942 UAOC sought to accept the 1921 UAOC clergy and faithful into the Church without performing the sacraments anew.

Political Contributions to Renewed Church Activity in Ukraine

Ironically, the renewal of Church activity throughout Ukraine was enabled in part by the German invasion of the Soviet Union. The documents manifest the readiness of the bishops to cooperate with the German authorities. The date of the conciliar greetings to Adolf Hitler occurred toward the end of a period in which Volyn' eparchy had been under Soviet rule. The routing of Soviet armies also carried the possibility of the creation of an independent Ukrainian state: the bishops, like the rest of the people, did not know that their liberators would eventually become merciless and ruthless captors. In truth, the warm welcome extended by the bishops to Hitler and the German army was also a result of the shock the Church experienced once it came under Soviet rule for the first time. Bohdan Bociurkiw identifies the Nazi-Soviet pact of 1939 as the beginning of a new campaign of Sovietization and Russification of the Orthodox communities that were previously part of Poland.[86] The Kremlin directed church leaders to put an abrupt end to Ukrainization and to "police" the new territories, especially given their tendency to harbor "intense Ukrainian nationalism."[87] The bishops witnessed the confiscation of churches and monasteries, the suppression of theological schools and publications, and a newfound zeal for the dissemination of anti-religious propaganda.[88] Bociurkiw captures a snapshot of the politico-religious environment when he says that "the major turning point came with the German invasion of the USSR in June, 1941," resulting in the "revival of religious life in Ukraine."[89] The prevailing theme of the literature covering religion in this period is the rehabilitation of the Church for the cause of the Great Patriotic War, but in Ukraine, there is instead a revival of hope for both an independent republic and an autocephalous Church, held even by the most conservative cohort of bishops in Volyn'. At the same time, the bishops of the Ukrainian Church could not reach an agreement on how to reconfigure church life in Ukraine on account of the liberation of the 1921 UAOC from the Moscow Patriarchate.

The Birth of the 1942 UAOC

The decision of the Orthodox bishops at Pochaiv to return to the Moscow Patriarchate was opposed by other Ukrainian bishops and the metropolitan of Warsaw. Metropolitan Dionysii complained about the "uncanonical" decision of the Pochaiv bishops to return to the fold of the Moscow Patriarchate. In a letter to

Archbishop Oleksii later published publicly (originally dated October 23, 1941), Dionysii stated the basis for his objection to the return to the Moscow Patriarchate and also iterated his rationale for the autocephaly of the Church in Ukraine.[90] Dionysii rejected the canonical basis of the Ukrainian Church's subservience to the Moscow Patriarchate because the "Orthodox Church in Ukraine, as history witnesses, was an independent church, dwelling in canonical union with the Great Constantinopolitan Church and His Holiness the Ecumenical Patriarch of Constantinople. This is established authoritatively by the . . . Tomos on the auto-cephaly of our Holy Orthodox Church on November 13, 1924."[91] This section of Dionysii's letter previews the canonical basis for his blessing of an autocephalous Ukrainian Church: the *tomos* of autocephaly recognizing the Church in Poland. Dionysii turns to a crucial political matter in the letter when he states, "I can under-stand how after the annexation of Western Ukraine and Belarus by the Soviet regime, the archpastors and flock of our holy church found themselves in captivity and by necessity received the directive of the Moscow Patriarchate that Moscow has subordinated us and we were required to commemorate Metropolitan Sergei as the locum tenens of the patriarchal throne." Dionysii adds that the Moscow Patriarchate violated the canons by interfering in the affairs of an autocephalous church, and he understood why Oleksii had to remain silent when he was under the Soviet regime, but could not excuse his silence now that the Church was no longer under Soviet rule. Dionysii attempts to instruct Oleksii that the proper canonical path was a return to the autocephalous Church of Poland.

Metropolitan Dionysii's Inauguration of the 1942 UAOC

Metropolitan Dionysii's response to the developing church situation in Ukraine appeared to be based upon a desire to uphold the canonical rationale for the auto-cephaly of the Church in Poland, which honored the antiquity and prestige of the Kyivan See. Metropolitan Dionysii viewed Archbishop Oleksii's return to the Moscow Patriarchate as uncanonical and sinful, as Archbishop Oleksii was under the omophorion of the Church in Poland, and was in the process of returning a significant portion of the Kyivan Church to Moscow's jurisdiction, which the 1924 *tomos* had assessed as uncanonical.[92] In the same letter to Policarp of November 13, 1941, Dionysii officially blessed Policarp's trip to Kyiv and ordination of bish-ops for the building up of church life, with the condition that Policarp was to present the biography of each candidate for the episcopacy to Dionysii.[93] Policarp was to ordain bishops together with Bishop Alexander (Inozemtsev) of Pinsk.

On December 24, 1941, Metropolitan Dionysii established a "Temporary Administration of the Orthodox Autocephalous Church on the liberated ter-ritory of Ukraine," apparently as a response to his consultation with the clergy and laity in Volyn'.[94] Dionysii's decision set the stage for the emergence of the second UAOC from the initial foundation of the temporary administration. The rationale for forming the 1942 UAOC was the canonical foundation of the 1924 *tomos*, which liberated Kyiv from its temporary historical subservience to Moscow. Dionysii appointed Archbishop Policarp (Sikorsky) to organize church life in Ukraine, which created a situation of two concurrent Orthodox churches in the same territory: the temporary Autocephalous Church in communion with global Orthodoxy via the Ecumenical Patriarchate, and the Autonomous Church in communion with global Orthodoxy via the Moscow Patriarchate. The two churches disagreed on the canonical path to regularizing church life in Ukraine: the autocephalists proceeded on the basis of the 1924 *tomos* that freed Kyiv from Moscow, and the autonomists acted on the decisions established by the 1918 All-Ukrainian Council. Both churches identified themselves as canonically legitimate, but ultimately came into conflict over a disagreement on how to integrate the existing clergy and faithful from the 1921 UAOC into the Church.

Archbishop Policarp acted quickly in his capacity as the temporary administrator of the Autocephalous Orthodox Church in the liberated Ukrainian lands. He addressed the Orthodox clergy and faithful in a letter dated January 29, 1942.[95] After identifying himself as the administrator of the Autocephalous Church, Policarp addressed the people following his visit to the office of the local German commissioner in Lutsk, to inform the commissioner of his new capacity as leader of the Church in Ukraine.[96] Policarp complained about a lack of proper order among the clergy in the church, and instructed them to obey his directives.[97]

Polycarp's letter is both similar to and different from Oleksii's and the directives from the 1941 eparchial gatherings in Pochaiv. On the one hand, both sides accuse one another of violating the canons by infringing upon the authority of another bishop. Policarp, who remained loyal to Dionysii, depicted Oleksii as a deceiver who was betraying the Church by returning her to the godless Bolsheviks of Moscow. Oleksii depicted Policarp as the traitor who abandoned the bishops who had voted to return to the principles of the 1918 council in Kyiv and Moscow that confirmed the full autonomy of the Ukrainian Exarchate. The dispute between the cohorts supporting Oleksii and Policarp-Dionysii concerned the proper interpretation of recent Church history. Oleksii and his bishops were attempting to honor the path adopted by the 1918 council in Kyiv, whereas Policarp and Dionysii sought to observe the *tomos* of autocephaly confirming the independence of the Kyivan Church. On the other hand, the two cohorts held much in common, despite their differences. They both openly despised and condemned the anti-religious campaign of the Soviet Bolshevik regime and welcomed the Germans as liberators who would free Ukraine from slavery and permit the Church to resume normal canonical life. Unfortunately, the dispute between the two churches would only become more bitter as Archbishop Policarp carried out Metropolitan Dionysii's agenda and created a Ukrainian episcopate that would eventually become the second UAOC of 1942.

The Response of the Moscow Patriarchate to the 1942 UAOC

The Moscow Patriarchate did not remain silent during the period of the rebirth of the UAOC in occupied Ukraine in late 1941 through 1942. Daniela Kalkandjieva meticulously documented the Moscow Patriarchate's dismissal of Policarp's legitimacy and shows how the Moscow Patriarchate used the polemics surrounding the war to depict Policarp as an ally of the Germans.[98] Metropolitan Sergei accused Policarp of offering his services to the German authorities who then assisted him and his "Petliurist" supporters in establishing the temporary administration of the UAOC.[99] Metropolitan Sergei galvanized formidable support for his anti-Policarp, anti-UAOC campaign by persuading the patriarchs of Jerusalem, Antioch, and Alexandria that Policarp had violated the canons by contributing to a war against Orthodox people.[100] Metropolitan Nikolai (still the official exarch of Ukraine, but living outside of its borders) joined the condemnation of Policarp, but he referred to Policarp's promotion of Ukrainian as a liturgical language as a method of creating enmity toward Russians among Ukrainians.[101] Moscow's condemnation of Policarp and the entire UAOC was part of a larger ideological campaign linking the bishops and clergy of the UAOC with Ukrainian and German fascism. The influence of the wartime polemics on ecclesiastical divisions fits the pattern identified throughout this study, and the official ideology of Moscow was at odds with that of the 1942 UAOC, which completely disavowed the MP, this time because of the MP's pledge of loyalty to the Soviet regime.[102] Significantly, the wartime polemics would linger into the postwar period and would ultimately contribute to intra-Orthodox divisions that erupted at the end of the Soviet era.

The Ordination of Bishops in Pinsk, February 7–10, 1942

The temporary administration of the Orthodox Autocephalous Church in Ukraine became an actual episcopate in February 1942, when Archbishops Policarp and Alexander presided at the ordination of several bishops, namely Nikanor (Abramovych), Yurii (Korenastov), and Ihor (Huba).[103] Proponents of autocephaly for the Orthodox Church in Ukraine have depicted the Pinsk council and the creation of an authentically Ukrainian episcopate for the Church in Ukraine as the correction of everything that went wrong when the patriarchal exarchate refused to ordain bishops for the Church in Kyiv in 1921. Vlasovs'kyi identified the episcopal consecrations that occurred during the Pinsk council as a turning point for the Ukrainian Orthodox Church, a reason for "great joy," since the new episcopate was canonical.[104]

The 1942 UAOC was not the direct descendant of the 1921 UAOC. The fact is, the 1942 UAOC was initially an outgrowth of the autocephalous Church in Poland, and occurred only with the blessing of Metropolitan Dionysii, primate of the Church in Poland. The dependence of the UAOC on the Church in Poland is evidenced by the consistent reports on the conditions of church life communicated to Metropolitan Dionysii by Archbishops Policarp and Nikanor, and later Bishop Mstyslav (Skrypnyk).

The council at Pinsk also discussed the problem of the scarcity of bishops available to administer the church, especially in Eastern Ukraine.[105] With Great Lent approaching, there would be fewer opportunities to ordain candidates to the episcopate, and the council of bishops discussed how they might address the problem. The bishops decided to restore the practice of ordaining multiple candidates to one liturgical order at the same liturgy, which had existed in the Kyivan Metropolia but was prohibited in accordance with the rules adopted by the Moscow Council of 1666–1667.[106] According to Bishop Yurii (Korenastov), the Orthodox Church was no longer obligated to observe the rules of the Moscow synod, so a return to the old practices was permissible. Thus, beginning in Lent of 1942, the Autocephalous Church in Ukraine began to ordain multiple deacons and priests at the same liturgy, to populate the church with pastors "for the rebirth of church life (in the wake of) its destruction by the Bolsheviks."[107]

Reception of Clergy from the 1921 UAOC: The Cause of an Irreconcilable Division

Following the ordination of bishops at the Pinsk council in February, Bishops Nikanor and Ihor travelled to Kyiv in March 1942 and celebrated Divine Liturgy at St. Andrew's Cathedral. Representatives of the 1921 UAOC approached the bishops of the temporary administration in Ukraine and expressed their desire to join the ranks of the second UAOC; on March 19, the 1942 UAOC accepted three priests of the 1921 UAOC into the Church, which opened the door for a larger reception of the 1921 clergy.[108] The reception of the 1921 clergy into the Church would become the most formidable stumbling block to healing the schism among the Orthodox in Ukraine, a bitter and polemical point of division between the autonomist and autocephalist parties.

The 1942 UAOC authorized a rite of return of priests of a different ordination to the UAOC of 1942.[109] The rite begins with one of the prayers of absolution from the Byzantine mystery of repentance: "Lord our God, who forgave the sins of Peter and the prodigal on account of their tears . . ." The bishop then lays his hands upon the head of the priest and reads the following prayer:

Eternal God, without beginning, older than every created being, who honors the honor of this presbyter, who has been made worthy of being selected to enter into your Church at this step, to perform the sacred acts of the word of your truth. You alone, master of all, bless your servant whom you have brought forward to receive the laying on of hands from us, help him to bear this great grace of the Holy Spirit in a blameless life and firm faith and show the perfection of your servant, that he would be pleasing in all things to you, and that great priestly honor would dwell in him, that is given to him from your great strength, for yours is the authority, of the Father, and of the Son, and of the Holy Spirit, now and ever and to the ages of ages. [Formula] Almighty and Merciful God, send down your Holy Spirit on your servant [N.] and by your compassion, make him worthy to be a performer of your holy Mysteries. I the unworthy bishop of the Church of Christ by my authority given to me from the Holy Orthodox Church and the power of the Holy Spirit bless, lay my hands and as not ordained, ordain you [N.] to be a presbyter of the Holy Community of Christ: in the Name of the Father, and of the Son, and of the Holy Spirit. Amen.

Clearly, the rite authorized by the temporary administration of the UAOC was a sacramental bridge between ordination in the Byzantine rite and the simple reception of a validly ordained priest from another jurisdiction of the Orthodox Church. This particular rite begins with repentance, which is designed to show the sinful path of the 1921 UAOC. The rest of the rite prays for the full abiding of the gift of the Holy Spirit to preside at the sacraments of the Orthodox Church. An assessment of this rite in isolation would suggest that it is ordination, since the language of the prayers seems to indicate that the clergy who are being received suffer from some kind of deficiency that needs to be corrected through the descent of the Holy Spirit. But the language of perfection suggests that this rite was created to complete an unfinished process of ordination. If the 1942 UAOC believed that the clergy of the 1921 UAOC had no sacramental authority to preside at liturgies, they would have used the rites of ordination normative in the Byzantine tradition. The creation of this rite suggests the completion of a process already under way: clergy who had some degree of sacramental grace were being received into the Church, and their priesthood was both renewed and perfected. More important for our purposes are the larger historical implications of the UAOC's decision to receive the clergy of the 1921 UAOC: their reception filled an immediate pastoral need for clergy to preside at parishes that had been devastated by Bolshevik persecution, and to unify all Orthodox Ukrainians into one canonical church. Another way of appraising the 1942 UAOC's reception of the 1921 UAOC into the church is to see this rite as honoring the good of the 1921 UAOC without accepting its canonical reforms. The 1942 UAOC was attempting to correct the uncanonical path of the 1921 church without forsaking and abandoning the entirety of its legacy.

The Autonomous Church's Rejection of the Reception of the 1921 UAOC Clergy

The Autonomous Church based at Pochaiv Monastery definitively rejected the decision of the 1942 UAOC to receive the clergy of the 1921 UAOC into the church, despite their use of a revised rite that included the laying on of hands and an epiclesis calling upon the Holy Spirit to grant the clergy the grace to preside at the mysteries. On April 30, 1942, Metropolitan Oleksii issued a statement on the Pinsk council, acknowledging their reception of the "self-consecrated" into the Church using a special rite of reception, but rejecting it as one foreign to the Orthodox world.[110] The statement claims that "the only path to a true and lawful priesthood for the Lypkivtsi is the reception of the grace of the priesthood through a new lawful ordination."[111] The statement of the autonomous bishops was probably accurate in its assessment of the motivation of the UAOC for receiving the 1921 clergy into their church: "they likely wanted to grant the self-consecrated a canonical sanction." The autonomous bishops asserted that the Pinsk council became obedient to those who were "cast out from the Holy Orthodox Church and deposed from holy orders." The next sentence of the statement marks a much stronger condemnation of the decision of the 1942 UAOC to receive the 1921 clergy: "accordingly, it is now apparent that the so-called 'Ukrainian Orthodox Church' is a restoration of 'Lypkivshchyna,' and its restorers belong to the 'heretical wisdom' of the Lypkivtsi, and so everything that has been written since our assessment of March 1 [1942] must be absolutely applied to the heresies and heretics of our time." The council then made several grave resolutions, referring to the authority of the council of bishops of the Orthodox Church in Ukraine from October 29, 1921, and refused to recognize the sacramental validity of all clergy ordained by the UAOC after March 15, 1942, and called upon the bishops of the Church to depose all canonical Orthodox clergy who either join the UAOC or concelebrate with it, or even commemorate its bishops.[112]

The absolute rejection of the UAOC's attempt to receive the clergy of the 1921 UAOC resulted in a bitter and polemical war of information between the autonomous and autocephalous churches in Ukraine. In a long letter addressing all the clergy and faithful of the Orthodox Church in the liberated lands of Ukraine, Archbishop Policarp responded to the autonomists angrily and accused Metropolitan Oleksii and the synod of autonomous bishops of attempting to claim that they were the only canonical church in Ukraine.[113] Most of Policarp's letter is an attempt to reject Oleksii's claims that the 1921 UAOC was heretical, especially since "no one has yet called the clergy and faithful of the Ukrainian Autocephalous Orthodox Church, destroyed by the Bolsheviks, heretics, except Archbishop Oleksii with his bishops."[114] Policarp explains that church tradition distinguishes between heretics and schismatics, and more importantly, depicts the

1921 UAOC as a church of martyrs. Policarp argues that "many of the clergy of the UAOC ended life with the blood of martyrs so that their blood consecrated their order."[115] Policarp's response to Oleksii and the synod of bishops at Pochaiv established a standoff between the two church camps: the autonomists depicted the autocephalists as contemporary heretics, ascribing to them the same stigma of ecclesial illegitimacy borne by the 1921 UAOC.[116] However, Policarp's response was equally sharp: the autonomists were denying authentic martyrdom and were thus collaborators with the Bolshevik regime, in the camp of Metropolitan Sergei, locum tenens of Moscow's patriarchal throne. Besides the obvious opposition of the two parties, they also came to ascribe identity markers to their opponents, negative identities that still complicate intra-Orthodox relations in Ukraine in the twenty-first century.

The story of the Orthodox Church in Ukraine continued to follow these lines as 1942 progressed. The German government in occupied Ukraine prohibited the use of the media for the exchange of polemics between Church leaders.[117] The UAOC held another council in May 1942, during which several new bishops were ordained and appointed to eparchies throughout Ukraine.[118] This council also issued resolutions, two of which are particularly notable. The first resolution declared that the autonomist council at Pochaiv of August 1941 was a "pseudo-council," and its resolutions were not to be implemented. This resolution referred to the authoritative directives of Metropolitan Dionysii of Warsaw. Second, the council officially regarded Metropolitan Dionysii as the "locum tenens of the Kyivan metropolitan throne until the next All-Ukrainian Church Council."[119] The May Council granted Bishop Nikanor the title of "archbishop of Kyiv and Chihirin," giving him the authority to lead the Kyivan see on a temporary basis.[120]

The May Council's identification of Metropolitan Dionysii as the temporary leader of the Ukrainian Church is significant for several reasons. First, the May Council recognized the divisions within the Church implicitly, evidenced by the resolution calling for unity in one autocephalous Ukrainian Church with a leader rightfully appointed by an All-Ukrainian Council of the Kyivan Church. Second, the May Council continued to depend canonically on the Church in Poland; all of its activities were reported to and blessed by Metropolitan Dionysii. Metropolitan Dionysii himself responded to the council's decision to name him locum tenens of the Kyivan throne. He expressed his pleasure with the canonical approach to the organization of autocephalous church life in Ukraine on the basis of the activities of the temporary administration, and acknowledged his appointment as locum tenens of the Kyivan throne in a letter sent to Archbishop Nikanor on August 25, 1942.[121] Dionysii implicitly acknowledged himself as the leader of the Ukrainian Church when he wrote the following to Archbishop Nikanor: "Only in my bosom does the Ukrainian Church have a relationship with the Ecumenical Orthodox Church. I also advocate for you before the holy ecumenical patriarch and the primates of other autocephalous churches . . . therefore I urgently pray to God that the time will soon arrive when I will be able to have a closer relationship with you, to participate without mediation in your conciliar tasks."[122] In a letter from Metropolitan Dionysii to Archbishop Policarp in September of 1942, he argued that he was the "organic bearer of this (Kyivan) throne" by virtue of his position as the head of the Autocephalous Church.[123] Dionysii blessed Archbishop Nikanor with the title of "archbishop of Kyiv," and urged Nikanor to make his residence in Kyiv, while referring to an imminent All-Ukrainian Church Council to definitively settle all of these matters. Dionysii's responses to the resolution of the May Council of the UAOC establish the UAOC's canonical dependence on the Church of Poland. The correspondence seems to suggest that Dionysii was actively encouraging the Ukrainians to establish their own autocephalous church, but as of 1942, the Autocephalous Church was a work-in-progress, aspiring to become the local church envisioned by the 1924 *tomos* of the Ecumenical Patriarchate while remaining within the jurisdiction of the Orthodox Church in Poland.

The Pochaiv Unity Council, October 1942

The obvious problem requiring resolution was the division among the Orthodox in Ukraine. This problem appeared to be resolved quite surprisingly by an unscheduled and unanticipated council at Pochaiv Monastery in October 1942. During the summer of 1942, the bishops of the UAOC scheduled a synodal meeting for October 4–8 in Lutsk.[124] The Germans prohibited them from traveling to Lutsk, so the bishops conferred among themselves unofficially. The most significant outcome of their meeting was to send a delegation of the Autonomous Church to Metropolitan Oleksii, led by Archbishop Nikanor and Bishop Mstyslav, to discuss potential resolutions to the schism. On October 8, an act of unification was agreed upon between the autocephalous and autonomous churches at the Pochaiv Lavra. The act of unification included the following important declarations:

1. The UAOC is active in Ukraine;
2. The UAOC is united with global Orthodoxy through Metropolitan Dionysii of Poland (Warsaw);
3. The supreme organ of government of the UAOC to the All-Ukrainian Local Council is the Holy Council of Bishops of Ukraine, which governs the church life of Ukraine through the Holy Synod;

4. All canonical differences separating the Churches were set aside for the purpose of unification.[125]

Responses to the act of unification at Pochaiv varied. On the one hand, bishops and clergy of the UAOC celebrated the act as a fait accompli, as evidenced by the celebration of a prayer service of thanksgiving in the Ukrainian Orthodox Church in Berlin on November 8, 1942, which also included the reading of the pastoral epistle of Metropolitan Policarp on the unification.[126] Priest Oleksander Vitenko visited Metropolitan Oleksii from December fifth to seventh to interview him on plans for actualizing the act of unification.[127] According to Vitenko, Metropolitan Oleksii stated that the German authorities were dubious about the unification since Oleksii had signed the act on his own, without his bishops' participation. He added that the ratification of the act by an all-Ukrainian council would have to be postponed until after the war and that Metropolitan Dionysii would be unable to exercise leadership over the church. One of the most important issues was the need for the act to be ratified, especially by the council of autonomous bishops themselves. Almost all of the plans for the realization of the act concerned matters of episcopal assignment and resolving questions of eparchial governance. A few items from Vitenko's report hint at what was to come. First, Metropolitan Oleksii called for a ceasefire in polemical exchange, so that the two leaders would no longer publicly criticize one another.[128] Second, Oleksii noted that the Autonomous Church did not recognize the authority of Metropolitan Dionysii because Dionysii did not agree to obtain certificates from the primates of all the Eastern churches indicating their agreement with the proclamation of the autocephaly of the Church in Ukraine. Finally, and perhaps most notably, Vitenko asked Oleksii, "Is it not possible to implement the act of October 8, 1942, into the life [of the church] without the assent of the council of bishops of your church?" Oleksii responded, "No, because there are opponents to unification, such as Bishops Ioan (Lavrynenko), Dmitry (Mahan), Leontii (Fylypovych), and others. Not all of my bishops are obedient, as it is in the Autocephalous Church."[129]

Metropolitan Oleksii's Reflections on the Pochaiv Unity Council

Metropolitan Oleksii explained his participation in the Pochaiv Council. In a short statement, he stated that he "agreed to Archbishop Policarp's attempt to unite the churches" out of obedience.[130] The rest of this remarks were quite pessimistic: Oleksii said that his bishops would demand the convocation of a council to discuss the terms of unification, and that a majority favoring unification at such a council was highly unlikely. He added that it was probably in the best interests of all concerned to defer the convocation of such a council to the end of the war when Ukraine would find itself free and in a "peaceful state."

In a letter dated December 17, 1942, sent to an unidentified bishop of his synod, Oleksii reports that the visit of the UAOC bishops to Pochaiv Monastery was a surprise to him.[131] Oleksii noted that the unification of the churches would be agreeable to all, but that the sides had to overcome considerable canonical and liturgical divisions:

> I responded that unification would be joyfully greeted by all, but that there is an obstacle of a canonical character. It demanded the reception of the self-consecrated in their current orders, the ordination of several candidates at one Divine Liturgy, and the change in the received order of the celebration of the Eucharistic canon. The delegates of the Lutsk Council, under the leadership of Metropolitan Alexander, agreed that all of the obstacles would be eliminated and that they would no longer exist. I then specified the resolution on our council of bishops concerning liturgical language. They responded that liturgical language cannot be a dividing issue at this time, for the bishops of the Lutsk orientation understand well that it is necessary to serve liturgy in the language the parishioners desire. At last I turned to the question about Vladyka Metropolitan Dionysii who . . . looks after the bishops of the Lutsk orientation. It was stated that Vladyka Dionysii will not govern in the future, but there is a desire that he should serve as the locum tenens of the Kyivan metropolitan throne so that he would have a relationship with the Eastern patriarchs.

Oleksii's letter is a statement establishing him as justly and accurately representing the perspective of his bishops. He addressed all of the primary problematic issues, namely the reception of the 1921 UAOC clergy, the controversy surrounding liturgical language, and the role of Metropolitan Dionysii.[132] Oleksii seems to be appealing to his brother bishops in an attempt to build consensus, as he refers a bit later in the letter to hierarchs, clergy, and faithful talking and writing about the necessity of unifying, as division is "fatally reflected in the contemporary life of the Church and demoralizes the people, so that even the German government is interested in this unification."[133] Oleksii documents the potential canonical steps that could be adopted to realize unity, and appeals to a sense of the urgency of the times and Christian love. It seems clear that the letter was intended to defend his actions in signing the act of unity while persuading the bishops of his synod to look for ways to resolve the canonical obstacles they had identified though canonical *oikonomia*.[134] Oleksii's assessment of the outcome of the act of unity had become more pessimistic by December, when he wrote Metropolitan Dionysii a summary report of the meeting, stating that "my hierarchs almost unanimously required a sobor, but it is impossible to convoke one during this time of war, which is why the time has arrived to defer unification to the end of the war, and to close the curtain on the act of October 8."[135] Later in the letter, Oleksii notes that Metropolitan Policarp had visited him, and that they had outlined "preparatory steps" for the realization of the unification act, though he feared that Policarp's bishops were going to deviate from the agreed-upon path.

Metropolitan Oleksii's correspondence establishes that the visit of the UAOC bishops to request unity was a surprise to him, that the bishops shared a frank discussion about all of the obstacles to unity, and that initial steps for implementing the act in the life of the church had been established. It is also clear that Oleksii did not have the authority to act on his own; his letters contain multiple references to the desire of the bishops on his synod for a special council to discuss these matters, and his letter to one of his own bishops indicates that he was attempting to persuade his synod that he was representing them and their positions without abandoning their principles. In addition to the obstacles posed by the question of receiving the 1921 UAOC clergy and liturgical language, the intensity of the war and the interference of the local German officials made it impossible for further steps to be taken.[136] The evidence of prayer services marking the unity of the churches and Oleksii's mention of how the division was demoralizing the people suggests that some of the rank-and-file clergy and laity of the Ukrainian churches wanted the autonomous and autocephalist camps to resolve their differences and unite. Vitenko's reference to a cease-fire in the polemical exchange between church leaders also suggests that there was some fatigue, perhaps on the part of all involved, over the intrachurch war being waged between the autonomist and autocephalist churches.

The Autonomous Church's Rejection of the Pochaiv Council

The combination of all of these factors doomed the attempt to actualize the resolutions of the October 1942 Pochaiv meeting. Ultimately, the bishops on Oleksii's synod not only opposed unity, but reprimanded him for acting unilaterally.[137] Some of the bishops on the autonomist synod, namely Archbishop Symon (Ivanovs'kyi) of Chernihiv, who was governing Kyiv eparchy, along with Bishop Panteleimon (Rudyk) and Bishop Benjamin (Novyts'kyi), wrote a memorandum accusing Metropolitan Oleksii of violating apostolic canon 34 and the directives of the council of bishops of the Autonomous Church in Ukraine from August 1941 because he did not consult with the rest of the bishops.[138] Metropolitan Oleksii himself was the recipient of particularly harsh condemnation, as the bishops claimed that faithful throughout Ukraine were publicly demonstrating against the act and had ceased commemorating Metropolitan Oleksii at the liturgy on account of his unification with the "Lypkivtsi," which was all attributable to the public dissemination of Oleksii's letter of October 10, 1942, asking the hierarchs to confirm the act. The three dissenting bishops wrote that "the holy Orthodox Church in Ukraine, which had offered hard sacrifices for the purity and the sanctity of her faith for the last quarter century, does not unite with teachers of schism [розколоучителів]."[139] The bishops resolved to request that Metropolitan Oleksii rescind his signature from the act of union and inform the faithful that he no longer supported it, cease using the title "Exarch of all Ukraine" until the bishops could discuss it at the next council meeting, and discuss how to receive those who had fallen away from the Church.[140] Bishop Panteleimon's letter to the deans of Kyiv eparchy follows the same line of thought: he instructed the deans that the clergy and faithful were not to enter into any acts of prayer with the autocephalists until they had corrected their dogmatic-canonical violations and errors. It also calls upon them all to firmly preserve "Holy Orthodoxy" and the purity of "our one, holy, Catholic, and Apostolic Church."[141]

By the end of 1942, the act of unity had been mostly dismissed, though Oleksii continued to maintain hope that the obstacles might finally be resolved, as he communicated to his bishops in a letter dated December 15.[142] Oleksii was prepared to wait for approbation until the bishops could gather at a conciliar meeting. In the letter, he repeated that the meeting needed to be postponed until the end of the war: "Canonical resolutions and the deliberation of unifying matters are postponed to the end of the war, and the act of October 8 of this year will be taken up by the first council of bishops of the exarchate after the war."[143]

By the beginning of 1943, the hope that Church leaders had invested in their German occupiers proved to be unfounded. As early as the summer of 1942, the German authorities had prohibited liturgical celebrations on feast days, and pressured pastors to serve the liturgy speedily so the people would be available for work.[144] In the beginning of 1943, Reichskommisar (commissioner of the Third Reich) of Ukraine Erich Koch decreed the reorganization of the UAOC and autonomists, deposing their central figures (the primate and council of bishops)—a brutal violation of church canons and unprecedented interference of the state in church affairs.[145] The Ukrainian Insurgent Army fought with German occupiers in West Ukraine, and in the process of the fighting, several clergy lost their lives and churches were destroyed.[146] The German occupiers of Ukraine were suspicious of the Orthodox Church and her leaders. A memo from SS Brigadier General Tomas to all the police commanders of the cities of Kyiv, Zhytomyr, Mykolaiv, and Dnipropetrovsk of February 11, 1942, indicates that the authorities should permit the Church to engage basic activities, but to observe the leaders of the Church as a way of preventing them from participating in political activities.[147] Tomas's memorandum focuses on the church principle of autocephaly and its parallel in the state, a sovereign republic. In an effort to prevent the Ukrainians from promoting national independence, the memorandum calls upon the police not to permit the Church to open theological schools in order to prevent the percolation of national and political ideologies.[148]

1944: German Defeat, Orthodox Reconfiguration in Ukraine

German prohibitions on church activity coincided with the turn of the tide in World War II. On May 7, 1943, Metropolitan Oleksii was assassinated. His tragic death remains controversial, as some reports attribute his assassination to the Ukrainian Insurgent Army led by Stepan Bandera.[149] The question of Oleksii's death is disputed: Kalkandjieva and Sophia Senyk assert that he was murdered by a Bandera agent, but John Armstrong's more extensive report suggests that Oleksii was traveling in a German vehicle and that the partisans were shocked to find a prominent church leader when they had targeted German officials.[150]

Metropolitan Feodosii (Protsiuk) offers the most explosive presentation with implications for the relationship between the 1942 UAOC and the Autonomous Church.[151] Protsiuk claims that UAOC Metropolitan Policarp and Bishop Mstyslav collaborated with the Ukrainian Insurgent Army to ensure the death of Metropolitan Oleksii. Protsiuk also attributed the assassination of autonomous Bishop Manuel to the devices of Mstyslav, based on Mstyslav's past nationalist partisan politics, in particular the demonstration he led at the Pochaiv Lavra in 1932, which caused a scene and a scandal.[152] Protsiuk's narrative fits squarely with the Moscow Patriarchate's depiction of all Ukrainian autocephalists and Greek Catholics who desired to separate from Moscow as supporters of Nazi fascism. Protsiuk's characterization of the mood among autonomous clergy captures the enmity separating the two churches. He claimed that "the popularity of the Autonomous Church and the murdered metropolitan—her head—increased, and in proportion to that growth, the popularity of Policarp (Sikorsky) and the entire UAOC decreased."[153] Protsiuk claimed that the clergy and laity of Volyn' called Policarp a murderer and politician, linking the UAOC with the Banderite party of Ukrainian nationalists. The murder of Metropolitan Oleskii sharpened the divisions between the autonomist and autocephalist Orthodox, since the autnomists believed the autocephalists ascribed to Banderite Ukrainian nationalism.

The patriotic activities and anti-Bolshevik polemics of the UAOC in Volyn' are undeniable during this period. Smyrnov chronicles Stepan Skrypnyk's creation of a newspaper titled *Volyn'*, a media outlet reporting on the activity of the Church and condemning the Soviet Union.[154] *Volyn'* contained articles pertaining to the life of the Church, and Skrypnyk's activity was influential enough to inspire Policarp to petition him to publish a liturgical Gospel book in Ukrainian for the furtherance of ecclesial Ukrainization, especially in the east.[155] Smyrnov asserts that there is evidence suggesting that the newspaper was funded by the OUN (Organization of Ukrainian Nationalists), a possibility requiring further investigation.[156] Smyrnov's appraisal of Mstyslav fits Ukrainians who were under Polish, Soviet, and German rule within a span of four years (1938–1942): like others in similar positions, Mstyslav negotiated with all political organs in an effort to compromise and improve the situation of Ukrainians living under occupation.[157] Karel Berkhoff's extensive treatment of German policies toward both Orthodox churches shows that the Germans were monitoring Mstyslav closely, and attempted to severely restrict his travels.[158]

As the Germans began to retreat from Ukraine and the Red Army approached, many of the bishops of both the UAOC and the Autonomous Church sought exile in the West. By 1944, the UAOC had gone into exile, initially with Metropolitan Dionysii in Warsaw, and then in Germany and Western Europe, with its bishops seeking union with existing Ukrainian Church structures in host countries.[159] On the eve of their departure from Ukraine, the bishops of the UAOC issued an encyclical to the faithful in and outside of Ukraine instructing them to impart their traditions to the next generation and struggle against Soviet anti-Ukrainian and openly anti-religious Bolshevik propaganda.[160] The anti-Soviet rhetoric of the epistle was striking and stands in direct contrast with the ecclesial ideology espoused by the Moscow Patriarchate in the immediate aftermath of the war.[161] The UAOC bishops referred to Sergei's election as patriarch of Moscow as a "Muscovite comedy," "necessary for the bishops to hide their horribly disastrous anti-religious activity from the world."[162] The UAOC sent bishops to minister to its people throughout Western Europe, Australia, and North America.[163] When the Soviets reoccupied Ukraine, the Moscow Patriarchate reabsorbed all former autocephalous parishes into the patriarchal structure. The Soviet victory over the Nazi regime in the "Great Patriotic War" became an important symbol for inscribing religious identity on the ecclesial legacy of Ukraine. The autocephalists were associated with Ukrainian nationalists who had allegedly collaborated voluntarily and even enthusiastically with the Nazi occupiers. The narrative celebrated a dual victory of state and church: the expulsion of the Nazi occupiers liberated all Orthodox Ukrainians from the evil temptation of fascism. The restoration of Ukraine to the Soviet Union marked the reunification of the nations of Russia, Ukraine, and Belarus. Similarly, the expulsion of the Nazis permitted Orthodox Ukrainians to return to the bosom of the Moscow Patriarchate. The state and church victories went hand-in-hand, with the return of Ukrainian Greek Catholics to Orthodoxy the only remaining task. This narrative became the cornerstone of the Moscow Patriarchate's ideology justifying the L'viv pseudo-council of 1946, but it was also a tool used to delegitimize Ukrainian Orthodox aspirations for autocephaly. The Soviet narrative depicted the desire for autocephaly as motivated by the Nazi invasion of Ukraine; thus, the desire for autocephaly included the acceptance of fascism by definition.

Orthodox Ukrainians and Their German Occupiers

This chapter has alluded to the warm welcome Ukrainian Orthodox offered initially to their German occupiers, especially in 1941 and 1942. History reveals a broad Ukrainian welcoming of the Germans, which is always coupled with a sharply worded condemnation of "Red Moscow." Contemporary Ukrainian historians have not attempted to conceal this difficult issue. Orest Subtelny depicts the context in his description of the Nazi racial doctrine that held that "all Slavs were subhumans," and Hitler's appointment of Erich Koch, "a notoriously brutal and bigoted administrator known for his personal contempt for Slavs," as the Nazi ruler of Ukraine.[164] The Nazis' brutal policies led to an increase in "anti-German feelings" among Ukrainians, who had dreamed of the abolition of collective farms.[165] Subtelny states that Ukrainians collaborated with the Nazi regime in order to survive, a situation complicated by the Ukrainian desire to be liberated from Stalinist totalitarianism, but that Ukrainian collaboration was relatively insignificant compared to that of Germany's allies because of Ukraine's lowly position in Nazi ideology.[166] Furthermore, resistance to the Nazi occupiers emerged among Ukrainians, as multiple Ukrainian nationalist partisan units fought both the Nazis and the Soviets, laying the foundation for a Ukrainian army the leaders believed would be necessary after the war.[167] The picture emerging from the larger context is that Ukrainians initially welcomed the Germans in hopes of an end to Soviet terror, but found their new overlord to be just as ruthless as its predecessor.[168]

The response of the Orthodox Church in Ukraine to the Nazi regime should be assessed in light of this broad context of Nazi-occupied Ukraine. One of the narratives in the history of the Orthodox Church in Ukraine during World War II was the thorny relationship between the Church and the Nazi state. Harvey Fireside's analysis of the Church's collaboration with state officials in Ukraine represents the narrative of the autocephalist camp benefitting from Nazi support.[169] Fireside asserts that the primary protagonists of the autocephalist movement, including the bishops Policarp, Ilarion, and Palladii (Vydybida-Rudenko) were all former state officials of the Directory in Ukraine.[170] He also argues that the 1942 UAOC benefitted most from the German policy on religion and state, and exploited it to their advantage by capitalizing on Oleksii's "vulnerability by having him sign a document recognizing autocephaly."[171] Armstrong proposes that the German officials initially supported the autocephalists as a way of intensifying enmity between Ukrainians and Russians, but that the Germans reversed roles and favored the autonomists when the autocephalists became too strong.[172] Investigation of the documents shows that both the autonomists and the UAOC hailed the German arrival in Ukraine, and there is no internal evidence to suggest that Oleksii was coerced into signing the act of unity with the UAOC.[173] Oleksii was certainly under duress, and the correspondence shows that the Nazis vacillated between supporting a Ukrainian Church merger and discouraging it, but Oleksii was also constantly critiqued within church circles for his support for a return to the Moscow Patriarchate, a move deemed suspicious within the Orthodox orbits in Poland and Ukraine because of the pledge of loyalty to the Soviet Union made by Metropolitan Sergei of Moscow in 1927. Furthermore, the correspondence of the churches suggests that the Germans harassed both the UAOC and the autonomist church, against Fireside's claim that the Nazis supported the UAOC, and the claim in Zinkewich and Voronyn that the Germans favored the Autonomous Church.

The Ukrainian experience of German invasion leaves us with two lessons. First, the narrative is consistent with the historical precedent of Ukrainians seeking an external leader to liberate them from a tyrant. In this instance, the Ukrainians placed their hope in Hitler, only to find that they had replaced one tyrant with another whose disregard for their national and ecclesial aspirations was equally fierce and dismissive.[174] Second, in performing an honest assessment of Ukrainian correspondence with German authorities, readers should keep in mind that for Ukrainians, it was impossible to establish church life without the approval of the state. A review of the historical documents in this chapter shows that Polish autocephaly was itself inspired, in part, by the existence of a sovereign state. Likewise, both the Ukrainians and the Russians were forced to negotiate deals of toleration with their anti-religious occupiers. In all cases of the Church attempting to redefine its relationship with the state, including that of the 1921 UAOC, a heavy price was ultimately paid in terms of the disintegration of church life and the eradication of clergy and church intelligentsia. Historians will continue to investigate instances of collaboration between select hierarchs and Nazi officials, just as they examine the degree to which Orthodox hierarchs obeyed the KGB in the Soviet period. From this brief look into this historical episode, one can only agree with the sentiment on relating to the state offered by the UAOC in its protest of Polish autocephaly in 1926: Church leaders should always be wary of placing their trust in princes and sons of men.

Conclusion

As World War II ended, all of Ukraine became a republic of the USSR and Poland became a communist state. The reconfiguration of state borders was accompanied by changes in church affairs: by 1944, all of the Orthodox in Ukraine fell under the jurisdiction of the Moscow Patriarchate, and by 1948, the Church in Poland had given up the autocephaly granted by Constantinople in 1924 and instead received it anew from the Moscow Patriarchate. Thus, the 1924 *tomos* and the development of autocephaly in the Church of Poland was a recent memory cultivated primarily by immigrants from Ukraine to the West. By 1946, the Moscow Patriarchate had complete ecclesial jurisdiction even over the Greek Catholics in Ukraine, and this reconfiguration prevailed in Eastern Europe until 1989, which witnessed to the rebirth and restoration of both the Greek Catholic and autocephalous Orthodox churches in Ukraine. The UAOC's pilgrimage to the West ended its canonical dependence on the Church of Poland. The most significant implication of this development is that the Orthodox churches in the West could not distinguish the canonical path of the 1942 UAOC from the 1921 version, so the stigma of ecclesial illegitimacy afflicted the UAOC in exile, despite the measures it took to resolve the canonical obstacles. The Ukrainian-Canadian Church historian Tymofii Minenko stated that the creation of a council of UAOC bishops in exile after World War II broke their dependence on Poland and contributed to confusion.[175] It is unlikely that the Ukrainians would have fared better had they remained dependent on the Polish Church, since the decision of the Polish Church to return to Moscow would have placed the Ukrainians under the authority of the Russian church yet again.

Minenko's hypothesis is that the history of autocephaly for the Ukrainian Church had two distinct lines: the 1921 UAOC, and the one originating in the 1924 Polish church.[176] Both the 1921 UAOC and 1924 cohorts of Ukrainians in Poland could trace their identities to the movement for autocephaly within the Kyivan Church from 1917 to 1921. The 1921 UAOC shares many of the same identity features as the 1924 Ukrainian cohort in Poland: they both desired an authentic restoration of the historic Kyivan Metropolia, especially its separation from Moscow. They both favored Ukrainization, though the 1924 group was more pastoral in implementing it by avoiding coercion, at least occasionally. They both sought state support to position themselves as the leader of the Kyivan Church: the 1921 UAOC briefly benefitted from the Soviet policy of isolating and weakening the patriarchate, whereas the 1924 group had limited freedom in Poland to pursue Ukrainization and receive protection from the Moscow Patriarchate.[177] The primary difference between the two groups was their divergent ecclesiologies: the 1921 UAOC interpreted the absolute power exercised by the hierarchy in Ukraine as endowed by the state, thus lacking a theological basis, and made the bold move of constructing their own distinct flattened ecclesiology, which strictly limited episcopal power. The 1924 group was steadfastly faithful to Orthodox ecclesiology and believed they proved their point when they were able to implement

Ukrainization and receive support for autocephaly through the primate of the Church in Poland. The 1924 cohort was also severely critical of the 1921 UAOC in its abandonment of a traditional episcopate and its variant of *sobornopravnist'*.

While the Ukrainian autocephalists' 1924 line followed a canonical path, it encountered two internal obstacles it was unable to overcome. The first and most serious obstacle was the question of patronage for the Church in Ukraine. For the autocephalists, the 1924 *tomos* of Constantinople was definitive and absolute, whereas an equally substantial group of Orthodox Ukrainians viewed the conciliar decisions in Moscow and Kyiv from 1918 to 1921 as definitive. The decision to return to ecclesial autonomy was based on the rationale that the Kyivan Church had voted for and received autonomy from Moscow before the Soviet disaster. The question of autocephaly for the Kyivan Church never left the proverbial table, but was impossible to deliberate because the Church could not convoke the appropriate councils. This is one of the reasons why the autonomists hailed the arrival of the Germans: the prospect of ecclesial freedom would permit the Church to resume the organic path to autocephaly that may have been in progress before it was interrupted by Stalinist terror. The inability of the Ukrainians to reach a consensus on their reception of the councils in Kyiv and Moscow of 1918 to 1921 and the *tomos* of 1924 made it impossible for them to agree on the proper path for autocephaly. Ironically, despite all of the differences separating the two churches, they both viewed autocephaly as possible.

The second obstacle was the legacy of the 1921 UAOC. For the autonomists, their betrayal of Orthodox ecclesiology had put them outside of the Church altogether, and rapprochement was possible only with repentance and an entirely new ordination. For the 1942 UAOC, the 1921 UAOC was a cohort of martyrs whose blood legitimized and sanctified them and their legacy, washing away the deficiencies in their orders and permitting the Church to receive them without ordaining them anew. World War II prevented the churches from convoking the all-Ukrainian council that would have decided the issue authoritatively, and the UAOC's decision to receive the 1921 clergy with absolution and restore their priesthood through the laying on of hands did indeed reinstate them to the ranks of the clergy, but the stigma of ecclesial illegitimacy came with them. This is one of the most severe crises of identity in the Orthodox Church of Ukraine, the legacy of the 1921 UAOC, and it had serious implications for church life among the millions of immigrants who made the West their new home after the war.

Finally, there is no doubt that the Orthodox Church in Ukraine was indelibly marked by the politics of war and its narratives. Those who fervently fought for an independent Ukrainian republic were conveniently branded as fascists; those who quietly served the Church under Soviet rule joined a narrative of the unified Slavic socialist republics liberating Orthodox Christians from fascist Western

Europe. One cannot underestimate the impact of the Soviet victory and the
implications of the Great Patriotic War for Ukrainian Orthodox identity: despite
severe persecution under the Soviet rule, renewed under Khrushchev, the Church
adopted the narrative that the Soviet state had protected it from the evils of fascism. From a certain perspective, there is some truth to the claim that survivors
of the ravages of World War II in Ukraine greeted Red Army troops as liberators,
since "Ukraine became a graveyard for millions of Ukrainians, Russians, Jews, and
Poles" on account of the war.[178] Plokhy captures the devastation Ukraine experienced with gravity:

> The Holocaust eradicated most of Ukrainian Jewry. Gone, too, were the German
> and Mennonite settlers of southern Ukraine and Volhynia—if the Soviets had not
> deported them in 1941, they now fled with the retreating Wehrmacht. The Polish
> population of Volhynia and Galicia was under attack from Ukrainian nationalists.
> As the Red Army began its advance into Ukraine after the victorious Battle of Kursk
> in July 1943, the Soviet leaders confronted a very different country from the one
> they had left in haste in the summer and fall of 1941. The cities were empty and their
> industrial enterprises completely destroyed.[179]

For the Ukrainian immigrants in the West, their new freedom provided them with
an opportunity to challenge the Soviet narrative; the next chapter tells their story.

3

The Ukrainian Diaspora (Canada and the United States)

THIS CHAPTER PROFILES THE ASPIRATIONS of Orthodox Ukrainians in the diaspora who strove to obtain both autocephaly and liberation from the Moscow Patriarchate and Soviet persecution of the Orthodox Church in Ukraine. The analysis will focus on the activity and thought of the Ukrainian Orthodox communities in Canada and the United States. The decision to focus on North America is pragmatic: in the postwar years, the most notable and influential leaders and events of the Ukrainian Church abroad were in Canada and the United States.[1] Featured topics are the emergence of a political theology in the Ukrainian Orthodox Churches of the diaspora, epitomized by preparations for the millennium of the baptism of Rus' in 1988; the burden of ecclesial illegitimacy and its isolation of Orthodox Ukrainians from global Orthodoxy; changes in Ukrainian Orthodox religious identity caused by the Canadian and American churches' decisions to join the Ecumenical Patriarchate; and the struggles of cultivating both Ukrainian identity and Orthodox church life in ethnically defined churches outside of Ukraine.

Summary of the Beginning: Western Ukrainians

The origins of the Ukrainian Orthodox Church in Canada begin with immigrants from Bukovyna and Galicia, regions under the rule of the Austro-Hungarian Empire, who settled in rural areas from Edmonton to Winnipeg.[2] The new immigrants were looking for fertile soil for farming, and began the process of constructing churches to sustain the church life accompanying them to Canada. Establishing stable church life during this period was a challenge on account of the difficulty in finding clergy for parishes, and bishops for administration. During the period of 1891 to 1923, a variety of churches attempted to proselytize the Ukrainians, including Roman Catholics, Russian Orthodox, and Presbyterians. The Presbyterians in particular sought to assimilate the Ukrainians into Canadian life.[3] Roman Yereniuk states that the Roman Catholics and Russian Orthodox alienated the Ukrainian immigrants, as the Catholics disrespected the Ukrainian Greek-Catholic distinction by imposing clerical celibacy, while the Russian Orthodox mission lost favor with the increase in Ukrainian national conscious-ness and the inability of the post-revolution Church in Russia to provide financial aid.[4]

In Canada, the Ukrainian immigrants reinvigorated the native Ukrainian tradi-tion of strong lay participation in the church by launching a lay initiative favoring the retention and cultivation of Ukrainian culture and language.[5] The so-called *narodovtsi* sought to have a Ukrainian national church, and following a meeting in July 1918, they established a Ukrainian Greek-Orthodox brotherhood that ulti-mately resulted in the emergence of the Ukrainian Orthodox Church of Canada.[6] Myroslaw Tataryn notes the crucial role played by the Winnipeg-based news-paper *Український голос* (Ukrainian voice), which sought to influence church life in Canada so it would resemble the Ukrainian model of clergy serving the people and their interests.[7] The most formidable challenge facing the aspirational Orthodox Church was securing a trustworthy bishop. Following a series of fail-ures, the Church ultimately persuaded the young archbishop John Teodorovych to assume pastoral responsibility for Canada along with the United States.[8] As read-ers would expect, the appointment of Archbishop John resulted in two outcomes. First, Archbishop John's stigma of canonical illegitimacy left an indelible mark on the Church in Canada. Second, Archbishop John proved to be an able archpastor who respected the people's national and cultural identities

The problem of Archbishop John's canonical status and attachment to the UAOC proved determinative for the future trajectory of the Ukrainian Church in Canada. He began to consider the possibility of having his ordination corrected, given the liquidation of his native church in Ukraine and his continued alien-ation from global Orthodoxy. This idea contributed to a tense argument between two of the chief ideologues of the Church in Canada, namely Vasyl Svystun (who supported the ideology of the 1921 church) and the priest Semen Sawchuk, who adopted more of a centrist Orthodox position while supporting the cultural aspi-rations of the Ukrainian Canadians.[9] The seventh Canadian council in Saskatoon in 1935 urged Archbishop John not to receive reconsecration, but to de-empha-size the centrality of the 1921 UAOC as a stone in the foundation of the Church in Canada.[10]

The initial pattern of Ukrainian immigration and the formation of church life in the United States was similar to the experience in Canada. The immigrants who came primarily from Western Ukraine in search of work after 1875 were Greek Catholic and experienced tension with the Roman Catholic hierarchy of the United States.[11] In 1915, a group of Ukrainian priests established an inde-pendent church in Chicago, and eventually received the support of Metropolitan

Germanos of the Antiochian Church.[12] When the Ukrainian community of the United States learned of the aspirations for the creation of an autocephalous Church in Ukraine, they planned to unite with the new church.[13] In 1924, the small Ukrainian Orthodox Church in America requested that the UAOC send a bishop to govern church life, and Archbishop John Teodorovych assumed those duties until his death in 1971. In 1931, a small group of Ukrainian Greek Catholics entered into communion with the Ecumenical Patriarchate. They received their first bishop in 1932.

An assessment of the origins of church life for Ukrainians in Canada and the United States reveals mostly similarities. First, immigrants from Western Ukraine constituted the original parish communities in both countries, people who were originally Greek Catholic. In both cases, the Ukrainians were unable to continue church life as they had experienced it in their homelands in the conditions of their new countries, as their Roman Catholic hosts imposed Latin canonical traditions and regarded the Ukrainians with mistrust. The Ukrainians who eventually came under the jurisdiction of Archbishop John (Teodorovych) identified themselves as culturally and nationally Ukrainian, which was one of the reasons they could not remain under the jurisdiction of the Russian Orthodox Church. In this regard, their experience was both similar and different from that of the well-known Greek-Catholic communities that became Orthodox when their Roman Catholic hosts did not respect their traditions.[14] The former Greek Catholics hailed from varying regions of Eastern Europe, so one cannot conveniently identify all of them as Ukrainians. Only those churches that voluntarily chose to be exclusively ethnic in Canada and the United States and cultivated their identity by requesting a nationally and culturally conscious bishop from Ukraine can be called Ukrainian. The vast majority of the first wave of immigrants hailed from Western Ukraine and were formerly Greek Catholic, so their cultural and liturgical traditions were formed by their native regions. These immigrants had experienced attempts at proselytism by other groups and made a conscious choice to be Ukrainian Orthodox as minorities both among North American Christian churches and their fellow Orthodox churches. The irregular canonical situation of Archbishop John (Teodorovych) also contributed to their evolving identities, as evidenced by the tension within the Church of Canada over fidelity to the principles of the 1921 UAOC and the decision of the smaller Orthodox group to enter into communion with the Ecumenical Patriarchate in the United States in 1931.

Post–World War II: The Arrival of Ukrainians

The arrival of Orthodox Ukrainians in Canada and the United States posed new challenges for the Ukrainian Orthodox churches already in existence here. In the

United States, the largest Ukrainian group was led by the aforementioned John (Teodorovych) of the Ukrainian Autocephalous Orthodox Church, one the first bishops of the 1921 cohort to be consecrated at the October Council. The UAOC sent Teodorovych to shepherd Orthodox Ukrainians in 1924, and he was the leader of the largest Church body in the United States until his death in 1971.

Archbishop John's most formidable challenge was his canonical isolation from the rest of Orthodoxy, a situation he was unable to elude. While ecclesial illegitimacy stigmatized all Orthodox Ukrainians, as evidenced by the convenient association of anyone professing sympathy for autocephaly with the *Lypkivtsi*, Archbishop John was particularly prone to this identity marker since he was a product of that very church. When other Ukrainians who had belonged to the UAOC settled in Canada or the United States, questions emerged about their jurisdictional fidelities and positions on the canonicity of the UAOC. In his coerced retirement, Metropolitan Vasyl Lypkivs'kyi himself expressed displeasure with the perception that Metropolitan John was compromising the right of the UAOC to establish its own internal canonical order without requiring assent from the other churches of the global Orthodox family.[15] Metropolitan John presided over the largest Ukrainian Orthodox church in the United States, but it was not the only one; a smaller church comprised mostly of former Greek Catholics existed under the leadership of the Ecumenical Patriarchate.[16] The coerced liquidation of the UAOC from 1927 to 1930 did not eradicate all of the clergy of this church, and the primary leaders of the Ukrainianizing and autocephalist movements in Poland and Western Ukraine deliberated methods of receiving Ukrainians into the church. The idea was to find a seamless way to receive the remnants of the 1921 cohort into a traditional canonical church, in communion with global Orthodoxy through the metropolitan of Warsaw. When thousands of these Orthodox who reverted to the traditional canonical structure preferred by global Orthodoxy arrived in Canada and the United States in the years following World War II, the existing Ukrainian churches sought to receive them. The Ukrainian Church led by Metropolitan John provided fundamental humanitarian aid for the impoverished and downtrodden immigrants, who commenced the process of assimilation into American life, which included introduction to Ukrainian church life outside of Ukraine. Since the Orthodox churches were largely populated by natives of Western Ukraine, who were formerly Greek Catholic, the arrival of immigrants from central and Eastern Ukraine contributed to a shift in the cultural center of the Church in America.[17]

A more urgent matter was unifying the Orthodox Ukrainians into one from their respective churches. In Canada, the position of primate of the Church became vacant when Archbishop John resigned from his duties in 1947.[18] The Extraordinary Council of November 1947 elected Archbishop Mstyslav

(Skrypnyk) as its new primate, a situation that became quite complicated with the simultaneous arrival and settling of Metropolitan Ilarion (Ohienko) at St. Mary the Protectress Orthodox Cathedral in Winnipeg.[19] The council of bishops of the UAOC in Exile exhibited some openness to Archbishop John as he presided at the Divine Liturgy on November 12–13, 1947, in Winnipeg, with Archbishop Mstyslav officially representing the synod of the UAOC in Exile.[20] Archbishop John performed the transfer of episcopal governance by handing over his staff to Mstyslav in a solemn ceremony after the liturgy.[21] Yereniuk notes that the presence of the two bishops in the same place caused tension: Metropolitan Ilarion was a respected scholar and had been at the center of the controversy about the position of metropolitan of Kyiv in the formative phase of the second UAOC. Ilarion was also very critical of the historical and ideological path adopted by the 1921 UAOC, and of Archbishop John, whose legitimacy he rejected.[22]

Mstyslav was an active pastor with political experience, and he clashed almost immediately with the influential laity of the Canadian Church, who were accustomed to exercising powerful influence in the life of the church.[23] Mstyslav involved himself in American Church affairs, and pressured Archbishop John to have his ordination corrected.[24] Yereniuk states that Mstyslav wanted "major episcopal control with a strong hierarchical leadership," whereas the laity and Sawchuk advocated for the continuation of the "tradition of collective leadership."[25] Furthermore, the Ukrainian Church under the Ecumenical Patriarchate held a council and elected Mstyslav as their chief hierarch, at the same time demoting Bishop Bohdan (Shpylka) to the position of Mstyslav's assistant. Bishop Bohdan, however, was able to nullify the council's resolutions and suspend the clergy who had arranged for the change.[26] Mstyslav focused his efforts on uniting the Canadian and American churches, an action that further distanced him from the Orthodox Ukrainians in Canada, who depicted his actions as obstructionist.[27] Tensions peaked in 1950 and Archbishop Mstyslav resigned, a decision narrowly accepted by the tenth council of the Ukrainian church in Canada held on June 18–21, 1950.[28] The Canadian Church expressed its commitment to full autocephaly at the 1950 council. Metropolitan Policarp (Sikorsky) of the UAOC appointed archbishops Michael and Platon, but Platon died before the extraordinary council of 1950 could elect a primate.[29] Metropolitan Ilarion (Ohienko) offered his services to the council, which then elected him, but under the conditions of a contract: Ilarion was to commit to conciliarism in the church, to pledge not to engage in affairs outside of the Canadian Church, and to recognize the canonicity of the UAOC in Europe: Ilarion accepted the terms and confirmed them.[30]

During his primatial tenure, Metropolitan Ilarion oversaw the expansion of the Canadian Metropolia with the strengthening of theological education at St. Andrew's College in Winnipeg, continued activity in publication, and the expansion of the hierarchy. He was an active ruling primate until his retirement in 1968 and death in 1972. Yereniuk describes the period after the war and up until the millennial celebrations in Canada as "an era of great growth, development, and creativity" in the life of the Canadian Church. However, the turbulent struggle between Mstyslav and the leaders of the Church in Canada exhibited divisions in the Ukrainian Orthodox agenda. The Canadians accused Mstyslav of authoritarianism (an accusation that beleaguered him for the entirety of his episcopal tenure), while he accused them of congregationalism. The argument between Mstyslav and the Canadian Church symbolized both Mstyslav's tendency to act authoritatively and the opposition of Orthodox parties pitting the competing ecclesiologies of conciliarity and church hierarchy against each other. The compromise reached with Metropolitan Ilarion also symbolizes this ecclesiological tension, as Ilarion had a history of severely criticizing *sobornopravnist'* in his writings.

The Canonical Metamorphosis of the Ukrainian Orthodox Church in America

With the prospect for a unified Ukrainian Orthodox Church of the USA on the horizon, Archbishop John Teodorovych was poised to become the leader of the new church, with Archbishop Mstyslav as his junior bishop. For the Church to function as a legitimate entity in the United States, a canonical resolution to the problem of Archbishop John's episcopal ordination was required. The bishops of the UAOC in Western Europe had discussed how to effectively transform Archbishop John's ordination into one recognizable by global Orthodoxy. For example, Mstyslav had openly recognized the validity of Archbishop John's ordination in a letter written to him on March 27, 1946.[31] Despite Mstyslav's approval, Archbishop John reached a compromise with the UAOC synod in exile on the conditions required for the unification of the churches in the United States. The UAOC synod anticipated divisions among Orthodox Ukrainians in the diaspora and asked Archbishop John to have his ordination canonically corrected. In a long letter addressed to Metropolitan Policarp of the UAOC synod abroad and Archbishop Gregory of the UAOC council in emigration, published in February of 1950, Archbishop John explained his actions as motivated by his desire to mediate between the divided cohorts within the Ukrainian Church.[32] He stated that significant compromises were necessary to remove all of the obstacles to the unification of the Ukrainian Churches, and that he would set an example by offering to have his ordination canonically corrected:

> For this reason, I took the initiative upon myself, in a letter to Metropolitan Policarp on June 6, 1946, to say, that in accordance with the path of these possible and necessary compromises, I also have before me the possibility to have my episcopal

ministry canonized, which I had received on the basis of the canonical concepts of the All-Ukrainian Orthodox Church Council in 1921. . . . The leadership of the Canadian Church, which was under my guidance at the time, did not find it possible to agree with my initiative by granting approval in advance for the possibility of the canonization of my episcopal order. This became the reason for my decision to exit as leader of the Church. I left. This was my sacrifice for the holy act of uniting all into one Ukrainian Orthodox Church.[33]

In a letter written to Bishop Platon in December 1948, secretary of the UAOC synod abroad, Archbishop John requested clarification on how he was to proceed with the canonical correction of his ordination, as the UAOC synod had requested.[34] The Ukrainian Church in America petitioned the patriarchate of Alexandria to receive it, and the Alexandrian exarch agreed.[35] Archbishop John's letter to Metropolitan Christopher (Contogeorge) of Alexandria broadens his desire for unity to global Orthodoxy, as he refers to the need to "liquidate our standing apart from the family of Orthodox churches because of the deviation of our past canonical understanding of the rite of episcopal consecration."[36]

The canonical correction of Archbishop John's episcopal ordination occurred on August 26–28, 1949, as Archbishop Mstyslav and Metropolitan Christopher, the exarch of the patriarchate of Alexandria, presided at the rite correcting his ordination from 1921.[37] The rite included his reception of the monastic tonsure and the laying on of hands by other bishops required by Orthodox canons.[38] The Divine Liturgy was concelebrated by Archbishops John and Mstyslav at the Cathedral of St. Volodymyr in New York on August 28, which Archbishop John described as a "unity permitting the prayerful reunion of the two Ukrainian Orthodox Churches, which were not in prayerful union up until that time."[39]

The canonical correction was a significant turning point in the public religious identity of Orthodox Ukrainians. First, Archbishop John's agreement to have his episcopal ordination corrected denoted a permanent shift on the part of the autocephalist Orthodox Ukrainians toward the traditional canonical pattern of global Orthodoxy. Archbishop John was the final bishop of the 1921 UAOC cohort and also its most visible surviving figure. The autocephalist Ukrainians who emerged from within the Church of Poland in the early years of World War II had returned to traditional ecclesial structures and were wary of the path selected by the UAOC. Metropolitan John's agreement to have his ordination corrected marked the decline of the revolutionary and innovative path blazed by the UAOC, as the UOC-USA was positioning itself as a legitimate Ukrainian Church advocating for autocephaly.[40] For the Ukrainians who had been alienated from global Orthodoxy throughout modern history, the correction of this canonical irregularity was designed to reintroduce Orthodox Ukrainians as legitimate members of the Orthodox Church worldwide.

The Unification of the Churches in the United States

The canonical correction of Archbishop John's ordination was an integral part of the festivities devoted to the unification of the Ukrainian Orthodox churches of the United States. The unification council occurred on October 14, 1950, in New York, on the feast of the Protection of the Mother of God.[41] The unification council members overcame obstacles and established a single Ukrainian metropolia, originally consisting of Metropolitan John and Archbishops Mstyslav and Hennadii (Shyprykevych).[42] The council did not limit its work to creating a unified metropolia in the United States: it viewed the unification as "the first stage toward a global council of all parts of the Ukrainian Orthodox Church operating outside the borders of enslaved Ukraine."[43] The council emphasized the unanimity of its delegates in unifying the two churches, numbering 61 clergy and 130 lay representatives.[44] The most significant public acts of the council were its configuration of the episcopate: the council elected Archbishop John as the metropolitan and ruling hierarch of the church.[45] Archbishop Mstyslav adorned Metropolitan John with the white *klobuk* at the Divine Liturgy on October 15.[46] The council also included an appearance by Archbishop Bohdan (Shpylka) of the Ukrainian Church under the Ecumenical Patriarchate.[47] Archbishop Mstyslav capitalized on Archbishop Bohdan's presence at the council to encourage him to "reveal his desire to enter into the ranks of the united Ukrainian episcopate in the USA."[48]

Archbishop Bohdan (Shpylka)'s request to attend the council as an observer is particularly noteworthy since the extraordinary council of his Ukrainian Church under the Ecumenical Patriarchate had elected Mstyslav as its new primate. Archbishop Bohdan's attendance at the unification council can be construed as a power play; in this instance, Mstyslav used the opportunity to call upon Bohdan to join the ranks of the newly united Ukrainian Metropolia in the United States.

Compromise and Unity without a Satisfactory Canonical Resolution

Archbishop John (Teodorovych)'s canonical correction can most accurately be described as a compromise. Orthodox Ukrainians had struggled to come to terms with the legacy of the 1921 UAOC. On the one hand, the 1921 UAOC had established a vibrant church without receiving external assistance, and exemplified the spirit of independence motivating Ukrainian Church and civil leaders. While the 1921 UAOC had benefitted briefly from Soviet favoritism, it became the target of the same destructive anti-religious wrath of the Soviet regime that had persecuted the patriarchate so brutally. The 1921 UAOC had sympathizers among the bishops of the 1942 UAOC because of their witness and suffering as their church was liquidated. The 1942 UAOC could not completely eradicate the legacy of the 1921 group, so it sought to include Archbishop John just as the clergy of the 1921 UAOC were received through an innovative liturgical rite of repentance and laying on of hands. Archbishop John was not excluded from church ministry, but had to agree to the canonical adjustment of his episcopal order. He agreed to the task for the sake of unifying the separated cohorts of the Church. His agreement sacrificed fidelity to the ecclesiological principles and canons of the 1921 UAOC, while the 1942 UAOC found new ways to honor the groundbreaking activity of the 1921 cohort.

Archbishop John's corrected canonical status had three immediate results that contributed to the next phase of development in the Ukrainian Orthodox agenda for autocephaly and liberation: first, for Orthodox Ukrainians, the move was a decisive return to traditional, episcopocentric, mainstream Orthodoxy. The bishops were the most influential and powerful leaders of the Church and a return to the familiar ecclesial structure of mainstream Orthodoxy also permitted the reintroduction of its mindset, which privileges the role and activity of the bishops. The return of a powerful episcopate diminished the principle of popular governance that was featured by the UAOC. Nevertheless, the spirit of popular governance endured within the Canadian and American churches, and their governing structures had lay representation through the creation of a metropolitan council that included clergy and laity. However, *sobornopravnist'* as a governing principle threaded throughout the church structures became secondary to episcopal governance with the unification of the churches.

The second result of the canonical correction was the attempt of the UOC-USA to stake a claim to complete canonical legitimacy. Unlike the 1921 UAOC, the UOC-USA's adherence to the principles of apostolic succession guaranteed through the Church of Poland enabled them to participate in the communion of global Orthodoxy while continuing to advocate for the restoration and legalization of a canonical church in Ukraine. Ultimately, the UOC-USA achieved only partial success on this matter, since some of the Orthodox churches would meet and dialogue with them, even pray. However, the Moscow Patriarchate sustained its position that the UOC-USA was uncanonical, as evidenced by the letter of Patriarch Pimen to Patriarch Athenagoras (Spyrou) in 1972. From Moscow's perspective, there was no global confirmation of the correction of Metropolitan John's ordination, so the UOC remained both uncanonical and schismatic.

When one traces the history of the UOC-USA, one finds that the approach to gathering and liturgizing with the UOC-USA adopted by Orthodox jurisdictions was not uniform. In some instances, Orthodox parishes would concelebrate vespers or other non-Eucharistic liturgical offices with the UOC-USA, and more importantly, would recognize the legitimacy of their sacraments by offering the faithful Holy Communion. An illustration of an exception to this rule can be found in the synodal decisions of ROCOR (the Russian Orthodox Church out-side of Russia). The synodal decision referred to the second UAOC as "self-con-secrated" and "neo-*Lypkivtsi* autocephalists," and stated that common prayer with them was forbidden until they had repented with "purity of heart."[49]

These perceptions of the UAOC found their way into parish communities in the years following World War II, illuminating the most rigid view of the second UAOC. In reality, the perception of the UAOC held by Orthodox in America began to soften throughout the period of the Cold War leading up to the mil-lennium, largely as a result of the church's fervent attempt to strengthen its ties with the Ecumenical Patriarchate. At the time of the millennium celebration in 1988, bishops of the Ecumenical Patriarchate were sent to participate in the celebrations hosted by the Ukrainians in South Bound Brook, New Jersey, with participation falling short of Eucharistic concelebration. Despite the absence of full communion with the Ukrainians, the Ecumenical Patriarchate responded favorably to official correspondence from the Ukrainian Church and went so far as to offer an official blessing of their activities in preparation for the millen-nial celebration. In summary, then, Metropolitan John's agreement to have his ordination corrected symbolized the Ukrainian Church's commitment to restor-ing the traditional ecclesiological structures favored by global Orthodoxy. Some Orthodox in North America began to warm to the Ukrainians; others continued to view them through the lens of ecclesial illegitimacy, as self-consecrated and neo-*Lypkivtsi*.

The third result is the most ironic. By returning to the episcopocentric system privileged by global Orthodoxy, the UOC-USA began the slow process of abdi-cating its independence. The step taken by the 1921 UAOC to consecrate bishops without the participation of bishops resulted in two outcomes. First, this deci-sion permanently imprinted the stigma of ecclesial illegitimacy upon the UAOC, depaying global Orthodoxy recognition of its canonicity. Second, the recreation of the episcopate using the ecclesiological mechanism of *sobornopravnist'*, along with the declaration of several new canons, ultimately freed the UAOC from the constrictive structure of global Orthodoxy. On the one hand, the UAOC had neither a place in nor the support of global Orthodoxy. On the other hand, the UAOC was truly independent and did not require confirmation or acceptance of its decisions. The decision of the UOC-USA to firmly commit itself to the eccle-siological structures and mechanisms of world Orthodoxy opened the door to its potential reception within the larger Church, but it also embarked on the path of dependence from world Orthodoxy. This journey was completed when the churches of Canada and the USA returned to the omophorion of the Ecumenical Patriarchate in 1990 and 1995, respectively.

In summary, the canonical correction of Archbishop John's ordination resulted in the unification of the Church on October 14–15, 1950, coinciding with the feast of the Protection of the Mother of God. An episcopate was established at this council, with Metropolitan John as ruling hierarch and Archbishop Mstyslav as his assistant. Voronyn notes that preparations commenced immediately for the next phase of the unified church life of Orthodox Ukrainians in the United States: the creation of a church center in South Bound Brook, New Jersey. The process of building St. Andrew's Memorial Church and the new headquarters would serve as the basis for the next phase of development in public religious identity for the American Ukrainians.[50]

FIGURE 1. St. Andrew Memorial Church in South Bound Brook, New Jersey. Photo by Elizabeth Symonenko. Used with permission.

Ukrainian-American Political Theology: "American Jerusalem"

With the arrival of immigrants from Soviet Ukraine after World War II in the United States and Canada, the internal life of the Church was altered. In addition to the reversion to an episcopocentric model of administration, the people of the UOC-USA adjusted to the arrival of immigrants who brought with them their own regional liturgical traditions. The new Ukrainian immigrants acclimated to their new North American context: they used the religious freedom available to them in the West to condemn Soviet persecution of the Orthodox Church in Ukraine, especially the UAOC was illegal. The UOC-USA was also openly critical of the Moscow Patriarchate and frequently accused the Russian Church of attempting to usurp the privilege of the Ecumenical Patriarchate and create a parallel structure governed by Moscow. In the process of sustaining the church life brought by the immigrants to the United States, the UOC-USA developed a political theology that lamented the woes of the more recent past, condemned the USSR, the primary antagonist, and sought the liberation of Soviet Ukraine and all countries under communist rule through the lens of American freedom.

Many events symbolized the émigré Ukrainian community's political theology. Among them was the process of erecting St. Andrew's Memorial Church and Center in South Bound Brook, New Jersey. Having accomplished the unification of the two largest Ukrainian churches in 1950, the construction of the administrative center commenced in 1952. The Church leaders appealed to Orthodox Ukrainians throughout the United States to gather in New Jersey under the protection of the Mother of God. The theme for this inaugural event was the Mother of God's protection of Orthodox Ukrainians in the past and present, headed by the title of the liturgical hymn "Beneath your compassion, we take refuge, o virgin Birthgiver of God." The church communique fused the Mother of God's patronage of Orthodox Ukrainians with the battle against communism and the building of the Memorial Church.[51]

The celebration scheduled for June 1, 1952, was disappointing because of heavy rain, which forced the organizers to move the festivities to Washington High School nearby. The political theology articulated at the inaugural events fused together several staples from Orthodox devotional history, namely the commemoration of those who defended the fatherland against a bloodthirsty foe. During the Cold War, the Orthodox Ukrainians who enjoyed the protection of the Mother of God in the United States named the foe: the Bolshevik regime located in Moscow. The rationale for the Ukrainian reference to the Protection of the Mother of God was their continued existence outside of their native homeland. In the context of the Cold War, the Orthodox Ukrainians in the United States drew from the traditional repository of Orthodox political theology and its champion, the Mother of God, and fused it with American civic values: freedom and democracy. Thus, the political theology proclaimed by the small Ukrainian émigré community had global resonances: the memory of their struggle to defeat the Soviets who sought their eradication provided fuel for the global Christian battle against Soviet Union. The émigré battleground was the United States, which as the global symbol of liberty and freedom was an appropriate opponent for the Soviet regime.

The centerpiece of the church center was the Memorial Church itself, and the process of building the church was prolonged by difficulties in raising the necessary funds. From 1954 to 1965, the Church administration repeatedly appealed to the people for donations. The Church established 1961 as the goal for the construction and dedication of the memorial church, the centennial of Taras Shevchenko's death. The UOC expressed hope that the edifice would serve as a memorial for those who perished under the Bolshevik regime, and a beacon of thanksgiving for the freedom to worship in America.[52] By November 1960, the urgency to complete construction by 1961 reached a new height: it was necessary to coincide with the hundred-year jubilee of Shevchenko's death, a symbolic year since Shevchenko was "the greatest martyr of Ukraine's battle with Moscow."[53]

In the September and October 1960 issues of the *Ukrainian Orthodox Word* (UOW), the UOC reported that the construction of the Memorial Church had garnered the attention of the Soviet Union and that Moscow viewed its completion as a serious threat. One report states that a priest in New York attempted to steal the primary contractor away from the Ukrainians, who had not raised enough money to continue construction. The urgency of the financial appeal and the latent criticism of those who had not yet donated to the cost of construction are expressed by the report's reference to a letter written to the editor.[54] The writer argues, "if each one of us donated just a portion of the sum we give each year [to income tax] . . . then our Church easily and quickly would not only complete the construction of the Memorial Church, but would be able to purchase the Empire State Building . . . and place a cross on her roof." The church continued to propose June 1961 as the completion date for the edifice.

In January 1961, a new element contributed to the political theology and the edifice itself. The construction process added fragments from beloved shrines in Ukraine, namely the Cathedral of St. Sophia, the Pecherska Lavra Monastery, St. Michael's Monastery, and the Cathedral of St. Nicholas (all in Kyiv). Each of these edifices has historical significance for Ukrainians, and the UOC sought the addition of the last three fragments in particular as symbols of reconstruction, since their original buildings—the Dormition Church of the Lavra, St. Michael's Church, and the Cathedral of St. Nicholas—were destroyed by the Bolsheviks.[55] The UOC added another commemoration to that of Shevchenko's death: the forty-year anniversary of the proclamation of ecclesial autocephaly in Kyiv by the first Ukrainian Autocephalous Orthodox Church.[56]

From 1961 to 1965, the political theology that began to take shape with the dedication of the church center in Bound Brook remained more or less stable as the émigré community slowly completed the construction. Church leaders continued to use the American values of liberty and religious freedom in their speeches and activities. On January 23, 1961, the day before Ukraine had declared independence in 1919, a special prayer for Ukraine's freedom was read in both chambers of the United States Congress.[57] The UOC declared June 4, 1961, a "great feast," as the fragments from the shrines in Kyiv were installed in their designated spaces in the memorial church. The theology of this great feast was consistent with the foundations established since 1952; the feast commemorated the Ukrainian people's sacrifice on the altars of its battle for the justice of God in the world. The Church stressed the significance of building the memorial church in the free world (America), an accomplishment permitted by "divine providence."[58] The addition of the ruined fragments to the Memorial Church's constituted the pilgrimage of relics from Ukraine's Jerusalem to the United States.[59] One quality of the Church's description of this great feast is notable: this was not an instance of an émigré community lamenting the loss suffered as a result of their exile from their native homeland. Rather, it was an occasion for thanksgiving for the gift of divine providence, and not an occasion for weeping while gazing upon the foreign "waters of Babylon."[60] The installation of relics from Ukraine's past shrines were designed to ignite renewed love for the fatherland in the present, an illustration of the ultimate objective of the Memorial Church: the liberation and resurrection of Ukraine, and of all people who were suffering under the tyranny of communism.

The church was finally dedicated on October 10, 1965, which was celebrated as a day of paschal joy, a "victory of light over darkness," and an opportunity to renew the majesty of ruined Ukrainian holy places in the free world. October 10 was designated as a special feast for the Ukrainian Orthodox Church as ten thousand people attended the dedication. Metropolitan John (Teodorovych's) speech included a concluding exhortation that synthesized the UOC's objective in erecting the edifice:

> May our memorial church remain standing for the ages! May the participants of the actions of our age establish the path for remembering these experiences! May our children and their children learn about the glory and sorrow of our day and evoke love in us for our native land and people! May the shrine erected by us loudly proclaim the need for our freedom-loving American people to attentively remain on the side of freedom! . . . From all ends of the United States of America, come here, and here find the breath of everything native, find in this place peace and faith: the day is coming that our land will be free and our nation on it![61]

The process of constructing and dedicating St. Andrew's Memorial Church in South Bound Brook, New Jersey, illustrates the addition of American values of independence and religious freedom to the extant aspirations for autocephaly among the Orthodox Ukrainians who belonged to the merged Church. First, this cohort of Orthodox Ukrainians maintained select aspects of the identity that accompanied them from Ukraine to the United States, namely resilient ecclesiastical independence from the Moscow Patriarchate. The UOC-USA aligned and fused its independence with American freedom, using the platform provided by the polemics of the Cold War to espouse a political theology of martyrdom that resulted in prophetic lament on the recent violence endured by their motherland, Ukraine. In terms of public self-identity, the UOC-USA was diametrically opposite the Moscow Patriarchate: the UOC-USA espoused both ecclesial and political independence, and characterized the Moscow Patriarchate as a collaborator with the Soviet regime, which represented both political and religious exploitation and slavery. From one perspective, the Ukrainian Orthodox community was simply continuing a proclamation of the same political theology it had articulated since the 1921 UAOC. What changed was the context: the Ukrainians were able to position themselves as allies of democracy and religious freedom pitted against an evil adversary in the Soviet Union. But the self-identity of the Orthodox Ukrainians in immigration assumed a new identifying marker: the challenge of sustaining community identity as a small émigré community in the massive space of American religious plurality. The community's struggle to raise the funds needed for the Memorial Church manifested this new reality, which became permanently affixed to their identity, a small group of immigrants with a limited capacity to sustain the fullness of church life they had experienced in Soviet and German-occupied Ukraine. The challenges posed by a hybrid Ukrainian-American identity would manifest themselves in new ways alongside the difficulty in raising funds to erect a memorial edifice.

The Ukrainian-American Conundrum: Hybrid Identity and Contribution to Mission

As the Cold War continued, the immigrants who began to arrive in the United States from the late 1940s to the mid-1950s raised a generation of children in the Church. These immigrants, many of whom were born in displaced-person camps, bore a hybrid Ukrainian-American identity. Unlike their parents, who accepted the work available to them as a small price to pay for freedom, the next generation was fully immersed in Cold War American life with all of its complexities, from postwar patriotism to the fears of nuclear Armageddon and the challenges of American social revolutions in race, gender, and sexuality. As the polemics of the Cold War intensified through nuclear armament, the Church in the United States attempted to navigate its hybrid internal life.

In terms of mission, the UOC-USA attempted to cultivate its canonical identity by strengthening its relationship with the Ecumenical Patriarchate. At the time of the first attempt at merging the Ukrainian churches in 1949, the ecumenical patriarch did not support the creation of one Ukrainian Orthodox episcopate in the United States. By the arrival of the millennium in 1988, the UOC-USA enjoyed a reasonably close relationship with the Ecumenical Patriarchate, nurtured by decades of friendly exchanges and overtures through the leadership of Metropolitan Mstyslav, who succeeded Metropolitan John as the leader of the UOC-USA upon the latter's death in 1971. An early manifestation of the closer relationship between the UOC-USA and the Ecumenical Patriarchate occurs in a 1972 letter from Patriarch Pimen of Moscow to Patriarch Athenagoras of Constantinople.

The Moscow Patriarchate was informed of the meeting between Metropolitan Mstyslav and Patriarch Athenagoras of February 2, 1972, by then-metropolitan Filaret (Denysenko) of Kiev and Galicia, patriarchal exarch of Ukraine.[62] In his report to the bishops of the Russian Church, Metropolitan Filaret referred to Metropolitan Mstyslav as one who "names himself" metropolitan of the "schismatic group that names itself the Ukrainian Orthodox Church of the USA."[63] The Russian Church expressed its disappointment at the meeting and concluded that "the supreme church government of the Constantinopolitan Orthodox Church does not have the pertinent information about the uncanonical status of the schismatic Ukrainian group."[64]

Patriarch Pimen acted on the directive of the Russian Church by addressing a long letter about the Ukrainian Orthodox Church to Patriarch Athenagoras.[65] Essentially, Pimen's letter characterized the UOC-USA as the direct descendant of the 1921 UAOC and bearing all of its ecclesial illegitimacy. Patriarch Pimen's detailed description of the 1921 UAOC recalls the position of global Orthodoxy and the terms it used to define the revolutionary church, depicting the UOC-USA as separatists motivated by ethnophyletism who have violated Church canons and fomented schism.[66]

Noteworthy in Pimen's letter is the amalgamation of terms: the 1921 UAOC was chauvinistic, illegal, a false council, blasphemous, and unrecognized by the legitimate Orthodox. One might summarize these terms as "illegitimate." The remainder of Pimen's letter attributes the same illegitimacy to the second UAOC that emerged during World War II, along with new negative features corrupting the Church's status in global Orthodoxy. Several of Pimen's assertions are historically accurate: for example, he states correctly that Lypkivs'kyi assigned Metropolitan John (Teodorovych) to shepherd the Ukrainian Church in the United States, and that

Metropolitan Mstyslav (Skrypnyk) succeeded Teodorovych in the office of primate. More problematic are the new accusations levelled by Pimen against the Ukrainian autocephalists: he stated that the second UAOC created itself in the "temporarily occupied territory of Ukraine," and that its leaders promulgated a "chauvinistic ideology, and were active assistants to the fascist occupants of the realm."[67]

Pimen's primary objective was to illustrate how the UOC-USA was thoroughly corrupt on account of the straight line connecting the 1921 UAOC to the Cold War–era UOC-USA. The illegitimacy of the UOC-USA was evidenced by its invalid ordinations and the absence of canonical integrity.[68]After gently admonishing the Ecumenical Patriarchate for sending Mstyslav formal greetings on the occasion of his election as metropolitan of the UOC-USA in 1971, Pimen states that the desire of the Russian Church is to persuade the Ukrainians (whom he likens to prodigal sons) to repent and return to the mother church. Pimen also makes it very clear that the mother church of the Ukrainians is the Russian Orthodox Church, not the Ecumenical Patriarchate.

Patriarch Pimen's letter demonstrates the Russian Church's maintenance of its position that the Ukrainian autocephalists are canonically illegitimate. His letter is also an attempt to inscribe new negative features on the religious identity of the Ukrainian Church. First, he emphasized the use of the relics of Metropolitan Macarius in the rite of ordination used by the 1921 UAOC, not the conciliar theme of the rite, which the Ukrainians themselves accentuated. Second, he states that the UAOC self-liquidated in 1930, which is historically inaccurate. Third, and perhaps most significant, is his fusion of political and ecclesial epithets: the Ukrainian autocephalists are consistently a minority, politically chauvinistic, and fanatics who cooperated with the Nazi rulers. The historical review of the relationship between church and state during the war shows that both the autocephalists and autonomists came into serious and dangerous conflict with their German occupiers, and that the autocephalists enjoyed the consistent patronage of the primate of the autocephalous Church of Poland, Metropolitan Dionysii. The omission of these facts from Pimen's letter is notable, but of greater interest is the deliberate construction of a clear narrative that depicts the mother church as the consistent victim of malicious separation. In this case, the accumulation of evidence implicating the Ukrainian autocephalists as vicious political chauvinists who were guilty of ecclesial phyletism is an attempt to persuade the audience of the just cause of the victim. Pimen and the Russian Orthodox Church saw themselves as victims, the mother church whose children abandoned her. Pimen's letter depicts the Ukrainian autocephalists as irresponsible children who pose a threat to the Ecumenical Patriarchate in the guise of friendship.

Pimen's letter only intensified the UOC-USA's resolve to strengthen their alliance with the Ecumenical Patriarchate and respond to these accusations with their own claims that Moscow was attempting to subvert the Ecumenical Patriarchate's authority. At the meeting of the council of bishops of the UOC-USA in April 1978, Mstyslav reported that the Moscow Patriarchate's granting of autocephaly to the Russian Metropolia (now the Orthodox Church in America, or OCA) was intended to harm the Ecumenical Patriarchate. Mstyslav condemned the activity of the newly founded OCA, stating that "all efforts of the Orthodox Church in America are aimed at the liquidation of all ethnic Orthodox Churches in North America, an effort which agrees with Moscow's intention."[69] In his report to the tenth council of the UOC-USA in 1981, Mstyslav said that two bishops had invited him to join the OCA.[70] He expressed "his sadness that brethren in Christ instigate him to scorn the graves of Ukrainian martyrs, among whom were bishops, thousands of priests and millions of pious faithful who sacrificed their lives for the faith of Christ, the Holy UOC and the pious Ukrainian nation," and repeated his assertion that the OCA was a deliberate creation of the Moscow Patriarchate designed to bring the churches of the free world under Moscow's rule.[71]

When Patriarch Pimen visited New York in 1982, Mstyslav went on the offensive, depicting him as part of a Soviet ploy to undermine Ukrainian interests, and describing OCA Metropolitan Theodosius as Pimen's spiritual son. Mstyslav's conspiracy theory had a political angle: he went public with his accusations in a special communique delivered to the US State Department.[72]

Metropolitan Mstyslav was indefatigable in his assault on Moscow, especially as the early years of the 1980s went by and the millennium of the baptism of Kyivan Rus' approached. When Patriarch Athenagoras died in 1986, Mstyslav remembered him "as a great benefactor and friend of their long-suffering Holy Ukrainian Orthodox Church which through a forcible and uncanonical act was annexed to the Moscow Patriarchate three hundred years ago."[73] In his reminiscence, Mstyslav promised Patriarch Pimen that "Kiev will once again illuminate and overshadow the European East."[74] On the surface, Mstyslav appears to be mimicking the polemical approach of Moscow by characterizing the Moscow Patriarchate as an institution employing uncanonical acts to subjugate peoples. Even if that was the case, Mstyslav was also attempting to argue that the Ecumenical Patriarchate was the legitimate mother church of the Kyivan Metropolia, an idea supported by the publication of an essay on the three hundredth anniversary of the annexation of the Kyivan Metropolia to Moscow, which asserted that the Kyivan Metropolia refused to swear allegiance to the tsar at the Treaty of Pereiaslav in 1654, and that the Ecumenical Patriarchate had not interfered in the affairs of the Kyivan Church for the entirety of its history.[75]

In addition to strengthening the relationship between the UOC-USA and the Ecumenical Patriarchate, Mstyslav attempted to illuminate the challenges of the Ecumenical Patriarchate in Turkey. At the council of bishops in 1978, Mstyslav "referred to the coming Ecumenical Orthodox Council and pointed out the discomforting situation of the Ecumenical Orthodox Patriarchate in Constantinople (Istanbul), where the Turkish government's attitude toward the patriarchate is becoming one of greater concern for all of the Orthodox faithful of the world."[76] In 1981, Ecumenical Patriarch Dimitrios (Papadopoulos) responded affirmatively to a petition from the council of the UOC-USA to convoke a tenth All-Church Council. This seemingly insignificant news should not be ignored; the UOC-USA's petition and the Ecumenical Patriarchate's response foreshadowed the restoration of the Ecumenical Patriarchate as the rightful patron and mother of Orthodox Ukraine. In 1987, on the eve of the millennium celebration, Mstyslav suggested that the Moscow Patriarchate was rejoicing at the struggles of the Ecumenical Patriarchate, and accused the Moscow Patriarchate of employing "a new form of simony" by awarding the Western European exarch of the Ecumenical Patriarchate with the order of the wonder-worker St. Sergius of Radonezh.[77]

The bishops of the UOC-USA positioned themselves as formidable partners in the ecumenical work of global Orthodoxy in their archpastoral Easter epistle of 1987. They argued that Ukraine's legacy of new martyrdom equipped her to contribute to creating peace in the world and eradicating evil threats to all humankind:

> The mission which our nation took upon its shoulders 999 years ago is far from complete. The world is in dire need of spiritual renewal and we believe that this renewal will shine forth from the Orthodox East. This East will again become master of its own territory and fate, ending its martyrdom. This East, which has always had a very deep and mystical understanding of its faith and duty before God, this East has always regarded Christ as the only source of hope and life. We believe that Orthodox Ukraine having shed its blood and tears and, strengthened through difficult afflictions, will be in the forefront of this spiritual renewal. We believe that a free Ukrainian Orthodox Church, which constitutes one fourth of the entire Orthodox Church will, as it did during the reign of our great princes, contribute immensely to the elevation of the life of the Ecumenical Orthodox Church in particular, and of Christianity in general to new heights. We believe that a free Ukraine, together with her free Ukrainian Orthodox Church, will live in a world which will rid itself of atom and hydrogen bombs and other horrifying means of destruction; in a world in which the struggle against evil will not be the concern of merely a few individuals, but rather of all renewed humanity.[78]

The 1987 Easter message built upon the efforts of the Ukrainian autocephalists to demonstrate that they were legitimate Orthodox who could partner with the rest of the Orthodox world not only in celebrating the glories of Orthodoxy's past,

FIGURE 2. Statue of Metropolitan Vasyl Lypkivs'kyi in South Bound Brook, New Jersey. Photo by Elizabeth Symonenko. Used with permission.

but also in contributing to the global common good. But the internal politics of global Orthodoxy have always been complicated, and Mstyslav did not hesitate to criticize the Ecumenical Patriarchate for making a pilgrimage to the Soviet Union. He was also sharply critical of the Vatican and the Ukrainian Catholic Church in particular for holding meetings with the Moscow Patriarchate in preparation for celebrating the millennium.[79]

Mstyslav's criticism of the Ecumenical Patriarchate illuminates the determination of the UOC-USA to sustain the fullness of its legacy without shame. While the UOC-USA took a definitive step toward the canonical structures preferred by global Orthodoxy in 1949–1950, the Ukrainian Church did not cease to honor the memories of the 1921 UAOC. In the official church periodical, Mstyslav and other writers consistently memorialized Metropolitan Vasyl Lypkivs'kyi and the UAOC as martyrs who sought the rightful restoration of the enslaved Kyivan Metropolia.[80] In an address to the tenth council of the UOC-USA in 1981, Mstyslav essentially presented an encomium honoring the labors of Lypkivs'kyi. His address had a few inaccuracies: for example, he stated that the 1921 UAOC council was the first All-Ukrainian gathering (the initial gathering occurred in 1918), and he also stated that the 1930 council resulted in Lypkivs'kyi's removal (this actually happened at the second UAOC council of 1927). Mstyslav's objective was to depict the UAOC as a persecuted church of martyrs, and it is possible to identify some mimicry in his depiction of the 1930 council as a "pseudocouncil," which parallels the language used by Patriarch Pimen in his description of the 1921 council. Perhaps the UOC-USA's most poignant demonstration of its fidelity to the legacy of the 1921 UAOC was its erection of a statue of Lypkivs'kyi at South Bound Brook, approved by the council of bishops in 1978.[81]

Pastoral Challenges of the Ukrainian Churches in North America

The hybrid identity of the UOC-USA also concerns the customary pastoral work that occurs on a daily basis. The continued labor of cultivating Ukrainian Orthodox identity in migration is a crucial component of an independent Ukrainian Church at the end of the Soviet era. But the churches of the diaspora had to address the challenges of member attrition and identity as a minority church in the sea of American Christian identity. The challenge of raising sufficient funds to subsidize the erection of St. Andrew's Church and Memorial Center in South Bound Brook was an initial symbol of the difficulty in maintaining dual identity in emigration. In 1978, the UOC-USA lamented the shortage of bishops and priests afflicting the church and authorized the creation and opening of St. Sophia's Seminary in South Bound Brook. Prior to the creation of St. Sophia's, the clergy of the UOC-USA were educated at St. Andrew's College of the UOCC in Winnipeg.

The same meeting of the council of bishops responded to a request from an source within the UOC-USA to abbreviate the Divine Liturgy. The bishops also upheld the absolute requirement of partaking of the sacrament of confession prior to receiving Holy Communion at the Divine Liturgy, prohibiting the use of

a "general confession."[82] The bishops briefly exhorted the clergy of the UOC-USA
to "strengthen internal church discipline," which the reader can interpret as an
instruction to maintain the customary order of services and the traditional structures of the divine offices without abbreviation. The bishops' instruction occurred
during the Eucharistic revival emanating from St. Vladimir's Seminary and popu-
larized by the teaching of Alexander Schmemann, which had a significant impact
on the Eucharistic discipline of many of the Orthodox churches in North America.

Some pastoral concern on the part of the bishops and leaders of the UOC-USA
is also apparent in the messages communicated to the Orthodox faithful on the
occasion of the millennium. In their archpastoral letter announcing the inauguration of the celebration, the bishops called upon the faithful to "grow closer to
God," "read the Bible," and attend church more frequently.[83] The exhortation also
mentioned the problem of the shortage of priests in the UOC-USA. Obviously,
using a significant anniversary as an opportunity to attempt to inaugurate a spiritual awakening is not unique to the UOC-USA, but the petition to engage the
daily Christian practices with more fervor is as much a representation of the inte-
rior challenges of church life as it is a pastoral strategy. As the millennium year
progressed, Church leaders continued to bring up the problem of attrition, stating
that "we need younger cadres of clergy: well-educated and devout pastors, eloquent
preachers, who would carry the eternal Word of God to the people of the nuclear
age in a manner understandable and comprehensible to them."[84] Oleksander
Voronyn, a respected lay historian of the Church who published numerous small
books and essays on the modern history of Ukrainian Orthodoxy, called for a
reinvigoration of education within the UOC-USA.[85] Voronyn observed that the
church dwelt too much on the past and had too many *panakhydas*, when it needed
to live in the present and celebrate "more molebens."[86] Voronyn's blunt assessment
of the church was that it was in a steady state of shrinkage: the diminishing church
simply did not have the capacity to generate new clergy.

As the millennial year concluded, the Twelfth Council of the UOC-USA convened, and its resolutions represented the hybrid identity of the Church. The first
set of resolutions referred to the issues pertaining to the primary identity markers
of the Ukrainian autocephalists, including another reference to the correct interpretation of the Kyivan Metropolia (resolution 2), an expression of gratitude to
Ecumenical Patriarch Dimitrios (resolution 3), and an appeal for increased cooperation among Orthodox Ukrainians (resolution 4).[87] Several of the resolutions
addressed urgent pastoral matters, such as the "serious crisis of the priest shortage" (23), an appeal for more clergy education (24), and the dire need to enhance
missionary activity within the church (29).

Two resolutions are particularly noteworthy: the council rejected any and all
appeals to alter the method of distributing communion and venerating the cross

and icons in light of fear caused by AIDS (22), and the council also appealed for the UOC-USA to remain a bilingual church (30). The resolution on language was a reaction by Ukrainians who lamented the decision of some parishes to move to predominantly and exclusively English-language worship; the disappearance of Ukrainian from church life would denote the loss of the most important identity marker. The resolution on language perhaps speaks more profoundly to the hybrid identity of the UOC-USA than any other, especially as it sought creative ways to sustain church life through a period of steady attrition.

Similar challenges confronted the Canadian Church. Archpresbyter Semen Sawchuk addressed the fifteenth council of the Church in Canada in 1975.[88] He presented four foundations for the ideology of the Church in Canada: it is Ukrainian, Orthodox, *sobornopravna* (governed by council), and independent.[89] Sawchuk emphasized the national character of the Church in Canada by dismissing other ethnic claims to the Ukrainian Church. The Church in Canada was not English, Polish, French, Greek, or Roman, but Ukrainian.[90] Sawchuk particularly lamented the diminishment of the Ukrainian language in the life of the Canadian Church, pointing out the irony of offering Ukrainian cultural immersion courses in the English language.[91] He also referred to concrete proposals presented at the fifteenth council on introducing English into the church's liturgy, abbreviating the Divine Liturgy, and abandoning the Julian calendar for the revised Julian.[92] Perhaps the most symbolic issue Sawchuk raised was the pan-Orthodox movement in America, and its appeal to all churches to encourage Orthodox unity and reduce the significance of national identity in the respective churches.[93] Sawchuk's conservative position illuminates the challenge that the Canadian Church faced in sustaining the four foundations of identity they had cultivated over a long period of time while opposing the possibility of change.

In 1980, the Church in Canada held its next council, at which Bishop Wasyly (Fedak) addressed the very same issues discussed by Sawchuk in 1975.[94] Bishop Wasyly dwelt upon the question of liturgical language at some length, and categorized the proposals for introducing English into the liturgy. His remarks exhibit the continued resistance of Canadian Church leaders to introduce English into the national church, referring to two perspectives on the assimilation of the Ukrainian community into Canadian culture: "The last two views which disparage the need for the Ukrainian language in the Church sadden our hearts because they imply a serious and painful surgery—a severing of oneself from maternal rootstock."[95] Bishop Wasyly acknowledged that retention of young people in the church was a problem, and called for the reinvigoration of Ukrainian language programs as part of the response to the crisis.[96] Bishop Wasyly also called for the strengthening of theological education at St. Andrew's College and missionary endeavors within the church in Canada.[97] He also sharply dismissed the pan-Orthodox movement

in America, which prioritized "English as the common language" and was motivated by the "imperialistic policies of Moscow."[98]

As late as 2000, the Canadian Church attempted to address the challenges of
modernity. The council of 2000 drafted several resolutions referring to the role
of women in the church, including a call for deliberation on the "renewal of the
women's diaconate," and an appeal for leaders to encourage women to "assume
leadership roles within the Church" and to demand that clergy and laity "be
informed of their duty to support, through prayer, action, and advocacy those
who suffer abuse."[99] These examples of conciliar discussions on contemporary
issues in the Church in Canada from 1975 to 2000 elucidate a church attempting to find creative ways to sustain its unique national identity, particularly while
beginning to negotiate issues of gender and abuse that were significant in contemporary society.

From 1950 to 1987, the UOC-USA and the Church in Canada adjusted to
the arrival of thousands of immigrants from war-ravaged Ukraine. These immigrants brought their memories of human catastrophe created by the war, man-
made famine, and the disappointment of remaining under tyrannical rule and
failing to achieve Orthodox unity. Motivated by the desire for unity and restoration of the Church in Ukraine, the immigrants capitalized on the freedom
of religion they enjoyed in North America and created a global platform for
denouncing the political and ecclesial acts of Moscow while aligning themselves with America as champions of freedom. The unification of two Ukrainian
churches in 1950 and the canonical correction of Archbishop John's 1921 ordination set the stage for the American Ukrainians to make friends in the global
Orthodox community. The most important development in the agenda of
Orthodox Ukrainians in the United States was the promulgation of a political theology that cast them as advocating for religious and political freedom
with the United States and in opposition to the Moscow Patriarchate, which the
Ukrainians depicted as agents of global slavery. The second significant development was the ecumenical impetus of the Ukrainian Americans: their open
support for the Ecumenical Patriarchate against the perceived machinations
of the Moscow Patriarchate demonstrates their desire to be embraced as full
members of the Orthodox communion, a formidable Ukrainian Church in the
free world. As their promulgation of political theology increased in intensity,
they also confronted the challenges of religious freedom: plurality and choice,
leading to attrition and the adjustment of their own internal mission as they
were required to minister to generations of descendants of immigrants whose
connections to Ukraine were weak. The Church in Canada struggled to sustain
its four foundational principles of Ukrainian identity, Orthodox faith, *sobornopravnist'*, and autocephaly in the North American context.

The Millennium Celebration, 1987–1989

The celebration of the millennium of the baptism of Rus' in the UOC-USA marked the pinnacle of its political theology. In addition to using the holiday as an opportunity to call for spiritual renewal throughout the church, the celebrations that occurred throughout 1988 marked the UOC-USA's attempt to definitively capture the historical narrative of the Ukrainian Church. A systematic effort to clarify the historical trajectory of the Kyivan Metropolia, especially its absorption into the Moscow Patriarchate in 1686, was one of many initiatives undertaken by the church to argue that the historical baptism in Kyiv was part of the establishment of Christianity in Kyiv, but not "Kyivan Russia." Earlier, the publication of an essay on the Kyivan Metropolia and the refusal of the metropolitan to accept the treaty of Pereiaslav between the Zaporozhian host and the tsar was mentioned. In the Nativity message of 1988, Metropolitan Mstyslav identified the Ukrainian Orthodox Church of the diaspora as the legitimate successor to the Kyivan Metropolia.[100] On the occasion of the tenth council of the UOC-USA in 1981, the delegates rebuked Moscow for dismissing the individuality of the Kyivan tradition, both during the movement for Ukrainian autocephaly in 1917–1921, and again during the emergence of the second UAOC in 1941–1943.[101]

The UOC-USA's repeated attempts to return to an analysis of the legality of Moscow's assumption of jurisdiction over the Kyivan see in 1686 are significant for several reasons. First, the generation of discourse on canonical questions within global Orthodoxy was a response to Moscow's claim that the UAOC had been uncanonical throughout its history. Even more significant was the argument over ecclesial motherhood: one could argue that the primary objective of Patriarch Pimen's 1972 letter to Patriarch Athenagoras was to remind the ecumenical patriarch that Moscow was the legitimate mother of the Kyivan See. The UOC-USA inherited the historical rationale for Kyivan autocephaly cultivated from 1921 through World War II and countered that Constantinople was the rightful mother of Kyiv, not Moscow. The sustained effort to create a strong relationship with Constantinople throughout this period was neither peripheral nor coincidental: the UOC-USA viewed Constantinople as a compassionate advocate of its attempt at liberation from Muscovite rule.

While there was no immediate resolution to this argument, the efforts of the UOC-USA eventually bore fruit. In the aftermath of the millennium, given the increasing possibilities for freedom and the legalization of persecuted churches in the Soviet Union, the third rebirth of the UAOC occurred in 1989, in L'viv. The leaders of the new church organized an initiative committee to renew the Church in Ukraine, and they sent an Easter epistle in 1990.[102] The third UAOC identified itself as "the only authentic national church of the Ukrainian people, as the direct heir of the 1,000 year old Kievan Metropolia."[103] In justifying their separation from the Moscow Patriarchate, the leaders of the UAOC depicted the merger of the Kyivan Metropolia with Moscow in 1686 as an act of coercion:

> Having forcefully subjugated the Ukrainian Church in 1686, they carried Ukrainian bishops off to Moscow, replacing them with Muscovite bishops, and brutally denied the Ukrainian Orthodox Church her independence in the election and assignment of her own bishops to eparchies.[104]

The members of the UAOC appealed for patriotism and criticized the reactionary response of the exarchate, which announced its approval of the use of vernacular Ukrainian in the liturgy. They cast this decision as "attempt to mislead those Orthodox Ukrainians who strive to establish their own Church."[105] They also accused the Moscow Patriarchate of continued devotion to the tsars and their successors, asserted that "foreign patriarchs will not bring order to our house," and called for the election and ordination of patriot-bishops. The rationale for selecting patriots was to avoid slavery: on numerous occasions, the epistle accused Moscow of enslaving the Orthodox Church in Ukraine through the power and authority of the imperial throne. Finally, the UAOC called for clergy to commemorate Ecumenical Patriarch Dimitrios in the liturgy, and sent him a telegram that petitioned him to take the UAOC under his omophorion.[106] The self-identification of the UAOC as the legitimate heir of the Kyivan Metropolia occurred when Metropolitan Mstyslav accepted the UAOC's election of him as their first patriarch in 1990. Mstyslav vowed to rebuild the Orthodox Church in Ukraine "upon the ruins of the once glorious Kyivan Metropolia, the Mother Church of our people."[107]

The UOC-USA's mission to redefine the legacy of the Kyivan Metropolia came full circle when they came under the omophorion of the Ecumenical Patriarchate in 1995 (to be treated more fully below). In the periodical announcing the act of canonical communion, the *Ukrainian Orthodox Word* published an English translation of the *tomos* of autocephaly granted by the Ecumenical Patriarchate to the Church in Poland in 1924. The *tomos* itself justifies the granting of autocephaly, in part, based on the "uncanonical subjugation of the Kyivan Metropolia to Moscow" in 1686.[108] Here again, the UOC-USA refers to the original relationship of Constantinople with the Kyivan Metropolia as the rationale for restoring that communion, and more importantly, for rationalizing separation from Moscow.

The millennium celebration was an opportunity for the UOC-USA to demonstrate its vitality, strengthen its political alliances, and identify Kyiv as the only authentic spiritual home for Ukrainian Christians. While the UOC-USA openly lamented attrition within the life of the church, the millennium ignited renewed energy. In Parma, Ohio, St. Vladimir's Cathedral sponsored and erected a mosaic scene of the baptism of Ukraine over the three doors to the front entrance on the building's façade to honor the millennium.[109] Another example of vitality was the construction and erection of St. Andrew's Church in Bloomingdale, Illinois, a suburb of Chicago. The church was consecrated in a Eucharistic concelebration presided over by the entire hierarchy of the UOC-USA on April 24, 1988. The UOC-USA showcased instances of church vitality like these two examples to establish its legitimacy as a growing Orthodox body.

The millennium was also an opportunity for the UOC-USA to attempt to strengthen its alliances, both within the Church and also in the public square. The UOC-USA concelebrated numerous prayer services in honor of the millennium in Greek Orthodox parishes of the Ecumenical Patriarchate, including one such office at the Greek Orthodox archdiocesan cathedral. Bishop Antony (Scharba) of the UOC-USA and Bishop Vsevolod (Maidansky) of the Ukrainian Church under the Ecumenical Patriarchate concelebrated the prayer service. This cooperation among Ukrainian Orthodox who did not share complete Eucharistic communion foreshadowed the eventual merger of these two church bodies into one under the Ecumenical Patriarchate in 1995. Bishop Antony also used the opportunity to speak about the spiritual unity of the UOC-USA and the Ecumenical Patriarchate.[110] The main celebration of the UOC-USA occurred in South Bound Brook, with Bishop Isaiah of the Greek Orthodox Archdiocese in attendance (though not concelebrating). The church periodical included a formal blessing from Patriarch Dimitrios congratulating the UOC-USA on its jubilee.[111]

The UOC-USA used the millennium celebration to influence political activities as well. Metropolitan Mstyslav participated in a symposium at the White House and followed up by writing President Reagan, warning him about "Russian colonial expansionism," and wishing Reagan a "good journey to the evil empire" on the eve of Reagan's political trip to the Soviet Union.[112] The National Ukrainian Millennium Committee established under the aegis of the Catholic and Orthodox bishops organized a rally of 20,000 people on October 7–9, 1988, in Washington, DC. They marched on the Soviet embassy and demanded freedom for the Ukrainian churches. Furthermore, 2,500 Ukrainians gathered at the Shevchenko monument for an ecumenical prayer service celebrating the millennium on the same weekend. Finally, the National Millennium Committee also wrote a formal letter to Mikhail Gorbachev demanding the legalization of the Ukrainian Catholic and Ukrainian Autocephalous Orthodox Churches in Ukraine. American politicians had varied responses to the Ukrainian entreaties. President Reagan wrote a formal letter of congratulations to the National Ukrainian Millennium Committee.[113] His message acknowledged that the USSR "outlawed the Ukrainian Catholic and Orthodox Churches and repressed the Protestant faith," and pledged

America's commitment to "emphasize that freedom of conscience and freedom of religion are basic human rights and that relations with the Soviet Union cannot prosper without improvement in the Soviets' human rights performance."[114] The Ukrainian community paid attention to the activities of the candidates for the Oval Office, criticizing George Bush for his absence from all millennial commemorations, whereas Michael Dukakis's campaign promoted the greetings they sent to the Ukrainians.

The organizers of the Ukrainian community's millennium committee had envisioned a unified celebration of the event with Orthodox and Catholics, but the UOC-USA bristled at the Catholic celebration that took place in Rome. The Ukrainians were politically united in condemning Soviet policies on religious freedom, but were fragmented in coming together for a common liturgical celebration. Mstyslav rebuked the Greek Catholics for going to Rome for the celebration, calling upon Ukrainians to acknowledge Kyiv as the Ukrainian Jerusalem.[115] Mstyslav's message did not only criticize other religious leaders, it also affirmed the unique identity of the UOC-USA: it was the rightful heir of the Kyivan Metropolia, which built a new capital in South Bound Brook, a Ukrainian Jerusalem of the diaspora.

In summary, the millennium celebration in the UOC-USA symbolized the legacy of the diaspora church while prefiguring the next epoch in the history of the Orthodox Church in Ukraine. The UOC-USA used the millennial anniversary to stake its claim as the rightful heir of the Kyivan Metropolia, call for religious freedom in the Soviet Union, and continue its mission of attempting to expose the ecclesial agenda of the Moscow Patriarchate. A second layer of concern about the longevity of the diaspora church lay underneath the public celebration: the Church was struggling to generate and educate pastors, and to adjust to the challenges of attrition in the American religious context. The UOC-USA had also established a pattern of friendly correspondence with the Ecumenical Patriarchate; this renewed relationship would take a new turn with the third rebirth of the UAOC in 1989–1990 and the decision of the UOC-USA to return to the Ecumenical Patriarchate in 1995.

A New Alliance with the Ecumenical Patriarchate

While the Orthodox churches in Ukraine adjusted to the collapse of the Soviet Union and the emergence of two pro-Ukrainian churches, the Orthodox Ukrainians of the diaspora made significant changes related to the current situation in Ukraine. These changes began in 1990 when the Ukrainian Orthodox Church of Canada entered into communion with the Ecumenical Patriarchate of

Constantinople. The patriarchate's reception of the Canadian Ukrainians ended their lengthy alienation from the rest of global Orthodoxy, as they had not been able to participate fully in the Eucharistic celebrations of the other churches. The Canadian Church's decision created some initial friction with the Ukrainian Orthodox Church of the USA, especially since its metropolitan, Mstyslav, was elected and enthroned as patriarch of the Autocephalous Church in the same year.[116]

The Ukrainian Church in Canada and the Ecumenical Patriarchate

The Canadian Church had a history of approaching the Ecumenical Patriarchate with aspirations for establishing a union. Negotiations began as early as 1935, when Archbishop John Teodorovych wrote Constantinopolitan patriarch Photius and asked him to receive the Canadian Ukrainians.[117] Successive church primates, including metropolitans Ilarion and Andrew, began similar negotiations and appeals.[118] When Metropolitan Wasyly traveled to Istanbul in October 1987, an outline of the terms of Eucharistic communion was established.[119] In 1989, the consistory of the Church in Canada stipulated the terms of the agreement in eight points to the Ecumenical Patriarchate.[120] The Canadian Church scheduled an extraordinary council for October 21–22, 1989, in Winnipeg, and unanimously adopted the resolution for Eucharistic communion with the Ecumenical Patriarchate.[121]

Ecumenical Patriarch Dimitrios's decree made the terms of the relationship between the Canadian Church and Constantinople public.[122] It notes that the Canadian Church retains its "internal and organizational structure without change," a way of honoring the distinct Ukrainian Orthodox heritage that developed in Canada.[123] The primary change was that the Ecumenical Patriarchate would now confirm the activities, appointments, and conciliar gatherings of the Canadian Church.[124] It would provide the Canadian Church with chrism and the Ukrainian-Canadian Church became a member of the conference of canonical bishops of the Americas. Essentially, the patriarchal decree cohered with the terms adopted by the extraordinary council of the Ukrainian Church in Canada. The dependence of the Canadian Church on the Ecumenical Patriarchate was limited to receiving chrism from her and to establishing Eucharistic communion with all of the other Orthodox Churches through the Ecumenical Patriarchate.

Following the extraordinary council's unanimous approbation of communion with the Ecumenical Patriarchate, the Church in Canada commenced preparations for the eighteenth regular council to take place in Winnipeg in July 1990.[125] At this time, the return of the UAOC to life in Soviet Ukraine was a matter of excitement for the émigré Ukrainian community. The official announcement of the eighteenth council was accompanied by a reminder of the significance of *sobornopravnist'* in the life of the Canadian Church. The bishops reminded the faithful that the whole church carries out the work of the council, which demands a high standard for lay delegates.[126] The instruction on *sobornopravnist'* and the desire for upstanding lay delegates are not unusual, but in this case, they prefigured trouble down the road when the Ecumenical Patriarchate was unable to resolve the divisions among Orthodox in Ukraine. The Canadian Ukrainians no longer had the freedom to lend their full support to the pro-Ukrainian cohort, which necessitated a clarification of their own self-identity at the 1990 July council in Winnipeg. Father Stepan Jarmus, president of the Canadian Church's consistory, clarified the role of the Church in Canada vis-à-vis the reborn UAOC in Ukraine in his report to the presidium of the council by stating flatly that the Canadian Church is not the UAOC.[127] Father Jarmus also mentioned the moral obligation of the Canadian Church to unify all Ukrainian Orthodox in the global Orthodox family.

The precarious position of the Canadian Church developed into a full-blown crisis by the year 2000, when multiple parish communities began to openly criticize the church's relationship with the Ecumenical Patriarchate and call for its end. Three cathedrals sent resolutions on this relationship for discussion at the twentieth regular council to be held in 2000. The resolutions submitted by the Cathedral of St. Sophia in Montreal appealed for the restoration of Canadian autocephaly and the strengthening of *sobornopravnist'* in the Church.[128] The first resolution called for the relationship with the patriarch of Constantinople to be the primary topic for discussion at the council. Resolutions four and nine concerned *sobornopravnist'*. Resolution four stipulated that "the principle of sobornopravnist be preserved" and number nine called for the establishment of a commission to determine whether or not the decisions made by the bishops were consistent with the charter and bylaws of the church.[129] Resolution five stated that "the prime objective of the UOCC must be the preservation of our freedom in all aspects of her life."[130] The resolutions insinuate that the bishops had relinquished the freedom guaranteed by autocephaly and were circumventing *sobornopravnist'* by making decisions without consulting the whole body of the church. The resolution calling for full disclosure of the conditions of the church's relationship with Constantinople demonstrate a lack of trust between St. Sophia and the Canadian hierarchy.[131] One of the resolutions insisted that the metropolitan of the Canadian Church be a Ukrainian, perhaps the most vivid symbol of this distrust.

While St. Volodymyr Cathedral in Toronto submitted the same list of resolutions as St. Sophia, St. John Cathedral in Edmonton submitted a much more elaborate list supported by a detailed rationale and plan of action.[132] The first resolution called for the termination of the agreement with the Ecumenical Patriarchate, based on changes in the situation of the Church in Ukraine and the claim that the agreement was controversial from the very beginning.[133] St. John's also made a fervent appeal for the restoration of *sobornopravnist'*, referring to the Ukrainian rejection of "tyranny, subterfuge and the corruption that had been rampant in institutional life in Tsarist- and Habsburg-ruled Ukraine."[134] The same section embraced the "Canadian values of democracy" and condemned the autocracy that typified "clerical-lay relations in both the Ukrainian Catholic Church and the Russian Orthodox Church."[135] Resolution 6 was perhaps the most passionate and strongly worded text, calling for the Canadian church to "firmly resist all efforts by the Russian Orthodox Church in Ukraine and Canada to compromise our effort for the creation of a united, fully autocephalous Orthodox Church in Ukraine free from colonial subjugation to any foreign patriarchates."[136] The text in this section also warned about the dangers posed by figures who sought to coerce a union of Ukraine with Belarus and Russia, and who were committed to "resurrecting the Soviet Union."[137]

The council of the year 2000 attempted to address the complaints coming from prominent cathedral communities by resolving to strengthen the role of the hierarchy in promoting unity among the Ukrainian Orthodox Churches and exploring the possibility of establishing an office to represent them in Kyiv.[138] The council iterated its strong support for the "establishment of one united Ukrainian Orthodox Church in Ukraine" but noted that the Church in Canada "cannot support one of the three branches" as "it would thereby enter into conflict with the other two."[139] The twentieth council appraised the relationship with the Ecumenical Patriarchate positively, and encouraged "a more proactive dialogue with the Patriarchate of Constantinople" to ensure that the concerns of the church were not ignored.

The decision of the Ukrainian Orthodox Church in Canada to restore Eucharistic communion with the Ecumenical Patriarchate generated new reflections on self-identity. Confirmation of their ecclesial legitimacy and the ability to represent Ukrainian concerns on the global stage was the greatest benefit to the Canadian Church. However, the Church's hesitance to take sides in the intra-jurisdictional battle in Ukraine led to the resurgence of *sobornopravnist'* and autocephaly as staple features of the public religious identity of Orthodox Ukrainians in Canada. The renewed emphasis on *sobornopravnist'* came from concerns about the balance of governing power between some lay delegates and the bishops. The relative freedom of the Canadian Church allowed by the terms of union with Constantinople did not satisfy those who wished to defend the freedom of the Ukrainian Church from Muscovite claims without having to obtain Constantinople's permission. Orthodox Ukrainians interpreted the ecclesial principles of autocephaly and *sobornopravnist'* through the Canadian civil values of democracy they had come to embrace as their own. These staples of Ukrainian public religious identity were fused with the civic values of democracy and independence in the Canadian milieu. Despite the ecclesial crisis posed by the divisions in Ukrainian Orthodoxy, the Church in Canada maintained its relationship with the Ecumenical Patriarchate and takes an active role in consulting on the Ukrainian issue in global Orthodoxy today.

The UOC-USA's Merger with the Ecumenical Patriarchate

The period of friction between the Canadian and American churches was short-lived. Mstyslav died in 1993, and his successors in the United States adopted the same path as the Canadians in 1995. First, the Church of the United States based in South Bound Brook, New Jersey, merged with the smaller Ukrainian Orthodox Church of America, led at the time by Archbishop Vsevolod (Maidansky). This merger prefigured the reception of the Church in the United States by the Ecumenical Patriarchate. By March 1995, the churches in the diaspora had migrated to the Ecumenical Patriarchate. In both cases, the leaders of the churches explained the decision to return to the Ecumenical Patriarchate as the fulfillment of the aspirations of the primary figures, namely Metropolitans Ilarion and Mstyslav.

The UOC-USA's return to the Eucharistic communion of the Ecumenical Patriarchate in 1995 was essentially an expected outcome of the events spanning the Cold War–era and the rebirth of the UAOC in 1989–1990. Metropolitan Mstyslav's cultivation of a close relationship with the Ecumenical throne coincided with his acceptance of the invitation of the pioneers of the third UAOC to serve as the first-ever Ukrainian patriarch. Mstyslav's tenure as patriarch had multiple outcomes for the emerging church. On the one hand, he proved himself to be an energetic and influential figure despite his age and the amount of time he had spent outside of Ukraine's borders. While some viewed Mstyslav's election as merely symbolic, he managed to galvanize energy and begin the process of establishing a structure for the UAOC in his two years of ministry. On the other hand, Mstyslav could not negotiate the complex church-state relationship already in place in Ukraine, especially the adjustment of the metropolia to the UAOC and the attempt of Metropolitan Filaret to secure autocephaly for the Ukrainian Church from Moscow in spring of 1992. At the council of the UAOC held in Kyiv in June 1992, the UAOC merged with a portion of the Moscow Patriarchate and received Metropolitan Filaret into its ranks, a decision that eventually resulted in the fragmentation of the church into two bodies, the much-smaller UAOC and the Kyivan Patriarchate.

The UOC-USA published Mstyslav's last will and testament in a tribute shortly after his repose. In the testament, Mstyslav lamented the divisions in the church in

Ukraine and called for the Ecumenical Patriarch to convoke an all-Orthodox coun-cil at an opportune time.[140] Mstyslav's advice to appeal to the ecumenical patriarch has resulted in tangible manifestations of these aspirations in 2016 with the con-vocation of a Holy and Great Council, but it also had more immediate outcomes. In December of 1994, Metropolitan Constantine and Archbishop Antony of the UOC-USA had an audience with Patriarch Bartholomew (Arhondonis) to estab-lish the process for the return of the UOC-USA to the Ecumenical Patriarchate. The bishops attributed the deepening division within the Orthodox Church in Ukraine to the death of Mstyslav in 1993 and informed the Metropolitan Council of the UOC-USA that Mstyslav had blessed them to seek communion with the Ecumenical Patriarchate. An important dimension of the rationale for commu-nion was to provide the UOC-USA with a unique platform for advocating for unity among Orthodox Christians in Ukraine. The Metropolitan Council voted unanimously to accept the resolution and the statements repeated the objectives of the Church's platform since the beginning of the Cold War. The *Ukrainian Orthodox Word* reported that "the Ukrainian Orthodox Church has resumed her rightful place in history," and stated that Moscow "is the spiritual daughter of the Kyivan Metropolia."[141] The union was sealed by the concelebration of the Divine Liturgy at the Sunday of Orthodoxy in Constantinople in 1995, and Patriarch Bartholomew announced the end of a "long period during which brothers of the same blood, not only by faith but also by ethnic origin, for reasons brought about by political circumstances, were forced to live separated and without coordinat-ing leadership."[142] Patriarch Bartholomew's comments on the significance of the Eucharistic concelebration refer to the historical memory of division and contrib-ute to defining the role of the Ecumenical Patriarchate in healing divisions among Orthodox Ukrainians once and for all: "May the all-holy and all-pure Body and Blood of Christ—of which from this day we are joyfully deemed worthy to par-take of the Common Cup of the One Faith—wash all of us of the past."[143]

The experience of the merger of the UOC-USA with the Ecumenical Patriarchate was turbulent for the Ukrainians in America. First, there was some hesitance among members of the Standing Conference of Canonical Orthodox Bishops in America to accept the merger of the Ukrainians with the Ecumenical Patriarchate. Second, Patriarch Alexy (Ridiger) II of Moscow wrote a lengthy let-ter to Patriarch Bartholomew on May 18, 1995, protesting the merger.[144] Patriarch Alexy's letter reprised the themes of Patriarch Pimen's 1972 letter to Patriarch Athenagoras. Alexy presented the case for Ukrainian illegitimacy based on their failure to reject the 1921 council, their decision to receive the clergy of the 1921 UAOC in 1942, and their shared communion with the leaders of the Kyivan Patriarchate. Besides naming the Ukrainians schismatics and self-consecrated, Alexy accused them of "the heresy of phyletism, which has brought so great a damage to the Holy Church of Constantinople."[145] The gravity of Alexy's letter is manifest in the overt threat to sever communion with Constantinople on account of their reception of the Ukrainians.

Patriarch Bartholomew responded to Alexy's letter on July 11, 1995.[146] After expressing bitterness and disappointment, Bartholomew stated that the Church of Russia has no authority over Ukrainians of the diaspora, who had "unbroken bonds" with the Ecumenical Patriarchate. Second, and perhaps most significantly, Bartholomew suggested that "the leaders of schisms and irregular situations are not the only ones to blame, and still less to blame are their distant descendants of today." Bartholomew's letter contains his own accusations of Russian violations of canons, including a reference to the autocephaly of the Orthodox Church in America.

The UOC-USA also experienced tension within its ranks on account of relations between the Ecumenical and Moscow patriarchates soon after the 1995 reception of the UOC-USA by Constantinople. The UOC-USA issued a lengthy statement addressing a meeting between Ecumenical Patriarch Bartholomew and Moscow Patriarch Alexy in Odessa in late September 1997. At the meeting, Patriarch Bartholomew publicly stated that the Church recognized the legitimacy of the Ukrainian Church under Moscow only, and the patriarchal delegation turned down a request to meet made by representatives of the Kyivan Patriarchate and the 1989 UAOC.[147] The UOC-USA made an urgent request for a meeting with the ecumenical patriarch in Constantinople, and he received them soon afterward, on October 7, 1997.[148] The Ukrainian bishops reported that Patriarch Bartholomew fervently prayed for all of the divided Ukrainian groups to resolve their differences and unite, "for the glory of the Lord's name."[149] The Ukrainian bishops seized the opportunity to unequivocally state their goal: "The only proper resolution of current Church division in Ukraine is that of Holy Orthodox tradition, which would clearly establish an independent Church on the independent nation of Ukraine. This is the goal of our actions relating to Ukraine. . . . We have not and will not silently accept the continued colonial and non-canonical subjugation of the Church of Ukraine to the Patriarchate of Moscow."[150] The bishops then cited a lengthy textual excerpt from the 1924 Tomos of Autocephaly to the Church of Poland, which renders the transfer of jurisdiction from Constantinople to Moscow as uncanonical.[151] The bishops concluded by remaining resolute in their devotion to pursuing autocephaly for Orthodox Ukraine through the Ecumenical Patriarchate:

> We are still of the firm belief that the most effective way which we as Bishops of Church outside of Ukraine can pursue our goal is through the canonical order of our Holy Church. We may be impatient with the pace of progress toward that goal and

the methodical and deliberate steps taken in that process, but we also understand that it is only such a necessarily slow process, which will ensure a long and lasting unification of all jurisdictions and which will obtain the recognition of the entire Orthodox world.[152]

The 1997 Odessa patriarchal meeting and the Ecumenical Patriarchate's continued support of the Moscow Patriarchate in Ukraine tested the new relationship between the UOC-USA and the Ecumenical Patriarchate. The American bishops responded in two ways: first, they appealed to the absolute necessity of proper canonical order in obtaining autocephaly, which could only be done through the Ecumenical Patriarchate. But the American bishops also resolutely rejected Russian ecclesial colonialism in Ukraine, and referred to the authority of the 1924 Tomos of Autocephaly to the Church in Poland as the path from canonical subjugation to Moscow to the establishment of an autocephalous church in an independent state. The UOC-USA's expression of support for Ukrainian autocephaly was new in one way: they made their appeal through their new canonical position within the Ecumenical Patriarchate.

Analysis of the Reunion with the Ecumenical Patriarchate

The Ecumenical Patriarchate's reception of two Ukrainian Orthodox metropolitanates added new dimensions to the evolution of Ukrainian Orthodox public religious identity. First, the mergers began the process of removing the stigma of ecclesial illegitimacy within global Orthodoxy carried by the legacies of these two churches. This new status was manifested by their freedom to concelebrate the Eucharist without prohibition with sister Orthodox churches. Their active participation among their fellow Orthodox demonstrated the possibility for Ukrainian Orthodox churches to be both canonically legitimate and publicly favor autocephaly for the Church in Ukraine. The return of these churches to the Ecumenical Patriarchate marked a new twist in the history of the Orthodox Church in Ukraine and was designed to denote Constantinople, and not Moscow or Rome, as the true patron of the Ukrainian Church.

This interpretation of church history had a strategic dimension: the Ukrainian Orthodox churches within the Ecumenical Patriarchate could work for the unity of the Orthodox churches in Ukraine by referring to the traditional role of the ecumenical patriarch in granting the canonical status of autocephaly to churches requesting it. A debate had raged for decades on the authority of any given church to grant another church autocephaly, a matter exacerbated by the historical precedent of Moscow granting the metropolia in the United States canonical autocephaly, which the Ecumenical Patriarchate refused to recognize. The work of the

Ukrainian churches of the diaspora within the Ecumenical Patriarchate would conform to the canonical principles observed by the Orthodox world. At the time, the adoption of this method distinguished the Ukrainian churches under Constantinople from the Kyivan Patriarchate, which proclaimed its own autocephaly. Particularly ironic was the reversal of roles for Patriarch Filaret, who had dismissed the legitimacy of the diaspora churches during his tenure as Muscovite exarch, and had essentially exchanged places with the diaspora churches.

Finally, a third change occurred as a result of the diaspora Ukrainian churches joining Constantinople. The narrative governing the historical fate of the Church in Ukraine had centered on the patriarch of Moscow as the central figure. With a united Ukrainian cohort ensconced in the Ecumenical Patriarchate, the ecumenical patriarch himself entered the picture as a figure who would stake his claim in the future path of Orthodoxy in Ukraine. The exchange of letters between patriarchs Alexy of Moscow and Bartholomew of Constantinople symbolizes the shift in the global power structure of Orthodoxy as it pertains to the Ukrainian issue. The similarity of the letters written by patriarchs Pimen (in 1972) and Alexy (in 1995) demonstrates that the prevailing Ukrainian narrative accepted by world Orthodoxy was controlled by Moscow. The ecumenical patriarch's reception of the Ukrainians in the diaspora permitted the Ukrainians to assume control over their own narrative and respond to the accusations of ecclesial illegitimacy.

Throughout this process of change, the Ukrainians in Canada and the United States struggled to come to terms with their own evolving self-identity. Their inability to defend pro-autocephaly Orthodox in Ukraine caused many in Canada and the United States to question the motivations of the Ecumenical Patriarchate and to call for a termination of the agreement. *Sobornopravnist'* and autocephaly were fused with the North American civil values of democracy and independence as diaspora Ukrainians looked to their past to intervene in the crisis dividing the churches in Ukraine.

Two recent additional events demonstrate both the complications of intra-church dialogue in Ukraine and the role of the Ecumenical Patriarchate in its future. The first event was an unprecedented symposium held in Toronto in May 2014 on the question of the past, present, and future of Orthodoxy in Ukraine.[153] The Canadian Church hosted the event and invited representatives of the Moscow Patriarchate, Kyivan Patriarchate, and UGCC, along with many other experts, to participate. This symposium was held with the blessing of the ecumenical patriarch and functioned as a workshop to ascertain what steps might be taken to unite the divided Orthodox churches. A spirit of goodwill and cooperation prevailed at the symposium, but it had no immediate impact, either in Toronto or in Ukraine.

Ukrainian bishops of the Ecumenical Patriarchate took a more assertive step in addressing the divisions in Ukraine by facilitating dialogues toward unity between the Autocephalous Church and the Kyivan Patriarchate in 2014 and 2015. The dialogues were prompted by a new sense of urgency due to the war and its toll on Ukraine. After the death of the UAOC's Metropolitan Mefodiy (Kudriakov), the new metropolitan of the UAOC, Makarii (Maletych), blessed and entered into official dialogue with the Kyivan Patriarchate.[154] Initial prospects for unity were mildly hopeful; despite numerous areas of disagreement, the two churches planned a unifying council in September 2015. The Ukrainian bishops of Canada and the United States made significant contributions to the process by facilitating the dialogue and presiding at the meetings. The process collapsed and the council did not occur, but even if it had, the actual outcome would have been uncertain.

Despite the collapse of the process of unification—which could be revived at any time—the role played by the Ukrainian bishops of the Ecumenical Patriarchate behind the scenes demonstrates their newfound power within global Orthodoxy. The diaspora bishops represented the Ecumenical Patriarchate in presiding at the unification negotiations, and their activity drew the ire of the Moscow Patriarchate. Bishops of the UOC-MP "expressed concern" about the activity of the diaspora bishops on their canonical territory and directed Metropolitan Onufry (Berezovsky) of Kyiv to request an explanation from Patriarch Bartholomew.[155]

It is essential to note that the unification meetings between the Kyivan Patriarchate and the UAOC collapsed in spite of the apparent patronage of the Ecumenical Patriarchate. An outcome-based assessment would conclude that the Ecumenical Patriarchate's attempt to foster unity has failed, at least to date. What is more important in this analysis is the return of the ecumenical patriarch as a primary figure in Ukrainian Church affairs. His participation is based on a rereading of the history of the Church in Ukraine, which views Constantinople as the authentic mother of the Kyivan Church. His authority has been enhanced by his acceptance of the previously orphaned Ukrainians of the diaspora, whose canonical deficiencies were dismissed once they were received by the mother church. It is equally essential to note that the ecumenical patriarch asserts himself in Ukrainian affairs through the Ukrainian bishops under Constantinople. To date, their relations with the bishops of the metropolia are minimal, whereas the pro-Ukrainian groups have sought their participation consistently. Their participation in Ukrainian affairs elicited a response in a recent interview with Bishop Klyment (Vecherya), the media spokesperson for the metropolia, who dismissed Metropolitan Yurii's (Kalishchuk) capacity to influence the unification talks.[156] However, a more irenic view emerged from an interview with Metropolitan Oleksandr (Drabinko), who was the protégé of the deceased metropolitan Volodymyr (Sabodan) and one of the most pro-autocephaly bishops within the metropolia. In referring to a statement made by Metropolitan Yurii of the Church in Canada in Kyiv on the Ecumenical Patriarchate's claim that it is the

rightful mother of the Church in Ukraine and is thus acting to unify divided parties, Metropolitan Oleksandr stated that "it would mean more to hear it from the
ecumenical patriarch himself."[157] Metropolitan Oleksandr's opinion illustrates the
limits of the influence of the Ukrainian diaspora bishops.[158] While they represent
the ecumenical patriarch, they do not bear the fullness of his authority. However,
the decision of the Canadian and American churches to join the Ecumenical
Patriarchate has given the ecumenical patriarch an opportunity to attempt to
address the Ukrainian situation while showing that the stigma of ecclesial illegitimacy can be erased through reception and recognition.

Conclusion

This chapter has surveyed the development of the autocephaly movement among
the Ukrainian Orthodox churches in the diaspora, especially Canada and the
United States. Originally, Greek Catholics who had settled in Canada and America
formed Ukrainian Orthodox churches in both countries, finding both the Roman
and Russian churches to be inadequate for their needs. Many of the immigrants
wanted to maintain their own native traditions and continued to hold nationalist and patriotic aspirations for their ancestral homelands. Furthermore, the
situation of the Orthodox Church in Canada and the United States was already
confusing, given the absence of unified juridical leadership of the Church, so the
formation of churches corresponding to ethnic identity provided a suitable pattern for Orthodox who self-identified as Ukrainian to adopt. In each country, the
distinct identity of the church came to be based on available episcopal leadership, which became more problematic during the era of Soviet persecution of the
church. Ironically, both the Canadian and American churches came to be led by
the same bishop, Archbishop John (Teodorovych), until the arrival of a new wave
of immigration following World War II. The decision to accept Archbishop John's
leadership introduced the stigma of ecclesial illegitimacy into the church, an issue
of concern to many (including the archbishop himself) and one which proved to
be divisive for Ukrainians sympathetic to the fiercely independent route taken by
the 1921 UAOC.

   In the post–World War II period up until the collapse of the Soviet Union, the
Canadian and American churches were shaped by the attitudes of immigrants and
developed hybrid identities. Both churches sought to sustain distinct Ukrainian
identity, and in the sphere of the Orthodox Church, steadfastly strove for ecclesial
legitimacy symbolized by the attempt to strengthen relations with the Ecumenical
Patriarchate and by the correction of the episcopal ordination of Archbishop John
in the United States.

Perhaps the most important aspect of the hybrid identity of the churches in North America is the cultural environment of religious freedom. The Ukrainian Orthodox community was quite small, a minority within the Orthodox minority, but the people and leaders of the churches used the freedom as a platform to begin the process of rewriting the narrative of Orthodoxy in Ukraine and to proclaim a political theology embracing freedom of religion. Ukrainian political theology emphasized the recent memory of martyrdom in the homeland and sharply juxtaposed that legacy to the possibility of Orthodoxy flourishing in the free world. The notion of reconstituting a free and independent Kyivan Metropolia was possible with the hypothetical collapse of the Soviet regime. In the macro-level landscape of global Orthodox communities, the Ukrainians allied themselves with all of those who valued freedom and sought liberation from an oppressor, including the American government and the Ecumenical Patriarchate. The consistent proclamation of this political theology coincided with the celebration of the millennium of the baptism of Rus', the rebirth of both the UGCC and UAOC in Ukraine, and the collapse of the Soviet Union. The culmination of this epoch was the reception of the Canadian and American Ukrainian churches by the Ecumenical Patriarchate in 1990 and 1995.

The hybrid identity of the churches coexists with a dual mission: to advocate for unity among Ukrainian Orthodox and the creation of a single autocephalous Orthodox Church while also sustaining church life in Canada and the United States. The existence of Ukrainian Orthodox Churches in North America is approaching its one-hundred-year anniversary, and the activities of these churches have added a decidedly Western dimension to their identities. The Ukrainian Orthodox Churches of Canada and the United States have been active proponents of unity as representatives of the Ecumenical Patriarchate. Their most recent legacy is to champion for autocephaly without the stigma of ecclesial illegitimacy, as they are now canonical. However, their aspirations for Ukrainian ecclesial liberty from Moscow inscribes a decidedly Western identity upon them, one which is inseparable from the larger notion of the Ukrainian diaspora seeking to separate Ukraine from Eurasia in favor of integration into the European Union.

4

The Orthodox Church in Ukraine during the Cold War (1945–1988)

This chapter examines the life of the Orthodox Church in Ukraine after World War II. The new era in the life of the Orthodox Church in Ukraine had two fundamental components. The first was the fading of Soviet openness to the Church and its replacement by a new wave of persecution under Khrushchev, which resulted in severe restrictions on church ministries including worship and education. This chapter briefly surveys Soviet religious policies in general on this matter, with specific attention to the Soviet curtailment of Ukrainization in the spirit of a multinational society. During this time, when Stalin inaugurated a period of toleration for the Church and permitted its activity and the reopening of Churches, the leaders of the Moscow Patriarchate proclaimed a holy war against Hitler, depicting him as "an offspring of the previous enemies of Orthodoxy."[1]

Second, this chapter features the next stage of evolution in the Orthodox Church of Ukraine following the war. This identity depends on a narrative simultaneously honoring the defeat of the Nazi fascists and the return of the Greek Catholics to Orthodoxy.[2] According to this narrative, the Soviet victory over Nazi Germany permitted Ukraine to become whole again and allowed Ukrainians to be free from the temptation of nationalism, which was similar to the evil of fascism. The return of the Greek Catholics to Orthodoxy went hand-in-hand with the Soviet defeat of Nazi Germany because the Moscow Patriarchate enhanced its identity as a multinational church during this period.

In this period, the identity of the church in Ukraine developed as the Moscow Patriarchate began defining itself as multinational home for diverse people: the historical background of the Orthodox Church in Ukraine contributed to the rehabilitation of the religious ideology now known as the *Russkii mir (Russian world)*, which refuted the necessity for the legal status of national churches in Ukraine. This chapter analyzes the identity of the Orthodox Church in Ukraine during the Soviet period by presenting the public face of the church as it was expressed in the most salient literature published by the Moscow Patriarchate and its exarchate in Ukraine, and by discussing the quest for survival of a "church within a church," drawing primarily from the recent scholarship of Natalia Shlikhta.[3] The public identity of the Orthodox Church in Ukraine celebrated the restoration of Ukraine after World War II, the peaceful existence of its Orthodox faithful within the Moscow Patriarchate, and the role of the Soviet regime in advocating for justice and equality of the nations. The "church within a church" struggled for survival by learning how to "speak Bolshevik" and manipulate the state system to glean modest gains for itself.

After Yalta: The 1946 Council in L'viv

The 1946 council of the UGCC in L'viv, which voted to liquidate the UGCC and return to the Orthodox Church, is one of the most formidable issues separating Ukrainian Greek Catholics from Eastern Orthodoxy today. The histories of Uniatism and the UGCC are beyond the scope of this work, but a few words to establish the background are necessary. The brief historical survey in the beginning of this book discusses the restoration of the Kyivan Metropolia following the decision of its hierarchy to enter into communion with Rome in 1596. Some church leaders viewed the union as actualizing the failed aspirations of the Council of Florence-Ferrara in 1448–1449 without denying the favorable position they thought they would gain by entering into communion with Rome under the Catholic Polish crown.[4] The larger issue is that most Orthodox Christians rejected the union, creating a situation where Orthodox lived side-by-side with Greek Catholics. The cultural and political shifts affecting both the Orthodox and the Catholic communities from the seventeenth through the twentieth centuries also had an impact on their relations, which were often strained. Furthermore, the conflicts occurring between Greek Catholics and Orthodox tended to align with Polish/Russian political polemics in the eighteenth and nineteenth centuries as well.[5] Despite UGCC metropolitan Andrei (Sheptytsky)'s public repudiation of the persecution of Orthodox believers in Poland (in 1938), Orthodox people and leaders tended to be suspicious of the Greek-Catholic Church as a Vatican plot to absorb and rule Orthodox people.[6]

The UGCC was regionally dominant in Galicia, which was also one of the locations of Ukrainian nationalism before and during World War II. The annexation of West Ukraine to the Soviet Union in 1945 did not diminish Ukrainians' hopes for an independent republic, and many patriots in Galicia happened to belong to the Greek-Catholic Church. The existence of national aspirations among the Greek-Catholic people was of no use to Stalin, who arranged for the arrest of the UGCC's leader, Metropolitan Joseph (Slipyi), in 1945, followed by the arrest of the entire episcopate of the church. When the UGCC convoked the council in L'viv in 1946, two Orthodox bishops presided over it, while the entire episcopate and most of the clergy were incarcerated. Russian church historian Dimitry Pospielovsky argued that the L'viv council "cannot be considered as historically valid," because it was obviously orchestrated by the Soviet government.[7] Pospielovsky also discusses the role of the Moscow Patriarchate in the "fraudulent act," and he notes the unfortunate timing of their statement, which coincided with the terror wrought by the NKVD.[8] Pospielovsky noted one positive occurrent in an otherwise dark time for the UGCC: many churches that would have otherwise been destroyed by the Soviets were spared by being taken over by the Moscow Patriarchate.[9]

Pospielovsky was correct about the significance of the timing of the council, but not merely on account of its proximity to the NKVD purge of the church. Patriarch Alexy's addresses called upon Ukrainians to rejoice over the result of the war, that is, the victory over fascism. This was the first of many messages determined to remove nationalistic tendencies from the faithful of the Ukrainian churches through reference to the Great Patriotic War as the event that freed them from the ideological tyranny of Nazi fascism.

For several decades, the literature of the Moscow Patriarchate celebrated the coerced council that temporarily reunified Greek Catholics with the Orthodox Church as the correction of a historical error. The reunification was marked by numerous pastoral visits of the patriarchal exarch to Western Ukraine. Shlikhta asserts that the L'viv council was aimed not only at reunion, but also at the inauguration of a "process of turning former Uniates into Orthodox and Soviets."[10] The actual outcomes of the L'viv council were complicated. Greek Catholics who immigrated to the West used their new freedom as an opportunity to publicly oppose Soviet policies and the narratives communicated by the Moscow Patriarchate. As

FIGURE 3. Initiators of L'viv Pseudo-Sobor in 1946. Photo by Svitlana Hurkina. Used with permission.

for those who were coerced into becoming Orthodox and Soviet, they struggled
to retain their distinct identity within the Moscow Patriarchate.

Religious Policy in Soviet Ukraine: Minimalism

Despite the narrative celebrating the restored wholeness of Ukraine, the religious
revival was not accompanied by real freedoms. Reports on Soviet religious policies in Ukraine during the Cold War depict a dismal existence, with the opening of
some parishes for worship the only thing of note to celebrate, and with monastic
life and theological education remaining minimal at best. In the immediate years
following the coerced return of the Greek Catholics to Orthodoxy, Stalin's policy of religious toleration remained essentially intact. The Moscow Patriarchate
became the preferred confession of the Soviet Union, a new status that came with
state control of the church.[11] The Moscow Patriarchate held two local councils
toward the end of the war, one in 1943 and a second one in 1945. The 1943 council consisted only of bishops, and Metropolitan Sergei (Stragorodsky) was elected
as patriarch of the church, which was short-lived, as he died on May 15, 1944.[12]
Pospielovsky reports that there were over 14,000 functioning Orthodox churches
in the Soviet Union by 1947, with over half of those coming from enemy-con-
trolled territories during the war.[13] At the next council in 1945, Metropolitan
Alexy was elected as the new patriarch.[14] One of the symbols of a slight increase
in tolerance for the Church was the agreement between Stalin and several senior
hierarchs to open seminaries in addition to the Moscow Theological Academy.[15]
Pospielovsky has a brief passage treating the "foreign policy agenda" for the
Church following the war, and this snapshot into the new international activity of
the Moscow Patriarchate during this period foreshadows its activity for much of
the remainder of the Soviet period, which includes pilgrimages to build alliances
with Orthodox patriarchs and an attack on the Vatican.[16]

   Pospielovsky notes that "the real gains of the Moscow Patriarchate" occurred
in "countries under Soviet control."[17] For example, all of the Orthodox parishes
of Czechoslovakia came under the Moscow Patriarchate and were then granted
autocephaly by Moscow.[18] Perhaps most significantly, the Church in Poland
negotiated the "annulment" of the autocephaly granted it by Constantinople in
1924, which was then replaced by autocephaly from Moscow in 1948.[19] These
actions prefigured continued developments within the Moscow Patriarchate
later in the Soviet period, including the establishment of an autonomous
Church of Japan under Moscow in 1970, and the granting of autocephaly to the
Orthodox Church in America (previously known as the metropolia) in 1970.
All of these canonical actions by the Moscow Patriarchate simultaneously
denoted the internationalization of the patriarchate and the pattern of Moscow

granting autocephaly to churches, a controversial action given Constantinople's reservation of this canonical rite.[20]

When Nikita Khrushchev became the new leader of the USSR after Stalin's death, the Soviet regime implemented a structured policy aimed at diminishing the influence of the Orthodox Church in society. Shlikhta asserts that Khrushchev's policies are comparable in scale with those imposed on the Church during Stalin's purges in the 1920s and 1930s.[21] As early as 1954, a variety of organizations were encouraged to struggle against the influence of religion by publishing anti-religious periodicals; by 1959, the overtly anti-religious journal *Science and Religion* was circulated.[22] Pospielovsky notes that the strategy of diminishing religious influence in society included the introduction of mandatory courses in scientific atheism in university curricula, sucking the life out of seminaries by making it difficult for prospective students to apply and enroll, and the forced closures of monasteries and churches.[23] The anti-religious program permeated everyday public life as well. Shlikhta notes that the ministry of education recommended that teachers emphasize learning about materialism in the first through fourth grades in 1960.[24] Atheism was to permeate every aspect of the curriculum in public education.[25] "Community fraternities" attempted to diminish the influence of church feasts and solemnities on the people by holding meetings with anti-religious themes on the same days, and especially by creating Soviet "holidays" that would coincide with Christian feasts.[26]

Perhaps the most blatant attack on the Church was the government's pressure on the bishops to accept an amendment to the Church's legal statute that would have a significant impact on the experience of church life at the parish level. The amendment stipulates that the "priest is restricted to functions concerning cult and is excluded from the parish council whose three members administer the parish autonomously."[27] This amendment and its implementation placed the local parish under the direct control of the municipal appointees of the Soviet regime, and reduced the priest to a symbolic figurehead who had the authority to administer sacraments, but realistically was unable to lead the people in the religious life of a community.[28] The implementation of this amendment compromised the rector's ability to shape community life, which was closely monitored by the officials. On the one hand, the Soviet government could claim that they promoted religious freedom since there were churches open for worship. On the other hand, the exclusion of the rector from leadership of any activity except for worship had the ripple effect of creating a generation of faithful whose participation in the life of the church was minimal, at least in principle. Instead of eradicating the Church with an aggressive and blunt assault, the regime attempted to bleed it slowly to death by reducing it to the performance of cultic observances and prohibiting its intellectual development, which would

theoretically limit the number of men interested in pursuing theological studies, especially with viable alternatives available in the sciences.

While the Soviet anti-religious campaign was designed to diminish the influence of the Church in all of the republics, its impact on church life in Ukraine was
unique because of the recent resistance to Sovietization in Ukraine, both before
and after the war. Bohdan Bociurkiw notes that Khrushchev's policy of closing
churches "shifted even further the social base of the Orthodox Church from the
more Russified cities to the overwhelmingly Ukrainian countryside," especially
strengthening the relative position of the Church in Western Ukraine.[29] Bociurkiw
estimated that the total number of operating churches in Ukraine had been
reduced from about 8,500 to 4,500 by the mid-1960s.[30] The majority of the monasteries and seminaries were closed, and approximately two-thirds of the existing
parishes were in Western Ukraine, which, as Bociurkiw notes, was the main base
of Ukrainian nationalism.[31] Bociurkiw linked the preservation of church life in
Western Ukraine with the coerced return of the UGCC to Orthodoxy, and noted
that the Moscow Patriarchate was prudent in permitting the Church to cultivate
its distinct features of Ukrainian identity, including the appointment of an ethnic
Ukrainian as the exarchate's metropolitan of Kyiv in 1966 (Filaret Denysenko),
and populating the ranks of the episcopate with ethnic Ukrainians. Furthermore,
the exarchate continued to publish its monthly Ukrainian-language periodical,
Православний вісник (Orthodox herald), after an interruption in publication
during the Khrushchev years. Thus, a modest program of Ukrainization within
the Moscow Patriarchate's exarchate in Ukraine was one of the outcomes of Soviet
anti-religious policies from Khrushchev's tenure.[32] The policy of permitting modest Ukrainization within the context of the canonical church in Ukraine contrasts
with the pattern observed throughout this study of viewing Ukrainization as
dubious or spurious at best, with Russification being the preferred ethnic identity marker. Bociurkiw notes that the Moscow Patriarchate's approach might
have been motivated by its hope of reconciling with the immigrant Ukrainian
Orthodox Church abroad and neutralizing the influence of the UGCC.[33]

Despite the toleration of a modest Ukrainization of church life in Western
Ukraine and the appointment of ethnic Ukrainians to the episcopate,
Ukrainization was not prevalent throughout the entirety of the Orthodox Church
in Soviet Ukraine. Bociurkiw notes that Russian was the only language authorized
for sermons and church administration in Odessa, and that the use of liturgical Ukrainian was strictly prohibited.[34] Frank Sysyn also treated the continued
existence of Russification in the Ukrainian Exarchate during the Soviet period by
providing examples of episcopal activities that seemed to endorse Russian chauvinism.[35] A letter written by the editors of the underground journal *Український*

вісник in the spring of 1974 accused Metropolitan Filaret of prohibiting the use of Ukrainian for church administration and preaching, and suggested that Filaret had removed a priest from his cathedral in Kyiv (St. Volodymyr's) for preaching in Ukrainian.[36] It appears that the Ukrainian Exarchate of the Moscow Patriarchate was accommodating some degree of diversity depending on the region, with modest Ukrainization in the west countered by Russification in the central, southern, and eastern regions of Ukraine. Sysyn discloses the strategy of attempting to win over the Greek Catholics and argues that many adherents would quickly return to the UGCC were it legal again.[37]

Thus, the Soviet decision to permit the Ukrainians to retain a certain degree of national identity facilitated some semblance of survival for Ukrainization itself within the exarchate. The limitation of Ukrainization to the western regions coincided with the remnants of two potent ecclesial institutions: the recently liquidated UGCC, and the Orthodox communities of Volyn', Lutsk, Rivne, and elsewhere that had retained some degree of Ukrainian identity within the autocephalous Church in Poland and in both the autonomous and autocephalous churches of Ukraine.

Shlikhta argues that the Ukrainian cohort within the Moscow Patriarchate should be considered a "church within a church," consisting of bishops, clergy, and faithful, who adopted a "subaltern" strategy aimed toward survival.[38] The people of this "church within a church" did not forsake their identity, but took on hybrid identities, expressing themselves externally as "Orthodox" and Soviet" while fiercely retaining their true national and ecclesial consciousness.[39] Shlikhta emphasizes that the retention of true identity occurred in everyday, local activities and customs, such as blessing special paschal breads and continuing beloved traditions of Christmas caroling.[40] They adopted this strategy with the knowledge that open, hostile opposition to the Soviet Orthodox alternative was impossible, as the state would never accept their "otherness."[41]

The coexistence of these distinctly Ukrainian Greek-Catholic and Orthodox populations within the Moscow Patriarchate, living side-by-side, not only formed a potentially strong lobby within the Church, but also served as a reminder to the Ukrainian intelligentsia of church history in Ukraine. Sysyn emphasizes Ukraine's distinctness in having a legacy of two national churches (Orthodox and Greek-Catholic), which demanded that the Ukrainian intellectual turn to Ukraine's past in order to preserve its distinct spiritual legacy.[42] Intellectual attention to Kyivan Christianity was primarily designed to understand a national religious past, not to work toward the unification of the Catholic and Orthodox churches. The activities of this strong lobby within the exarchate of the Moscow Patriarchate served as the foundation for the emergence of yet another pro-autocephaly cohort in Ukraine that was allowed to emerge in the public square when the Soviet regime truly began to loosen its grip on participation in religious activities in the late 1980s. It was not a coincidence that the third rebirth of the UAOC emerged in L'viv, alongside the return of the UGCC.

The Impact of Soviet Religious Policy on Orthodoxy in Ukraine

Having noted a surprising outcome in Soviet religious policy in Ukraine, namely the retention of a strong Orthodox core in Western Ukraine, it is necessary to mention the limitations of this policy. The tolerance of Ukrainization occurred under the auspices of the Moscow Patriarchate, as a part of the patriarchate's international expansion program. This program was both political and ecclesiastical, with the church organization taking on the same quality of internationalization claimed by the USSR itself. The Moscow Patriarchate's close relationship with the churches in Czechoslovakia and Poland, along with its successful strengthening of ties with the churches in Japan, the United States, and England, gave it the appearance of being a kind of ecumenical patriarchate that was multinational in character. The patriarchate strongly desired to reconcile with the Russian Orthodox Church outside of Russia and the 1942 UAOC, which had established itself throughout the world, especially in North America. Sysyn depicts the patriarchate's decision to make the Orthodox Church in America autocephalous as part of a larger plan of bringing more of the Orthodox world under its wing.[43] In 1972, Patriarch Pimen described the ecclesial illegitimacy of the Ukrainians in the diaspora to Patriarch Athenagoras in great detail, but he still ended his letter with an open invitation for the Ukrainians to return to the Moscow Patriarchate. The dual strategy of permitting some Ukrainization while attempting to stifle the emergence of an autocephalous Ukrainian Church was designed to provide a space for Orthodox Ukrainians in a multinational ecclesial home that would make it unnecessary for them to seek their own independent church, at least theoretically. The problem was that the same Ukrainians who had worked toward ecclesial autocephaly had also expressed their dream for an independent and sovereign Ukrainian republic: even the most brutal Soviet campaigns had failed to eradicate the combined national and ecclesial aspirations of the Ukrainians.

A notable Ukrainian Church figure who symbolized the paradoxical question of the UAOC in Soviet Ukraine was the Orthodox priest Vasyl Romaniuk, who was a prisoner in the Soviet Gulag because of his advocacy of religious freedom. Romaniuk was originally arrested in 1944 for religious and nationalist activity, and again in 1946 for anti-Soviet agitation.[44] He was arrested yet again in 1972 for writing a letter on behalf of the political prisoner Valentyn Moroz.[45] Before he became a bishop and a significant figure in the third rebirth of the UAOC, Romaniuk publicly voiced his allegiance to the UAOC and its leader, Metropolitan

Mstyslav (Skrypnyk), as early as 1977.[46] Romaniuk eventually immigrated to Canada in 1988, only to return to Ukraine in 1990, on the eve of the collapse of the Soviet Union.[47]

Romaniuk is best known for the tragic circumstances surrounding his death. Many years after his defiant condemnation of Soviet religious policies and his joining of the Ukrainian Orthodox diaspora community, he was elected as the second patriarch of the UOC-KP. He died under mysterious circumstances in 1995, and a fierce disagreement on the appropriate place for his burial resulted in an outburst of violence in Kyiv in what is now known as Black Tuesday.[48] For the purposes of this chapter, Romaniuk is an important figure because he was an ordained clergyman who was also a human rights dissident. His multiple arrests and time served in labor camps exhibit the limits of religious freedom for the Orthodox Church in Ukraine. Romaniuk also serves as a bridge figure: his open declaration of loyalty to the UAOC in the diaspora prefigured the storm that was forthcoming in Ukraine's Orthodox Church. Romaniuk's election to the office of patriarch in 1993 fits the pattern, witnessed earlier in this study, of laity and mid-level clergy whose activities often resulted in their ascension to offices of church leadership.

Natalia Shlikhta presents several reports of resistance to Soviet policies within the Church in activities undertaken at all levels of church life, including the hierarchy and the laity. She introduces Bishop Feodosii (Kovernynsky) as an example of a hierarch who uses unconventional methods to dispute an attempt to restrict the celebration of liturgy in rural areas.[49] In this case, Bishop Feodosii feigned misunderstanding a directive to keep services short.[50] In another example, the hierarch initiated a protest of the planned closure of the Kasperovsky Cathedral in Mykolaiv.[51] Shlikhta notes that protests to local plenipotentiaries were common; it was unusual for a hierarch to initiate them.[52] She also profiles the opposition of Archbishop Paladii, who served as bishop of Volyn'-Rivne and L'viv-Ternopil', and had several tussles with local officials while continuing to maintain the public persona of a hierarch who was a model Soviet and Orthodox citizen. Shlikhta's objective is to demythologize the notion that the Church blindly obeyed the state and embraced its new official identity; her study shows that hierarchs resisted the state's anti-religious campaign, despite the ecclesial annexation of the UGCC.[53] The laity also played a prominent role in resisting assimilation in order to retain its ecclesial and national distinctiveness. Shlikhta proposes that every state-mandated closure of a church resulted in a letter of protest signed by lay members, epitomized by a letter of 1964 from two Ukrainian Orthodox women to the patriarchs of the Eastern Church and the United Nations, appealing for external assistance to prevent the closure of the Pochaiv Lavra.[54] In her examination of this corpus of correspondence, Shlikhta argues that the authors tended to accuse the authorities of violating Soviet law in closing churches, a tactic in sharp contradiction to condemning the Soviet state and its ideology.[55] In other words, the faithful wrote in a style representative of Soviet citizens who are aware of their rights and the kind of language needed to state a persuasive argument. Shlikhta's scholarship illustrates the continuity of lay resistance to state persecution of the Church: the people's ability to sustain a hybrid identity of loyal Soviet/Orthodox citizenry and national/ecclesial distinctiveness was a powerful force in sustaining the "church within a church" in the conditions of the Moscow Patriarchate in the postwar Soviet Union.

The Soviet state's attempts to control the Church and mute its distinctive identity is in direct contrast with the idealistic picture of peace between church and state expressed by Metropolitan Filaret in a 1978 interview.[56] Filaret stated that the Church was free to conduct its activities in the Soviet Union without prohibitions, pointing to several examples of freedom to publish, worship, and educate. In response to a question on the persecution of faithful (as reported by the Western press), Filaret stated that "there is no persecution on the basis of religious persuasion in the Soviet Union. The laws of the country prohibit any kind of discrimination against the faithful. Non-believers and believers in the USSR constitute a united society. They labor together for the good of the fatherland."[57] Filaret's published remarks are not surprising: they delineate the difference between the lived experience of the church and the experience that its leaders were allowed to depict publicly. Filaret himself personifies the hybrid identity of Ukrainian Orthodox in the postwar period, as his private correspondence to the local plenipotentiary contradicts his public applause for Soviet policies on the Church.[58]

The Healing of the Uniate Schism as the Primary Source for Official Political Theology

The introduction to the impact of Soviet religious policy on the Orthodox Church in Ukraine sets the stage for a presentation on the development of the political theology of the Moscow Patriarchate in the final phase of the Soviet period leading up to the millennium of the baptism of Rus'. The Moscow Patriarchate's policy of Ukrainization included a narrative featuring several historical events in the life of the Church that allegedly led to the return of the Greek Catholics to Orthodoxy. These events included archpastoral visits of the exarch to Western Ukraine, a series of articles published in *Православний вісник* on the deficiencies of the Unia and the triumph of Orthodoxy, and the emergence of a political theology that praised the Soviet government for delivering the Orthodox in Western Ukraine from fascism and providing them a safe and holy space in the bosom of the Moscow Patriarchate. This ecclesial-political theology embraced the union of Ukraine and Russia at the Treaty of Pereiaslav in 1654 and the victory of the

Soviets in the Great Patriotic War as symbolizing the multinational character of both the USSR and the Moscow Patriarchate.

Select Publications in Православний вісник, 1969–1988

One of the best sources for gleaning a narrative of official religious identity in the Ukrainian Orthodox Exarchate of the post–World War II Soviet era is the Ukrainian-language version of the exarchate's periodical, *Православний вісник* (The Orthodox herald—henceforth, PV). In his brief overview of the Orthodox Church in the Soviet period, Bociurkiw mentions that the resumption of the dissemination of PV symbolized both the modest Ukrainization permitted by the Moscow Patriarchate and their attempt to seal the reunion of the Greek Catholics with the Orthodox Church. Accordingly, reunion was one of the most important themes of the dozens of essays published in PV during this period, with numerous references to both church and state reunions.

The first example is a summary of an article by Archbishop Hryhorii (Zakaliak) of Mukachiv and Uzhorod published in January 1969.[59] Archbishop Hryhorii establishes his theme from the beginning of the article by lamenting the fact that important regions of Right-Bank Ukraine were not included in the political reunion of Ukraine with Russia in the Treaty of Pereiaslav in 1654.[60] He states with some pride that the Ukrainian people remained faithful during this time in spite of an economic, political, and ecclesial crisis afflicting them, summed up by the pressures of Polonization.[61] For Archbishop Hryhorii, the Orthodox Church, which had previously united all of the peoples of Kyivan Rus', was the primary bearer of identity for the Ukrainian people.[62] Archbishop Hryhorii speaks directly about the matter of national belonging for the Ukrainian people at a time when foreigners governed them, stating that the word "Orthodox" alone denoted national belonging. He then argues that the motivation of the original uniates was to divide the Ukrainian people, to demoralize her, to induce her to forget her ancestry, and to undermine Orthodoxy through the process of Polonization.[63]

Archbishop Hryhorii then argued that Unia was a political device designed to sever the spiritual relationship between Ukraine and Russia.[64] He claimed that important Ukrainian figures retained a historical memory of their connection with the spiritual East and attributed the idea of a new union between Ukraine and Russia to the renowned opponent of Uniatism, Metropolitan Iov (Boretsky).[65] After referring to Bohdan Khmelnitsky's agreement to the Pereiaslav Treaty as the foundation for a common life between Ukraine and Russia, Archbishop Hryhorii depicted the significance of the Pereiaslav agreement as a reunion that created a new great Slavic regime in the East.[66] This new realm stood as a symbol of hope for the Ukrainians who continued to be ruled by foreign peoples, including the Poles and the Austro-Hungarian empire. The union of Ukraine and Russia remained a beacon of hope for the Ukrainians who were under Polish rule from 1919–1939; the Ukrainians needed only to look to the East for liberation. The end of Archbishop Hryhorii's essay celebrates the Soviet army's entrance into Galicia to liberate the Ukrainians from Hitler's fascism: "reunion with the Soviet regime assisted in the battle of all of the fraternal nations of the Soviet Union with Hitler's hordes in the Great Patriotic War."[67] Archbishop Hryhorii praises the victory of the Soviet army over "human-hating fascism," which resulted in the liberation of all the Ukrainian regions and their reunion into "one native Ukrainian Soviet republic."[68] The archbishop came full circle in his argument, stating that the military victory over the fascists resulted in a political reunion that enabled the Orthodox Church to put an end to ecclesial division, namely the Latin Unia to which Ukrainians had belonged for several centuries.

This essay published in PV in 1969 is one of dozens of examples of a political-religious narrative designed to express joy over the reunion of all Ukrainians into one Soviet republic and the return of the Greek Catholics to Orthodoxy. This narrative continues the fusion of the political and religious during the heat of World War II by representatives of the Moscow Patriarchate, who aligned the autocephalist Ukrainian bishops with Nazi fascism, thereby contrasting them with church leaders who were loyal to the people of the Soviet Union. Archbishop Hryhorii's essay establishes foundations for the continued development of this political-ecclesial narrative over the course of more than a decade in the Ukrainian Orthodox Exarchate. First, his reading of history assumes that Kyivan Rus' was a single political entity uniting the three Slavic nations of Ukraine, Russia, and Belarus, who were also united spiritually in the Orthodox Church. His essay emphasizes the Orthodox East as the spiritual home of the Ukrainian nation and insists that the events that fractured the political unity of Kyivan Rus' (beginning with the Tatar-Mongol horde) did not diminish its spiritual unity. The Ukrainian fidelity to Orthodox identity was the most important feature of the national identity it derived from Kyivan Rus'. The narrative views the political subjugation of Ukraine by Poland (primarily), and also Austro-Hungary and Nazi Germany as continuing the pattern of outside forces attempting to change Ukraine's identity. Two political events strengthened Ukrainian identity by reuniting them with their Russian brothers: the Treaty of Pereiaslav in 1654, and the Soviet victory over the Nazi fascists in the Great Patriotic War. The epic victory of the Great Patriotic War resulted in Ukraine's restoration to wholeness in the Soviet Union, which then enabled the MP to put an end to the final remaining ecclesial division: the liquidation of the UGCC. Obviously, Archbishop Hryhorii's reconstruction of history as a series of events causing division can be contested, as can any one of the events within the sequence. The larger point here is the relationship between the political and the religious in the creation of a narrative designed to reach Ukrainian-language Orthodox, most of whom were recently forced to abandon their Greek Catholic faith and convert.

The September 1969 issue of PV contained the sermon of Metropolitan Filaret, exarch of the Moscow Patriarchate in Ukraine, celebrating the twentieth anniversary of the reunion of the "former" Greek Catholics of Transcarpathia with the Orthodox Church.[69] Metropolitan Filaret's sermon was not nearly as politically charged as Archbishop Hryhorii's essay, but the message contributes another layer to the narrative, given its context (delivered at a women's monastery in Mukachevo, in the Transcarpathian region of Ukraine), and the appearance of the same themes in the message. The explicit identification of the union of former Greek Catholics with the Orthodox Church of Rus' is notable here— Filaret did not mention the Moscow Patriarchate, but the Rus' Orthodox Church (written Руською Православною Церквою). Filaret claimed that the people of Transcarpathia "waited for three hundred years to be able to return to the faith of their fathers," and also to be reunited with the nations of their fatherland.[70] Filaret said that the people of Transcarpathia were freed from "foreign dependence" after World War II.[71] After greeting the hierarchs, clergy, and people who struggled for reunion with their "Mother Rus' Church," and honoring the departed, Filaret caricatured the Unia as an "instrument of oppression" and offered an elaboration of the significance of the reunion of the Greek Catholic with the Orthodox.[72]

Filaret went on to express hope for authentically constructive ecumenical dialogue with the specter of Roman domination now removed from the scene while also expressing support for the Orthodox Church in Czechoslovakia, which had recently suffered on account of Uniate aggression.[73] Filaret's homily is short, but pithy, as he interpreted the twenty-year anniversary of the return of the Greek Catholics in Transcarpathia to Orthodoxy as the healing of divisions between fraternal Slavic nations, which resonates with the narrative of Archbishop Hryhorii. A new addition to the narrative is the condemnation of Unia as a means of healing the schism between Orthodoxy and the Catholic Church, a development within Orthodoxy that had potentially positive implications for ecumenical dialogue at the global level.

The literature published in the 1969 editions of PV celebrated the twentieth anniversary of the reunion of the Transcarpathia Greek Catholics with Orthodoxy, but also anticipated the twenty-fifth anniversary of the 1946 L'viv council to come in 1971. The continued celebration of this reunion was one of the many themes discussed at the 1971 local council of the Moscow Patriarchate, as evidenced by its resolutions.[74] Resolution 3 of the Holy Synod meeting explicitly referenced the "return to Orthodoxy" of Greek Catholics from Galicia and Uzhorod.[75]

The resolutions of the 1971 meeting place the return of the Greek Catholics to Orthodoxy within the context of all the activities of the Moscow Patriarchate, which were numerous and global in character. Resolution 2 expresses satisfaction with the activities of the Moscow Patriarchate in granting autocephaly to local Orthodox churches, namely Poland (June 22, 1948), Czechoslovakia (November 23, 1951), and the OCA (April 10, 1970).[76] In resolution 5, the synod confirmed their activities and those of the patriarch in strengthening the relationships between the Moscow Patriarchate and the other local Orthodox churches for the purpose of addressing the issues confronting contemporary society and for deepening unity among them. In resolutions 6 and 7, the 1971 council continued to encourage the patriarch and synod to engage in ecumenical dialogue and to pray for peace in the world. These decrees of the 1971 local council manifest the emphasis on internationalization embraced by the Moscow Patriarchate during the period following Khrushchev's persecution of the Church. The resolution concerning the jubilee of the reunion of Greek Catholics to Orthodoxy was a prominent component of a growing ecclesial institution: the Moscow Patriarchate increasingly assumed the role of negotiating peace, meeting with non-Orthodox Christian groups, granting autocephaly to other Orthodox churches, and facilitating the end of schisms within the patriarchate, symbolized by the reunion with the former Greek Catholics. Two formidable churches claimed by the Moscow Patriarchate remained outside of her grasp, and the 1971 council addressed their situations in resolution 4:

> To recognize the issue of exceptional attention: the intense efforts on the part of His Holiness Patriarch Alexy and the Holy Synod of the Russian Orthodox Church during this period for the return into the bosom of the Mother Church, hierarchs, clergy, and faithful who departed from her at various times and created diverse schismatic groups outside of the borders of the church, and also the USSR. We charge the superior church council of the Russian Orthodox Church to continue efforts for the reunion of the so-called "Russian Orthodox Church Abroad" (Karlovatsky Schism) and the Ukrainian Autocephalous Orthodox Church in the diaspora with the Mother Church (along with other scattered children of the Church), that in the name of our Lord Jesus Christ they would gather in her saving bosom.[77]

This snapshot into the resolutions of the 1971 Moscow Council exhibits its identity as the sole mediator of all divisions and arbiter for granting autocephaly and brokering peace both within and outside of Orthodoxy. The return of Greek Catholics to Orthodoxy was one of a number of orchestrated actions that would also apply to the UAOC: all would be well if the autocephalists would join the MP.

The Twenty-Fifth Anniversary Celebration of the Reunion of Greek Catholics with Orthodoxy in L'viv in 1971

The Moscow Patriarchate marked the twenty-fifth anniversary of the L'viv council of 1946 with a solemn church celebration at St. George Cathedral in L'viv on May 15–16, 1971, which included speeches by Metropolitan Filaret and Archbishop Nikolai (Yuryk) of L'viv, along with reflections on the council by select participants, and a solemn hierarchical liturgy with numerous eparchial bishops from Western Ukraine concelebrating.[78] The patriarchal locum tenens in Moscow, Metropolitan Pimen, also greeted the hierarchs, clergy, and people of the Western Ukrainian eparchies with an epistle on the occasion.[79] Metropolitan Pimen's message contained many of the same themes already mentioned: he depicted the Unia as involuntary and coerced, and described the 1946 L'viv council as "an ecclesial-popular council, the free manifestation of the will of a faithful nation, which set itself on the path of returning to the faith of its fathers." As in Filaret's sermon of 1969 at Mukachev, Pimen depicted the Unia as an evil attempt to display an exterior unity without any real basis. Pimen closes his letter in praise of Protopresbyter Gabriel Kolestnyk and depicts the church union of the former Greek Catholics with the Orthodox as a "gathering of the whole Ukrainian nation and living sentiments of brotherhood and its unity with all of the great, ancient united peoples of Rus'."[80]

Metropolitan Filaret addressed the gathering in L'viv with a speech and a sermon for the liturgy.[81] Two new elements of his speech are notable, as most of the message is recycled material from the narrative established a few years earlier. First, Filaret referred to the assertion of Ukrainian Catholics abroad that the L'viv council of 1946 did not have the authority to annul the Union of Brest.[82] After asking rhetorically if it was possible for an obstacle to block Christian freedom, he dismissed the claims coming from the Ukrainian diaspora as a "feeble desire to renew the Unia," which had only existed to plant "enmity between the fraternal Slavic nations."[83] Second, Filaret also reflected on the progress made over these twenty-five years in eradicating the elements of Uniatism that had permeated Orthodox consciousness and ritual. He emphasized that clergy of the former Greek-Catholic eparchies had attended Orthodox seminaries and theological academies for over twenty-five years and were being educated in the spirit of Orthodoxy and love for the fatherland.[84] It is also worth mentioning the opening of his speech, in which he emphasized the participation of the bishops, clergy, and faithful of the former Greek-Catholic Church in the forthcoming local council of the Russian Church, an event occurring for the first time in the history of the Moscow Patriarchate.[85]

The speech of Archbishop Nikolai of L'viv on May 15, 1971, echoed the themes presented by Filaret, and attributed the liquidation of the Unia to a grassroots church movement that had simmered for quite some time within the Greek Catholic community.[86] After a brief presentation on the characteristics of the Latinization of the Unia by Austro-Hungarian officials, Archbishop Nikolai discussed the formation of a group among Uniate clergy called ritualists, who "advocated for the purity of the Eastern rite and opposed its Latinization."[87] He praised those among the group who called upon the people of Galicia to abandon the Unia and return to Orthodoxy.

Nikolai expressed thanks to the Lord for the opportunity to "reconstruct church life."[88] This reconstruction included the restoration of authentic Orthodox liturgy, with only the architectural style of churches belonging to particular regions remaining unchanged.[89] The evidence of the reconstruction of church life was the publication and dissemination of an eparchial periodical and the distribution of the exarchate's Ukrainian-language PV, for the purpose of performing the tasks of mission in the Western eparchies.[90] Nikolai's alignment of the 1946 church reunion with the liberation of Western Ukraine from Nazism is notable, if repetitive: the point of the message was to persuade the Western Ukrainians that they had returned to their rightful home.[91]

The Ukrainian Exarchate adopted a defensive posture when it was challenged by a pastoral epistle issued by the synod of the Ukrainian Catholic bishops in October 1971.[92] Most of Nikolai's response defends the canonical foundation of the 1946 L'viv council and dismisses the accusations of the Ukrainian Catholic bishops as ignorant of the realities of Orthodox church life in Soviet Ukraine. When asked about the renewed activity of the Ukrainian Catholic episcopate outside of Ukraine, especially its attempt to create a patriarchate, Metropolitan Nikolai characterized the Ukrainian Catholic community outside of Ukraine as the successors of the violent *banderivtsi*.[93]

Metropolitan Nikolai also asserted that the basis for the creation of a Ukrainian Catholic patriarchate was completely political, with nationalistic aims, which was alien to Christianity.[94] Metropolitan Nikolai's interview is helpful for understanding the development of official religious identity in the Ukrainian Orthodox Exarchate of the Moscow Patriarchate following the 1946 L'viv council. The narrative celebrated the reunion of Greek Catholics with Orthodoxy facilitated by the defeat of fascism. The exarchate essentially celebrated two epic events: the freeing the Greek Catholics from oppression thanks for the Great Patriotic War, which also facilitated their return to their proper home in fraternal union with all the Slavic nations of Kyivan Rus'. The 1946 L'viv council was a natural outcome of the Great Patriotic War, just as a reunited Ukraine in the USSR healed the divisions created by external political aggressors. When challenged by the Ukrainian diaspora on this narrative, Nikolai sharpened its polemical quality. The Greek Catholics had been liberated not only from external aggressors, but also from Ukrainian nationalistic groups who murdered their own people.[95] Thus, his 1972 interview is an early expression of the identity inscribed by the Orthodox leaders of the Ukrainian Exarchate onto the Ukrainian diaspora: their motives were politically and religiously dubious, alien to Christianity, and seeking to divide Ukrainians from their brother Russians. Nikolai depicted the exarchate as having adopted the proper Christian path, evidenced (in part) by its honoring the distinctiveness of Ukrainian identity in the publication of a Ukrainian-language periodical issued monthly (PV).[96] Nikolai's polemical intensity would return with greater vigor at the end of the Soviet era when the UGCC returned to Ukraine and came into conflict with the Orthodox exarchate.

When the thirty-fifth anniversary of the L'viv council arrived in 1981, PV published more material following the same themes.[97] The intriguing content of these publications is the increasingly intense dismissal of Ukrainian Catholics in the diaspora as nationalists, including accusations that they collaborated with the Germans during World War II, an act that "tarnished" the reputation of the Greek-Catholic leadership, in the words of I. Fedorovych.[98]

The language of Fedorovych's essay is strikingly polemical and accusatory, having shifted from the more banal attribution of the 1946 oseudo-council of L'viv to the Great Patriotic War and the allegedly longstanding desire of Latinized clergy and faithful to become Orthodox again to an accusation of Greek-Catholic clergy working with Nazis. Here, the author of the essay claims that the clergy and faithful of the Greek-Catholic Church were aghast at the collaboration of their hierarchy with the Nazis and the OUN, and this disgust was one of the motivating factors inspiring them to return to the Orthodox Church. He employs hyperbole to fuel the ideology supporting the narrative. Bohdan Bociurkiw states that the UGCC had "openly sided with the enemies of the Soviet system," which included the implicit blessing of the formation of a volunteer SS division to fight the Soviets, and the commissioning of priests to serve as chaplains.[99] Sophia Senyk accuses the UGCC of openly supporting the OUN, from the guerilla warfare after World War II up until the present day.[100] Despite the UGCC's support for the Ukrainian nationalists, Bociurkiw notes that the Church did not support all of the nationalists' methods, and "repeatedly protested against Nazi excesses."[101] Bociurkiw's description of Galician attitudes toward the Soviets establishes the context for the UGCC's assistance of Ukrainian nationalist partisans in the battle: "the overwhelming majority of Western Ukrainians, including the Greek-Catholic hierarchy and clergy, never considered themselves Soviet citizens and viewed the Soviet annexation of their lands in 1939 as an illegal act of force."[102]

But the literature of the patriarchal exarchate in Ukraine did not address the pre-Soviet history of Western Ukraine. Fedorovych's article also dismissed the possibility of reconstituting the UGCC in Ukraine and establishing a Uniate patriarchate, stating that Kyiv never had a Uniate bishop and that all of the Uniate churches in communion with Rome were experiencing a spiritual crisis on account of the problem of Latinization.[103] The second argument dismissing the possibility of reopening the UGCC in Ukraine was rationalized by the return of Latinization, which the Ukrainian Orthodox Exarchate had attempted to point out as one of the deficiencies of Uniatism in all of its polemical literature.

This review of the literature published by the exarchate in commemoration of the reunion of the Greek Catholics with Orthodoxy, has alluded to the significance of the Soviet Union in defeating external aggressors and facilitating the restoration of Ukraine and the reconciliation of divided Slavic nations. The literature depicts the state as parallel to the church in its multinational quality and its restoration of the glory of the legacy of Kyivan Rus'. One of the most important factors communicated by church leaders is the unity of Kyiv and Moscow in the Russian Orthodox Church, a unity to which the former Greek Catholics now belonged after the 1946 council. An essay celebrating the thirty-fifth anniversary of the L'viv council emphasized the unity of the Western Ukrainian eparchies with both Kyiv and Moscow:

> Kyiv and Moscow, the Orthodox Ukrainian and Russian East, from which the enemies of our father's faith at one time turned away our heart and attention and turned them to Rome, Vienna, or Warsaw, have become close and dear to our souls and hearts forever.[104]

The Soviet regime believed that it had achieved the Ukrainian reunion with Moscow through its media campaign in the Moscow Patriarchate, and the patriarchate and Ukrainian Exarchate openly praised the advocacy of the Soviet Union for the Orthodox Church throughout this period. On June 20, 1980, the USSR awarded Moscow Patriarch Pimen the Order of the Friend of the Peoples (Орден дружби народів).[105] In his letter of thanks to the head of the council of ministers of the USSR Alexei Kosygin, written in commemoration of the victory of the Soviet Union in the Great Patriotic War, Patriarch Pimen expressed his best wishes on the occasion of the victory over "fascist Germany," stating that price of the war was the "protection of our freedom and independence and the bringing of liberation to many countries of Europe from fascist slavery."[106] Pimen added that the "faithful children of the Russian Orthodox Church in our country, the clergy and laity, wholeheartedly express our love for our homeland, and entirely share in the principled policy of peacekeeping of our republic."[107] In the same letter, and also in an official statement to the media on the thirty-fifth anniversary of the Great Patriotic War, Pimen referred to the Helsinki Act and stated that the Church would do everything in its power to ensure disarmament.[108] In his media statement, Pimen referred to the memory of those who died during World War II as the inspiration for the Russian Church's mission of peacekeeping in the world.[109] Pimen called upon all Christian churches to cooperate in a common peacekeeping enterprise.[110]

As the millennium of the baptism of Rus' approached, the Moscow Patriarchate continued to define its identity as an international church with peacemaking as its primary mission. The basis for peacemaking was the tremendous loss suffered in the Great Patriotic War and the lessons learned from the defeat of the Nazi regime. In a letter issued by Patriarch Pimen and the Holy Synod of the Russian Orthodox Church on the seventieth anniversary of the October Revolution, the patriarch and bishops stated that the fall of Nazi Germany required each citizen of the Soviet Union to come together in strength and self-sacrifice.[111] After referring to the typical experience of Soviet citizens who had to work together to rebuild society in the aftermath of the war, Pimen and the bishops stated that "in the ensuing environment of the 'Cold War,' the peacemaking service found its distinct place in the life of the Russian Orthodox Church," pursuing efforts for the sake of the common good together with like-minded representatives of other religions.[112] The letter connects the peacemaking mission of the Church with its patriotism, as church leaders convey warm greetings to the leaders of the Soviet Union, granting them their blessing, while greeting all of the children of the church on the occasion of the "great feast," the anniversary of the October Revolution.[113]

The lengthy letter includes a review of the thorny relationship between the Orthodox Church and the state during the Soviet period, and justifies the controversial declaration of Metropolitan Sergei to the Soviet Union in 1927 as the continuation of a policy inaugurated by Patriarch Tikhon in 1925 to work together with the state for the sake of the common good.[114] According to the letter, the Russian Church found its proper place from the experience of war and its devastating effect on the populace, with the result that "the voice of the Russian Orthodox Church began to be heard in the international arena."[115] The international voice of the Russian Church was manifest in "the experience of our Church in helping fraternal Churches of socialist states," an implicit reference to the Moscow Patriarchate's activity in granting autocephaly to the churches of Poland and Czechoslovakia.[116] The epistle attributed the other aspect of the church's peacemaking mission, her service to the world, to the pioneering inauguration of Patriarch Alexy I.[117]

The delivery of this epistle on the seventieth anniversary of the October Revolution actually followed the patriarchate's announcements of its activities for the forthcoming millennium celebrations in various parts of the Soviet Union.[118] Despite the order of the two epistles, the two themes of the October Revolution and the millennium celebration coincided, and thus many of the same themes appear in both letters. One of the differences in the millennium epistle is its international character: the letter on the revolution was addressed to the Russian Orthodox Church, but the addressees of the millennium letter included those outside the borders of the Soviet Union. In addition to the announcement of jubilee celebration plans and events, the letter claims that the Russian Church has always participated in the activities of the citizenry, especially in its peacemaking mission.[119] On the eve of the millennium, the patriarch and synod explicitly identified the Orthodox churches outside of the borders of the Soviet Union that they desired to restore to their canonical fold as part of their international peacemaking mission: the Russian Orthodox Church Abroad and the UAOC.[120] The patriarch and bishops offered a fervent prayer that the "Great Chief Shepherd" would unite them in his love in a spirit of humility and repentance.[121]

Metropolitan Filaret of the Ukrainian Exarchate also offered a sermon on the occasion of the millennium and a rather detailed speech reviewing the history of the Orthodox Church from Kyivan Rus' to the present, which echoed the themes expressed the patriarchal and synodal epistles. Filaret's brief sermon was delivered before the statue of St. Volodymyr in Kyiv.[122] In it, he declared that the baptism of Rus' "is a feast not only of the Russian Orthodox Church and out multinational homeland, but a feast of all Orthodoxy," emphasizing again the international character of the Russian Church and its stature within global Orthodoxy.[123] Filaret said that the millennium was part of the history of a great culture that became an integral part of European and world culture, manifested in the achievements of the republic. He also made it clear that people of all nations could belong to the Russian Church, including Ukrainians and Belarusians.[124]

Filaret's sermon expressed the identity of the Moscow Patriarchate that had developed during the Soviet period, particularly after World War II. According to the official narrative of the patriarchate, the Church was an active agent of peace, a mission that was in continuity with the entirety of her history. The religious narrative of the patriarchate and the Ukrainian Exarchate connects the historical events to form a pattern of the Church upholding and preserving the spiritual unity of the people even when external events threatened society. The celebration of the millennium of Rus' provided an opportunity for the patriarchate to collect and fuse its dimensions of international identity and proclaim this identity as the result of divine providence. For Orthodox Ukrainians, the millennium celebration was supposed to mark arrival of a time of peace shared with all of the other socialist republics who had been served by the patriarchate's peacekeeping mission. Filaret's sermon at St. Volodymyr's monument in Kyiv defined the Ukrainian space in the multinational ecclesial community of the Moscow Patriarchate: the only patriotism or nationalism one could legitimately speak of was the one created and cultivated by the Soviet government itself. The unity of the Slavic peoples in the Soviet Union was the restoration of an original union existing during the days of Kyivan Rus', and the healing of wrongs inflicted upon the East Slavs by their Polish, Lithuanian, and Austro-Hungarian overlords. In this narrative proclaimed by the Moscow Patriarchate and figures within the Ukrainian Exarchate, the formation of an odd pairing emerges, a symphonia of church and state manifested through active cooperation in peacemaking by the Soviet Union and the Moscow Patriarchate. However, the Soviet leaders of 1988 were granting new freedoms to religious organizations, and while Filaret could legitimately render thanks to the Soviet regime for returning a portion of the Kyiv Pecherska Lavra Monastery to the Church, the spirit of religious freedom would permit the legal restoration of the UGCC and the UAOC also. When these two church groups returned to Ukraine in 1989, they challenged the peacemaking narrative of the Moscow Patriarchate. The impact of the rebirth of the UAOC on Orthodoxy in Ukraine will be explored in the next chapter.

Conclusion

This chapter has surveyed the situation of the Orthodox Church in Ukraine after World War II. When the bishops and many of the clergy and faithful of the UAOC left Ukraine, the remaining Orthodox churches were absorbed into the Moscow Patriarchate, including those that had belonged to the Autonomous and Autocephalous churches of Ukraine and Poland. The reconfiguration of Soviet borders expanded the size and constituency of the Ukrainian Soviet Republic after the Yalta agreement of 1945, and the Orthodox and Greek-Catholic Churches of Western Ukraine now belonged to the Soviet regime. The period following the war and continuing up until the millennium celebration was a time of serious adjustment for both the Church and society. As the Soviet leaders rebuilt society and the Cold War descended upon the international community, the Soviet Union presented itself as an agent of peace within the Soviet bloc, and encouraged the Moscow Patriarchate to pursue an agenda of active engagement in world affairs.

It is crucial to note that this was the public face of the Orthodox Church during this period. The first part of the chapter discussed Soviet religious policy and its periodization: Stalin continued modest toleration of the Church, but Khrushchev reintroduced an anti-religious campaign that resulted in the closing of thousands of churches and severe restrictions on monastic life, theological education, and religious freedom, while implementing overtly anti-religious campaigns into schools. While the severity of restrictions on the Church decreased after Khrushchev's removal in 1964, the Soviet regime certainly favored the promotion of atheism in the period leading up to Gorbachev's policies of glasnost and perestroika. There were many symbols of religious repression throughout the postwar period, perhaps epitomized by the severe restrictions placed on parish rectors, who reported to a committee consisting of "lay" leaders who had been imposed upon the statute of the Moscow Patriarchate in 1961.[125] In assessing the official stance of the Moscow Patriarchate and the intentions of its narrative throughout this period, one must consider the impact these policies had on church life. One also must weigh the impact of governmental interference at the local level—the parish—and the lack of access to quality theological education confronting church leaders. From a practical perspective, it simply was not possible for the Church to prepare intellectual heavyweights who would share the forum of the public square with atheists and agnostics. Church leadership was essentially reduced to cooperating with the Soviet authorities and presiding at liturgies, with meaningful interaction with the people held at bay. The Soviet religious policy of diminishing the prestige and influence of the church on the public is hidden behind the public face of church-state symphonia in an international peacekeeping campaign.

The review of the literature shows that the closure of churches and the addition of parishes from the annexation of Western Ukraine to the Soviet Union created a disproportionate percentage of parishes in Western Ukraine in relation to the rest of the Soviet Union. This state of affairs was the result of by the 1946 L'viv council, at which Soviet officials orchestrated the liquidation of the UGCC and the "reunion" of its clergy and parishes with the Moscow Patriarchate. The reunion of the former Greek Catholics with the Orthodox Church, including those who had entered into communion with Rome after the Union of Brest in 1596, became the most important component of the postwar narrative of the Ukrainian Exarchate of the Moscow Patriarchate. The religious narrative attributed the reunion of the former Greek Catholics to the heroic actions of the Soviet army, which expelled the Nazi fascists from Soviet territory once and for all. The restoration of Orthodoxy in Ukraine became an occasion to celebrate the reunion of all Ukrainians into one Soviet republic, and the restoration of communion of all Ukrainians with their natural siblings, Russians and Belarusians. The leaders of the Ukrainian Exarchate, namely metropolitans Filaret and Nikolai and Patriarch Pimen, are the authors of this narrative. The Soviet defeat of the Nazis created an opportunity to align the historical enemies of the nations of Kyivan Rus' who had destroyed the home of the Eastern Slavic peoples. Thus, the Nazis were the last in the line of external adversaries that included Tartars, Mongols, Lithuanians, Austrians, and especially Poles. An increase in polemics resulted in the inclusion of Ukrainian nationalists such as *banderivtsi* and OUNers in the band of external adversaries to the peaceful Orthodox of the USSR. The primary ally of the adversaries of Rus' was the Roman Catholic Church. It opposed the Orthodox Church, which had sustained the spiritual unity of people who were separated by involuntary wars. The story of reunion also reinterpreted the history of the Union of Brest itself. In the revised version, the decision of the hierarchy to enter into communion with Rome was the outcome of a Polish political agenda and resulted in the eradication of Orthodox identity, which was replaced by ecclesial Latinization and ethnic Polonization. The narrative of official religious identity cultivated in the patriarchal exarchate of Ukraine continued the polemical assault of bishops representing the Moscow Patriarchate against the autocephalists during the heat of World War II. The authors of the story fused the religious with the political, as the bishops linked the autocephalists to Nazi fascism and to Christian bishops who supported Ukrainian separatism. The tale depicts the Soviet Union as the only legitimate state structure that promotes authentic Ukrainian identity. Any expression of separatism is dismissed as inspired by fascism, which was a historical anachronism (especially for Western Ukraine), but convenient for the Soviet and Orthodox victors of World War II.

The coerced reunion of the Greek Catholics with the Orthodox Church also occasioned an increased emphasis on internationalization and peacemaking. The program of Ukrainization in the Ukrainian Exarchate designed to seal the Orthodox into the multinational space of the Moscow Patriarchate was a strategy of modest internationalization. By authorizing Ukrainian-language periodicals and prayer books, along with Ukrainian pronunciation of Church Slavonic, the exarchate could claim that multiple nationalities could belong to a church governed by Moscow. Moscow's patronage of the churches of Poland, Czechoslovakia, Japan, and America furthered the internationalization campaign of the Moscow Patriarchate, along with its peacemaking mission, especially since the United States was the primary country engaging the USSR in the Cold War and nuclear armament. The success of the Moscow Patriarchate in obtaining authority over the Orthodox churches of socialist countries gave it the courage to set its eyes on the ecclesial prizes outside of the USSR: ROCOR and the UAOC. The resolutions of the local council of the patriarchate in 1971 charged Patriarch Pimen and the Holy Synod with the task of creating peace with these churches and returning them to the bosom of the canonical church of Moscow. Patriarch Pimen and the synod of bishops made a fervent appeal for the reunion of the churches outside the USSR with the patriarchate in preparation for the celebration of the millennium in a message that was considerably warmer and more charitable than the pattern of communications concerning ROCOR and the UAOC. Historically, one could argue that the religious narrative claimed that the former Greek Catholics were perfectly at peace in their new home, and that the Orthodox Church's mission of peacebuilding had not only reunited Greek Catholics with Orthodox and improved international ecumenical relations, but had also definitively resolved any feelings of bitterness between Russians and Ukrainians. The Greek Catholics who had annulled their union with Rome and returned to Orthodoxy through the 1946 L'viv council were thus the poster children for the patriarchate's campaign of internationalization and peacemaking.

The official narratives of the patriarchate and exarchate during this period are significant for three reasons. First, the official narrative of the exarchate does not represent the reality of the "church within a church," as demonstrated by Shlikhta's examination of the subaltern strategy of retaining ecclesial and national distinctiveness within the exarchate. Shlikhta presents examples of the people who have embraced the necessity of hybrid identity, resisting state policies imposed on the Church as loyal Soviet and Orthodox citizens without relinquishing their true, inner identities. This strategy permeates the entirety of the Church; in addition to laity, hierarchs also said one thing publicly while engaging local plenipotentiaries in battle quietly, as a matter of survival. In principle, the program of internationalization adopted by the Moscow Patriarchate would have accommodated Ukrainian distinctiveness within the Church. The reemergence and rapid rise to popularity of the UGCC and UAOC in 1989 demonstrates the fatal flaw of the internationalization program: it could never tolerate an "otherness" rooted in ecclesial and national independence, especially when postwar Soviet policy privileged Russian nationality.[126] Second, the international campaign of the patriarchate and its peacemaking mission would become the thematic foundations for the *Russkii mir* ideology expounded by Moscow patriarch Kirill in the twenty-first century. In other words, the official ideology of the Moscow Patriarchate during the postwar period has continued to shape the policies and ideology of the contemporary Moscow Patriarchate, which includes the paradox of cultural and national plurality that has no tolerance for Ukrainian national and ecclesial distinctiveness.

In summary, the official religious identity of the Orthodox in Ukraine during the Soviet period took on several new markers because of the religious narrative coauthored by Soviet leaders and representatives of the patriarchate and its Ukrainian Exarchate. The narrative stated that the Orthodox in Ukraine had restored unity with the Russians (symbolized by the unity of Kyiv and Moscow) and were safe and sound in a multinational patriarchate, and that they executed their charge of international peacekeeping and patriotic service to the Soviet homeland with enthusiasm. Perhaps most importantly, it claimed that the Orthodox Ukrainians had permanently excised all Latin and Polish elements from their religious identities and had relinquished nationalism and aspirations for an independent and democratic Ukrainian republic in favor of the utopian church-state symphonia epitomized by the relationship between the Soviet Union and the Moscow Patriarchate. The religious narrative communicates a political theology of the Cold War era supported by the foundations of the Great Patriotic War and the 1946 L'viv council, a theology depicting the Ukrainian Exarchate as an egalitarian and multinational church that seeks peace while contributing to a Soviet socialist society. The Moscow Patriarchate's political theology of the Soviet period demonstrated its new prestige in the international arena and advocacy for other Orthodox churches. Ecclesiologically, the Moscow Patriarchate sought to replace the ministry typically exercised by the Ecumenical Patriarchate by being the first among equals in the autocephalous churches.

This survey of Soviet religious policy and its restrictions on freedoms demonstrates that there were many dissidents in the ranks of the clergy and laity; some of them were imprisoned and punished for speaking out, whereas others learned how to "speak Bolshevik" and struggle against Soviet policies as loyal and faithful citizens. Persecution of religious dissidents adds a new identity marker to Orthodoxy in Ukraine during this period: it was persecuted, silenced, and strictly controlled by the Soviet officials. Furthermore, the religious narrative includes instances of angry dismissal of Ukrainian religious leaders outside of the Soviet Union who challenged the legitimacy of the 1946 L'viv council and pressured Soviet leaders to legalize the UGCC and the UAOC. Their return to Soviet Ukraine in 1989 not only challenged the political theology communicated by the patriarchate and the Ukrainian Exarchate, but it marked the revelation of the inner identities of those who belonged to Shlikhta's notion of the "church within the church." The resurgent UGCC and UAOC offered a challenge and alternative to the patriarchate's claims that it was tolerant, multinational, and peaceful.

5

Orthodoxy in Ukraine: The Late and Post-Soviet Period (1989–2016)

THIS PENULTIMATE CHAPTER EXAMINES THE turbulent period of 1989–2016 in the Orthodox churches of Ukraine. It begins with the rebirth of the 1989 UAOC and the creation of the Kyivan Patriarchate (KP) in 1992. It discusses how public religious identity evolved within the KP with special attention to its response to political crises in Ukraine, especially the Euromaidan, Crimean annexation, and war in Eastern Ukraine, and its attempts to resolve the increased air of illegitimacy attributed to Patriarch Filaret (Denysenko). It explores the UOC-MP's transition from a patriarchal exarchate to a church with an ambiguous canonical status of broad autonomy, with special attention to internal tensions caused by the return of Ukrainization. By the end of the chapter, it will have become clear that the opposing Orthodox churches in Ukraine have clung to their core public identities originally forged in 1921, but have also cross-pollinated, so that the primary features of public religious identity are the only real marks of distinction between the pro-Ukrainian, pro-autocephaly Orthodox and the Orthodox who remain within the MP.

The End of the Soviet Period and the Reconfiguration of Orthodox Churches in Ukraine

The Return of the Ukrainian Autocephalous Orthodox Church

The third rebirth of the 1989 UAOC was similar to its two predecessors in 1921 and 1942 in the identity markers defining the movement. Seizing the openness and freedoms generated by Gorbachev's policies of glasnost and perestroika, the Ukrainians who left the patriarchal exarchate in Lviv embraced a platform of Ukrainization.[1] In 1989, the parish of Saints Peter and Paul in Lviv, shepherded by the priest Volodymyr Jarema, officially left the exarchate and inaugurated the third rebirth of the Autocephalous Church (1989 UAOC).[2] Among the initial changes enacted by the new church was the use of vernacular Ukrainian in the liturgy. The third Ukrainian cohort maintained the course established by the second group by aligning themselves with the bishop of Zhytomyr, Ioan (Bodnarchuk), who had belonged to the MP. Openly patriotic, Bishop Ioan quickly assumed the mantle of leadership among the autocephalous Orthodox in Western Ukraine.[3] By November of 1990, a fairly sizable autocephalous church had been organized and had elected and enthroned a patriarch, Metropolitan Mstyslav (Skrypnyk) of the United States.[4] The pace of growth in the third cohort followed the pattern of its two predecessors: parishes began to leave the exarchate and join the Autocephalous Church particularly in Western Ukraine, and it grew quickly. The situation of the 1989 UAOC represents a new element in the history of the movement for autocephaly among Orthodox Ukrainians: L'viv was the center of the movement, a new occurrence since Kyiv and Lutsk were the centers of the first two movements, and a bit surprising given the concurrent return from the catacombs of the Greek-Catholic Church.[5] The coincidence of Greek Catholic and Orthodox renewal in Western Ukraine testifies to the region's character as the new primary location of Ukrainian national identity in the native country; but it also demonstrates the desire of a critical mass of Ukrainians to belong to an Orthodox Church of Ukraine, governed by neither Rome nor Moscow.[6]

The second primary identity marker of the 1989 UAOC was its deliberate attempt to designate itself as the legitimate successor of the previous autocephalous churches. As mentioned earlier, the Church in the United States attempted to rehabilitate the image of the 1921 UAOC, which was symbolized by the literature written during the erection of St. Andrew's Memorial Church in Bound Brook and the establishment of a permanent memorial to Metropolitan Vasil (Lypkivs'kyi) on the property of the church headquarters. The American Church assumed a canonical path by arranging for the canonical correction of Metropolitan John Teodorovych's ordination in 1949, and Teodorovych served as a link between the divergent paths of the first and second autocephalous cohorts.[7] Essentially, the leaders of the American Church symbolized the fusion of the two autocephalous movements in Ukraine. They retained the best identity markers of the 1921 UAOC: Ukrainization, the use of liturgical Ukrainian, and select elements of the *sobornopravnist'* that characterized the 1921 UAOC, while reintegrating the episcopate into the Church, leading her in worship and administering her affairs in cooperation with the people. Metropolitan Mstyslav (Skrypnyk)'s advocacy of Vasyl Romaniuk symbolized the trust of an unknown number of Ukrainians in the diaspora church to restore the Autocephalous Church to her legal place in Soviet Ukraine. The 1989 UAOC essentially absrobed all of the identity markers of the previous manifestations of the UAOC when she recognized Mstyslav as the most senior leader and central figure of the global Ukrainian autocephalous movement.

The 1989 UAOC completed the process of transferring the center of Ukrainian autocephaly from Bound Brook, New Jersey back to Kyiv when it elected the ninety-year-old American prelate as the first Orthodox patriarch of Kyiv at a council held in 1989. The election of Mstyslav as patriarch honored the decades he devoted to promoting the Ukrainian Church and symbolized the Church's reception of the enormous legacy carried by Mstyslav. When the 1989 UAOC enthroned Mstyslav as its first patriarch in St. Sophia Cathedral in Kyiv in November of 1990, the stage was set for the former patterns to occur for a third time in Ukraine. In all three instances of the birth and rebirth of an autocephalous church in modernity, the Ukrainian nation was on the verge of sovereignty. In the previous two instances, national independence was brief (in 1919) and illusory (during World War II). In November 1990, Ukraine was on the verge of independence and statehood the Soviet Union was cracking and as the state and political apparatuses shook and trembled, the notion of a living, national, autocephalous church was quickly revived. In this third instance, the center of the movement was in Western Ukraine, the region that had been subject to the mild program of Ukrainization employed by the exarchate to foster the integration of former Greek Catholics into the patriarchate following the pseudo-council of 1946. The stage appeared to be set for a concurrent transition from the Soviet period to a new, independent republic of Ukraine accompanied by an authentically Ukrainian Orthodox Church.

Through the conciliar decision to elect a patriarch of Kyiv, the 1989 UAOC added a new feature to Ukrainian Orthodox public religious identity designed to strengthen her canonical legitimacy. Historically, Kyiv had always been a metropolia, not a patriarchate, and neither of the two preceding autocephalous movements had developed strategies for the creation of a patriarchate of Kyiv. In retrospect, the cohorts sought the restoration of Kyiv's heritage as a metropolia; the only canonical change they desired was autocephalous status, which is both possible and legitimate for a metropolia within global Orthodoxy. By enthroning Mstyslav as patriarch and not metropolitan of Kyiv, the Autocephalous Church attempted to elevate its prestige among Orthodox churches by declaring itself the equal of the patriarchate in Moscow, at least in name. The decision to elevate the 1989 UAOC from a metropolia to a patriarchate was taken up at the June 5–6, 1990, Ukrainian Council in L'viv.[8] Larysa Lokhvytska, who attended the council, reported that the bishops wanted to strengthen the authority of the Ukrainian Church by refusing to repeat the mistakes of the past.[9]

Reports from the council indicated that a consensus emerged among the hierarchy and clergy at the council of the 1989 UAOC on the necessity of a patriarchate.[10] Clearly, the council desired to show that the 1989 UAOC was not a

spontaneous religious movement, but the continuation of the organic development of autocephaly in Ukraine. One could also argue that Kyiv was superior to
Moscow on account of Kyiv's privileged place in the narrative of the history of
Orthodoxy in Rus'; establishing an Orthodox patriarchate in Kyiv was a strategy
for solidifying a public religious identity rooted in antiquity and prestige. The
1989 UAOC adopted a statute at the June 1990 council that refers to its antiquity
and its ministry of bearing witness to the 1921 and 1942 churches. First, in terms
of its relationship to global Orthodoxy, the UAOC defined itself as a "local part"
of the church founded by the patriarchate of Constantinople:

> The Ukrainian Autocephalous Orthodox Church (henceforth UAOC) is a local
> part of the one, holy, Catholic and Apostolic Church, whose head is our Lord Jesus
> Christ. The UAOC is equal in rights with all of the local Orthodox Churches and
> is independent from other local Churches in her organization and governance. The
> UAOC recognizes her special relationship with the Ecumenical Constantinopolitan
> Mother Church, from whom Rus'-Ukraine entered the Catholic Apostolic Church
> of Christ. . . . The UAOC recognizes the special authority in matters of faith of the
> Ecumenical patriarch of Constantinople.[11]

In emphasizing the special authority of the Ecumenical Patriarchate, the 1989
UAOC privileged the identity of the 1942 UAOC by restoring Constantinople as
the maternal patron of the Church. This action was a deviation from the heritage
of the 1921 UAOC, which consistently insisted on the authority of its own independence without special reference to Constantinople.

The 1989 UAOC also explicitly mentions *sobornopravnist'* as its method of
ministry in the world.[12] The UAOC attempted to balance Orthodoxy's hierarchical structure with the principle of conciliarity by designating the local council
and Bishops' council as highest authoritative organs of the church, with the patriarchal council functioning as the governing structure in between councils.[13] At
each level of the church's structure, a council headed by the appropriate member
of the clergy leads the ministry. In summary, the UAOC returned to Ukraine in
1989 and defined itself as the church established by Constantinople, which had
matured into a patriarchate without relinquishing the importance of conciliarity
in church life.

The 1989 UAOC's aspiration to transition from a vassal nation and enslaved
church to a sovereign republic and united, independent church never came to fruition. The 1989 UAOC essentially peaked in the brief period between Mstyslav's
election and enthronization and the proclamation and achievement of Ukraine's
independence on August 24, 1991. One the one hand, while Mstyslav was a living symbol who bore all of the essential elements of a living, legitimate Orthodox

Church that was simultaneously Ukrainian and canonical, his advanced age, poor health, and American affiliation left him ill-equipped to lead the 1989 UAOC beyond the euphoria of its liberation from the MP. On the other hand, some credit Mstyslav with rekindling church life in Ukraine. For example, Frank Sysyn attributes the rapid growth of the Autocephalous Church in 1990 to Mstyslav's efforts in traveling throughout Ukraine and encouraging pastors to participate in civic life.[14]

The Moscow Patriarchate responded to the emergence of the 1989 UAOC by deposing Bishop Ioan (Bodnarchuk) from holy orders and declaring all of his episcopal activities to be invalid.[15] The patriarchate depicted the 1989 UAOC as continuing the ecclesial illegitimacy of the 1942 UAOC that had previously condemned by the patriarchate. After referring to Metropolitan Mstyslav's elevation of Bishop Ioan to archbishop, the Russian synod described the 1942 UAOC as unrecognized, condemned, and uncanonical.[16]

Particularly noteworthy in the Russian synod's condemnation of the new movement was the charge that Bishop Ioan had led the Church into schism.[17] The MP dismissed the UAOC's restoration of apostolic succession; the narratives of history had aligned separation on national lines with the absence of canonical legitimacy. From the MP's perspective, the 1989 UAOC was playing the same old song.

When the autocephalists quickly gained the support of pro-Ukrainian groups, including a portion of the Ukrainian intelligentsia, the exarchate changed its strategy by discarding exarchal status and becoming instead a local church within the MP that had broad privileges of autonomy.[18] The synod of the Moscow Patriarchate bestowed this new canonical status on the metropolia in October of 1990.[19] In explaining the significance of this canonical change to the Ukrainian press on October 29, 1990, Metropolitan Filaret (Denysenko) said that "we are returning to the position that existed in the Kyivan Metropolia before its reunion with the Moscow Patriarchate. Then, the metropolitan of Kyiv was elected by the council of bishops of the Ukrainian Metropolia, confirmed initially by the Constantinopolitan patriarchs, and after 1686, by the patriarch of Moscow."[20] In response to a reporter's question about the 1989 UAOC's claim to be the legitimate heir of the Kyivan Metropolia, Filaret said that the 1989 UAOC is altogether "uncanonical," had no relationship of any kind with the Kyivan Metropolia or any other Orthodox churches, and that "the UAOC is truly independent, but independent from all of Orthodoxy."[21] Filaret sealed the fate of the 1989 UAOC by using the refusal of the Ukrainian Church in Canada to concelebrate with the 1989 UAOC as proof of the UAOC's ecclesial illegitimacy.[22] Emboldened by the privileges of autonomy the MP granted to his church, Filaret claimed that the Kyivan Metropolia was the church of the Zaporizhian Cossacks who had historically opposed the Unia and the advance of the Catholic Church, and that "the independence in administration granted to the Ukrainian Orthodox Church will help us to defend our holy faith."[23] In response to a question about the language to be used for the liturgy, Filaret responded that the metropolia would retain Slavonic and permit Ukrainians to select their own pronunciation.[24] He added that "the Ukrainian Orthodox Church is the national Ukrainian Church, but she is constituted from several nationalities. She leads those who turn to her for salvation. The Church is supposed to save peoples' souls. If she does not do this, then she is not a church, but an ordinary political or community organization. Our church does not interfere in politics, because her mission is the salvation of souls."[25] In this statement, Filaret contrasted the metropolia's traditional stance as a multinational and apolitical church with the 1989 UAOC as a church armed with a particular political agenda. The metropolia also published the appeal of the Ukrainian episcopate to the patriarch of Moscow requesting autonomy, as a way of counteracting the challenges posed by "extremists" of the UGCC in Western Ukraine.[26] The appeal included an excerpt on the nature of the transformed metropolia from the resolutions of the June Hierarchical Council of the Russian Church: "Our multinational church blesses the national-cultural rebirth of nations that belong to her, but casts aside chauvinism, separatism, and nationalistic enmity."[27]

Thus, the metropolia's response to the emergence and organization of the 1989 UAOC and to the transformed religious landscape of Ukraine was swift and consistent with the tactics that had been employed throughout the modern history of the Orthodox Church in Ukraine. Only the patriarchal church was canonically legitimate and the rightful heir of the historical Kyivan Metropolia. The statements made by the patriarchate and the metropolia described the transformation of the metropolia's canonical status as consistent with the patriarchate's identity as a peacemaking church that honored diversity and discouraged the perils of nationalism. In this vein, the decision to grant broader autonomy to the Kyivan Metropolia continued the narrative crafted by the patriarchate for the Ukrainian Exarchate during the Cold War. In both instances, the actions taken by the Moscow Patriarchate were in response to Ukrainian self-identity among Orthodox and Greek Catholics primarily in Western Ukraine.

More troubling for the 1989 UAOC was its inability to adjust to the inner turmoil of the church.[28] While the election of Mstyslav as patriarch was symbolic, he lacked the connections and inner workings of the people of his church to effectively lead it. Particularly problematic was the typical problem of dissatisfaction among the ranks. The 1989 UAOC rapidly populated the ranks of their episcopate through ordination, but loyalty to Mstyslav was absent except among the bishops in America he had cultivated.[29] Other leading bishops had their own ideas on the path of the church, especially Ioan (Bodnarchuk), who returned to the MP through repentance in 1992.[30] Furthermore, Mstyslav's advanced age and

FIGURE 4. Painting of Patriarch Mstyslav (Skrypnyk) at L'viv Orthodox Theological Academy (UOC-KP). Photo by Nicholas Denysenko.

continued leadership of the Church in America he had carefully cultivated since 1950 kept him away from Kyiv and he was often too ill to lead.

The convergence of these factors created a leadership vacuum and an opportunity for a new leader to replace Mstyslav. Even though the exarchate in Ukraine
changed its name and increased its autonomy, the 1989 UAOC continued to capture the attention of people attuned to a combined revival of nation and church.
In 1991, Metropolitan Filaret formally requested canonical autocephaly for the
Orthodox Church in Ukraine with the support of the majority of the bishops of his
church, although a small but vocal minority were opposed. Metropolitan Filaret
engaged in a fierce battle on autocephaly with the patriarchate and his own bishops in late 1991 and early 1992 that led to his forced retirement, and eventually
his suspension, deposition, and anathematization from the MP in 1997.[31] Filaret
seized the opportunity created by the leadership vacuum to join a small part of
the former exarchate to the 1989 UAOC during a council in June of 1992. The
council resulted in a schism among the autocephalists, as the majority embraced
Filaret and appointed him as deputy patriarch to Mstyslav, while Mstyslav himself, absent from the council, denounced its decisions, instructed Filaret to follow
the orders given him by the MP, and remained within the Autocephalous Church.

After Mstyslav's death, the priest Volodymyr Jarema, who was one of the chief
ideologues and organizers of the 1989 UAOC, received monastic tonsure on
August 23, 1993, with the name Dmitry.[32] Archimandrite Dmitry was ordained
bishop of Pereiaslav and Sicheslav on September 5, 1993, elected as patriarch
of the second council of the UAOC on September 7, 1993, and enthroned on
October 14, 1993. Jarema's path from populist priest to patriarch of the UAOC
marks yet another example of a member of the lower clergy ascending through
the ranks to occupy the highest office in his church. Patriarch Dmitry was an
active leader and a creative and insightful theologian, but he lacked Metropolitan
Filaret's political connections and experience. From the end of Mstyslav's brief
tenure as patriarch of the Autocephalous Church through Dmitry's tenure and
death in February 2000, the KP grew while the UAOC shrank and splintered yet
again. After Dmitry's death, the Autocephalous Church relinquished its patriarchal ambitions in order to resolve the schism of the Orthodox Church in Ukraine.
In 1994, Patriarch Dmitry, Bishop Ihor (Isichenko), and Evhen Sverstyuk published a thoughtful reflection on the state of the Orthodox Church in Ukraine in
the immediate post-Soviet period.[33] Their reflection, which came relatively soon
after the June 1992 council that resulted in the emergence of the UOC-KP, emphasized the unique features of the identity of the original 1989 UAOC. Dmitry,
Ihor, and Sverstyuk claimed that the Russian Church had established a pattern
of aggression against Orthodox Ukrainians from the tsarist synodal era through
Sergianism, all on the basis of "canonicity."[34] The authors claimed that Patriarch
Mstyslav's inauguration of the 1989 UAOC opened the doors of the church to
the "intelligentsia, young people, and progressive politicians," but that graduates

of the "old seminaries" interrupted the process, resulting in the creation of the UOC-KP, which aspired to become Ukraine's state church.[35] Dmitry, Ihor, and Sverstyuk suggested that a new generation of clergy was needed to foster reconciliation among the Orthodox, and they proposed a phase of preparation for an all-Ukrainian church council that would result in one, unified church.[36] The proposal included the creation of two interchurch councils, one in preparation for the council, and also called for the renewal of the Eucharistic union of all Orthodox in Ukraine.[37] This proposal had the same fate as many from this period: it was essentially ignored. As Patriarch Dmitry prepared for his death, he instructed his fellow bishops and the patriarchal council of the UAOC to work toward the unification of the Orthodox churches in Ukraine with the diaspora churches under the EP.[38]

Following Patriarch Dmitry's death, the UAOC sought to strengthen its connections with the Ecumenical Patriarchate by essentially placing itself under the jurisdiction of the UOC-USA, which was then led by Metropolitan Constantine. The UAOC officially adopted commemoration of Metropolitan Constantine on February 12, 2000.[39] The UAOC endured yet another division in 2002, as Archbishop Ihor (Isichenko) of Kharkiv refused Metropolitan Mefodii's proposition that the UAOC stop commemorating Metropolitan Constantine (Buggan) as its primate, thus changing its canonical status.[40] The UAOC's orbit was limited to Western Ukraine and a handful of eparchies. Despite its small size, the UAOC would become significant again through a series of negotiations for a merger with the KP.

The third rebirth of the Autocephalous Church in Ukraine included the retention of existing identity markers such as Ukrainization, the use of the Ukrainian language, the notion of an autocephalous church existing in a sovereign state, and some elements of popular governance. By associating with the diaspora church and electing its metropolitan as patriarch, the Autocephalous Church added new identity markers. First, the UAOC defined itself as canonical on the basis of its election of Metropolitan Mstyslav as its leader. Second, the Autocephalous Church declared itself a patriarchate, a strategy designed to communicate its antiquity, authority, and prestige to the Ukrainian people and global Orthodoxy. Internal divisions and a lack of political finesse extinguished the dream of this church, though it retained a modest following in Western Ukraine. But the emergence of the Autocephalous Church is significant for these reasons in addition to those already mentioned above: it grew rapidly during the concurrent restoration of the UGCC in the same region, illustrating that there was a critical mass of people who identified themselves with the Autocephalous Church's public religious identity; its creation of a patriarchate became a permanent fixture with the establishment of the KP; and its claims to canonical legitimacy failed to persuade the exarchate and the churches of global Orthodoxy to receive it as an equal. This final point on canonical legitimacy demonstrates the resilience of the idea of ecclesial illegitimacy born in the 1921 cohort and passed on to the successive autocephalous bodies through featured identity markers.[41]

The Metropolia, Autonomy, and Autocephaly: From Exarchate to Local Church

During the turbulence of the late-Soviet period, the patriarchal exarchate in Ukraine endured its own transition, both in name and in its internal approach to autocephaly. The exarchate had largely dismissed the aspirations of the autocephalous groups on account of their canonical illegitimacy, manifest most clearly by the letter of Patriarch Pimen to Patriarch Athenagoras complaining of the Ecumenical Patriarchate's willingness to dialogue with diaspora Ukrainians.[42] The Orthodox of the patriarchal exarchate continued to cultivate the perspective established in 1917–1918: Ukrainians share one common church and patriarch with Russians, just as they share the same history and legacy. Separation from the Church would serve to divide the Ukrainian and Russian peoples.

In the early twentieth century, the synod in Ukraine and the Moscow patriarch established a pattern of assuaging Ukrainian complaints by offering a platform for modest Ukrainization within the Ukrainian Church and granting the it autonomy. In October 1990 the MP altered the Church's canonical status, granting it broad privileges of autonomy and changing the title of the church's head from metropolitan of Kyiv and Halych to metropolitan of Kyiv and all Ukraine. The metropolitan was also saluted as "his beatitude," had the right to wear two panagias, and held a permanent seat on the Holy Synod of the patriarchate, which made him the most senior hierarch after the patriarch.[43] At this point, the Church in Ukraine was no longer an exarchate and came to be known as the 'Ukrainian Orthodox Church," though its unofficial title was "Ukrainian Orthodox Church—MP." The Ukrainian Church received the canonical privilege of convoking its own synods, including local councils; electing and consecrating bishops; canonizing saints, and revising liturgical rites.[44] All of these pastoral activities are marks of autocephalous local churches; the primary exception is that the patriarch of Moscow reserved the right to confirm the bishops elected by the synod.

Before proceeding further, it is important to note that these developments were not particularly original. In fact, the patriarchate's decision to grant Ukraine privileges of broad autonomy merely restored the status of the Ukrainian Church affirmed by the MP in 1918 and Patriarch Tikhon in 1922, and restored by the council of bishops of the Autonomous Church at Pochaiv in 1941. Hyacinthe Destivelle's study of the Moscow Council adds that the metropolitan of Kyiv had special privileges that honored Kyiv as the city-state in which Orthodoxy originated in Rus'.[45] The Kyivan metropolitan was the permanent senior bishop of the patriarchal synod and his privileges included the right to consecrate chrism for the Church in Ukraine, a liturgical rite traditionally reserved for the first bishop of an autocephalous Orthodox church.[46] The Moscow Council had ruled that all decisions of the patriarchate would be applied to the life of the Church in Ukraine, a notable limit on its internal freedom.[47] Therefore, the decisions of the patriarchate in 1990 largely restored the structure of the church legislated by the Moscow Council in 1918.

One difference in the new status of the Ukrainian church was its new name. With the removal of vocabulary referring to the exarchate, the church was now named "Ukrainian Orthodox Church": the use of "Ukrainian" as an adjective suggested that the former exarchate of the Moscow patriarchate had become Ukrainian.[48] The change in the name of the Church in Ukraine bore the appearance of transitioning to a decidedly more Ukrainian character, though translating this quality to the actual life of the church would be challenging given its legacy of deeply embedded Russification.

The metropolia's decision to formally request autocephaly from Moscow in April 1992 was motivated by the Ukrainians' refusal to accept the transformation of the former exarchate as an authentic act of progressive Ukrainization. The new canonical status, name change, and elevated prestige of the metropolitan of Kyiv failed to diminish the fervor of the autocephalous movement in Ukraine. Despite the flaws within the Autocephalous Church discussed above, it became clear rather quickly that maintaining the ecclesial status quo would prove to be an ineffective strategy for the exarchate.[49]

Metropolitan Filaret (Denysenko) began an internal process to acquire canonical autocephaly from Moscow for the Ukrainian Church in late 1990 and into 1991.[50] He needed to persuade his episcopate to reach the consensus needed to formally request autocephaly from the patriarchate in April of 1992. Despite the patriarchate's resistance to Ukrainian autocephaly, it would have been difficult to justify the denial of a request on behalf of a unanimous episcopate, which would represent the hypothetical unanimity within the church itself from an ecclesiological perspective. Controversy surrounded the Ukrainian episcopate's petition for complete canonical autocephaly from Moscow, and the appeal of the Ukrainian episcopate issued to Patriarch Alexy II and the Holy Synod of the Russian Orthodox Church captures the intense political atmosphere surrounding the possibility of autocephaly for the metropolia.[51] In the appeal, the Ukrainian bishops complained that "certain forces" had planted discord among Ukrainian monks, clergy, and laity by spreading lies and misinformation about Metropolitan Filaret.[52] The bishops noted that an accusation was made at the December 1991 meeting of the Russian Holy Synod that the Ukrainian episcopate's petition for autocephaly "was made because of pressure

from the state, as if not all of the Ukrainian hierarchs who had signed the documents of the council agreed with its decisions."[53] The Ukrainian bishops also
complained that some hierarchs of the Russian church expressed their desire
to hold a church referendum on the question of canonical independence for
Ukraine, which was unknown to both the histories of the ancient church and
the Russian Church.[54] Metropolitan Agafangel (Savvin) was allegedly one of the
forces opposing the Ukrainian metropolia's path to autocephaly, as Archbishop
Feodosiy of Vinnytsia put forth a formal complaint about Agafangel's refusal to
leave the Vinnytsia eparchy, threatened to take his eparchy directly under the
jurisdiction of Moscow, and referred to the metropolia as "illegal, schismatic,
"Filarestistic," and without grace.[55]

Despite the obvious opposition to Ukrainian autocephaly in Moscow and
within the ranks of his own episcopate, Filaret almost accomplished this objective,
and fell just short, with three bishops opposing autocephaly when he formally
requested it on behalf of the Ukrainian Church in Moscow at the meeting of the
Ukrainian Bishops' synod in April of 1992.[56] Unfortunately for Filaret, the three
bishops opposing him did so vigorously. One of these bishops was Bishop Onufry
(Berezovsky), who gathered a small group of protesters outside of the synodal
meeting in Moscow for a public demonstration against autocephaly.

The subsequent series of events shaped the future of the ecclesial landscape in
Ukraine. First, the Moscow synod rejected the appeal for autocephaly, with the
possibility of deferring it to further deliberation at a future synodal convocation.
Second, Filaret's change of mind and heart led to his departure from the exarchate. As a longtime supporter of the notion of a single, united Church, Filaret's
strategic shift resulted in an avalanche of criticism from within his church and
outside of it. Filaret had vast international experience as an ecumenical officer
within the patriarchate, and traveled to the West frequently. His change of position within the exarchate elicited a response from his opponents, who unleashed
several personal attacks against him. Filaret was accused of abrogating his monastic vows and keeping a wife and children; he was also accused of belonging to a
group of bishops within the church who had cooperated with Soviet authorities
"even though they had certain reservations."[57]

The April 1992 Moscow council charged Filaret with leading the Church
toward schism, referring to conflicts between Filaret and select Ukrainian bishops as support for the accusation.[58] The series of events beginning at the April
Council can only be described as bizarre. The council asked Filaret to resign from
his post as patriarchal exarch and he agreed, with the stipulation that he be permitted to serve at a cathedral within the Ukrainian Church.[59] But when Filaret
returned to Kyiv from the council, he refused to resign, claiming that his promise in Moscow was made under duress and that he had endured a "Golgotha."[60]

Serhii Plokhy's account of the Moscow-Kyiv controversy surrounding Filaret also provides precious information on the roles played by Filaret's opponents. Plokhy identifies Bishop Onufry (Berezovsky) as the bishop who "demonstrated the most active opposition."[61] Filaret, annoyed with the refusal of Onufry, Bishop Serhii, and Bishop Alipit to join him in pursuing autocephaly, removed them from their eparchies and reassigned them after the Ukrainian synod's adoption of a resolution requesting autocephaly.[62] Plokhy suggests that Bishop Onufry was a central figure in seeking Filaret's ouster; one rumor even suggested that Onufry was prepared to establish a separate metropolitanate in Bukovyna.[63]

Leaving some of the internal drama aside, the following facts concerning the pivotal month of April 1992 are clear: Filaret galvanized a majority of the Ukrainian bishops to support autocephaly, but lacked absolute unanimity; rumors circulated about Filaret's moral improprieties and KGB affiliation; the April Council rejected the petition for autocephaly and accused Filaret of fomenting schism; Filaret promised to resign, but reneged upon returning to Kyiv. Filaret's battle with the MP had two results: he separated from the patriarchate, and ended up as the primary figure and eventually leader of the new KP. The Moscow Patriarchate instructed the Ukrainian episcopate to convene a hierarchical synod to elect a new primate, and a council was held in Kharkiv on May 27, 1992, resulting in the election of Metropolitan Volodymyr (Sabodan) as the primate of the metropolia. He led the metropolia during a period of modest internal Ukrainization while retaining steadfast loyalty to the MP.

In 2012, Metropolitan Volodymyr reflected on the episodes of 1990–1991 that shaped the next stage of post-Soviet history in the Orthodox churches of Ukraine in his report on the twentieth anniversary of the hierarchical council in Kharkiv.[64] He noted that the metropolia's revised statute granted its primate unprecedented authority in organizing committees and implementing initiatives. For example, the statute authorized the metropolitan of Kyiv (then Filaret) to populate the synod with five bishops from the episcopate, including the metropolitan himself.[65] According to Metropolitan Volodymyr, "the primate obtained the possibility to centralize truly limitless authority in his hands."[66] Metropolitan Volodymyr asserted that Metropolitan Filaret "began to force the idea of complete independence [autocephaly] for the Ukrainian Church" following the declaration of Ukraine's independence in 1991.[67] Volodymyr attributed the metropolia's internal movement toward autocephaly to Metropolitan Filaret's vision for the church's future, arguing that Filaret forsook the possibility of "engaging open fraternal discussion" in the church on the possibility of autocephaly.[68] As for the 1992 hierarchical council in Kharkiv, Metropolitan Volodymyr reported that it included seventeen bishops and that only Metropolitan Filaret and Bishop Yakiv (Panchuk) of Pochaiv refused to participate.[69]

Metropolitan Volodymyr's account of the crucial period of 1990–1992 is in direct contrast with that of Filaret. Volodymyr claimed that Filaret abused his power and alienated his own bishops on account of his ambitions for the church; Filaret claimed that Moscow created a false and slanderous campaign designed to discredit him and attempted to coerce him into retirement. Whatever the case, these events resulted in Filaret's departure as primate of the metropolia and decision to join the UAOC. Furthermore, the Kharkiv council of May 1992 would emerge as a benchmark of canonical legitimacy for both the MP and the KP. The MP would come to hail the 1992 Kharkiv council as inaugurating a period of peace within the metropolia, whereas the KP rejected the Kharkiv council as uncanonical, since it was convened without the blessing and initiative of the metropolitan of Kyiv.

New elements emerged that contributed to the shaping of the approach to autocephaly of both the metropolia and the KP during this period. First, under Filaret, the metropolia requested autocephaly after Ukraine had attained sovereignty and achieved independence. Ukrainian president Leonid Kravchuk steadfastly supported Filaret during Filaret's dispute with Moscow. Plokhy notes the irony of this support: "The Ukrainian government and most leaders of the opposition in parliament unquestioningly supported Filaret in order to defend autocephaly, even though his character not only threw a shadow on the cause but also complicated it immensely."[70] Plokhy was referring to the assumption that national sovereignty would create ecclesial autocephaly, but a parallel church and state independence had never occurred simultaneously in Ukrainian history.[71] One preceded the other, and in most cases, aspirations for a Ukrainian state encouraged autocephalous church movements.

With Metropolitan Volodymyr in place and a government with mixed political loyalties, the MP in Ukraine continued to sing the refrain of canonical legitimacy and dismiss the claims of the KP. One of the most significant symbols of the MP's loyalty to Moscow during this period was its withdrawal of the official petition for autocephaly to the MP in 1996.[72] This decision demonstrates the precarious position of the metropolia as a church transcending the borders of Russia and Ukraine. The withdrawal of autocephaly seemingly appeased Russian constituencies within the metropolia, but it caused further separation with supporters of Ukrainian independence as well. The metropolia would find its future path to be a challenge in pastorally negotiating these two opposing approaches, namely remaining Ukraine's authentically local church while maintaining close connections with and subservience to Moscow.[73]

The following developments that occurred under the leadership of Metropolitan Volodymyr were particularly important. First, to be clear, the Ukrainian Metropolia remained faithful to the MP under Volodymyr's leadership. There were never any serious signs of a separation of the metropolia from Moscow. Volodymyr, however, initiated modest Ukrainization for parishes that desired it. Those desiring to liturgize in Ukrainian could do so with reference to the synodal decision of 1921, where a two-thirds majority could receive permission to celebrate the liturgy in Ukrainian. While liturgical Ukrainian remains limited in the metropolia, individual eparchies have commenced the process of translating the liturgy into vernacular Ukrainian. However one assesses the impact, or lack thereof, of this development, it is a significant step toward offering a real response to the possibility of internal Ukrainization. Second, the metropolia capitalized on its status as a church with broad privileges of autonomy and began to define itself as the local Orthodox Church in Ukraine. Such a definition did not occur on the initiative of the metropolia, but in response to assertive claims by the KP that it represented the Ukrainian populace. As the church remaining within the MP, the metropolia took on a dual identity: it retained its relationship with Moscow while becoming increasingly Ukrainian to cultivate an identity as a local church.

An examination of recent events will show that attempting to maintain both identities has thus far proven elusive for the metropolia. The final identity marker is familiar: the metropolia is the only canonical church among the Orthodox churches in Ukraine, and it continues to promote itself as the only canonical Church in Ukraine. However, Ukrainian independence proved to be resilient in the post-Soviet period, though occasionally fragile, and the growth of the KP and continued existence of the Autocephalous Church lowered the prestige of the metropolia among the Orthodox churches in this period. After the Orange Revolution of 2004 and during the presidential tenure of Viktor Yushchenko, there were numerous appeals for Orthodox Church unity within Ukraine. Eventually, the metropolia responded to those appeals by agreeing to participate in dialogue with both the autocephalous and KP churches, which was a new step for the metropolia. Critics have pointed to the absence of tangible results or even improved relations among the Orthodox as evidence of the failure of the dialogues. But the metropolia had steadfastly refused to dialogue with groups it designated as schismatic for the entirety of modern Ukrainian church history. Its willingness to engage in even a pro forma, tepid dialogue is the result of Metropolitan Volodymyr's attempts to foster reconciliation in the Church.

An episode at the very beginning of Volodymyr's tenure indicated his conciliatory disposition. He agreed to meet with Patriarch Mstyslav (Skrypnyk) in Kyiv and called for a dialogue with the UAOC.[74] Volodymyr's policy of dialogue permitted the emergence of a new attitude toward ecclesial autocephaly within the metropolia. Plokhy describes it concisely: "the Kharkiv Sobor affirmed the episcopate's demand for 'canonical autocephaly.'"[75] Ukrainian autocephaly went from an absurdity to a possibility within the metropolia, with one stipulation: it could only occur through canonical channels. Throughout its history, the metropolia has failed to adequately define those channels and how working through them could result in an autocephaly recognized by the world. In this vein, the new identities adopted by the metropolia in the post-Soviet period have their limitations. Dialogue with schismatics is possible, but its results are conditional: the schismatics must return to the Church before an internal discussion of autocephaly can take place. Autocephaly is equally possible, and it is also conditional: it can only be achieved if the Church is unanimous in expressing its desire for autocephaly. This is where the metropolia fails in adequately describing the mechanisms that could result in either outcome: the options for reconciliation are prohibitive to the churches that separated from the metropolia. These options are prohibitive because the separatist autocephalous churches demand that they be welcomed and hosted as equals, and the use of terms such as schismatic are received as pejorative acts of aggression.

As for autocephaly, the metropolia appears to have defined the canonical path as one requiring absolute and unanimous support for autocephaly in the Church. As with the episode involving Filaret above, any dissension within the episcopal ranks can be interpreted as a lack of consensus with autocephaly dismissed on these grounds. The metropolia has not conceived of a proposal indicating how it would quantify absolute consensus as a prerequisite to autocephaly, nor has it referred to historical precedents of churches receiving autocephaly as an obvious expression of absolute internal unity of mind. The metropolia has referred to potential problems resulting from an autocephaly that is not born of an absolute consensus, and the theology underpinning such language is dubious. It is difficult to accept the notion that autocephaly would result in a tragic severing of relations with the MP when autocephaly promotes full communion through the Eucharist in Orthodox ecclesiology. The metropolia needs to refine its language on these matters, but the lack of sophistication and absence of flexibility does not diminish the metropolia's development of identity markers in the post-Soviet period.

Metropolitan Filaret and the KP

Following his departure from the MP in 1992, Metropolitan Filaret sought entrance into the Autocephalous Church. On June 25–26 of 1992, a council was held in Kyiv under the pretext of the unification of the metropolia and the autocephalous churches. The council's objective was to unify the two churches once and for all with the establishment of a local Ukrainian Church. The metropolia was represented primarily by Metropolitan Filaret himself. The council of June 1992 produced a new church, the KP. The council's resolutions reflect a merger of two church bodies and respect for the unique heritage of the UAOC.[76]

The council appointed Filaret to be Mstyslav's deputy patriarch, explaining that Mstyslav's age and residence overseas necessitated a deputy to ensure continued church administration.[77] The UAOC's reception of Filaret is a controversial issue in the history of both the UAOC and the KP. One report indicated that the June Council was frustrated with its inability to communicate with Mstyslav, who was absent from the gathering.[78] There is some evidence suggesting that Mstyslav worked to reconcile with Filaret, and that the ecumenical patriarch took initial steps toward recognizing the new KP.[79] Once Filaret was deposed from holy orders, a decision of the MP accepted by global Orthodoxy, Mstyslav disavowed him and called for his resignation, along with that of Metropolitan Antony (Macendych). The merger of the churches generated confusion about canonical order, and Mstyslav was worried about the reordination of Metropolitan Antony (Macendych) and Archbishop Volodymyr (Romaniuk) by Metropolitan Filaret and Bishop Yakiv in the patriarchal chancery on October 19, 1992, which allegedly made the two bishops canonical.[80] Mstyslav also stated that the June Council creating the KP was illegitimate because it took place without his knowledge or blessing.[81] Dmytro Stepovyk, who published a biography of Mstyslav, claims that select clergy and laity within Mstyslav's American cohort turned the aged prelate against Filaret.[82] The evidence seems to indicate that Mstyslav's remained opposed to the merger several months afterward.[83]

The birth of the Kyivan Patriarchate resulted in the establishment of three Orthodox churches in Ukraine since the Western eparchies of the Autocephalous Church rejected the union. As of 1992, then, the KP emerged as the new church structure, acknowledging Mstyslav as its patriarch with Filaret essentially administering the church behind the scenes. The KP continued to commemorate Mstyslav as its patriarch (despite his disavowal of the merger) until his death in 1993. The KP elected Archbishop Volodymyr (Romaniuk) as its second patriarch in 1993 until his untimely death, which occurred under suspicious circumstances, in 1995.[84] A council met to elect a new patriarch in October 1995 and selected Filaret as the new patriarch, an office he held through 2016.

The KP has developed its own public religious identity during the years of Filaret's oversight of the church, an identity that has changed since the 2008 celebration of the baptism of Rus' in Kyiv. The KP adopted the identity features already established by the 1989 UAOC, particular the consistent advocacy of an autocephalous church for a sovereign Ukrainian republic. The KP also continued the Ukrainization of church life, manifest in the translation of liturgical books into Ukrainian and the establishment of theological schools and monasteries. The KP ensconced itself in Kyiv through three important centers during this time, the first of which was St. Volodymyr's Cathedral. St. Volodymyr's continued to function as the patriarchal cathedral, a vestige from Filaret's tenure as prelate of

the metropolia, and the KP's continued occupancy forced the metropolia to designate a new home for the metropolitan of Kyiv. Consequently, they established
their see in the Kyivan Pecherska Lavra, while planning the construction of a new
primatial cathedral.[85] The KP also occupied the Vydubytsky Monastery in Kyiv
and was the beneficiary of the reconstructed monastery of St. Michael in Kyiv, an
edifice destroyed by the Soviet regime and rebuilt by the Kyiv city authorities in
2000.[86] The KP's numerical growth during this period demonstrated its devotion
to becoming the people's church.

Ecclesial illegitimacy continued to affect the KP during this period because
of its inheritance of the UAOC's legacy, and the problem was enhanced by the
presence and elevation of Filaret. The MP was relentless in its delegitimization
campaign against Filaret, publicizing the allegations of his violation of monastic
vows and collaboration with the KGB, and referring to his leadership of an already
dubious church committed to separation as evidence of his desire to foment
schism within the Church. These identity markers originating with the 1921
UAOC became more prominent under Filaret's leadership. Any legitimate discussion of Ukrainization and canonical autocephaly was dismissed on account of
the perception that schism was the source of these features. In reality, the UAOC's
agreement to accept Filaret in the ranks of its bishops was due to a handful of reasons; Plokhy mused that the decision was designed as "a last-ditch effort to save
Filaret."[87] In all likelihood, Filaret was received by the UAOC because of the confidence invested in him by figures within the Ukrainian government who viewed
him as having the necessary experience to develop the KP into a church with a
strong international presence, a necessary feature for a church that needed international acknowledgement for legitimacy. In the initial period of his patriarchate,
Filaret proved himself to be an able leader in building up the life of the church by
establishing parishes and educational institutions and increasing the stature of the
KP as an ecclesial fixture in Kyiv and Western Ukraine.

Filaret's primary challenge was global Orthodoxy's rejection of his legitimacy
as a church leader, on account of the MP's campaign of delegitimization. Filaret
dismissed the campaign as politically motivated, but the other churches within
global Orthodoxy observed and honored the MP's decision, which isolated the
KP from the rest of the Church. The KP thus fell into the same pattern as its
Ukrainian predecessors. This situation affected the internal life of the KP as candidates for the mysteries of initiation and ordination had to weigh the risk of
non-recognition and alienation among their Orthodox peers.[88] Officially, the KP
expressed confidence that the problem would be resolved with time. Filaret stated
repeatedly that the process of receiving recognition for canonical autocephaly is
slow, but inevitable, and the church just needed to sustain her course.[89] The MP

adhered to its policies on the KP: laity of the KP who desired to participate in the liturgical life of the MP were not permitted on the basis of the absence of baptism.

The MP adopted a rigorous canonical perspective on the KP: any laity desiring to participate in the life of a local MP parish could do so only following rebaptism.[90] Any clergy of the KP who wished to return to the MP had to be reordained. The MP referred to the absence of any ecclesial legitimacy in the life of the KP caused primarily by Filaret's deposition from holy orders and anathematization from the Church. Any bishops ordained with Filaret's participation were canonically invalid; any baptisms performed by those priests were false. Essentially, this was the same rigorous sacramental/ecclesiological policy adopted by the Orthodox churches toward the 1942 UAOC, despite its adherence to apostolic succession.[91] In this instance, Filaret affirmed his own ordination as valid and reflected on the irony that bishops whom he had ordained were leading the charge in pointing out his illegitimacy.[92]

The KP attempted to clarify the authority of the canons in ascertaining the presence of grace in the life of the church. In response to assertions of uncanonical identity, the KP stated that the four marks of the church are "one, holy, catholic, and apostolic," all expressed in the Nicene-Constantinopolitan Creed professed by global Orthodoxy. Nowhere does the Church define herself as "canonical" in her liturgical texts, the KP claimed.[93] Later in its history, the KP began to engage the debate on its canonical basis by claiming that the metropolia and MP were the uncanonical churches because they violated apostolic canon 34 by assembling the Kharkiv council of 1992 without the consent, blessing, and knowledge of the first hierarch.[94] The KP published numerous articles arguing that the MP's delegitimization campaign against Filaret was dubious. The KP's most substantial argument was based upon accusations leveled against Filaret as early as 1990, when he was the metropolitan of Kyiv under the Moscow Patriarchate.[95] The KP attributed the slander campaign to Bishop Ionafan (Ieletskykh), and his narrative formed the basis of the MP's case against Filaret. The KP argued that Ionafan's testimony was baseless, especially as Ionafan later testified that he had fabricated the accusations against Filaret.[96]

As the KP's stature has grown over recent years, the KP has countered the delegitimization campaign against Filaret with a series of events honoring Filaret's service as primate of the Kyivan Church. The KP's veneration of Filaret's leadership culminated with a celebration honoring his fiftieth anniversary as primate of the Kyivan cathedral in May 2016. The celebration included a prayer service with the Holy Synod in the symbolic St. Sophia Cathedral, at a state museum, and at several public events. The Holy Synod of the KP publicly proclaimed its formal greetings to Filaret at a major public event.[97] The text of the address celebrates

Filaret's fifty-years of service to the Church, and illuminates the turbulent year of 1990 as a pivotal time in his leadership.

> In the year 1990, when you were one step away from leading the church of Moscow, it was as if the Lord placed a choice before you: take either the broad path of earthly glory, or take the narrow and thorny path of fulfilling the divine will. So that the detractors and opponents would not speak, but the Lord, who sees hearts, your conscience, and we, your flock, are witnesses that you completely relied on God's will. But God provided you with another ministry: the service of patriarch in the Ukrainian Church, for the good of the native people.[98]

This statement of the Holy Synod illustrates the consistent position of the KP in response to attempts to discredit Patriarch Filaret: from the KP's perspective, Filaret forsook the power he could have wielded within the MP for the cross-laden path of service to the Ukrainian Church. This construal of Filaret's tenure as primate of the KP coheres with the themes of martyrdom previously attributed to the 1921 UAOC and its leaders, although the KP stops short of drawing an explicit connection between the two historical churches.

The KP also assembled a Bishops' council on May 13, 2016, at the complex of St. Sophia, with the permission of Ukrainian state officials.[99] This Bishops' council updated the canonical position of the church and publicly explained it.[100] The statement condemned the activity of the Moscow Patriarchate in Ukraine, explicitly identified the KP as the sole heir of the Kyivan Metropolia, and most significantly, defended the KP's patriarchal status while offering to relinquish it for the sake of canonical compromise.[101]

The rationale for the KP's offer to relinquish its patriarchal status is based upon the possibility of receiving recognition of autocephaly from the Ecumenical Patriarchate: the bishops stated that the KP "recognizes only the Constantinopolitan Patriarchate as its mother church and awaits recognition from her" of the historical and canonical reality of the KP's autocephaly.[102] The conciliar statement cemented the KP's historical and canonical legacy: they defined themselves as the only rightful heirs of the Kyivan Metropolia, they condemned the external entities that interfered with the assembly of the Church in Ukraine, they defined the KP as the sole successor to each historical manifestation of the UAOC, and they condemned the MP's Kharkiv council as a pseudo-council in violation of the canons. Most of their markers of public religious identity had appeared earlier in the history of the Orthodox Church in Ukraine, so the features of self-identity were not original. The KP used an innovative tactic in order to receive the long-awaited recognition from Constantinople: a willingness to temporarily relinquish their patriarchal status. This offer demonstrated the KP's priorities: recognition of autocephaly by the EP is more important than the stature of patriarchal status.

KP Relations with the Ukrainian State and Black Tuesday, 1995

For much of its history, the KP has attempted to align itself with the state. President Kravchuk's support of Filaret was mentioned earlier in this chapter. In 1994, Leonid Kuchma was elected as president of Ukraine, and with him, a new religious policy was inaugurated that shifted the balance from favoring the KP to the MP in Ukraine. Plokhy refers to one of Kuchma's first decisions as president as definitive for this period: the Council for Religious Affairs, which had supported Filaret, was dissolved and replaced by a Ministry for Nationalities, Migration, and Cults.[103] The impact on the KP is best explained through a tragic incident that occurred in conjunction with the burial of the KP's patriarch, Volodymyr (Romaniuk), on July 18, 1995. Plokhy explains that the incident was caused by the ongoing feud between the KP and MP about ownership of precious church properties, a situation alluded to above.[104] St. Sophia Cathedral, not assigned to any particular church, was the most symbolic and precious church owned by the state. The KP wanted to bury Patriarch Volodymyr on the property of St. Sophia; Plokhy describes this proposed tactic as an attempt to "stake a claim to the greatest shrine of East Slavic Christendom."[105] Plokhy also notes that Filaret opted to honor the wishes of the paramilitary Ukrainian National Assembly-Ukrainian National Self-Defense, along with influential members of the government, including ex-president Kravchuk, and process to St. Sophia's for the burial in spite of government opposition.[106] A tragic and symbolic event took place; here is Plokhy's description of the account:

> The police had removed the cordon it had initially put up along the funeral-procession route, but a special police unit set up barricades to prevent the funeral participants from entering the cathedral's grounds. After drawn-out negotiations between the Supreme Rada deputies in attendance and government officials failed, the funeral participants began digging a grave for the patriarch on St. Sophia Square near the entrance to the cathedral's grounds. To this the government responded by ordering the police to disperse the crowd and not permit the interment of the patriarch on the square. However, by the time the police had entered the square in force and began beating up and violently dispersing the assembled funeral participants, singling out UNA-UNSO members in particular, it was too late: the patriarch's casket had already been lowered into a hastily dug grave by the entrance to the cathedral's grounds.[107]

FIGURE 5. The tomb of Patriarch Volodymyr (Romaniuk) of the UOC-KP in front of St. Sophia Cathedral in Kyiv. Photo by Nicholas Denysenko.

In Ukraine, this incident was known as "Black Tuesday," and it was an enormous scandal for the government. Despite the darkness of the tragedy of that day, Plokhy emphasizes the transformation of Filaret from a likely villain to a hero aligned with Ukraine's proponents of democracy.[108]

Plokhy adds that the event set the stage for Filaret's election as patriarch of the KP at its council in October 1995.[109] In the period following Black Tuesday, the KP continued to struggle in its battle with the government. In the midst of the struggle, the KP took refuge in the traditional agenda of autocephalous Orthodox Ukrainians: support for Ukrainian national independence and democracy. Plokhy notes that Filaret's ascension to the position of patriarch led to the departure of a handful of bishops who joined the small UAOC, but that the KP continued to grow and create alliances with nationalistic groups in Ukraine. It was during this period that Filaret was anathematized by the MP, which had two effects on the KP. First, Filaret's anathematization severed his ties with Moscow and garnered strong support from the nationalists who viewed him as a patron and hero of Ukraine.[110] However, the final act of casting out Filaret from the Church had support within global Orthodoxy. Filaret's isolation enhanced the perception of Ukrainian autocephaly in general as a movement based on a dubious, anti-Orthodox, and anti-canonical rationale. The dual effect of this final act on the part of the MP increased Filaret's prestige within Ukraine and among nationalists in the diaspora, but rendered him a local player on the global stage of Orthodox church politics.[111] This new development in the KP's public religious identity, closely connected to the person of Filaret, became a pattern that manifested itself repeatedly in future events, especially the Orange Revolution, the national celebrations of the baptism of Rus' in Ukraine, and the Euromaidan and war.[112]

FIGURE 6. Patriarch Filaret (Denysenko) of the UOC-KP. Photo by Håkan Henriksson.

In conclusion, the KP emerged from the autocephalous movement and advanced its initiatives from 1992 until the present. This section has covered the initial years of the history of the KP and the significance of its relations with the state, its acquisition of property, its assertive campaign of ecclesial Ukrainization, and its rapid growth as a sizable church in Ukraine. Throughout the process, the KP took on the strategy of proclaiming itself a patriarchate, and its prestige grew rapidly in conjunction with epic events in Ukraine under the leadership of Patriarch Filaret. Filaret's assumption of leadership enhanced two aspects of Ukrainian Orthodox public religious identity: the stigma of illegitimacy has increased with the scandals attached to Filaret's personal history and his anathematization from the MP; and his steadfast pursuit of true independence established him as the most visible, and perhaps the most beloved, religious figure in Ukraine.[113] Filaret's stature in Ukraine became predominant after the year 2000, and the next section elucidates the KP's public religious identity in the events from 2008–2015.

Church/State Relations: Four Examples

In addition to Black Tuesday, four other significant events involving serious church-state relations contributed to the shaping of public religious identity in the Orthodox churches. These events are the Orange Revolution of 2004, the 1020th anniversary of the celebration of the baptism of Rus' in 2008, the 1025th celebration of the same event in 2013, and the letter from Ukraine's parliament to Ecumenical Patriarch Bartholomew requesting that he grant autocephaly to the Church.

The events leading up to the presidential election of 2004 witnessed the flaring of tensions in Ukraine. The election pitted Viktor Yushchenko, who had overseen a period of economic growth, against Viktor Yanukovych, a vestige of President Kuchma's tenure of corruption. The candidates had different plans to ameliorate concerns and stabilize Ukrainian society. Yushchenko envisioned a Ukraine with increasingly closer ties to the European Union, whereas Yanukovych preferred alliances with Russia as the most familiar and economically advantageous neighbor. The campaign was compromised when Yushchenko became deathly ill and permanently scarred from an unsuccessful assassination attempt via poison. Yanukovych won the election, but observers questioned the validity of the results, noting numerous instances of false reporting. This corruption resulted in an explosive revolution in Kyiv, as people gathered at Independence Square (Maidan) and wore orange to support Yushchenko and his party. Under increased international scrutiny, the votes were recast, and Yushchenko defeated Yanukovych and became Ukraine's president.

The role of the Church during this episode was crucial, especially for the metropolia. Numerous reports emerged of clergy instructing people how to vote, admonishing them with the threat of divine punishment to cast their votes for Yanukovych. In one infamous episode of blatant clerical manipulation of believers, a bishop of the MP instructed the faithful to cast their vote for Yanukovych by invoking a command he attributed to Mary, the mother of God. The MP parishes in Ukraine also distributed campaign literature in favor of Yanukovych.[114] However, Patriarch Filaret and UGCC primate Archbishop Lubomyr (Husar) openly supported the Yushchenko campaign, thus aligning themselves with the crowd and the figures who sought to deepen Ukraine's ties with Europe and the West.[115] Archbishop Yevstratii (Zoria), the spokesperson for the KP, stated that the Orange Revolution was a "moment of truth" for the churches, especially the KP.[116] The moment of truth was an opportunity for the Church to support political, religious, and economic freedom, a conscious choice between good and evil.

The 2004 Orange Revolution witnessed the strengthening of church-state alliances, with political ideologies setting the stage for the gatherings of cohorts.[117] President Yushchenko was supported by the UGCC and KP, two churches that had only been legalized at the end of the Soviet period and enjoyed strong ties the West on account of their diaspora existences in exile.[118] These churches cast their vote for political candidates who would support freedom and Ukrainian sovereignty. They also vouched for Yushchenko's identity as a pious Orthodox Christian before the populace. The MP in Ukraine exhibited its support for Yanukovych when its bishops accompanied him on visits to holy places such as Jerusalem and Mount Athos in an attempt to establish his legitimacy as a canonically Orthodox politician. Yanukovych's political interests aligned with the legacy inherited from the Soviet era, the notion of a common Orthodox faith holding together the historical peoples of Russia, Belarus, and Ukraine. In 2004, the Orange Revolution was victorious and Yushchenko represented the face of church-state independence, freedom, and relations with the West. Yushchenko's victory would prove temporary, though. Perhaps of greater importance is the obvious alignment of church-state interests behind the candidates: Yushchenko became the symbol and champion of independence for the Ukrainian Orthodox Church, while Yanukovych became Ukraine's champion of closer relations with Russia and the MP.[119] The coalescing of church cohorts around these politicians set the stage for three occurrences in Ukraine's Orthodox life that have significantly impacted its present state: the 2008 and 2013 celebrations of the baptism of Rus', and Moscow patriarch Kirill's *Russkii mir* initiative.

The Post-Soviet Celebration of the Baptism of Rus', Part 1

In 2008, Kyiv played host to an international celebration of the baptism of Rus'.[120] Ukraine orchestrated the event as a reprise of the millennium celebration of 1988 that occurred in Moscow at the end of the Soviet period. For embattled President Yushchenko, the 2008 celebration was an attempt to definitively solidify the most important religious constituency in Ukraine, the Orthodox Church. The establishment of an independent Church would serve two important purposes: it would create the possibility of mitigating internal divisions by unifying all Orthodox believers into one structure, and it would also symbolize the end of Ukraine's ecclesial dependence on Moscow. Yushchenko invited Ecumenical Patriarch Bartholomew, who wielded the most ecclesial power to legalize the KP and catalyze unity in the Church, to preside at the festivities. But Yushchenko's plans failed. First, while Bartholomew attended and presided at the celebrations, he navigated church politics carefully by honoring Moscow patriarch Alexy II and stopping short of calling for an autocephalous Ukrainian Church. Rumors circulated that Bartholomew had offered to receive the KP under his jurisdiction as an interim move toward legitimizing it, a natural step toward unifying the Orthodox in Ukraine with autocephaly as the imminent outcome. The KP, however, reportedly rejected this initiative on the grounds that accepting it would relinquish both autocephaly and the patriarchal status the church had claimed. The risk was too great for the KP, which held its own celebration of the festivities, and the result was that Orthodoxy remained divided in Ukraine.

Patriarch Kirill's Russkii mir *Initiative*

Like Ukraine, Russia also adjusted to the collapse of the Soviet Union, and as the Russian Federation became the largest of the states emerging from the Bolshevik rubble, the Moscow Patriarchate had to adjust to the surfacing of old ideologies in Russia.[121] Cyril Hovorun describes this ideology as a Russian civil religion that inherited features from both the imperial and communist eras, and concerned itself with political and social issues rather than theology.[122] As the prelate overseeing the administration of the patriarchate during the transition from a multinational Soviet Union to the establishment of independent republics, Patriarch Alexy II (Ridiger) had the responsibility of maintaining the internationalist dimension of the Moscow Patriarchate. The patriarchate's dismissal of Ukrainian autocephaly shows that the Russian Church was not going to tolerate the possibility of local churches adopting the pattern of independence established by the state. A resurgence of Russian nationalism challenged the patriarch, who was confronted by the presence of extremist zealots within the Russian Church, including Metropolitan

Ioann (Snychov) of St. Petersburg.[123] The result of Russian nationalist fervor was the evolution of the ideology of the internationalist Moscow Patriarchate, which became anti-Western and anti-globalization.[124] The patriarchate would continue to be a space for all Orthodox peoples who traced their roots to Kyivan Rus', but its primary center would be Moscow, and its official language would be Russian. In other words, Moscow would continue to be the primary cell directing the political and ecclesial activities of the nations and churches that had existed within the borders of the Soviet Union. This transition of political-ecclesial ideology occurred under Patriarch Alexy II and took shape under Patriarch Kirill, who had been one of the key figures developing the ideology during his tenure as the head of the Moscow Patriarchate's Department of External Church Relations.

When Kirill was enthroned as patriarch in 2009 following Alexy's death in 2008, he formalized the ideology into an initiative that called for the creation of a *Russkii mir* (Russian world) located within the MP.[125] The patriarch outlined *Russkii mir* in two speeches he delivered at the Assembly of the Russian World in 2009 and 2010. *Russkii Mir* would serve as an alternative multinational society for those who shared its values, with the MP serving as its locus. In his speeches, Patriarch Kirill identified Russia, Ukraine, Belarus, and Moldova as the core nations of the *Russkii mir*, but also emphasized its multinational character, which coheres with its ecumenical impetus. Kirill's initiative refers to Kyiv as a crucial center of the *Russkii mir*, a place that will unify people instead of promoting Ukrainian nationalism. One should note that the *Russkii mir* initiative was the result of a process that started in the early post-Soviet period. Its implementation also coincided with Kirill's emphasis on evangelizing portions of Eastern Ukraine that had been disproportionately impacted by the Soviet persecution of the Church.

The initial Ukrainian responses to the *Russkii mir* initiative were largely negative and dismissive. Patriarch Filaret caricatured the initiative as an attempt to rehabilitate a medieval empire, while the head of the Ukrainian Church in Canada vigorously protested the extension of the *Russkii mir* into Canada through the visit of the relics of St. Volodymyr. The implementation of the *Russkii mir* initiative had the most immediate impact on the Kyivan Metropolia itself, especially since Metropolitan Volodymyr had permitted mild Ukrainization within the Church. Members of the UOC-MP synod battled Metropolitan Volodymyr on his plea to renew unification dialogue with the UAOC and KP, and questioned his authority in upholding the canonical statute of the metropolia. When his illness rendered him unable to execute his office, Metropolitan Onufry was elected as locum tenens and eventually as the new metropolitan of Kyiv in 2014.

The implementation of the *Russkii mir* project contributed to church politics in all of the Orthodox churches of Ukraine. For the KP, Patriarch Kirill's renewed interest in evangelizing Ukraine was an opportunity to identify themselves in

FIGURE 7. The tomb of Metropolitan Volodymyr (Sabodan) of the UOC-MP. Kyiv Percherska Monastery, Kyiv. Photo courtesy of Dukh i litera Publishing in Kyiv. Used with permission.

contrast to the *Russkii mir*. Filaret's blunt dismissal of the initiative was designed to expose it as a Trojan horse strategy, with the MP solidifying its control of Ukraine through a nostalgic ideology that attempted to reconstitute a Rus' of the past that no longer existed. The KP's post-Soviet pattern of Ukrainization, patriotism, and endorsement of creating stronger ties with the West was incompatible with the *Russkii mir*. For the metropolia, the initiative had a dramatic effect, as supporters of Metropolitan Volodymyr found themselves at odds with bishops completely devoted to the MP. As Metropolitan Volodymyr's illness worsened into 2013, it became increasingly difficult to identify someone sympathetic to Ukrainization and encouraging of the rapprochement with the KP.

The Baptism of Rus' in 2013 and the Russkii mir

July 2013 witnessed to yet another Kyivan celebration of the baptism of Rus', one that was markedly different from its predecessor in 2008.[126] The 2013 celebration was a carefully orchestrated, multi-city event featuring the core of the

FIGURE 8. Dormition (Uspensky) Cathedral in Kyiv (UOC-MP). Photo by Nicholas Denysenko.

Russkii mir, as the MP hosted several international guests on a patriarchal train traversing Moscow, Kyiv, and Minsk. Each visit was punctuated by church-state events championing the host country's confirmation of the values of the *Russkii mir*, without actually enunciating the term. Presidents Vladimir Putin (Russia), Viktor Yanukovych (Ukraine), and Alexander Lukashenko (Belarus), representing the core nation-states of the *Russkii mir*, addressed large gatherings of bishops in each country, remarking on the spiritual heritage of the church and its contemporary contribution to the present course of the state. Perhaps the most controversial statement occurred in Kyiv when the UOC-MP's synod of bishops hosted Russian president Vladimir Putin, who visited the rebuilt Dormition Cathedral at the Pecherska Lavra Monastery, and bestowed several honors on select bishops for their contributions to the life of the Church in the post-Soviet period. Victor Yelensky sharply criticized the meeting as a blatant attempt to fully execute the *Russkii mir* initiative in Ukraine.[127]

The primary takeaway of the event for our purposes is the obvious alignment of church and state consistently throughout the celebration. The participation of heads of state, especially the meeting of President Putin with the Ukrainian bishops, gives credence to the perception that the UOC-MP is controlled directly by the Kremlin, via Patriarch Kirill. In terms of intra-Orthodox relations in Ukraine, the event was a stalemate. The KP and UOC-MP had effectively taken sides, even when one accounts for the internal tension of the UOC-MP on the matter of Ukrainization. The possibility of reunion with new points of intersection emerged only with yet another revolution in Kyiv: the Euromaidan of November 2013.

Orthodox Church Politics in Tension: Euromaidan, Crimea, and the War

The Euromaidan in November 2013 shook up the religious landscape of Ukraine. With the bishops of the UGCC and KP expressing their solidarity with the Ukrainian people and openly criticizing President Yanukovych, Ukraine's attempt to begin the process of joining the European Union would simultaneously denote her detachment from the *Russkii mir*. At this point, it is crucial to note that the evolution of the Ukrainian state, including her relations with Russia and other neighboring nations, impacted relations among the churches. The leaders of the UGCC and KP acted swiftly to demonstrate their solidarity with the people by appearing at the Maidan. Several representatives of the MP also ventured into the chaos. Many rank-and-file clergy joined the protest as citizens of Ukraine adding their voices to the revolution of dignity, a statement that denounced corruption and called for freedom within Ukraine. Metropolitan Volodymyr invited representatives of the government and the people to the Pecherska Lavra to resolve their differences. The KP's St. Michael Cathedral was temporarily transformed into a hospital to care of the wounded. When the Berkut Riot Police opened fire on the crowd, Bishop Borys (Gudziak) of the UGCC proclaimed them to be new martyrs, the "Heavenly Hundred." Bishop Ioann (Shvetz) of the KP later composed an entire liturgical office in honor of the Heavenly Hundred, though the KP was quick to announce that the office was not sanctioned by the Church and parishes were not authorized to celebrate it.[128] Prominent theologians viewed the Euromaidan as the manifestation of a new ecumenical convergence. Cyril Hovorun referred to the Maidan as catalyzing a new ecumenical impetus in Ukraine, the spontaneous creation of a potential model for rapprochement and cooperation moving forward.[129] Reports also surfaced of spontaneous liturgical celebrations of an ecumenical character on the ground, including priests offering sacramental confession and the regular celebration of the Divine Liturgy.[130]

Despite these positive signs of unity emerging from the chaos, ensuing events pointed toward a deepening of fissures, especially among the Orthodox, as the primary ideologues of the churches involved developed narratives and counternarratives that blamed opposing churches for contributing to the violence.

The MP's Ideological Position on the Maidan and the War: Canonical versus Schismatic

Metropolitan Hilarion (Alfeyev) was the official spokesperson for the MP and crafted its statements on the crisis in Ukraine. It was Hilarion who apportioned blame for the war in Eastern Ukraine. A few citations from his statements illustrate the position of the Russian Orthodox Church on this matter. The most controversial of them comes from Hilarion's greetings to the participants of the fourth European Orthodox-Catholic Forum (Minsk, June 2–6, 2014). Concerning affairs in Eastern Ukraine, Hilarion states:

> Sadly, the Greek Catholics have played a very destructive role in allowing this situation to develop. The words of their leading archbishop, hierarchs and clergy and an extremely politicized position have brought about the polarization of society and a worsening of the conflict which has already led to numerous victims. Unlike the canonical Ukrainian Orthodox Church, which has been able during these difficult months to unite people of various political persuasions, including those who have found themselves on both sides of the barricades, the Uniates have ostentatiously associated themselves with only one of the belligerent forces. The aggressive words of the Uniates, actions directed at undermining the canonical Orthodox Church, active contacts with schismatics and the striving to divide a single multinational Russian Orthodox Church have caused great damage not only to the Ukraine and her citizens, but also to the Orthodox-Catholic dialogue. All of this has put us back a

great distance, reminding us of the times when the Orthodox and Catholics viewed
each other not as friends but as rivals.

Allow me to use this platform to appeal to all our partners in the Orthodox-
Catholic dialogue to do all that is possible to cool down the "hotheads" among
the Uniates, to halt the actions of the Greek Catholics in making the crisis in the
Ukraine worse.[131]

Metropolitan Hilarion's statement is pivotal to interpreting the MP's identification of who is to blame for the bloodshed and violence. The Maidan unleashed a
fierce and bloody struggle for Ukraine's identity, and the possibility of reshaping
Kyiv into a strong center of Ukrainian national identity posed a serious challenge
to the MP's understanding of Ukraine's role in the *Russkii mir*, which was to disavow nationalism in favor of transnational unity. Notably, Metropolitan Hilarion
mentioned Uniates and schismatics whose words and activities represent "an
extremely politicized position" and result in the "polarization of society." Hilarion's
assertion appears to be an implicit condemnation of the Maidan itself, since it was
indeed the UGCC ("Uniates") and UOC-KP ("schismatics") who were the most
active religious groups at the Maidan.

Hilarion continued to exert pressure on the Ukrainian churches that supported
the cause of the Maidan and condemned Russian aggression in Eastern Ukraine
by asking the Catholic bishops who were gathered for the Synod on the Family
in October 2014 to end the Uniate project and convince the UGCC to cease their
activities in Ukraine. One of the most significant elements of Hilarion's speech
was his assertion that the Unia was and remains "a special project of the Catholic
Church aimed at undermining canonical Orthodoxy." This assertion is pivotal
because it enhances the illegitimacy associated with Hilarion's explicit and deliberate use of the word "Uniate" in his appeal.[132]

Since November of 2013, there have been numerous examples of intra-Christian polemical exchanges illustrating the inscription of adversarial identity on the
other. A recent example illustrating this view of the other is Moscow patriarch
Kirill's statement at the recent meeting of the heads of the Orthodox churches in
Chambesy, in which he implicates "schismatics and nationalists" for attempting to
seize parishes of the canonical church in Ukraine.[133]

Note the strategic construction of this statement: the schismatics are also ban-
dits, raiders, and unlawful. It is consistent with other documents he has issued,
including his letter to Ecumenical Patriarch Bartholomew on August 20, 2014,
in which he blamed "Greek Catholics and schismatics" for promoting hostility in
Ukraine and requested Patriarch Bartholomew's assistance.

These statements by Patriarch Kirill and Metropolitan Hilarion reveal their
perception of the UGCC and KP as ecclesially illegitimate communities. For Kirill

and Hilarion, illegitimate religious communities (the UGCC and KP) caused a political upheaval at the Maidan that resulted in a protracted war, killed many innocent people, and threatened the existence of legitimate Christian society by desecrating shrines and terrorizing clergy and laity. The reader or hearer of the appeal knows the identity of the legitimate Christian society (the MP) because it is "canonical," and explicitly manifest in the "multinational Russian Orthodox Church" (Hilarion's speech). The juxtaposition of these two societies—one belli-cose, hateful, and tinged by religious illegitimacy, and the other legitimate, peace-ful, and tolerant—forms the basis for a narrative that has implications for the average believer who wants to belong to the right church. This analysis of eccle-sial legitimacy and identity must also take note of the target audiences. Patriarch Kirill has delivered this consistent message on Ukraine to the leaders of global Orthodoxy who are poised to confirm the legitimacy (or canonicity) of the MP against the aggression of illegitimate groups (the UGCC and KP). Metropolitan Hilarion has raised the question of the legitimacy of the UGCC in light of Orthodox-Catholic dialogue, appealing directly to the Catholic bishops to inter-vene. Metropolitan Hilarion's position is not original: he continues the ideology espoused by the MP during the period of the Cold War, and finds support among scholars of the Church in Ukraine such as Sophia Senyk, who has criticized the UGCC for hypocrisy in denouncing the 1946 L'viv council and for colluding with the UOC-KP.[134] The UGCC has offered a different view of the church's role in political crises, which challenges the MP's accusation that they incite political and civil turmoil. Patriarch Lubomyr (Husar) expressed the position of the UGCC in an interview with Antoine Arjakovsky, identifying "the defence of human dignity and justice" as the primary issue at stake for the churches when clergy and laity gathered at the Maidan during the Orange Revolution.[135]

While the most vocal leaders of the MP in Russia consistently follow this narrative pattern, representatives of the MP in Ukraine do not. When her pri-mate, Metropolitan Onufry, recently took a pilgrimage to Mount Athos, the MP called upon the renowned elder Ephraim, hegumen of the Vatopedi Monastery, to address the Ukrainian people. The elder Ephraim's remarks illuminate global Orthodoxy's perception of the MP's identity: the UOC-MP is the canonical Church in Ukraine.[136]

Fr. Ephraim's statement wields the spiritual authority of Mount Athos; given his use of the word "canonical" five times in two short sentences, it is clear that this is the primary identifying marker of the MP in Ukraine. Furthermore, the MP in Ukraine has reported numerous instances of attempts on the part of the UGCC and KP to seize parishes, which (again) fits the narrative pattern. Other leaders of the MP have challenged the narrative. For example, Metropolitan Oleksandr (Drabinko) apologized to the KP for the destruction of their church

in the Crimea in June 2014.[137] An even more significant event was the so-called
Rivne Memorandum cosigned by the bishops of the KP, MP, and UGCC, communicating their support for the unification of the Orthodox churches into one
local church and the condemnation of Russia for aggressive acts on November 13,
2014.[138] The memorandum's life was unhappily brief, with the MP and UGCC delegates withdrawing their support just one day later.[139] The creation of this memorandum demonstrates the existence of a counternarrative to that prevailing within
the MP, as not all parties agree on the convenient categorization of the churches in
alignment with traditional labels of ecclesial illegitimacy and canonicity.

Onufry's ascension to the Kyivan cathedra resulted in several internal shifts,
including the diminishment of Metropolitan Oleksandr (Drabinko), Volodymyr's
spiritual son and protégé, and the dismissal of Archpriest Heorhii Kovalenko
from his position as head of the press office of the UOC-MP. In addition to
Onufry's visit to Mount Athos, he accompanied Patriarch Kirill to the meeting
of the Synaxis of the Primates of the Orthodox Churches in Geneva in January
2016.[140] The synaxis did not make any public declaration on Ukraine at this meeting. Reports indicate that Patriarch Kirill himself announced that the ecumenical
patriarch supported Onufry as the only canonical prelate in Ukraine, promised to
refrain from recognizing the KP as canonical, and apologized to the UOC-MP for
the actions of the diaspora bishops, who had traveled to Ukraine in an attempt to
preside over the unification of the UAOC with the KP.[141]

As of this writing, Onufry's public stance is a mixed bag. On the one hand,
Onufry briefly presided at meeting of the All-Ukrainian Council of Churches and
Religious Organizations and signed their statements condemning Russian aggression. Onufry also blessed Kyivan clergy to liturgically commemorate the metropolitan of Kyiv without reference to the patriarch of Moscow.[142] More recently,
Onufry made a public video confirming his church's acknowledgement of Petro
Poroshenko as the legitimate president of Ukraine, with the church continuing to
pray for his exercise of the presidential office.[143] On the other hand, Onufry has
contributed to a fierce public campaign protesting the illegal seizure of parishes
by the KP, as numerous parish communities have changed allegiance from the
MP to the KP. Patriarch Kirill and Onufry consistently claim that this is an act of
persecution of the canonical church in Ukraine that stands in the way of unification negotiations. Two events centering on Onufry garnered serious media attention. First, he attended a session where President Poroshenko addressed Ukraine's
Verkhovna Rada, and when the president called upon everyone to stand in honor
of the soldiers who had died in battle, only Onufry and the MP bishops accompanying him remained seated.[144] The UOC-MP's press service defended this action
as a protest against war and consistent with the Church's stance of remaining
outside of politics. Also, during the December 2015 assembly of Kyivan clergy,

Onufry dismissed the use of vernacular Ukrainian in the liturgy as unnecessary, and claimed that the use of Slavonic was consistent with the universal ecclesial practice of employing sacred languages for worship, distinct from the ordinary, everyday language of life.[145]

In sum, Onufry's assumption of leadership of the Kyivan See seems to manifest the UOC-MP's turn toward solidifying its ties with the MP. As of this writing, the episcopate of the UOC-MP is mostly conservative, and autocephaly is not a prominent agenda item. The most vocal advocate for autocephaly is Metropolitan Oleksandr (Drabinko), who has published several essays charting a path for canonical autocephaly and a vision for resolving the schism in Ukraine on the basis of the foundation established by Metropolitan Volodymyr (Sabodan), Oleksandr's spiritual father.[146] Metropolitan Oleksandr is one of a few UOC-MP bishops who remains open to dialogue with the UAOC and UOC-KP. In terms of public religious identity, the UOC-MP's constant iteration of the refrain of canonical identity, its claim to be outside of politics and multinational, and its allegation of persecution are consistent with the legacy of public religious identity in the MP. What is new in this equation is the UOC-MP's attempt to identify itself as one of the victims of the war in Ukraine. This claim is also the result of public adherence to an ecclesial policy of remaining outside of politics: as a non-political entity, the UOC-MP can attempt to make the claim that it is an innocent victim of policies it never endorsed. However, its recent history of close ties with President Putin himself makes the claim of victimhood dubious at best.

The KP's Public Profile after the Maidan

In many ways, the KP employed the same argumentative style as the one used by Russian Church leaders by clearly identifying who is to blame for the problem (President Putin). The KP's position has a unique theological feature consistently offered to readers: the imminent day of judgment that will hold all accountable for their actions. In a letter written to the faithful of the KP, Filaret states that Putin is the "new Cain." Accusing Putin of committing acts of murder and falsehood, Filaret placed the blame for the bloodshed and loss of life in Donbass squarely on Putin's shoulders.[147] At the end of his letter, Filaret refers the people to the promise of their liberation from Putin, which will occur by the mighty hand of God, as promised by the narrative story of the book of Exodus. In this letter, Filaret uses familiar theological figures and places Putin in a community of antagonists including Cain and Pharaoh.

There is also evidence of a more recent pastoral initiative in the KP that is addressed inwardly and designed to build the body of Christ by excising the sin of corruption from the body. A letter from the synod of bishops to the Ukrainian people argues that corruption has manifested itself in many ways in contemporary Ukraine and that those who are guilty of corruption have simultaneously violated the laws of humanity and God. After presenting a brief warning and exhortation about corruption, the letter threatens those who commit acts of corruption with sacramental excommunication. The synod explains its directive on denying communion to those who practice corruption as a result of Ukraine's experience of turbulence in the present and depicts those who take bribes as traitors.[148]

The KP's synod then appeals to their faithful to refrain from participating in acts of corruption and from protecting those who commit such acts. The consequence for failing to adhere to this directive is divine: God's judgment will ultimately hold everyone accountable for their actions. In these recent statements, the KP has used a somewhat unusual form of argumentation in disclosing their pastoral approach to their faithful. The Church has participated in the blame game, holding President Putin responsible for the chaos in Ukraine. An untold number of opportunists are also accused of corrupt activities in the synodal decree.[149]

The rhetoric the KP employs in these narratives is somewhat traditional and yet unlike that of the MP. It uses the familiar method of building the profile of an antagonist who is then compared unfavorably to a biblical figure: Putin is in the company of Cain, Satan, and Pharaoh, and his bellicose actions are subject to divine judgment. For one who belongs to the *Russkii mir*, the experience will be one of slavery, not sanctity, especially since the patrons are under the spell of the devil. Equally intriguing is the KP's decree on corruption. The decree elucidates a pastoral initiative to address one of the primary problems afflicting contemporary society, which has been heightened by the conditions of war that exacerbate the problems of societal inequality. The synodal decree turns to a familiar strategy by threatening the removal of sacramental privilege for those who commit acts of corruption while belonging to the KP. Again, the guilty are actually in the company of familiar biblical antagonists such as Judas Iscariot, and concealing one's guilt will bring about a worse judgment than excommunication: shame and eternal condemnation. The directive denying communion sends a message about the integrity and dignity of the community of believers who belong to the KP as it attempts to illuminate the inherent sanctity of this church. By denying communion to those who would exploit multitudes of homeless and destitute people during a war for their own political and material gain, the KP identifies itself as a community that is the patron of the homeless, destitute, and at-risk population of Ukraine. The emerging picture of the KP in the Maidan was that of a patron for those caught in the crossfire. In other words, the KP is a communion of sanctity: belonging to this communion is a privilege that one may not purchase, and the communion is a preferential option for those who do not desire slavery. The KP reinforces their public religious identity by drawing distinct lines dividing belonging from exclusion: those who care for the poor and needy and support peace belong to a holy communion. External figures who perpetrate war (such as Putin) are excluded because they succeed a long line of antagonists epitomized by biblical figures such as Cain, Pharaoh, and Judas Iscariot. Insiders who violate the moral precept of protecting the innocent are denied Holy Communion, a punitive act designed to encourage repentance.

This review of the narratives and counternarratives communicated by select statements from leaders of the Orthodox churches in Ukraine illuminates the respective and often contradictory notions of identity and ecclesial legitimacy associated with each group. The Euromaidan, annexation of Crimea, and war in Ukraine prompted a series of letters and statements delivered by each body to deliberately targeted audiences that seek to precisely define one's own identity in contrast with the other local competitors. The national political and societal crisis in Ukraine precipitated urgent appeals to external allies for support of one's own ecclesial agenda, and affirmation of one's own identity and perception of the other. The current status quo is as follows for the central ecclesial bodies discussed here: the MP in Ukraine marks its own religious identity as canonical, peaceful, and multinational; it appealed to the leaders of the global Orthodox churches and the bishops of the Roman Church (and on many occasions, to the Ukrainian citizenry); and it depicts the other as illegitimate, responsible for contributing to the political and societal crisis, and as desiring the eradication of the MP from Ukraine. The KP defines itself as united with contemporary Ukraine, which is verified by their activity on the Maidan, and it rejects the claims of the MP and dismisses it as an institution seeking to promote a geopolitical strategy of imperial absorption under the mask of an ecclesial conglomerate that is searching for an alternative to the plurality generated by globalization. The KP blames Russia for the outbreak of war in Ukraine, while the UOC-MP calls for equal treatment and ministry to multinational constituencies in Ukraine. The KP's instruction on corruption served to demonstrate its commitment to maintaining its identity as a house of sanctity.

The Holy and Great Council in Crete and the Appeal of the Verkhovna Rada

As mentioned earlier, the the Moscow Patriarchate explained its opinion on the church situation in Ukraine during the synaxis of primates that gathered in Geneva in 2016 in preparation for the Holy and Great Council, which was held in Crete in June 2016. Patriarch Kirill and Metropolitan Onufry attended the synaxis in Geneva, and Patriarch Kirill reiterated the Moscow Patriarchate's position that the Orthodox bishops support only the Ukrainian Church under the Moscow Patriarchate and that attempts to recognize one of the other churches (i.e., the KP or UAOC) would have a negative outcome. The question of the Ukrainian Church was temporarily overshadowed by intrigue surrounding the council itself. As June approached, the Georgian Church withdrew its commitment to attend, the Antiochian Church decided not to take part because of a long-standing dispute with Jerusalem over a parish in Qatar, and the Bulgarian and Russian churches withdrew, while the Serbian Church expressed concern about the council's work. The council gathered in Crete and issued several documents, none of which touched upon the Ukrainian question, although many of the bishops openly discussed Ukraine. The question of the status of the Ukrainian Church became explosive when Ukraine's Verkhovna Rada (parliament) issued an appeal to the ecumenical patriarch and petitioned him to grant autocephaly to the Ukrainian Orthodox Church on June 16, 2016.[150] The Rada's petition highlighted several of the identity markers of the movement for Ukrainian autocephaly discussed throughout this study, two of which were particularly prominent. The first was the request that Constantinople pronounce the 1686 annexation of the Kyivan Metropolia to Moscow as invalid, and the second was the rationale for the petition, that "Ukraine will never be either a political or religious colony of Russia." President Poroshenko thanked the Rada for the appeal in his address on September 6, 2016, and assured the delegates that "autocephaly does not mean [the] appearance of [a] state church."[151] The Ecumenical Patriarchate established a special commission to study the matter.

The Rada's appeal to the ecumenical patriarch provides a fitting conclusion to this chapter, which has presented dozens of events and developments in the Orthodox Church of Ukraine. The chapter establishes the pattern of a new type of church-state relationship, as both the churches and state officials in Ukraine attempted to manipulate one other for the purpose of strengthening their respective strategic positions. The landscape of church-state relations has been shaken by the costs of war in Eastern Ukraine. While the MP continues to retain millions of adherents in Ukraine, the war and its consequences have emboldened each church to entrench themselves in their respective positions on intrachurch relations.[152] On the surface, the Rada's appeal to the council in Crete appears to be a gross violation of the precept of the separation of church and state. The state's decision to make an official appeal for the intervention of the ecumenical patriarch is based upon obvious motivations. State officials hope that a unified Orthodox Church in Ukraine will contribute to the unification of the people, as divergent Orthodox Church allegiances are contributing to societal division.[153] The parliament's appeal reveals the progress made by the adherents of the KP and the autocephalous churches of the twentieth century in inscribing the narrative of Ukrainian Orthodoxy on the Ukrainian public. Parliament's request for the annulment of the 1686 transfer of jurisdiction to Moscow and the granting of autocephaly to eradicate Russian colonization of Ukraine is a public reiteration of two primary identity features of the autocephalous movement. The post-Soviet pattern of church-state relations in Ukraine is inconsistent and turbulent, and parliament's request is not likely to prefigure a dramatic shift in this area. However, the state has essentially affirmed the narrative proclaimed by pro-autocephaly cohorts in Ukraine for nearly one hundred years, and their reception of this narrative creates the possibility for some kind of change to emerge in the intra-Orthodox landscape of Ukraine.

Attempts at Church Unity, Twenty-Five Years after Ukraine's Independence

Following the millennium celebration in 1988, the Orthodox Church in Ukraine has evolved along the path of plurality. In 1988, there was only one official Orthodox Church in Ukraine. By 1989, the UAOC had entered the scene, and in 1992, there were three Orthodox churches, a situation that remains to this day. In their official literature, each church stakes a claim to authority in Ukraine, referring to a variety of surveys on religious adherence. The prevailing trend seems to indicate a slow but gradual movement of people and parishes from the MP to the KP, with neither side agreeing on the legality of parish decisions to formally change jurisdiction. The polemical saturation of intra-Orthodox discourse in Ukraine suggests that there have been no attempts to resolve differences and unite, but there have been instances of intrachurch dialogue.

Following the June 1992 council of unity that resulted in the emergence of the KP, some eparchies remained loyal to the UAOC and recognized only the authority of patriarchs Mstyslav and Dmitry. However, the UAOC and KP commenced dialogue for the purpose of unity, and as early as 1995, there appeared to be prospects for a reunion of the UAOC and KP into one church. Under the leadership of Patriarch Dmitry, in 1995 the UAOC agreed to an act of union with the KP, with the understanding that the unified church would be renamed the "Ukrainian Autocephalous Orthodox Church—Kyivan Patriarchate," and that Patriarch Dmitry would lead the unified church.[154] The document was signed by several representatives of both churches, including UAOC patriarch Dmitry and KP metropolitan Andrii (Abramchuk) of Halychyna. The proposed union failed on account of the absence of agreement on all points of union between the two churches. On October 19, 1995, KP metropolitan Andrii informed the synod of the KP that his eparchy did not recognize the election of Filaret to the office of patriarch and did not regard his directives as authoritative.[155] Metropolitan Andrii was representing the clergy and laity of the Ivano-Frankivsk eparchy of the KP, as he was its temporarily administrator until he left the KP and joined the UAOC in 1995.[156] On August 10, 1995, the council of deans of Ivano-Frankivsk eparchy wrote Filaret (who was then locum tenens of the KP following the death of Patriarch Volodymyr [Romaniuk] in July), and expressed their consternation with Filaret's dismissal of negotiations for union and suggestion that the UAOC be absorbed into the KP.[157] The council of deans also requested that Filaret recuse himself as a candidate for the patriarchal office of a united Orthodox Church in Ukraine.[158]

While Filaret was elected as the patriarch of KP in October 1995, negotiations for union of the UAOC with the KP continued through 2015. On August 15, 1996, the Bishops' council of the UAOC resolved to change the official name of the church from "UAOC" to UAOC-Kyivan Patriarchate, a move signaling their desire for compromise in negotiations with the KP, and their identity as equal partners in dialogue.[159] The UAOC infused renewed urgency into the dialogue by making several appeals to the Ecumenical Patriarchate to bless the unification dialogue and eventually assume leadership of the process. On June 13, 2001, UAOC metropolitan Andrii reported that a meeting of representatives of the UAOC and KP took place in Istanbul for the purpose of renewing the dialogue on unification.[160] The dialogue took place with Metropolitan Constantine (Buggan) of the UOC-USA observing. The joint committee stated that "no ideological differences exist among them in terms of dogma," and that the dialogue would resume with the participation of Archbishop Vsevolod (Maidansky) of the UOC-USA as the official representative of the Ecumenical Patriarchate.[161]

The UAOC-KP unification dialogue stumbled in 2005 and again in 2014. The UAOC representatives claimed that the conditions for unification presented by the KP were not about the unity of two equal partners, but constituted the absorption of the UAOC into the structure of the KP.[162] The eparchial council of the UAOC's Ivano-Frankivsk eparchy embellished Metropolitan Andrii's letter to Mefodii with a proposal containing eight points.[163] Four of the points manifest the urgency of unity and the obstacles preventing agreement:

1. The episcopate of the UAOC and UOC-KP should appeal in writing to the primate of the UOC-MP (His Beatitude) Metropolitan Volodymyr (Sabodan) at their hierarchical councils, to join the unification process of the Orthodox in Ukraine and appoint a representative for work on the unification commission.

2. It was resolved to create a preconciliar commission consisting of representatives of the UAOC and UOC-KP that would perform work ahead of time in preparation for the carrying out of an All-Ukrainian Local Council.

3. It was resolved to request that Ecumenical Patriarch Bartholomew appoint a *protosyncellus* of the Ecumenical Patriarch, possibly a representative of Ukrainian descent, who could function as a mediator.
4. It was resolved to conduct an All-Ukrainian Council in Kyiv under the presidency of the honorable representative of the Ecumenical Patriarchate (to confirm the statute, elect a primate and other organs of Church administration)
5. The Unification Council should take place in conditions of the equality of all Orthodox groups without accounting for the number of parishes and bishops of the churches.
6. The election of the new patriarch should be carried out with the method of drawing from a lot before the Holy Liturgy by the will of the Holy Spirit following the apostolic example of the selection of the twelfth apostle to replace the fallen Judas (Acts 1:21–26) and the election of the seven deacons (Acts 6:2–7).[164]

Two dimensions of the proposal manifest the aspirations of the UAOC for the unification of the churches. The UAOC sought equal representation without accounting for size and numbers in the process. Since the question of who would assume the office of patriarch had been raised in the past, the proposal to elect the patriarch via lot would ensure fairness. Furthermore, the UAOC sought to make the unification complete by appealing to the UOC-MP, and referred to the authority of the Ecumenical Patriarchate to ensure good order. The UAOC remained faithful to these principles in the successive attempts at dialogue for union with the KP, and the UAOC even made an official appeal to the ecumenical patriarch to find a way to recognize the UAOC as a canonical metropolia of the church.[165]

The possibility of unification between the UAOC and KP was nearly realized in 2015, as the two churches scheduled a unification council in Kyiv for September 14. The joint committee for unification reached a decision at St. Michael's Monastery in Kyiv on June 8, 2015, for unification under the leadership of bishops representing the Ecumenical Patriarchate.[166] The joint committee agreed that representation would consist of all the bishops of both churches, and one delegate for every fifteen parishes officially registered with the Ministry of Cults of Ukraine as of January 1, 2015.[167] The joint commission on unification dialogue would immediately become a preconciliar preparatory committee, and the heads of the two churches (Metropolitan Makarii of the UAOC and Patriarch Filaret of the KP) would serve as cochairs of the council until it ratified the union and elected a new primate. The agreement did not include a method for voting for a primate, but it did state that the council would vote upon difficult issues, including the official name of the unified church, taking into consideration the UAOC's desire to retain the word "autocephalous" in the name.[168]

The agreement collapsed almost immediately, however, as the UAOC withdrew its commitment to the council on July 10, refusing to compromise with the KP on the name of the unified church, representation at the unified council, and candidacy of bishops for the office of patriarch.[169] The KP in turn claimed that the UAOC had abandoned all of the agreed-upon points in the dialogue, and had disappointed the Ecumenical Patriarchate as a result.[170] On August 27, 2015, the meeting of the Holy Synod of the KP addressed the failed attempt to unite the two churches and expressed its position on the future of dialogue.[171] After thanking Patriarch Bartholomew and the Ukrainian churches of the diaspora for attempting to promote dialogue and union, the KP Synod concluded that the UAOC does not truly desire unity, and that the church that "today bears the name [of the UAOC] is a new creation that fell under the influence of external, anti-Ukrainian forces in 1992–1993."[172] The KP stated that the UAOC is primarily comprised of clergy and laity who once belonged to the KP, which implies that the existence of the UAOC is a protest against the policies of the KP. The synod also claimed that the KP is the legitimate heir of the original unification of the two churches in June 1992, and called upon the clergy and faithful of the UAOC to promote

FIGURE 9. St. Michael's Cathedral (UOC-KP). Photo by Nicholas Denysenko.

the creation of a single, local Ukrainian Orthodox Church by joining the KP.[173] The KP noted that this was the fifth attempt to unite the two churches, and they had all failed. The event symbolized the patronage for union on the part of the Ecumenical Patriarchate, which started to actively participate in unification negotiations in 2001. Despite the desire of the Ecumenical Patriarchate to foster union, the two sides were unable to overcome their disagreements, the most formidable being the sheer size of the KP and the desire of the UAOC to be an equal partner in negotiations despite its much smaller size.

The UOC-MP's Position on Intra-Orthodox Dialogue

In the post-Soviet period, the UOC-MP's position on dialogue has varied, largely on account of its insistence on fidelity to canonical norms and traditions and its support of the MP's deposition and anathematization of Filaret from holy orders and church membership. The UOC-MP created a commission on dialogue with the UAOC in 1995, and in his reflections on his leadership of the church, the late Metropolitan Volodymyr (Sabodan) noted that the meetings had positive results, but that the commission had not continued its work in recent years.[174] He expressed satisfaction with changes within the UAOC over the years, especially with its official disavowal of ethnophyletism, and its clarification that the UAOC's claim to being a "national church" was to be interpreted within the canonical tradition of Orthodoxy.[175]

Metropolitan Volodymyr also stated that a commission for dialogue with the KP was created in 2009.[176] This dialogue marked a shift in the internal policy of the UOC-MP, as it had declined dialogue with the KP as late as 2008, "until her head repents of the sin of schism before the mother church and is no longer under anathema."[177] In 2009, Cyril Hovorun suggested that the UOC-MP felt it had a responsibility to take action to resolve the schism in Ukraine, and not merely comment on it. Hovorun added that the UOC-MP had noted the failure of the UAOC and KP to agree on union, and entered the scene in an attempt to resolve their differences.[178] Metropolitan Volodymyr stated that "it is necessary for us to learn not to fear open dialogue with our opponents. Only in open, sincere discussions can we understand one another better and find paths to the resolution of church divisions."[179] The dialogue between the UOC-MP and KP faltered when Metropolitan Volodymyr's illness prevented him from consistently acting as the leader of the UOC-MP, though the UOC-MP formally reinvigorated the dialogue in accordance with the decision of the Holy Synod in March 2014.[180] The dialogue has been compromised by the decision of some parishes in Ukraine to transfer from the jurisdiction of the UOC-MP to that of the KP. The KP regards these transfers as the right of parishes to determine their own affiliation, but the MP has consistently condemned such transfers as illegal and a symbol of the persecution of the church.[181]

In summary, the post-Soviet period has witnessed numerous attempts to generate dialogue among the churches in Ukraine for reunification. The failure of the dialogues to generate a favorable outcome reveals the irreconcilable positions and ideologies separating the churches, and from a historical perspective they are consistent with the modern history of Orthodoxy in Ukraine. Only one conclusion can be drawn from these episodes of dialogue: ideological plurality reigns among the ranks of clergy and other leaders of the separated Orthodox churches, and no leader has yet to emerge who is able to find a solution to the problem.[182] Certainly, the dialogues have accentuated the primary identity features presented throughout this study: the UOC-MP seeks a canonical resolution on the matter, while the KP and UAOC look to the modern pattern of autocephalous churches existing in independent nations, with the Ecumenical Patriarchate acting as an anchor through the process of autocephaly. To date, even the Ecumenical Patriarchate has failed to resolve the differences among Ukrainian Orthodox. All three sides can claim only one tangible success: they have met with one another on several occasions and created proposals for union. To date, the accomplishment of the primary objective remains elusive.

Orthodox Participation in Ecumenical Dialogue

Orthodox clergy and theologians have participated in ecumenical dialogue in the Ukrainian religious milieu of the post-Soviet period, despite the prevailing pattern of intrachurch conflict. The reemergence of the UGCC in Ukraine was the catalyst for this ecumenical dialogue, a key development in a story that tends to accentuate disputes between Catholics and Orthodox. The return of Christian pluralism to Ukraine demanded an attempt to understand the other Christian communities there, and the UGCC was also motivated by a desire to connect with its own Constantinopolitan origins The Kyivan Church Study Group was founded in 1992 in cooperation with the Ukrainian Orthodox Churches of Canada and the USA and the Ecumenical Patriarchate, and this group illuminated the largely unknown narratives of religious persecution endured by the UGCC and the autocephalous churches.[183] The group met several times from 1992 to 1995 and engaged many prominent churchmen and theologians who were experienced interlocutors in ecumenical dialogue. Archbishop Lubomyr reintroduced the idea of establishing a national Ukrainian Church that would be in communion with Constantinople, Moscow, and Rome in letters addressing Patriarch Filaret and Metropolitan Volodymyr.[184] While both Filaret and Volodymyr dismissed his appeal, their responses manifest a willingness to engage the other on questions of church unity.

The National University of the Kyiv-Mohyla Academy founded the Ukrainian Christian Academic Society (UCAS) to encourage dialogue and collaboration among all Christian institutions in Ukraine, and Orthodox representatives participate in its activities.[185] The presence of several academic delegates from the UOC-MP demonstrates an understated point in the larger narrative of contemporary intra-Christian issues in Ukraine: some Orthodox are committed to ecumenical dialogue with other Christians. The crises in Ukraine have challenged Orthodox representatives to the Ukrainian Council of Churches and Religious Organizations (UCCRO), especially in the Maidan and post-Maidan milieu, when Orthodox Church leaders hold diverse positions on the controversies of state and society.[186] Nevertheless, Orthodox participation in the UCCRO facilitates personal encounter and dialogue between church leaders who are otherwise unable or unwilling to meet in traditional church-sponsored forums.

In summary, consistent Orthodox participation in ecumenical activities demonstrates a counternarrative to the official accusations of inciting civil unrest and promoting illegitimate activities. Some Orthodox continue to engage other Orthodox and Christians in dialogue in academic or state-sponsored spaces. The mere existence of these dialogues suggests that a resolution to long-standing disputes may still be possible.

Conclusion

The religious identities of the 1921 and 1942 UAOCs returned to Ukraine with the UAOC that emerged in 1989. This church initially bore the following marks: it was patriotic, advocated Ukrainization, and had overcome canonical illegitimacy by uniting itself to the Ukrainian Orthodox Church of the United States, which honored the aspirations of the 1921 church while reverting to a traditional, canonical path. The positive perspective on the 1921 cohort made the UAOC illegitimate in the eyes of its neighbors. The most important move made by the UAOC was its metamorphosis into a patriarchate, designed to permanently preserve its canonicity and autocephaly, reestablish Kyiv's antiquity and prestige within global Orthodoxy, and proclaim itself as Moscow's equal.

When Metropolitan Filaret left the metropolia and the KP emerged from the 1992 council, the KP's infection with ecclesial illegitimacy was deepened by their reception of Filaret, a problem worsened by his deposition from orders and eventual anathematization in 1997. However, the public religious identity of the KP coalesced around its commitment to being the local church of Ukraine. The KP negotiated national politics with savvy, strengthening its internal position with alliances with presidents Kravchuk and Yushchenko, and somehow emerging from Black Tuesday during Kuchma's tenure as the people's church. The perception of the KP as the people's church increased dramatically through its activity during the Orange Revolution, at the Euromaidan, and during the war in Eastern Ukraine. Its patriarch, Filaret, emerged as both a hero, on account of his support for Ukraine, and a villain, because of his refusal to relinquish his patriarchal office despite tepid support from external global Orthodox churches. The KP poses an enigma in this postmodern period of Ukrainian religious history for assessing the permanence of ecclesial illegitimacy: how does one compare the KP's occasionally dismissive attitude toward the absolute character of Orthodox canons with its stature among the people as a church that embodies the values of the Gospel?

Another enigma occurs in the metropolia, which attempted to become the authentic local church of Ukraine while remaining within the Muscovite orbit in the post-Soviet period. Initially, the metropolia adopted a path of modest internal Ukrainization under Metropolitan Volodymyr, a process governed by pastoral concern for non-Ukrainians, adherence to canons, acknowledgment of the need for consensus on changes in church life. Furthermore, the metropolia openly pursued autocephaly from 1992 to 1996, with the stipulation that it take a canonical course. The implementation of Patriarch Kirill's *Russkii mir* initiative exposed the internal tensions within the metropolia. Some leaders within the church used the opportunity to draw closer to Moscow. Metropolitan Volodymyr withstood the tensions and continued on his course of cautious Ukrainization and increased openness to dialogue, but he died in 2014. The ascension to the cathedra by Metropolitan Onufry in 2014 marked an uncertain time within the metropolia. On the one hand, he participated in the All-Ukrainian Council of Churches and Religious Organizations and used Ukrainian to address the public. On the other hand, the metropolia has used social media to communicate the appeals of other Orthodox churches to honor the canonicity of the Ukrainian Church, symbolized by Onufry's visit to Mount Athos and his participation in the synaxis of Orthodox primates in Geneva in January 2016. Onufry himself has commenced the process of moving the metropolia away from internal Ukrainization. The internal religious identity of the metropolia is obviously plurivocal. First, it seems that the metropolia will continue its course of claiming to be the only local Orthodox Church of Ukraine while remaining under Moscow. While this strategy pleases the MP, it has cost the metropolia faithful who have crossed jurisdictional lines in spite of the warnings of canonical violations. Second, it seems that the metropolia's approach is more cautious than anything else. It cannot credibly dismiss Ukrainization or even the possibility of autocephaly, but it insists on fidelity to canons and *absolute* consensus among the people to even begin such discussions. This returns us to the enigma of the KP: the metropolia needs to explain the relationship between church canons and the ordinary life of the daily Orthodox Christian in order to sustain its credibility among the people. The decision of the diaspora churches to join the EP in 1990 and 1995 demonstrates the ease with which canons and their interpretation can be manipulated. When the ecumenical patriarch received the diaspora churches, they became canonical and were empowered to influence church affairs in Ukraine, which they have done, especially in recent history. Here one might note the limitations of appeals to canons in discussion on church divisions and their resolution.

This assessment leads to a significant observation about the entire Ukrainian scene: the end of the Soviet Union unleashed an atmosphere of freedom and opportunity that permanently shaped the landscape of the Orthodox Church. Without a doubt, this post-Soviet period has been chaotic and tragic. But the new freedom has permitted Orthodox Ukrainians to revisit their interpretation of the epic events shaping Ukrainian Orthodox public religious identity. The development of official religious identity has been most dynamic in this atmosphere of relative freedom, and the individual churches' responses to epic events have provided a platform for them to articulate and rearticulate their self-identities. This pattern of responding to events and articulating identity has been a staple of Ukrainian history, and had continued in the events since the collapse of the Soviet Union. Cyril Hovorun aptly noted that the Ukrainian churches have entrenched themselves more deeply into their comfort zones. The KP and UAOC are patriotic, and the MP is multinational, and somehow their differences are too formidable to overcome; unity remains out of reach. The elusiveness of unity is magnified when one considers that the UAOC and KP have declared that they have no ideological or dogmatic differences: somehow, they are unable to unite despite unity of faith. As each church responded to Ukraine's post-Soviet struggles for economic stability and sovereignty, the question of nationalism infecting the church arose again, as it did in each period of our study. Certainly, the passions and wounds of war inflamed patriotic consciousness among many Ukrainian church leaders, but the post-Soviet period exhibits continuity in the primary identity features of the autocephalist Orthodox in Ukraine. They followed their predecessors in disavowing the 1686 annexation of Kyiv to Moscow, and bemoaned the problem of Russian colonization of Ukraine. One cannot speak of Ukrainian nationalism without reference to the problem of Russian colonization of Ukraine: the Church was viewed as a symbol of this colonization, so the topic cannot be reduced to ethnophyletism, as the problem is much more complex and includes a collision of ideologies. One can say that the Church's own organic evolution was marked by state events perhaps more profoundly in this period than at any other time in Ukrainian history.

The Ukrainian responses to current events tend to include sustaining the current course or reconstructing some version of the Kyivan Metropolia. Iterations of a new church emerging that is adjusted to the conditions of post-modernity in the twenty-first century are rare. Only a few such suggestions exist, including the remarks of Archbishop Ihor (Isichenko) of the UAOC eparchy in Kharkiv.[187] Reflecting on the failure of the UAOC to fortify its identity in the wake of the twentieth-century struggles, Archbishop Ihor calls for the church to begin construction of a new identity based upon the casting away of a psychology of church subservience to the state and the improvement of educational models in dialogue with contemporary pedagogy.[188] Metropolitan Oleksandr (Drabinko) is another voice, appealing to the UOC-MP to retrieve the legacy of Metropolitan Volodymyr and establish a local church that can engage society more effectively.[189] But only time will tell if the innovative voices of Archbishop Ihor and Metropolitan Oleksandr will find new company in bishops who are interested in establishing a new path of engagement for the Church in the twenty-first century. The stakes are high for the Ukrainian churches, but even higher for the Ukrainian people, as the violence caused by the adoption of Russian nationalism in the *Russkii mir* ideology has eradicated not only Ukrainian Christians in Crimea, but has also threatened Muslims there and Jews in Eastern Ukraine, and has resulted in a bloody war with over 1.5 million internally displaced persons.[190] The collision of civil religions in Ukraine has resulted in the deepening of divisions and outbreaks of violence: the question of whether or not church leaders will respond to the proverbial sound of the trumpet signaling the urgency of the need for interfaith and interreligious peace remains unanswered.

Conclusion

ORTHODOXY IN UKRAINE HAS ENDURED a turbulent journey of awakening, modernization, controversy, division, and terrible suffering. This study has treated the most prominent events, figures, symbols, and developments among the Orthodox Ukrainian communities from 1917 through 2016. Throughout, the study has presented the developments synchronously and emphasized significant identity markers as they appeared historically. In concluding this deeply complex study, this section summarizes its most significant contributions on the evolution of autocephaly and the stigma of illegitimacy in Orthodox Ukraine first, and then offers brief reflections on how the legacy of the twentieth and twenty-first centuries might shape the future of the Orthodox Church in Ukraine.

Modernization

The movement for autocephaly in Orthodox Ukraine occurred in tandem with modernization. Although some may object to the opacity of this term, modernization is the cultural phenomenon that inaugurated the environment that shaped the future trajectory of the Orthodox Church in Ukraine. The introduction of this study and the close review of the events leading up to the fateful 1921 UAOC council in Kyiv covered the starts and stops in attempting to stimulate a national awakening among the Ukrainian intelligentsia. The late nineteenth and early twentieth century was a time in which intellectuals sought to cultivate Ukrainian culture throughout the fabric of society, primarily through language. Ukrainian politicians and parties imagined diverse reconfigurations of Ukraine, from Ukraine as an autonomous republic retaining some kind of relationship with Russia to Ukraine as an independent nation-state. The primary "stop" in the intellectual process was the varying policies on the use of the Ukrainian language, which varied from discouragement to prohibition. The discouragement of public use of Ukrainian resulted in an urban culture of people conversing in Russian, unless they were at home with their families.

The period of modernization also witnessed to Ukrainian Church figures participating in the discussions on church renewal occurring throughout the Russian Orthodox Church. Like Russians, Ukrainians paid attention to cultural developments, and some clergy strove for educational reforms and the cultivation of a generation of clergy that was devoted to a significant increase in advocacy for the people and participation in their lives. Among Ukrainian churchmen, Vasyl Lypkivs'kyi exemplified this cohort of clergy. Ukrainian participation in the deliberations on church reform revolved around the question of liturgical language. The committee weighing questions of liturgical reform reviewed a variety of proposals that would permit the use of vernacular Ukrainian and Russian in the church's official liturgy. The inclusion of the Ukrainian language alongside Russian illustrates its importance in the life of the church: one of the primary ways for the clergy to deepen their connection with the people was to use the language with which they were most familiar.

From an ecclesial perspective, modernization also included an assessment of the church's structure. While the Russian Orthodox Church retained the traditional hierarchical structure of Byzantine Orthodoxy, it had not had a single identifiable leader since the reforms of Tsar Peter I (the Spiritual Regulations) had paused the continued succession of the patriarchate. The Russian Church was ruled by a synod and monitored by a lay imperial official, the over-procurator of the church, which compromised the church's independence. The most important issue to be deliberated for church modernization was the possibility of recreating the patriarchate, so as to establish a leader who could represent and organize the church, and prepare it to address the turbulent questions posed by modernization without depending solely on the will of the state. The recreation of the Moscow Patriarchate would also reconfigure the church-state relationship.

The most prominent Ukrainian leaders were also interested in modernizing the church structure, but their priority was to restore Kyivan distinctiveness that had been muted since the annexation of the Kyivan Metropolia to Moscow in 1686. The movements to recreate the Moscow Patriarchate and restore the Kyivan Metropolia had one common theme: the reforms of Tsar Peter I were viewed as making the bishops into the servants of the tsar, and thus the Petrine system needed to be removed. Furthermore, the problems for both the Russian and Ukrainian Church modernizers were deeply embedded in church structures. Changing the structure was the best path for modernizing the church, and changes were indeed implemented, with divergent outcomes.

Modernization and the Council of 1917–1918

Both the Russian and Ukrainian Church modernization movements were taken up by the councils in Moscow and Kyiv in 1917–1918. Obviously, the work of these councils was hindered by the political chaos and the destructive impact of the revolution and war on the Church. In terms of structure, change was effected in the churches both in Ukraine and Russia—the patriarchate in Moscow was recreated with the election and enthronization of Patriarch Tikhon in November 1917, and the 1918 All-Ukrainian Council voted for ecclesial autonomy, retaining its relationship with the Moscow Patriarchate.

The 1918 All-Ukrainian Council is an enigma and a turning point in the history of Orthodoxy in Ukraine and the inability of the Ukrainians to heal divisions within the Church. A review of the history of this period demonstrates that there was resistance to the convocation of a council in Ukraine, especially by Metropolitan Volodymyr (Bogoiavlensky) of Kyiv, and that the council's work was interrupted by the constantly changing political scene in Ukraine, with the Soviets, Hetmanate, Directory, and White Army all ruling in Kyiv at one point or another. The initial evidence suggests that a majority of Ukrainians favored autocephaly, with a sizable minority advocating for autonomy. The autocephalist movement in Ukraine gained momentum when the Moscow Council did not adopt the proposals for vernacular language in the liturgy.

The 1918 council in Kyiv became a turning point for three reasons: first, the change in the delegates for the second session in July kept the most vocal proponents of autocephaly out of the council. Second, the council affirmed the enthronement of Metropolitan Antony (Khrapovitsky) as metropolitan of Kyiv and Halych, a significant event given that he did not support Ukrainization. Third, the council rejected the use of vernacular Ukrainian, permitting only Church Slavonic as the sole legitimate liturgical language. The proponents of Ukrainization who had been forced out of the council deemed it illegitimate because only the Kyiv eparchy voted for Metropolitan Antony, which the council interpreted as a power play to eradicate the Ukrainian movement. The Ukrainianizers viewed the ability of the bishops to sway the council to a pro-Moscow position as a vestige of the system created by Tsar Peter I, which required each ordained bishop to swear his fealty to the monarch. When the bishops of the Ukrainian Exarchate appealed to conciliar authority and argued that the Kyiv Council itself voted for autonomy and contributed to the recreation of the patriarchate, the Ukrainianizers responded that those same bishops were products of a tsarist system that required them to serve the empire's interests, the same monarchical system that had appointed a predominantly Russian episcopate to oversee the life of the Church in Ukraine.

Ironically, it was the political change in Ukraine that enabled the Ukrainianizers to continue their agenda and establish the building blocks for the 1921 UAOC by exploiting anti-patriarchate Soviet officials to seize parish churches and serve the liturgy in Ukrainian. The uneasy peace between the Ukrainianizers and the exarchate's bishops in Kyiv was broken when Bishop Nazarii, Metropolitan

Antony, and Metropolitan Michael suspended and deposed the clerical leaders of the Ukrainian movement. The Ukrainianizers interpreted this event as just another episode in a pattern of using episcopal power to snuff out a legitimate church movement. Ultimately, the Ukrainianizers rejected the 1918 council altogether as invalid, a robber council, and embarked on a bold path of modernization. However, the bishops continued to refer to the authority of this council as justifying their disciplinary actions. In their attempts to negotiate peace with the Ukrainianizers, the exarchate's bishops approved of Ukrainization and its legitimacy, but this move failed to close the gap separating the two parties. Thus, a rejection of the Ukrainian subjugation to the Russian monarch, and the invalidity of the 1918 All-Ukrainian Council became primary identifying markers for what would become the 1921 UAOC.

Ukrainization

Ukrainization was the staple feature of the history of Orthodoxy in Ukraine in the twentieth century, for several reasons. Modernization included the introduction of vernacular languages into the liturgy and, for Ukrainians, the restoration of native traditions that had been muted or prohibited. Especially dear to Ukrainians was the cultivation of liturgical music based on folk melodies. Ukrainization has easily been the most disruptive and controversial matter dividing Orthodox for the entirety of the period under study. When the 1921 UAOC established its path toward independence despite the canonical risk, it implemented Ukrainization throughout the fabric of its life so that Ukrainization and the 1921 UAOC became synonymous. Parishes praying in vernacular Ukrainian were considered uncanonical because only the communities of the UAOC were using Ukrainian. Of course, the history of this period demonstrates that Ukrainization was also implemented throughout the Ukrainian eparchies of the autocephalous Orthodox Church in Poland and the 1942 UAOC. Furthermore, the assembly of the Ukrainian Exarchate in 1922 recommended Ukrainization, and it was implemented by Bishop Feofil (Buldovsky) and other bishops who ultimately became part of the Lubny Schism. But the approach to Ukrainization adopted by these churches was much more careful, with Ukrainianizing bishops often allowing parishes to retain Slavonic as the liturgical language.

   The tendency for Ukrainization to become polarizing has been strong in each phase of the history of the Ukrainian Church. The 1942 UAOC was well known for its advocacy of Ukrainization, and an appeal for a more measured, pastorally sensitive approach to Ukrainization was one of the two most important issues discussed by the autocephalist and autonomist bishops who signed the act of unity at Pochaiv in October of 1942. Modest Ukrainization was employed by the exarchate during the Soviet period to ease the transitions of Greek Catholics into Orthodoxy after the L'viv council of 1946, and the rebirth of the UAOC and emergence of the KP as the national Orthodox Church of Ukraine after the turn of the twenty-first century marked the permanent return of Ukrainization and its implementation in the Church in Ukraine. The divergent approaches to Ukrainization within the UOC-MP illustrate the reluctance of many Orthodox in the Moscow Patriarchate to embrace it as a legitimate movement. On the one hand, Metropolitan Volodymyr (Sabodan) authorized Ukrainization as legitimate, referring to the 1921 decision of the bishops in Ukraine that permitted parishes to pray in Ukrainian provided the majority of the parish desired it. On the other hand, the narrative of the Church under Moscow has continued to prefer that Slavonic be the language used for worship by all Orthodox Slavs. Four factors contribute to the continued use of Slavonic instead of vernacular Ukrainian. First, the use of the vernacular itself is viewed as an innovation and conservatives throughout the Orthodox Church oppose the introduction of modern languages, including Greek and Russian. Second, the laity were suspicious of liturgical innovations. In the milieu of the revolution, the laity took up the mantle of defending Orthodoxy from usurpers, and the liturgy served as a symbol of continuity during a period of drastic change. Regardless of the reasons for the conservatism of the people, the fact is that only parts of the church accepted Ukrainization as legitimate during the twentieth and twenty-first centuries. Third, the use of Slavonic as a language used by all Slavs adhered to the multinational character of the Moscow Patriarchate, with four nations as its foundation: Russia, Ukraine, Belarus, and Moldova. Fourth, Ukrainization is controversial as a political issue, so the Orthodox who favor Ukrainization are depicted as favoring the pro-Ukrainian nationalists, suggesting the presence of ethnophyletism in the Church.

The presence of four different justifications for the continuation of Slavonic in favor of Ukrainian in the liturgy all point to the ever-evolving environment in Ukraine, in which the Church under Moscow seeks to be a constant, non-changing institution. Furthermore, it also shows that Ukrainization has consistently been associated with innovation and nationalism, and that it has not taken root throughout the Orthodox Church in Ukraine as a churchwide initiative. Ukrainization is thus one of the most useful issues for studying Orthodoxy in Ukraine, as it has proven to be polarizing despite being confirmed as canonically legitimate in each stage of the history of Orthodoxy in Ukraine. The consistent suspicion and rejection of Ukrainization also confirms the pattern whereby initiatives proposed by the pro-autocephalist cohort become affixed to the stigma of ecclesial illegitimacy.

Ecclesiology and *Sobornopravnist'*

Sobornopravnist' is the only issue that has proven to be more polarizing than Ukrainization in the history of the Ukrainian Church. The movement to restore traditions of the Kyivan Metropolia resulted in the favoring of *sobornopravnist'* as the primary governing principle of the 1921 UAOC. The church used *sobornopravnist'* as its rationale for reconstructing an episcopate despite the absence of any participating bishops, and its statute limited the broad and deep power bishops traditionally have in Orthodox ecclesiology. The revision of the rite of episcopal ordination, where the entire assembly essentially ordained the first two bishops of the 1921 UAOC, was a second permanent turning point for the history of Orthodoxy in Ukraine, with severe implications for Ukrainian relations with the rest of global Orthodoxy. The 1921 UAOC hoped that global Orthodoxy would come to receive a version of its flattened ecclesiology, but this never happened, even within the cohort of Ukrainians who desired autocephaly. The 1924 branch of Orthodox autocephalists preserved the traditional Orthodox approach to ecclesiology and dismissed the 1921 cohort as having misinterpreted and misapplied the meaning of *sobornopravnist'*. Certainly, many Orthodox in the world have moved closer to a conciliar model by increasing the rights of lower clergy and laity and their participation in the life of the church, a principle that was even legislated into the life and activities of the 1917–1918 Moscow Council. But no church ever went so far as to remove the episcopacy from the ritual of ordaining bishops, which caused other Orthodox Ukrainians to describe the 1921 UAOC as Protestant, while the Moscow Patriarchate identified them as self-consecrated and without grace. These terms represented the stigma of illegitimacy attached to the UAOC that has proven to be permanent. When the 1942 UAOC received the surviving clergy of the 1921 UAOC into their "true orders," without a new ordination, they were perceived as permitting the pollution of canonical illegitimacy to permeate their church, a problem that likewise afflicted all of the Orthodox Ukrainians in the diaspora, the 1989 UAOC, and the KP.

For its part, the 1921 UAOC embarked on a path toward constructing its own episcopate as a way of separating from the hegemony of tsarist Orthodoxy that had dominated Ukraine since 1686. Therefore, the construction of a new episcopacy had a political dimension, liberating the Church from the shackles of subservience to the Russian imperial throne, which was anti-Christian. But while the 1942 UAOC shared the same rejection of Russian imperial hegemony over the fate of the Ukrainian Church, it also rejected the adoption of *sobornopravnist'* by the 1921 UAOC as misdirected and uncanonical. The contemporary UAOC maintains a nominal adherence to *sobornopravnist'*, but it is no longer a staple feature of the other churches. Thus, the ecclesiology of the 1921 UAOC is a product of ecclesial modernization that was received neither within the community of Orthodox Ukrainians nor in global Orthodoxy, and it has clouded the permanent path of Orthodoxy in Ukraine for the foreseeable future.

The rejection of *sobornopravnist'* did not eradicate the paradigm shift of social power within the Orthodox churches of Ukraine, however. The 1921 UAOC established a pattern that has recurred throughout the contemporary history of the Orthodox Church in Ukraine: popular and frequently controversial laity and married clergy rising to positions of power within the Church and influencing its life for generations. Metropolitan Vasyl (Lypkivs'kyi) (married priest), Volodymyr (Chekhivsky) (layman), Metropolitan Ilarion (Ohienko) (layman), Patriarch Mstyslav (Skrypnyk) (layman), Patriarch Volodymyr (Romaniuk) (married priest), and Patriarch Dmitry (Jarema) (married priest) all began their careers within the Church as populist laypeople or married priests who eventually ascended to the heights of church power. In one way or another, each figure struggled on behalf of the cause of Ukrainian Orthodox autocephaly despite resistance from the established hierarchy. It is ironic that two of these figures, Metropolitan Ilarion and Patriarch Mstyslav in particular, gained reputations as tyrannical hierarchs, but their adoption of a hierarchical mindset does not cancel out the environment within the Ukrainian Church that permitted the laity to exercise considerable influence within the church. The shift of power from hierarchy to laity has not been absolute: many of the current divisions within Ukrainian Orthodoxy have been caused by the inability of the people in ecclesial power structures to compromise on divisive issues.

In summary, modernization set the tone for the emergence of an independent church in Ukraine. Many aspects of Ukrainian modernization existed in the Russian Church as well, and certain aspects of Ukrainian Church modernization have been declared as legitimate as long as they are not imposed on parish communities. The most notable aspects of Ukrainian Church modernization have been the polarization resulting from the implementation of initiatives, and the absence of consensus on the reception of these initiatives within the Orthodox Ukrainian community.

Canonicity

The second macro-level identity for the Ukrainian Church is canonicity. Canonical status has been used by all church leaders as a way to define the identity of their churches and inscribe identity on the opposing churches in Ukraine. This occurred in each stage of the history of Orthodoxy in Ukraine. First, from 1917–1930, the 1921 UAOC rejected the canonical validity of the 1918 All-Ukrainian Council and created its own native canons. The Moscow Patriarchate and Ukrainian

Exarchate rejected the canonical status of the 1921 UAOC because its clergy had been deposed and the rite used to ordain bishops was not Orthodox. The rejection of the 1921 UAOC was upheld by global Orthodoxy. The 1921 UAOC became the anti-model for canonicity, as all pro-autocephaly Orthodox churches in Ukraine and the diaspora have reverted to the traditional ecclesiological model employed within global Orthodoxy, with the exception of very small minorities maintaining fidelity to 1921.

Canonicity is particularly powerful in the perception of receiving or even approving of the 1921 UAOC. The decision of the 1942 UAOC to receive the clergy in their true orders proved to be an insurmountable obstacle to unity, despite Metropolitan Policarp's appeal to the martyrdom of the 1921 church, which connected to the universal recognition of martyrdom as superseding all canonical prohibitions. Because of the power of the perception of the absence of canonical legitimacy, the depiction of a Ukrainian church as being uncanonical, self-consecrated, and without grace has become the most vicious polemical device in intrachurch politics. The 1942 UAOC and its defendants accused the Moscow Patriarchate of being uncanonical because of its official loyalty to the USSR proclaimed by Metropolitan Sergei in 1927. Metropolitan Dionysii (Valedynsky) of Warsaw condemned Metropolitan Oleksii (Hromadskii) for his uncanonical decision to return to the Moscow Patriarchate when the Soviets assumed control over Western Ukraine in 1939. Patriarch Pimen (Izvekov) and Metropolitan Filaret (Denysenko) declared the Ukrainian diaspora and the 1989 UAOC as uncanonical entities because their sympathy for the 1921 UAOC meant that global Orthodoxy was not in communion with them.

The 1992 Kharkiv council and the Moscow Patriarchate accused Metropolitan Filaret of leading the Church into schism and later deposed and anathematized him, adding a new dimension of canonical illegitimacy to Orthodoxy in Ukraine. Patriarch Filaret and the KP have condemned the 1992 Kharkiv council as a pseudo-council because it was convoked without the blessing and presidency of the first hierarch of the Church. Two conclusions emerge from this vicious pattern of canonical polemics. First, canonicity has become the preferred instrument of choice to establish legitimacy in the eyes of the global Church. Second, the Ukrainians have failed to find ways to resolve canonical problems that deepen divisions within their Orthodox communities, despite many efforts.

Canonicity has a third dimension worth mentioning. The critical mass of Orthodox Ukrainians abandoned the canonical platform of the 1921 UAOC. The canons and ecclesiology of that church are not a part of the fabric of any formidable Orthodox body in or outside of Ukraine. The 1942 UAOC remained faithful to traditional Orthodox canonical structures, with the exception of overt sympathy and a desire to forgive the uncanonical path of the 1921 UAOC. Therefore, it would be sensible for Orthodox Ukrainians to remove the stigma of illegitimacy complicating intrachurch negotiations as an unnecessary obstacle. This could contribute to clearing the path for a more constructive journey to unity. In reality, the 1921 UAOC should no longer figure into the larger canonical discussion. The more urgent question is the application of the 1924 *tomos* recognizing the autocephaly of the Church in Poland, which renders the 1686 annexation of the Kyivan Metropolia to Moscow as uncanonical. The argument between the autocephalists and autonomists from 1941 to 1944 exposes the real canonical dispute, as the autocephalists referred to Constantinople as the true Mother Church of Ukraine, while the autonomists sought to continue the work of the 1918 All-Ukrainian Council, which had been tragically interrupted by the revolution, wars, and the persecution that followed. A real breakthrough will be possible when Orthodox Ukrainians can return to a discussion of the application of the 1924 *tomos* of autocephaly and the 1918 All-Ukrainian Council to contemporary church life in Ukraine.

Political Theology

This study has illuminated the emergence of several political theologies responding to the conditions of Orthodox church movements in Ukraine throughout the twentieth century. The emergence of political theologies also shows the Ukrainian tendency to seek an alliance with the state and ask for its intervention on behalf of the church. From 1918 to 1921, the autocephalist and pro-Moscow cohorts each received support from the state. The autocephalists were supported explicitly by the Directory and implicitly by the Soviet regime, whereas the patriarchal churches were supported by Denikin's army, with mild and insignificant support coming from the Hetmanate. The tsarist regime was removed from this picture, which contributed to one of the most important theological foundations of the 1921 UAOC. Having been delivered from its enslavement to the Russian empire and its policies, the Ukrainians were now free from Russification and all of the decisions decreed by the Russian episcopate, since these bishops had sworn their fidelity to the monarchy. The political theology of liberation and socialist democracy was expressed through innovative Ukrainian liturgical practices and its ecclesiology limiting episcopal power. However, the most definitive decisions made by the 1918 All-Ukrainian Council occurred after Metropolitan Antony returned to Kyiv with Denikin's army. The collision of Ukrainian and Russian parties in the Church was often a confrontation of two political bases, one monarchist, and the other for an independent Ukrainian republic. Ultimately, the 1921 UAOC briefly championed itself as a revolutionary church that was not opposed to the Soviet regime and thanked it for the separation of church and state, but all Orthodox churches in Soviet Ukraine were eventually hurt by the anti-religious policies of the Bolshevik regime.

While Metropolitan Sergei's oath of allegiance to the Soviet Union permitted the patriarchate's survival, it also set the stage for the next round of political theologies in Ukraine. When the bishops of Volyn' rejoined the Moscow Patriarchate in fidelity to the decision of the 1918 All-Ukrainian Council, they had experienced just under two years of Soviet persecution of the Church and were essentially hoping for the establishment of a Ukrainian republic and the eradication of the "red Bolsheviks." Thus, all Orthodox of Ukraine hailed the invading Germans as liberators in 1941. This set them against the Moscow Patriarchate itself, which began to depict the Germans as the latest foreign invaders seeking to exploit the peoples of Kyivan Rus'. Tragically, these same Ukrainians found the German occupiers to be as malevolent as their Soviet predecessors: there was no liberation for Ukraine. Throughout the processes though, the Orthodox in Ukraine had cooperated with their German occupiers in attempting to establish themselves as legitimate churches of the republic, a continuation of the Church's tradition of attempting to work in symphony with the state.

This symphony occurred involuntarily, when the political theology of the Moscow Patriarchate took on the features of internationalization and peacekeeping, symbolized by the reunion of Greek Catholics with Orthodox in the wake of the L'viv council of 1946. The new political theology of the Ukrainian Exarchate permitted Ukrainization in the spirit of the multinational character of the Moscow Patriarchate, which could be a home for the Church of any nation. This political theology honored the peacemaking initiatives of the Soviet Union, which had achieved peace when it evicted the Nazi invaders from Ukrainian borders during the Great Patriotic War. If the exarchate's political theology expressed the official position of the Church, individual hierarchs, clergy, and communities adopted subaltern strategies of survival and "speaking Bolshevik." The unique attempts of various individuals and groups within the Church to resist state imposition of a Soviet and Orthodox identity on the people though unconventional means yielded two noteworthy outcomes. First, the postwar period of the Orthodox exarchate was one of multiple identities that were essentially irreconcilable, as the outward expression of Soviet Orthodoxy did not erase the underlying ecclesial and national identities of Orthodox Ukrainians in the exarchate. Second, Shlikhta's contributions demonstrate the value of underrepresented sources in presenting the complete picture of the Orthodox Church in the postwar period.

The political theology of the Ukrainian churches of the diaspora diversifies the postwar narrative, as these churches in the West used their new platforms of freedom in Canada and the United States to condemn Soviet religious policies and the captivity of nations. The Ukrainian diaspora cooperated with the democratic governments of the United States and Canada and adopted the rhet-oric of Cold War ideology to seek the liberation of oppressed churches in the Soviet Union. The erection of the Shevchenko monument in Washington, DC, and the construction of St. Andrew's Memorial Church in South Bound Brook, New Jersey, became symbols communicating the political theology of martyrdom and liberation via democracy. The two opposing political theologies clashed with the celebration of the millennium of the baptism of Rus' in 1988; the multinational, peacemaking ideology of the Moscow Patriarchate vying with the pro-democ-racy, liberation theologies rooted in martyrdom proclaimed by the diaspora. The diaspora Ukrainians do not have sole claim to inspiring the rebirth of the UAOC in 1989: the consistent retention of ecclesial and national identity on the part of those engaging in quiet resistance permitted them to reclaim their space in the religious marketplace of Ukraine at the end of the Soviet period.

When the UAOC was reborn in Ukraine in 1989 and the division among the Orthodox deepened through the epic events of Black Tuesday in 1995, the Orange Revolution in 2004, and the Maidan in 2013, the Orthodox churches and their political theologies experienced their most recent stages of evolution. The KP became the church of patriotism and the active supporter of the Ukrainian military, whereas the UOC-MP became the church that served the entire flock in Ukraine and was unashamedly anti-war. Through each phase of post-Soviet development, each church sought the advocacy of the state, and the favoring of churches has alternated from one political leader to the next.

Four constants have emerged in the evolution of political theology in the post-Soviet period as the churches attempted to adjust to reconfiguration of political boundaries and spaces. First, the Moscow Patriarchate retained certain aspects of its internationalist identity from the Soviet era while becoming more anti-Western and anti-globalization under the influence of Russian nationalism. The emergence of a *Russkii mir* ideology resulted in actions in which the Moscow Patriarchate laid claim to the ecclesial space of the Ukrainian churches, while the ideology of the initiative functioned as a rationale for Russia's annexation of Crimea and the eradication of all churches and religious groups from Crimea and Eastern Ukraine that did not belong to the Moscow Patriarchate. Second, all of the Ukrainian churches have sought state support, including direct intervention in intrachurch affairs, which would increase the prestige and legitimacy of one church over the other during this period. Third, each church has attempted to establish an anchor in canonical identity, symbolized by the UOC-MP's frequent visits to Mount Athos. The outcome has remained the same: no bishop or state leader has been able to overcome the obstacles dividing the Orthodox churches and construct a path to unity. Many Orthodox Ukrainians have appealed to the authority of the ecumenical patriarch, and the ecumenical patriarch has attempted to gently encourage union among the divided parties, as evidenced by the years of official negotiation between the UAOC and KP. But the attempts of the Ukrainian bishops of the Ecumenical Patriarchate to facilitate dialogue have yet to produce tangible union from the existing divisions, and the results include accusations of foreign bishops interfering in the sovereign, canonical life of another local church. In other words, no new developments in political theologies and church-state or church-church alliances have definitively resolved the division in Orthodoxy that has reigned since 1921.

The fourth outcome is that political theology evolves in tandem with the identified antagonist persecuting the church. The most prevalent pattern of shifting antagonists occurs in the history of the pro-autocephaly churches. If the tsar was the original captor the Church needed to escape, he has been succeeded by the bishops, the patriarch of Moscow, the Soviet Union, and the president of Russia (Putin) in a seemingly endless rotation of tyrants keeping the Ukrainian Church captive. In some cases, two antagonists share the role of tyrant—that is the case for the contemporary autocephalist churches in Ukraine, who refer to Patriarch Kirill and President Putin as their captors. Even the UOC-MP has adopted the language of political theology by implicating the Ukrainian state and Patriarch Filaret as the antagonists who seize places of worship illegally and grant them to illegitimate churches. This pattern of expressing a theology grounded in liberation from an external or internal captor has become a permanent fixture in intrachurch polemics in Ukraine, and it prevents church leaders from engaging a critical evaluation of their own culpability in expanding the separation between the churches.

Nationalism and Autocephaly: A Resolution to the Crucial Question?

The introduction to this book promised an assessment of the impact of nationalist ideology on the autocephalist movement in the Orthodox Church of Ukraine. In this study, the swelling in the ranks of autocephalists has coincided with the process of Ukrainian nation-building. In many instances, church leaders have appealed to patriotism as a way of dismissing the history of external oppression on both political and ecclesial fronts. These appeals suggest that the autocephalist movement seeks to establish a national church of Ukraine, while the church leaders themselves refer to the modern Orthodox pattern of configuring canonical church borders in alignment with the official spatial boundaries of sovereign nations. As global Orthodoxy confronts the twenty-first century, there has been some discussion of returning to regional structures and abandoning the practice of aligning autocephalous churches with the territorial borders of nation-states. This approach could contribute to the eradication of ethnophyletism in the Church and prevent the potential damage done by the emergence of a civic religion with a narrow ideology, at least in principle. Many Ukrainians believe that appointing Orthodox Ukrainians to the regional structure of the Moscow Patriarchate would embitter Ukrainians by demanding they remain in a tyrannical church structure that does not respect their ecclesial and national otherness. The evidence yielded by this study on the nationalist ideology of Ukrainians in the church is mixed. On the one hand, many of the primary ideologues of Ukrainian Orthodoxy have also been patriots who have been eager to create advantageous alliances with the state. On the other hand, Ukrainians have proven that they have a particular regional and cultural tradition that distinguishes them from Russians and other Eastern Slavs. As the Orthodox Church considers the criteria for autocephaly in the twenty-first century, it must take into account both the problem of nationalist ideology and the risk of tolerating the cultural enslavement of a people through a church structure. In contemporary Ukraine, the damage inflicted by the *Russkii mir* ideology of the Moscow Patriarchate has contributed to gross violations of human dignity through violence and displacement. Orthodox leaders are right to be cautious about the emergence of a blatantly nationalist civic religion in Ukraine, so it seems that an innovative solution that mutes nationalism without prohibiting healthy patriotism is in order.

Anticipating the Next Phase

The story of the Orthodox Church in Ukraine in the twentieth and twenty-first centuries is a bewildering tale of modernization and conservatism, opportunity and threat, elation and melancholy, and serfdom with the promise of liberation. The 1921 UAOC constitutes the most bold, creative, brazen, and controversial attempt to recreate the Kyivan Metropolia in response to the needs of modernity. The remainder of the legacy of Orthodoxy in Ukraine in this period is a series of attempts to restore order and establish an authoritative voice. Each church described in this study makes its case as the Orthodox Church in Ukraine: none of these churches can claim that they have established themselves definitively as the Orthodox Church in Ukraine, affirmed by the Orthodox faithful and the global Orthodox community alike. In many ways, the story of Orthodoxy in Ukraine is one of persuasion, making the case to the people and the other Orthodox churches of the world that they are and want to be the people's church. The division among the Orthodox in Ukraine is the primary obstacle preventing any one of the churches from being able to make this claim persuasively. In fact, the most tragic and lamentable outcome of the story of Orthodoxy in Ukraine is the failure of the Church's leaders to overcome their divisions and unite into one church. The prevailing pattern of Orthodox Church development in Ukraine is to deepen separation and sharpen the distinctions between the Orthodox churches, a problem severely exacerbated by the fusion of pro-autocephaly features and objectives to the stigma of ecclesial illegitimacy. Cyril Hovorun depicts the churches as planting themselves more firmly into their positions of self-identity, finding refuge in their comfort zones, which are affirmed by the people who are faithful to their particular positions, be they modern, patriotic, canonical, or something else.[1] Given the consistency of this pattern of separation and triumphant declaration of legitimacy by the Orthodox churches in this period, there is no reason to expect the pattern to be broken as the Orthodox Church in Ukraine continues its life deeper into the twenty-first century.

The preceding statement is quite pessimistic: is it possible the world will encounter something new in the near future in Orthodox Ukraine? From an ecclesiological perspective, the other pattern illuminated by this study is the attempt of the Church to adjust and respond to the needs of society. The following possible outcomes for the Orthodox Church in Ukraine are based on contemporary Ukrainian society's ever-increasing demand for the emergence of a local Orthodox church and the post-Soviet challenges of religious and cultural pluralism that church leaders already face. Here are three plausible developments for the Orthodox communities of Ukraine, namely the cessation of dependence on external church leaders, the emergence of a canonical alternative to the Moscow Patriarchate, and the organic development of a new intellectual center of Orthodox clergy and laity.

Forsaking Cyrus

As the Church attempted to establish its legitimacy in Ukraine, its leaders turned to an array of ecclesial and civil leaders to resolve Ukrainian differences once and for all. Since 1919, church leaders have turned to the Ukrainian and German state leaders, and to the primates of autocephalous churches in Russia, Constantinople, Poland, and Georgia to proclaim the legitimacy of the autocephaly and/or autonomy of the Church in Ukraine. From the failed attempts of the 1921 UAOC to obtain Constantinopolitan and Georgian support to the welcome of Hitler to Ukraine, and up through the alliances with Kravchuk, Yushchenko, and Yanukovych, the Ukrainian attempts to find a contemporary Cyrus to liberate them from their captor and return them to their own homeland have failed. Authoritative figures of the state and the global Orthodox churches have been unable to resolve the separation between the Orthodox Ukrainians. The pattern of irreconcilable differences separating Orthodox Ukrainians has parallels in Ukrainian society and within the global Orthodox communion, demonstrated by the difficulty experienced by Ukrainian political leaders in building lasting coalitions and the constant turbulence within the Orthodox community, which compromised the convocation of the Holy and Great Council in Crete in 2016.

History has demonstrated that the problems dividing the Orthodox Ukrainians do not require external resolution. It remains reasonable for Ukrainian churches to appeal for the assistance of the ecumenical patriarch in resolving this issue, as a nod to the canonical mechanism in the Church. In June 2010, an intra-church conference was held in Kyiv on the role of Constantinople in the life of the Orthodox Church in Ukraine.[2] The participants presented a number of creative ways the Ecumenical Patriarchate could facilitate the creation of a united, local church in Ukraine, with multiple references to canonical patterns in church con-figuration throughout history. Ultimately, however, Orthodox Ukrainians could ease the entire process for the rest of the Orthodox world by attending to their own internal matters without depending on external intervention. There is no need for a foreign patriarch or political figure to make a judgment on the legiti-macy of Ukrainization of the liturgy, or even the canonical status of the Church in Ukraine. Ultimately, the Ukrainians themselves need to work through these issues, even if several decades of negotiations are required before some kind of consensus emerges. When the Ukrainians reach a mutual understanding on the structures and agendas of the Church in Ukraine, all that will be needed from foreign patriarchs is formal recognition.

Some of the responsibility for the situation in Ukraine falls on her sister Orthodox churches. Essentially, the story told in this book is one of competing narratives. To date, the non-Ukrainian churches have accepted the narrative on Ukrainian Orthodoxy presented by the Moscow Patriarchate. This narrative depicts autocephalist Ukrainians as nationalists and chauvinists, promulgating an ideology polluted by their encounter with Nazi fascism that results in vio-lence. The Ukrainian narrative pleads for liberation from Russian tyranny, and depicts Russian church leaders as imperialistic, power-hungry, and bigoted. The non-Ukrainian and non-Russian church leaders do not have to begin favoring the Ukrainians for political reasons, but they are responsible for making their canon-ical mechanisms elastic enough to hear the narrative written by the churches in question. The Ecumenical Patriarchate set the tone for allowing Ukrainians to tell their own story by receiving the diaspora Ukrainian Orthodox Church in 1990 and 1995. If global Orthodox leaders demonstrate that they are willing to hear everyone's case without bias, they will be empowered to assist the Orthodox Church in Ukraine to embrace authentic Christian witness in an autocephalous church that interrelates with all other Orthodox churches, while setting aside any vestiges of chauvinistic ethnophyletism.

A Canonical Alternative?

One possible way forward for the Church in Ukraine is the legitimizing of a canonical alternative to the UOC-MP. The KP could become this canonical alternative, even if it relinquishes its patriarchal status. Another possibility for the canonical alternative is to simply recognize the Orthodox Church in Ukraine itself as autocephalous while creating an eparchy of the Moscow Patriarchate, a solution suggested by Metropolitan Oleksandr (Drabinko).[3] Both scenarios would permit the clergy and laity who belong to these Orthodox churches to choose their own path without fear of canonical impediments. The creation of a canonical alternative would also honor the reality of pluralism within the Orthodox Church in Ukraine—Ukrainization could not be universally imposed, and no one would be forced to be Orthodox under Moscow's jurisdiction. This solution would permit church life to evolve somewhat naturally without necessitating the interference or intervention of an external ecclesial entity into Ukrainian church affairs. Creating an ecclesial situation that honors the legitimacy of the Ukrainian movement and those who wish to retain a strong connection to Moscow would also break the pattern of dependence on external authorities prevailing in modern Ukrainian Orthodox life.

After Canonical Legitimacy: Developing an Intellectual Elite

Ukrainian Orthodox have devoted much of their energy to presenting their canonical case to anyone in the Orthodox world who was willing to listen. For better or worse, pluralism will continue to spread throughout Ukrainian society, and a closer association with Europe along with the adoption of democratic values will allow Ukrainians to choose their religious adherence freely. Eventually, a generation of Ukrainians will no longer feel obliged to be Orthodox; they will choose their ecclesial homes in step with most of the rest of the Christian world.

    From the perspective of pastoral theology, appeals to Ukrainian patriotism, canonical legitimacy, and even the shrines of Kyiv will not be enough to sustain the people. Like other Christians of the world, Ukrainians will seek a church where they can encounter God, the saints, and one another in meaningful personal relationships. Ukrainian Orthodox people are already tired of triumphant political theologies and are taking note of the failure of the churches to achieve union. For the next generation of Church leaders, developing an intellectual elite of clergy and laity who can creatively respond to contemporary challenges while remaining faithful to Orthodox tradition will give the Church the best chance to secure its relationship with the people. The basis of an intellectual elite exists in the UGCC and has a center at the Ukrainian Catholic University in L'viv; only time will tell if the Orthodox Church will join the conversation and establish centers of learning and discourse for both clergy and laity. If history has taught us anything, it's that a cohort of bold intellectuals will attempt to form an intellectual center designed to modernize the church and serve contemporary Ukrainian society. One can only hope that the Orthodox people of Ukraine will embrace its work as a welcome sign of the arrival of the Orthodox Church in Ukraine.

Notes

Notes to Introduction

1. According to a Pew Research Center study published May 10, 2017, "Religious Belief and National Belonging in Central and Eastern Europe," 78 percent of Ukrainians claim to be Orthodox. See http://www.pewforum.org/2017/05/10/religious-belief-and-national-belonging-in-central-and-eastern-europe/ (accessed September 25, 2017).

2. For Moscow's position on the Ecumenical Patriarchate's authority, see Metropolitan Hilarion (Alfeyev), "Primacy and Synodality from an Orthodox Perspective," The Russian Orthodox Church: Department for External Church Relations, November 9, 2014, https://mospat.ru/en/2014/11/09/news111091/ (accessed October 5, 2017). The Ecumenical Patriarchate responded with an essay by Metropolitan Elpidophoros (Lambridianis), "First without Equals: A Response to the Text on Primacy of the Moscow Patriarchate," Ecumenical Patriarchate, December 2, 2014, https://www.patriarchate.org/-/primus-sine-paribus-hapantesis-eis-to-peri-proteiou-keimenon-tou-patriarcheiou-moschas-tou-sebasmiotatou-metropolitou-prouses-k-elpidophorou (accessed October 5, 2017).

3. For an overview of the problems associated with the power struggle and canon 28, see Paul Brusanowski, "Autocephaly in Ukraine: The Canonical Dimension," in Churches in the Ukrainian Crisis, ed. Andrii Krawchuk and Thomas Bremer (New York: Palgrave MacMillan, 2016), 47–77.

4. For an overview of Ukrainian nationalism, see John Armstrong, Ukrainian Nationalism, 3rd ed. (Englewood, CO: Ukrainian Academic Press, 1990).

5. In 2009–10, Patriarch Kirill (Gundiaev) of Moscow developed and articulated a vision for a civilization rooted in the traditional valued of Kyivan Rus' that would serve as an alternative to globalization. In a series of speehces, he referred to the civilization as the Russkii mir, or Russian world. The multinational Moscow Patriarchate serves as the primary community of belonging for those whose values cohere with the Russkii mir.

6. The Council of Florence in 1438–9 culminated in the restoration of union of the Catholic and Orthodox Churches. The Union collapsed when local Orthodox bishops and laity refused to receive it. Greek Catholics view the Union of Brest as congruent with the Council of Florence, an organic step towards restoring the Union achieved in Florence throughout the entire Church. The literature covering the history of the Union of Brest in 1596 is deep and varied. From the Ukrainian Orthodox perspective, select older historical works represent a common interpretation of the historical context, such as Ivan Vlasovs'kyi, Outline History of the Ukrainian Orthodox Church, vol. 1, The Baptism of Ukraine to the Union of Berestye (988–1596) (New York: Ukrainian Orthodox Church of the USA, 1956), 156–265; Vlasovs'kyi, Outline History of the Ukrainian Orthodox Church, vol. 2, XVII Century, ed. Ivan Korowytsky, trans. Mykola Haydak and Frank Estocin (New York: Ukrainian Orthodox Church of the USA, 1979), 13–24. For a Russian perspective, see Dimitry Pospielovsky, The Orthodox Church in the History of Russia (Crestwood, NY: St. Vladimir's Seminary Press, 1998), 90–100. Also, see Borys Gudziak, Crisis and Reform: The Kyivan Metropolitanate, the Patriarchate of Constantinople, and the Genesis of the Union of Brest, Harvard Series in Ukrainian Studies (Cambridge, MA: Harvard University Press for the Harvard Ukrainian Research Institute, 2001); Bert Groen, ed.,

Four Hundred Years Union of Brest (1596–1996): A Critical Reevaluation; Acta of the Congress Held at Hernen Castle, the Netherlands, in March 1996 (Leuven: Peeters, 1998); Jean-Claude Roberti, *Les Uniates* (Paris: Cerf, 1992); Oleh Turii, "Die Union von Brest 1595/96: Entstehung und historische Hintergründe," in *Glaube in der 2. Welt: Zeitschrift für Religionsfreiheit und Menschenrechte* 4 (1977): 12–16; and John-Paul Himka, "The Greek Catholic Church and Nation-Building in Galicia, 1772–1918," *Harvard Ukrainian Studies* 8, nos. 3–4 (1984): 426–52.

7. On this topic, see Ronald Popivchak, "The Life and Times of Peter Mohyla, Metropolitan of Kiev," *Logos: A Journal of Eastern Christian Studies* 43–45 (2004): 339–59; Frank E. Sysyn, "The Formation of Modern Ukrainian Religious Culture: The Sixteenth and Seventeenth Centuries," in *Religion and Nation in Modern Ukraine*, ed. Serhii Plokhy and Frank E. Sysyn (Edmonton, AB: Canadian Institute of Ukrainian Studies Press, 2003), 1–22; Ihor Ševčenko, "The Many Worlds of Peter Mohyla," *Harvard Ukrainian Studies* 8, nos. 1–2 (1984): 9–40 (this issue is devoted to the study of the Kyiv Mohyla Academy); Peter Galadza, "Seventeenth-Century Liturgicons of the Kyivan Metropolia and Several Lessons for Today," *St. Vladimir's Theological Quarterly* 56, no. 1 (2012): 73–91; and Paul Meyendorff, "The Liturgical Reforms of Peter Moghila: A New Look," *St. Vladimir's Theological Quarterly* 29, no. 2 (1985): 101–14. Mohyla was glorified as a saint in the Ukrainian Orthodox Church in 1996.

8. Orest Subtelny, *Ukraine: A History*, 3rd ed. (Toronto, ON: University of Toronto Press, 2000), 123–38.

9. For the most recent scholarship on this matter, see the essay by Konstantinos Vetochnikov, "La 'concession' de la metropole de Kiev au patriarche de Moscou en 1686: Analyse canonique," paper presented the at Twenty-Third International Congress of Byzantine Studies, Belgrade, August 22–27, 2016, 37–41. Vetochnikov notes that the clergy and laity of the Kyivan Metropolia protested the attempt to place the Church under Moscow's jurisdiction, and adds that the canonical documents limit the degree of jurisdiction exercised by Moscow over Kyiv by simply permitting the Moscow patriarch to ordain the metropolitan of Kyiv, with the Kyivan Church retaining all of its privileges. On the history of this event, also see Victor Zhivov, "The Question of Ecclesiastical Jurisdiction in Russian-Ukrainian Relations (Seventeenth and Early Eighteenth Centuries)," in *Culture, Nation, and Identity: The Ukrainian-Russian Encounter, 1600–1945*, ed. Andreas Kappeler, Zenon E. Kohut, Frank E. Sysyn, and Mark von Hagen (Edmonton, AB: Canadian Institute of Ukrainian Studies, 2003), 1–18. Also see James Cunningham, *A Vanquished Hope: The Movement for Church Renewal in Russia, 1905–1906* (Crestwood, NY: St. Vladimir's Seminary Press, 1981), 23–30, and Zenon Kohut, *Making Ukraine: Studies on Political Culture, Historical Narrative, and Identity*, foreword by Frank Sysyn (Edmonton, AB: Canadian Institute of Ukrainian Studies, 2011), 135–50.

10. Subtelny, *Ukraine*, 172–73.

11. Ibid., 160–65, 232–37. Also see Sysyn, "The Formation," 18, and Andreas Kappeler, "*Mazepintsy, Malorossy, Khokhly*: Ukrainians in the Ethnic Hierarchy of the Russian Empire," in *Culture, Nation, and Identity: The Ukrainian-Russian Encounter, 1600–1945*, ed. Andreas Kappeler, Zenon E. Kohut, Frank E. Sysyn, and Mark von Hagen (Edmonton, AB: Canadian Institute of Ukrainian Studies, 2003), 162–63.

12. On the Church renewal movements, see Gregory L. Freeze, *The Parish Clergy in Nineteenth-Century Russia: Crisis, Reform, Counter-Reform* (Princeton, NJ: Princeton University Press, 1983); Freeze, "All Power to the Parish? The Problems and Politics of Church Reform in Late Imperial Russia," in *Social Identities in Revolutionary Russia*, ed. Madhavan K. Palat (New York: Palgrave, 2001), 174–208; Edward Roslof, *Red Priests: Renovationism, Russian Orthodoxy, and Revolution, 1905–1946* (Bloomington: Indiana University Press, 2002); Nikolai Balashov, *На пути к литургическому возрождению* [On the path of liturgical renewal] (Moscow: Kruglyi stol po religioznomu obrazovaniiu i daikonii, 2001), 23–170; Hyacinthe Destivelle, *The Moscow Council (1917–1918): The Creation of the Conciliar Institutions of the Russian Orthodox Church*, ed. Michael Plekon and Vitaly Permiakov, trans. Jerry Ryan, foreword by Metropolitan Hilarion (Alfeyev) (Notre Dame, IN: University of Notre Dame Press, 2015).

13. Andryi Starodub, *Всеукраїнський Православний Церковний Собор 1918 року: Огляд джерел* [The All-Ukrainian Orthodox Church Council in 1918: An examination of sources] (Kyiv: Україн, In-t ukr. arkheografiï ta dzheroloznavstva im. M. S. Hrushevs'koho, 2010).

14. See the review of Starodub's study and remarks on the significance of the 1918 council by Volodymyr Bureha, "Нічий Собор" [No one's council], Religiia v Ukraïni, November 25, 2010, http://www.religion.in.ua/main/6987-nichij-sobor.html (accessed October 8, 2015). Also see the detailed survey of the 1918 council by Metropolitan Feodosii (Protsiuk), *Обособленческие движение в Православной Церкви на Украине* [The separation movement in the Orthodox Church in Ukraine] (Moscow: Krutitskoe podvor'e, 2004), 14–122.

15. P. S. Sokhan', Serhii Plokhy, and L.V. Yakovleva, eds., *Перший Всеукраїнський Православний Церковний Собор УАПЦ, 14–30 жовтня 1921 року* [The first All-Ukrainian Orthodox Church Council of the UAOC, October 14–30, 1921], (Kyiv: NAN Україн, In-t ukr. arkheografiï ta dzheroloznavstva im. M. S. Hrushevs'koho, 1999) (hereafter cited as Sokhan' et al., *УАПЦ 1921*).

16. In the first section of her book, Prelovs'ka presents the primary sources and assesses the secondary literary sources. She is particularly dismissive of Metropolitan Feodosii (Protsiuk)'s study, which she deems a polemical work aimed at delegitimizing the autocephaly movement. Iryna Prelovs'ka, *Джерела з Історії Української Автокефальної Православної Церкви (1921–1930)–Української Православної Церкви (1930–1939)* [Sources from the history of the Ukrainian Autocephalous Orthodox Church (1921–1930)—Ukrainian Orthodox Church (1930–1939)], (Kyiv: Inst. Ukraïns'koi Arkheohrafiï ta Dzhereloznavstva im. M. S. Hrushevs'koho NAN Ukraïny, 2013). We will occasionally refer to Feodosii (Protsiuk)'s study since he includes numerous primary sources. Another important source is the encyclopedic compilation of documents in Osyp Zinkewich and Oleksander Voronyn, eds., *Мартирологія Українських Церков*, vol. 1, *Українська Православна Церква* [Martyrology of the Ukrainian churches, vol. 1: Ukrainian Orthodox Church] (Baltimore, MD: Smoloskyp, 1987). In addition to the works previously cited by Prelovs'ka, Vlasovs'kyi, and Feodosii (Protsiuk), see the seminal works by Bohdan Bociurkiw, "The Autocephalous Church Movement in Ukraine: The Formative Stage (1917–1921)," *The Ukrainian Quarterly* 16, no. 3 (1960): 211–23; "The Ukrainian Autocephalous Orthodox Church and Modernization, 1920–1930: A Case Study in Religious Modernization," in *Religion and Modernization in the Soviet Union*, ed. Dennis Dunn (Boulder, CO: Westview Press, 1977), 310–47; and "The Soviet Destruction of the Ukrainian Orthodox Church, 1929–1936," *Journal of Ukrainian Studies* 12, no. 1 (1987): 3–21. See also Tetiana Ievsieieva, "Ідеологія і практика православних конфесій України стосовно національного питання у 1920-i pp." [Ideology and practice of Orthodox confessions of Ukraine on the national question in the 1920s], http://history.org.ua/JournALL/pro/pro_2010_19_2/2.pdf (accessed October 20, 2016), and Ievsieieva, *Російська православна церква в Україні 1917–1921 pp.: Конфлікт національних ідентичностей у православному полі* [The Russian Orthodox Church in Ukraine 1917–1921: A conflict of national identities in the Orthodox sphere] (Kyiv: Instytt istoriï Ukraïny NAN, 2005).

17. A "tomos of autocephaly" is an official letter from the mother Church recognizing the autocephaly of a daughter Church. Contents of a tomos include the effective date, a rationale for recognizing autocephaly, any terms or provisions (such as the capital city or see), and the official signatures of the bishops.

18. The primary sources for this section will be documents published in Zinkewich and Voronyn, *Мартирологія Українських Церков*; Dmytro Stepovyk, *Патріарх Мстислав: Життя і архипастирська діяльність* [Patriarch Mstyslav: Life and archpastoral activity] (Kyiv: Mystetsvo, 2007); Feodosii (Protsiuk), *Обособленческие движение*; and archival materials in the Bohdan Bociurkiw Memorial Library and the Tymofii Minenko Collection, accession 2011–27 at the Canadian Institute of Ukrainian Studies of the University of Alberta in Edmonton.

19. See Bohdan Bociurkiw, "The Orthodox Church and the Soviet Regime in the Ukraine, 1953–1971," *Canadian Slavonic Papers* 14, no. 2 (1972); 191–212; Bociurkiw, *The Ukrainian Greek Catholic Church and the Soviet State, 1939–1950* (Edmonton, AB: Canadian Institute of Ukrainian

Studies, 1996); Frank Sysyn, *The Ukrainian Orthodox Question in the USSR* (Cambridge, MA: Ukrainian Studies Fund, Harvard University, 1987).

20. "Unia" refers to Greek Catholics in Ukraine, who restored communion with the Church of Rome at the Union of Brest in 1596. Greek Catholics observe the Byzantine liturgical rite in its fullness, considering themselves as Orthodox in communion with Rome.

21. See Frank Sysyn, "The Third Rebirth of the Ukrainian Autocephalous Orthodox Church and the Religious Situation in Ukraine, 1989–1991," in Plokhy and Sysyn, *Religion and Nation*, 88–119.

22. See Serhii Plokhy, "Ukrainian Orthodox Autocephaly and Metropolitan Filaret," in Plokhy and Sysyn, *Religion and Nation*, 128–35.

Notes to Chapter 1

1. For a comprehensive survey of the sources for the history of the 1921 Ukrainian Church, see Iryna Prelovs'ka, *Джерела з історії Української Автокефальної Православної Церкви (1921–1930)-Української Православної Церкви (1930–1939)* [Sources from the history of the Ukrainian Autocephalous Orthodox Church (1921–1930)—Ukrainian Orthodox Church (1930–1939)] (Kyiv: Inst. Ukraïns'koi Arkheohrafiï ta Dzhereloznavstva im. M. S. Hrushevs'koho NAN Ukraïny, 2013). Prelovs'ka presents a rigorous assessment of the secondary scholarship on 22–173.

2. On the historical development of sovereign states having autocephalous churches, see Metropolitan Kallistos Ware, "'Neither Jew nor Greek': Catholicity and Ethnicity," *St. Vladimir's Theological Quarterly* 57, nos. 3–4 (2013): 245–46; Paul Meyendorff, "Ethnophyletism, Autocephaly, and National Churches—A Theological Approach and Ecclesiological Implications," *St. Vladimir's Theological Quarterly* 57, nos. 3–4 (2013): 390; and Daniel Payne, "Nationalism and the Local Church: The Source of Ecclesiastical Conflict in the Orthodox Commonwealth," *Nationalities Papers* 35, no. 5 (2007): 831–52. See also Peter Galadza, "The Structure of the Eastern Churches: Bonded with Human Blood or Baptismal Water?" *Pro Ecclesia* 17, no. 4 (2008): 373–86.

3. Arsen Zinchenko, *Визволитися вірою: Життя і діяння митрополита Василя Липківського* [Deliverance through faith: The life and activity of Metropolitan Vasyl Lypkivs'kyi] (Kyiv: Dnipro Publishing, 1997), 85–100.

4. Ibid., 85.

5. Ibid.

6. Ibid., 86.

7. Ibid., 87.

8. Ibid., 94.

9. Ibid., 94–95.

10. Ibid.

11. Ibid., 99–100.

12. Ibid., 99.

13. Ibid., 99–100.

14. Ivan Vlasovs'kyi, *Нарис історії Української Православної Церкви*, 2nd ed. (New York: Ukrainian Autocephalous Orthodox Church, 1990), 4:1:11. Also see Metropolitan Feodosii (Protsiuk), *Обособленческие движение в Православной Церкви на Украине* [The separation movement in the Orthodox Church in Ukraine] (Moscow: Krutitskoe podvor'e, 2004), 14–24.

15. Vlasovs'kyi, *Нарис історії 4:1,* 12. Rasputin was a friend and confidant of Tsar Nicholas II, a mystic who had no official church position and whose relationship with the tsar was controversial.

16. Ibid.

17. Ibid., 13.

18. Ibid., 14.

19. Vasyl' (Lypkivs'ky), *Історія Української Православної Церкви*, vol. 7, *Відродження Української Церкви* [History of the Ukrainian Orthodox Church, vol. 7, Rebirth of the Ukrainian Church] (Winnipeg, MB: Fund of Ivan Hryshshuk, 1961), 7–8.

20. Ibid., 8.

21. Vlasovs'kyi, *Нарис історії 4:1*, 17.

22. Lypkivs'ky noted that the new AUOCC "called against itself a great adversary of Russian and conservative elements," in Vasyl' (Lypkivs'ky), *Історія*, 9.

23. Ibid., 11–12.

24. Ibid., 18–20.

25. Feodosii (Protsiuk), *Обособленческие движение*, 27–28.

26. Vlasovs'kyi, *Нарис історії 4:1*, 13.

27. Ibid., 13–14.

28. See Prelovs'ka, *Джерела*, 353–54, for the details on the epistle.

29. Ibid., 353.

30. Ibid. Prelovs'ka adds that "in his [Metropolitan Volodymyr's] opinion, love for one's native country should not supersede love for Russia and the Orthodox Church."

31. Hyacinthe Destivelle, *The Moscow Council (1917-1918): The Creation of the Conciliar Institutions of the Russian Orthodox Church*, ed. Michael Plekon and Vitaly Permiakov, trans. Jerry Ryan, foreword by Metropolitan Hilarion (Alfeyev) (Notre Dame, IN: University of Notre Dame Press, 2015), 77–90.

32. Dmitry Pospielovsky, *The Orthodox Church in the History of Russia* (Crestwood, NY: St. Vladimir's Seminary Press, 1998), 105–12.

33. For the story of the patriarchal election, see James Cunningham, "Reform Projects of the Russian Orthodox Church at the Beginning of the Twentieth Century," in *The Legacy of St. Vladimir: Byzantium, Russia, America*, ed. John Breck, John Meyendorff, and Eleana Silk (Crestwood, NY: St. Vladimir's Seminary Press, 1990), 116–23.

34. Destivelle, *The Moscow Council*, 65.

35. Ibid., 117.

36. Evlogy (Georgievsky), *My Life's Journey: The Memoirs of Metropolitan Evlogy*, comp. T. I. Manukhina, trans. Alexander Lisenko, intro. Thomas Hopko (Crestwood, NY: St. Vladimir's Seminary Press, 2014), 1:346.

37. Ibid.

38. Nikolai Balashov, *На пути к литургическому возрождению* [On the path of liturgical renewal] (Moscow: Kruglyi stol po religioznomu obrazovaniiu i daikonii, 2001).

39. Ibid., 152–55.

40. Ibid., 153.

41. Ibid., 158.

42. Starodub published the acts of the All-Ukrainian Council in *Всеукраїнський Православний Церковний Собор*, 106–65.

43. Orest Subtelny, *Ukraine: A History*, 4th ed. (Toronto, ON: University of Toronto Press, 2009), 355–59.

44. Vlasovs'kyi, *Нарис історії 4:1*, 20–4.

45. Destivelle, *The Moscow Council*, 117.

46. See Prelovs'ka, *Джерела*, 352.

47. Destivelle, *The Moscow Council*, 117.

48. Evlogy, *My Life's Journey*, 360–62.

49. Vlasovs'kyi, 38–40.

50. See Vladimir Tsurikov, ed., *Metropolitan Antonii (Khrapovitskii): Archpastor of the Russian Diaspora*, Readings in Russian Religious Culture 5 (Jordanville, NY: Foundation of Russian History, 2014).

51. Destivelle, *The Moscow Council*, 359.

52. Ibid., 358–59.

53. Ibid., 359.

54. On the role of the Hetmanate in Church affairs, see Friedrich Heyer, *Die Orthodox kirche in der Ukraine von 1917 bis 1945*, Osteuropa und der Deutsche Osten 111 (Cologne: Rudolf Müller, 1953), 46–48.

55. Evlogy, *My Life's Journey*, 364.

56. Ibid.

57. Another recent account of the council comes from Sophia Senyk, "The Orthodox Church in Ukraine in the Twentieth Century," in *The Orthodox Church in Eastern Europe in the Twentieth Century*, ed. Christine Chaillot (Oxford: Peter Lang, 2011), 328. Senyk suggests that the vast majority of the delegates were in favor of autonomy, a position contradicting the others presented here.

58. Vlasovs'kyi, *Нарис історії 4:1*, 28. Also see Ohienko's own account of his speech in Metropolitan Ilarion (Ohienko), *Українська церква: Нариси з історії Української Православної Церкви* [The Ukrainian Church: Outlines from the history of the Ukrainian Orthodox Church], 2 vols, ed. Stepan Jarmus (Winnipeg, MB: Konsystoriia UHP Tserkvy v Kanadi, 1982), 329.

59. Vlasovs'kyi *Нарис історії 4:1*, 38–40. On this matter, also see Evlogy, *My Life's Journey*, 363–64. Metropolitan Evlogy reported that the patriarch had permitted each eparchy to elect its own hierarch while Vlasovs'kyi mused that the entire All-Ukrainian Council should have elected the metropolitan. Starodub, in *Всеукраїнський Православний Церковний Собор*, affirms Vlasovs'kyi's claim on 74.

60. Vlasovs'kyi, *Нарис історії 4:1*, 43.

61. Ibid.

62. Vlasovs'kyi refers to another example where forty-five well-known supporters of the pro-Ukrainian coalition were excluded from the council. Ibid.

63. To his credit, Vlasovs'kyi chronicled the role of the local Ukrainian Council from the beginning of its convocation in 1918 to its continuation in July. The interruption of the council was necessitated by the invasion of Kyiv by the Bolsheviks. The church council was replaced by the brotherhood of Saints Cyril and Methodius during this period. Vlasovs'kyi argued that the council should have resumed representation since the July assembly was a continuation of the January council, and not the inauguration of a new all-church assembl in *Нарис історії* 4:1, 43–4.

64. Ibid., 44.

65. Feodosii (Protsiuk), *Обособленческие движение*, 119. On this topic, also see Vasyl' (Lypkivs'kyi), *Історія*, 11," who caricatured the second session of the council as "an altogether different Russian council in Ukraine."

66. As reported by Prelovs'ka, *Джерела*, 354–55.

67. Osyp Zinkewich and Oleksander Voronyn, eds., *Мартирологія Українських Церков*, vol. 1, *Українська Православна Церква* (Baltimore, MD: Smoloskyp, 1987), 47–49.

68. The excerpt of Kramarenko's sermon illustrates the anti-tsarist polemics of the autocephalists: "God-loving brothers and sisters! This day is a tragic day for the Ukrainian people! On this day over two hundred years ago there was a victory at Poltava, the victory of Peter over Ivan. The great hetman Ivan Mazepa in the churches that he himself built in Ukraine . . . in these very churches the Muscovites cursed him as a traitor during the course of two hundred years. Moscow gave Hetman Ivan Mazepa over to anathema as a traitor. Who among them was a traitor? Was it the one who protected his people from the enemy or the one who went to destroy this people? No, brothers, Ivan Mazepa was not a traitor of the Ukrainian people, but the traitor was the one who enslaved our people. Peter was not given over to anathema because power was on his side, like a victorious one! The good fortune of Ukraine and her independence are not yet constructed and there is much to come to us, brothers—fight for this! Let us be faithful sons of our mother Ukraine! Let us fight until the dreams of our great Ivan are fulfilled! Knowing how many of ours were laid to rest at Poltava, knowing how hard it was for Ivan Mazepa to see the ruin of his native people, we cannot refrain from saying with the saints, give rest!" (Zinkewich and Voronyn, *Мартирологія Українських Церков*, 1:48).

69. Ibid., 44–45.

70. Evlogy, *My Life's Journey*, 364.

71. Vlasovs'kyi republished portions of Lotocky's speech in *Нарис історії 4:1*, 52–54. For a profile of Lotocky's efforts as minister of cults, see Andre Partykevich, *Between Kyiv and Constantinople: Oleksander Lototsky and the Quest for Ukrainian Autocephaly* (Edmonton, AB: Church Studies Program, Canadian Institute of Ukrainian Studies, 1998).

72. Vlasovs'kyi argued that the Moscow Council revised the statute on autonomy presented by the 1918 Ukrainian council, and that this statute required affirmation from the Ukrainian government. Vlasovs'kyi also asserted that Lotocky's speech represented the government's rejection of the church statute, rendering the autonomous status of the Ukrainian Church invalid in *Нарис історії 4:1*, 54–55.

73. Subtelny, *Ukraine*, 360–61.

74. See Balashov, *На путі*, 158–59.

75. Vlasovs'kyi, *Нарис історії 4:1*, 58–59.

76. Evlogy, *My Life's Journey*, 367–70.

77. Vlasovs'kyi, *Нарис історії 4:1*, 62–63.

78. Ibid., 64–65.

79. Destivelle, *The Moscow Council*, 187.

80. Vlasovs'kyi, *Нарис історії 4:1*, 66–67.

81. Subtelny, *Ukraine*, 362.

82. Ibid., 374, 380.

83. Vlasovs'kyi, *Нарис історії 4:1*, 69.

84. See Edward Roslof, *Red Priests: Renovationism, Russian Orthodoxy, and Revolution, 1905–1946* (Bloomington: Indiana University Press, 2002), 6–9.

85. Gregory L. Freeze, "Subversive Atheism: Soviet Antireligious Campaigns and the Religious Revival in Ukraine in the 1920s," in *State Secularism and Lived Religion in Soviet Russia and Ukraine*, ed. Catherine Wanner (New York: Oxford University Press, 2012), 30.

86. Ibid.

87. Vlasovs'kyi, *Нарис історії 4:1*, 74.

88. Ibid., 74–75.

89. Ibid, 74.

90. Ibid., 73.

91. Ibid., 78–79. Also see Subtelny, *Ukraine*, 373–74.

92. Vlasovs'kyi, *Нарис історії 4:1*, 91. On the communication of the news of the canonical deposition within Kyiv, see Prelovs'ka, *Джерела*, 352.

93. Vlasovs'kyi, *Нарис історії 4:1*, 73.

94. Ibid.

95. Ibid., 74.

96. Ibid.

97. Ibid., 74–75.

98. Vlasovs'kyi notes that the Mykola Leontovich both wrote the music and conducted the choir for this occasion; only parts of the liturgy were in Ukrainian. Ibid., 74–75.

99. "Having learned that the Ukrainians were demanding to receive the right to use St. Andrew's Cathedral, Bishop Nazarii with the Russian clergy established some kind of brotherhood of five individuals . . . who locked the cathedral . . . and presented their pretensions to the government. Having examined the matter in detail, the government granted use of the cathedral to the second Ukrainian parish. To prevent the advancement of the Ukrainians obtaining use of the churches, Bishop Nazarii and his 'eparchial council' came up with this plan: they said, unless there were all-parish meetings in all the parishes of Kyiv to decide 'to remain Orthodox in the faith of our fathers, or go to the Ukrainians,' and to select one of the clergy and four of the laity in a council of all the Kyivan parishes, where they would deliberate the question of whether to remain with Orthodoxy or to go to the 'Ukrainian' faith." Ibid., 75. It is worth noting Vlasovs'kyi's lament over the situation posed to the Russian clergy in Kyiv, who were being coerced into viewing Ukrainians as non-Orthodox on the matter of language.

100. Tetiana Ievsieieva, "Ідеологія і практика православних конфесій України стосовно національного питання у 1920-і рр." [Ideology and practice of Orthodox confessions of Ukraine on the national question in the 1920s]. http://history.org.ua/JournALL/pro/pro_2010_19_2/2.pdf (accessed October 20, 2016).

101. Ibid.

102. Ibid.

103. Ibid.

104. Ibid., 83.

105. Ibid., 85.

106. Ibid., 87.

107. Ibid.

108. Ibid., 90–91.

109. Sokhan' et al., *УАПЦ 1921*, 440–41.

110. Ibid., 431.

111. For an overview of the May Council, its sources, and an assessment of its scholarship, see Prelovs'ka, *Джерела*, 174–83.

112. Vlasovs'kyi, *Нарис історії 4:1*, 92.

113. Ibid.

114. Prelovs'ka, *Джерела*, 181.

115. See "Звернення Московського патріарха Тихона до віруючих України про збереження єдності церкви" [Appeal of Moscow patriarch Tikhon to the faithful of Ukraine on maintaining the unity of the church], in Sokhan' et al., *УАПЦ 1921*, 503.

116. Ibid.

117. Ibid.

118. Ibid.

119. Ibid.

120. Ibid., 504.

121. Ibid., 501.

122. Ibid., 500.

123. Ibid., 501.

124. Ibid., 501–2.

125. Ibid., 39.

126. Ibid., 105.

127. Ibid.

128. The proceedings indicate that his address is included, but the editors of the proceedings state that it has been omitted.

129. See Prelovs'ka, *Джерела*, 214, for a brief note about Mykola Levitsky. For Levitsky's petition to Metropolitan Michael, see Sokhan' et al., *УАПЦ 1921*, 164.

130. "Vladyko" is the Slavonic version of the Greek "dhespota," or "master." In church culture, it is customary to address a bishop as "Vladyko."

131. Sokhan' et al., *УАПЦ 1921*, 164.

132. Ibid., 166.

133. Ibid., 167.

134. Ibid., 156.

135. Balashov, *На пути*, 157; Destivelle, *The Moscow Council*, 134–35.

136. The resolution also includes a statement on the urgent need for the translation of liturgical books into Ukrainian.

137. Prelovs'ka, *Джерела*, 195.

138. Ibid. Prelovs'ka adds that the delegates at the October Council referred to Shevchenko as "our prophet."

139. "Then our Ukrainian people was left without a hierarchy, as it is now, because, as now, bishops went to lords, but the poor people that formed a democratic government, began to care about the renewal of the hierarchy—and they saved the church and renewed the hierarchy . . . when the church was delivered from the rule of the tsarist regime, we witnessed a sad thing, we saw that the Orthodox Church was left like an orphan, like a melting widow. You all know that we began to care, to help her, but those who send us polite letters curse us. They hurl at us that we are not Orthodox." Ibid., 31.

140. Ibid., 32.

141. Ibid.

142. For a survey of his work and theological interlocutors, see Prelovs'ka, *Джерела*, 315–22.

143. "The life of the Holy Spirit occurs through the Holy Scriptures; holy tradition; in the holy life of the Church; a succession of holy acts through the Church itself, but not from separate representatives. . . . The entire church performs a sacrament. In the first ages of liturgy even private needs were not permitted, but everything was performed in unison and the first great service, the 'Eucharist' is called 'liturgy'—an act done together, but not the act of an expert, the act of a person who creates this sacrament. It is a joint work, a work of the whole Church. . . . When we arrive at the sacrament of the priesthood itself, then we see here that the gifts of the Holy Spirit are through the Church itself, the whole Church, with the participation (of course) of the bishops in their customary order, when they are present and take part in the laying on of hands," Sokhan' et al., *УАПЦ 1921*, 191–92.

144. This section comes from Chekhivsky's historical account, ibid., 193–97.

145. Ibid., 194–95.

146. Ibid., 198. For a brief biography of Sokolowsky through 1922, see ibid., 42n27. This chapter will return to Sokolowsky's attempts to implement Ukrainization within the Ukrainian Exarchate of the Moscow Patriarchate.

147. Ibid., 199.

148. Ibid., 236.

149. Note: the 1942 UAOC successfully employed this point of the proposal in 1940.

150. Ibid., 236–37.

151. Ibid., 204. Homichevsky's comments caused a tumult at the council, and some people shouted, "enough!" Michael Moroz, the council's presiding chair, asked Homichevsky "to not offend members of the council."

152. On this matter, also see Prelovs'ka, *Джерела*, 201.

153. "It is affirmed that the so-called All-Ukrainian Church Council of 1918 was not an authentic Ukrainian council, but meetings of enemies of the Ukrainian Church liberation movement, and so neither its resolutions nor the creation of the higher governing organ of the council is to be recognized; it is affirmed that the so-called Holy Synod of Bishops of All Ukraine, members of which were not elected by Ukrainian Orthodox people, is not an authentic representative of the Ukrainian Orthodox Church, but an adversarial institution." Sokhan' et al., *УАПЦ 1921*, 471.

154. Ibid.

155. Ibid.

156. "Therefore it is not for the eradication or revision of the old canons, but concern for saving and presenting to people what is better (canon 126 of the First Ecumenical Council) that we resolve: that the episcopal-governed organ of the Church that was created under the influence of historical circumstances and the monarchical climate of those times that was adopted by the old canons, can no longer remain and must be changed into a conciliar-governed Church coherent with the spirit of the Orthodox Christian faith; that some councils with bishops, as this was once and is now, do not observe the true spirit of the Orthodox Christian faith, do not grant the ability to the Church to live a full life, and it is necessary from this point forward to replace these councils with representatives of the entire Ukrainian populace; we assert that councils consisting of representatives from the entire Ukrainian populace are not in violation of church canons, but are only their organic development, we the representatives of the Ukrainian Orthodox populace, convoked by the All-Ukrainian Orthodox Church Council, recognize ourselves as a canonical local council of the Ukrainian Orthodox Church and thus her superior organ through which the voice of the Ukrainian Church resounds by the grace of the Holy Spirit." Ibid., 375–76.

157. Ibid., 379.

158. Ibid.

159. Bohdan Bociurkiw, "The Ukrainian Autocephalous Orthodox Church and Modernization, 1920–1930: A Case Study in Religious Modernization," in *Religion and Modernization in the Soviet Union*, ed. Dennis Dunn (Boulder, CO: Westview Press, 1977), 325.

160. Vasyl Lypkivs'kyi was born in 1864 in Lypovetsky, in the family of a priest. He studied in the Kyivan seminary and again in the theological academy (from 1884 to 1889). He was ordained a priest in 1891 and became rector of the cathedral in Lypovetsky in 1892. He served for eleven years as the director of the Kyivan school for church teachers. Following the revolution of 1905, Lypkivs'kyi became an advocate for ecclesial Ukrainization. Lypkivs'kyi presided at the Kyivan eparchial gathering of 1917 and formed the Brotherhood of the Resurrection in 1917, a movement for the rebirth of the native Kyivan Church. He was an active proponent of autocephaly at the 1918 All-Ukrainian Council in Kyiv, and he greeted Symon Petliura with a solemn speech at Sophia Square when Petliura arrived there on December 21, 1918. He was elected, ordained, and enthroned as metropolitan of Kyiv and all Ukraine at the UAOC council of October 14–30, 1921, and served in this office until the second All-Ukrainian Council of the UAOC of October 17–30, 1927. Lypkivs'kyi was murdered in the Luk'ianivsky prison on November 27, 1937. See the complete profile compiled in V.A. Smolii and P.S. Sokhan', eds., *Другий Всеукраїнський Церковний Собор УАПЦ, 17–30 жовтня 1927 року: Документи і матеріали* [The second All-Ukrainian Orthodox Church sobor, 17–30 of October 1927: Documents and materials] (Kyiv: Instytut Ukraïns'koï arkheohrafiï, Instytut istoriï Ukraïny, 2007), 641–42.

161. Vasyl' (Lypkivs'kyi), *Проповіді на неділі й свята, слово Христове до Українського народу* [Sermons on Sundays and holy days, the word of Christ to the Ukrainian people] (New York: Ukr. Pravoslavne bratstvo im. Mytr. Vasylia Lypkivs'koho, 1988), 305–8. The homily has no date.

162. His references include a dismissal of the authority of the monastic cell and the aristocratic bloodlines he attributes to the old Russian bishops.

163. "Thus I testify and my testimony is true . . . I was never nor am I now a political revolutionary, nor a political counterrevolutionary, for I did not and do not want to extend myself into any kind of politics. But I am a Church revolutionary, because the Ukrainian Church arose and was liberated and the battle with the old regime occurred on revolutionary grounds. . . . Therefore, the political and socialist revolution, the general liberation and greater justice for the satisfaction of laborers; this I greet. All of my life I was interested only in Church matters, dreaming about the liberation of the Church, that is to say, about her status, when there would no longer be in her any lordship, no princes, but only brotherhood, and when the state would not interfere in her affairs. I am fortunate that I lived on to see to the possibility of the fulfillment of this status of the Church during the time of the Soviet Union, with her law on the separation of the Church from the state." From *Заява Митрополита Василя Липківського до Уряду УРСР* [Statement of Metropolitan Vasyl Lypkivs'kyi to the government of the URCR], in Zinkewich and Voronyn, *Мартирологія Українських Церков*, 1:433.

164. By comparison, presbyters are ordained after the Great Entrance (offertory) but before the Eucharistic prayer since Eucharistic presidency is the primary element of presbyteral ministry, whereas deacons are ordained after the Eucharistic prayer but before Holy Communion since assisting in the distribution of communion is the primary aspect of diaconal ministry.

165. Zinkewich and Voronyn, *Мартирологія Українських Церков*, 1:116–17.

166. Zinkewich and Voronyn, *Мартирологія Українських Церков*, 1:116–17. The dikir and trikir are candles used by the bishop when he presides at liturgical offices. The dikir is two candles and the trikir is three candles, the two sets attached to special holders, with the candles waxed together and tied with ribbons. The bishop uses them to bless the people at various points in liturgical celebrations.

167. See "Організація Української Церкви і церковного урядування [Organization of the Ukrainian Church and church governance] in Sokhan' et al., *УАПЦ 1921*, 382–94.

168. Ibid., 384.

169. Ibid. The canons also permitted clergy to wear civilian clothing and adopt any hair style they wished; pastoral appointments to parishes were contingent on parish approval.

170. See the May resolutions, ibid., 47.

171. Ibid., 338.

172. See Bohdan Bociurkiw, "Ukrainization Movements within the Russian Orthodox Church and the Ukrainian Autocephalous Orthodox Church," *Harvard Ukrainian Studies* 3–4 (1979): 92–111. Also see Feodosii (Protsiuk), *Обособленческие движение*, 232–45.

173. Bociurkiw, "Ukrainization Movements," 99.

174. Ibid.

175. Ibid., 100.

176. Ibid.

177. Ibid.

178. Ibid, 101.

179. Ibid., 103–4. On Buldovsky and the Lubny schism, also see Feodosii (Protsiuk), *Обособленческие движение*, 324–73.

180. Bociurkiw, "Ukrainization Movements," 104. Also see Feodosii (Protsiuk), *Обособленческие движение*, 278–85.

181. Bociurkiw, "Ukrainization Movements," 106–8.

182. Ibid., 108.

183. Ibid.

184. Ibid., 108n70.

185. Vlasovs'kyi, *Нарис історії 4:1*, 278.

186. Ibid., 279.

187. The Living Church was the largest faction of the renovationist movement in Russia that came into being in 1922. The Church's leaders and followers consisted of progressives and radicals who wanted to break from the conservatism of the patriarchal church. See Pospielovsky, *The Orthodox Church in the History of Russia*, 236–38, and Roslof, *Red Priests*, 61–70.

188. Ibid., 276.

189. "Слово Митрополита Київського і всієї України Василя Липківського (до п'ятиріччя існування УАПЦ)" [Word of Metropolitan Vasyl Lypkivs'kyi of Kyiv and all Ukraine on the five-year anniversary of the existence of the UAOC], in Zinkewich and Voronyn, *Мартирологія Українських Церков*, 1:238–41.

190. Bohdan Bociurkiw, "The Soviet Destruction of the Ukrainian Orthodox Church, 1929–1936," *Journal of Ukrainian Studies* 12, no. 1 (1987), 3–21. For a comprehensive explanation of all documents pertinent to the liquidation of the UAOC, see Prelovs'ka, *Джерела*, 205–45.

191. Bociurkiw, "Soviet Destruction," 4.

192. Ibid.

193. Ibid.

194. Ibid., 5–6.

195. Ibid., 5–7.

196. "To compromise the UAOC in the eyes of its believers, the GPU staged a humiliating mockery of the church's 'self-liquidation' at the so-called 'Extraordinary Church Sobor', which met on 28–29 January 1930 in Kiev. Hastily convoked to 'solve the question of the church's status in connection with the discovery of its counter-revolutionary activity of autocephaly and, in particular, its role in the organization of the SVU', the Sobor supplied the GPU with a collective confession of guilt and duly 'voted' to dissolve the UAOC." Ibid., 7. For detailed documentation of these events, see Prelovs'ka, *Джерела*, 491–508.

197. Bociurkiw, "Soviet Destruction," presents the details of the show trial on pages 9–11.

198. Ibid., 10.

199. Ibid., 10–11.

200. Ibid., 12–14.

201. Vasyl' (Lypkivs'kyi), *Історія*, 7:118–19. Lypkivs'kyi claimed that the USSR's internationalization campaign was based upon the Hebrew notion of communes, and recognized only the proletariat, and not national identity.

202. Gregory L. Freeze, "The Stalinist Assault on the Parish, 1929–1941," in *Stalinismus vor dem Zweiten Weltkrieg: Neue Wege der Forschung*, ed. Manfred Hildermeier and Elisabeth Müller-Luckner (Munich: Oldenbourg, 1998), 214–17, 225–28.

203. Roslof, *Red Priests*, 147.

204. Ibid., 156–57. Roslof notes that the Soviet government referred to the lay rejection of renovationism as *Tikhonovshchina*.

205. Freeze, "The Stalinist Assault," 224. Roslof also notes that clergy with advanced education tended to be drawn toward liberal reforms, but many parish clergy did not have the benefit of seminary education (*Red Priests*, 157). See also Gregory Freeze, *The Parish Clergy in Nineteenth-Century Russia: Crisis, Reform, Counter-Reform* (Princeton, NJ: Princeton University Press, 1983), 454–55.

206. Ievsieieva, "Ідеологія і практика."

207. Ibid.

208. See Bohdan Bociurkiw, "The Russian Orthodox Church in Ukraine: The Exarchate and the Renovationists, and the 'Conciliar Episcopal' Church, 1920–1939," *Harvard Ukrainian Studies* 26, no. 1 (2002), 65–67.

209. Freeze, "Subversive Atheism: Soviet Antireligious Policy in Ukraine," 34.

Notes to Chapter 2

1. See Karel C. Berkhoff, "Was There a Religious Revival in Soviet Ukraine under the Nazi Regime?" *The Slavonic and East European Review* 78, no. 3 (2000): 536–67.

2. As estimated by Oleksander Voronyn, *Історичний шлях УАПЦ* [Historical path of the UAOC] (Kensington, MD: Voskresinnia, 1992), 88.

3. Ibid.

4. Ibid., 89.

5. Ibid.

6. Ibid.

7. Ibid., 90.

8. Friedrich Heyer, *Die Orthodox kirche in der Ukraine von 1917 bis 1945*, Osteuropa und der Deutsche Osten 111(Cologne: Rudolf Müller, 1953).

9. Voronyn, 88.

10. Ibid., 89.

11. Holy Synod of Orthodox Church in Poland, "Змагання за Українізацію Православної Церкви на Волині і Поліссі" [Debate on the Ukrainization of the Orthodox Church in Poland and Polissia] March 3, 1924, revised by Tymofii Minenko January 6, 1998), University of Alberta Archives (UAA), accession no. 2011-27-104-2020.

12. Ibid.

13. Volodymyr Vasylenko, "Події у Володимирі" [Events in Volodymyr], *Українська нива*, no. 14, April 8, 1927, 12.

14. Ibid.

15. "Вісті з Володимира, в справі Володимирського собору" [News from Volodymyr on issues at Volodymyr cathedral], *Українська нива*, no. 17, May 1, 1927, 2.

16. As reported in *Православний вістник* (Winnipeg), no. 7, July 1927, 2.

17. Ibid.

18. Ibid.

19. The text mentions places with a significant Russian immigrant community.

20. Ibid.

21. Ibid.

22. Published in *Православний вісник* (Winnipeg), no. 7, July 1927, 3.

23. Ibid., 2.

24. Ibid.

25. Ibid.

26. Ibid.

27. Ibid.

28. Ivan Vlasovs'kyi, *Нарис історії Української Православної Церкви* [Outline of the history of the Ukrainian Orthodox Church] (New York: Ukrainian Autocephalous Orthodox Church, 1990), 4:2:6.

29. Ibid., 184–85.

30. Ukrainian Orthodox Church of Canada, *Ювілейна книга на пошану Митрополита Іларіона* [Jubilee book in honor of Metropolitan Hilarion] (Winnipeg, MB: Trident Press, 1958), 182–85.

31. The liturgical language of the eparchy was to be Church Slavonic, with Ukrainian pronunciation; wherever the majority desired it, the celebration of the liturgy in Ukrainian was to be blessed; the council recommended the celebration of all other liturgical offices in Ukrainian (e.g., prayer services, akathists, services for the dead, hours, and the canon of St. Andrew); Russian pronunciation of Slavonic was not permitted; the language of church governance was to be literary Ukrainian. This is an abbreviated summary of the pertinent section. Ibid., 195. See also Ilarion's more extensive elaboration of his pastoral approach to liturgical language in Ilarion (Ohienko), *Ідеологія Української Церкви* [Ideology of the Ukrainian Church], ed. Mykola Timoshik (Kyiv: Nasha kul'tura i nauka, 2013), 123–31.

32. A. I. Smyrnov, *Мстислав (Скрипник): Громадсько-політичний і церковний діяч (1930–1944)* [Mstyslav (Skrypnik): Community-political and Church activist (1930–1944)], 2nd ed. (Kyiv: Smoloskyp, 2009), 96–99.

33. Ibid., 96–97.

34. Ibid., 94–95.

35. Ibid., 97.

36. Ibid., 95.

37. "К прискорбнымъ событіям в Ровенском соборе" [On the deplorable events at the Rivne cathedral], *Slovo*, no. 48 (259), 1934.

38. Copy of a letter from Metropolitan Dionysii to Archbishop Ilarion dated March 1, 1941, UAA, accession no. 2011-27-6-235.

39. On the significance of Archbishop Oleksii's governance of Volyn' eparchy in the Church in Poland, see Vlasovs'kyi, *Нарис історії*, 91–97, and passim.

40. Ibid., 108.

41. The translation of liturgical books was part of the larger campaign of Ukrainization. Ibid., 114–27. Vlasovs'kyi presents the highlights of the periodicals on 128–34.

42. The Orthodox Church in America (OCA) became autocephalous in 1970 via a *tomos* issued by the Moscow Patriarchate. The autocephaly of the OCA is one of the most contested issues between the Ecumenical and Moscow patriarchates.

43. Vlasovs'kyi, *Нарис історії*, 29.

44. See *Патріархъ Тихонъ объ автокефаліи полской церкви Православный Русскій календарь на годъ 1925* [Patriarch Tikhon on the autocephaly of the Polish Church, Russian Orthodox Calendar for the Year 1925] (n.p.: Senator U. Lazho, 1924), 78–80.

45. Ibid., 79.

46. Ibid.

47. Ibid., 80.

48. Vlasovs'kyi, *Нарис історії*, 29.

49. Ibid., 30.

50. Ibid.

51. English translation taken from *Vistnyk*, November 1, 2004, 15.

52. Vlasovs'kyi emphasizes that the *tomos* acknowledged Polish autocephaly, it did not grant it—see Vlasovs'kyi, *Нарис історії 4:2*, 30.

53. "Протоколъ Собора Епископовъ Св. Автокефальной Православной Церкви въ Польшѣ, отъ 18 сентября 1925 года" [Protocol of the Synod of Bishops of the Holy Autocephalous

Orthodox Church in Poland, from September 18, 1925], in *Вѣстникъ Православной Митрополоіи въ Польшѣ*, nos. 21–22 (November 30, 1925), 1–5.

54. "Послання Всеукраїнської Православної Церковної Ради до Його Блаженства Царгородського Патріарха Василія III" [Epistle of the All-Ukrainian Orthodox Church Council to his Beatitude Patriarch Basil III of Consantinople], *Наша батьківщина*, nos. 280, 281, 282 (1972): 24–26.

55. Ibid., 24.

56. Ibid., 25.

57. Ibid., 26.

58. Ibid.

59. Orest Subtelny, *Ukraine: A History*, 4th ed. (Toronto, ON: University of Toronto Press, 2009), 454.

60. See Subtelny's comments, ibid., 454–55.

61. Ibid., 460.

62. Daniela Kalkandjieva, *The Russian Orthodox Church, 1917–1948: From Decline to Resurrection* (London: Routledge, 2015), 115.

63. For an overview, see Berkhoff, "Was There a Religious Revival?," 541–42.

64. Subtelny notes that the "collapse of the Soviet Union was imminent" in the first stages of Hitler's attack during the summer of 1941. Subtelny, *Ukraine*, 460.

65. "Resolved: to thank the Lord for the gift to the world of the great man, who is providentially called to renew human life on the foundations of righteousness, and to turn to the Führer with this telegram: 'The Bishops of the Orthodox Church in Ukraine, liberated from the fiercest godless and theomachist regime in the world by your invincible soldiers, having gathered at Pochaiv at the shrine of the Ukrainian nation in Volyn' for a synodal meeting on Church affairs, enthusiastically greets its great liberator, and conveys warm words of sincere thanks and heartfelt feelings and devotion from ourselves and the faithful. We reverently beseech God the Creator for the continuation of your life for many years, for the glory of the great German nation and for the benefit of the Ukrainian people and the profit of all nations, which have long awaited their better fate from the hand of the chosen one of God—the Führer Adolf Hitler.'" "Діяння обласного собору Православних єпископів в Україні, в Почаївській Лаврі" [Acts of the Council of Bishops of the Orthodox Church in Ukraine at the Pochaiv Lavra]. August 8, 1941 UAA, accession no. 2011-27-27-1-42.

66. Ibid.

67. "Neither individual bishops nor even the council of bishops of a region may create auto-cephaly themselves, but must [defer] the resolution of this matter to a local council of the Ukrainian Orthodox Church composed of the hierarchy, clergy, and laity. The Church should remain under the jurisdiction of the Moscow Patriarchate, but with the privileges of autonomy that the Russian Church once granted to her." Ibid.

68. See Kalkandjieva, *The Russian Orthodox Church*, 115, for a discussion of the questions surrounding Ukrainian autonomy. Patriarch Tikhon had revoked Ukrainian autonomy in 1924, an act Kalkandjieva believed was due to the political climate and pressure on the Church.

69. Ibid., 115–16.

70. "Діяння пр
ослвних єпископів" August 8, 1941, UAA, accession no. 2011-27-1-42.

71. Ibid.

72. "Діяння обласного собору Православних єпископів в Україні, в Почаївській Лаврі," [Acts of the Eparchial Council of Bishops of the Orthodox Church in Ukraine at the Pochaiv Lavra], November 25, 1941," UAA, accession no. 2011-27-27-1-42.

73. "Church life in the capital of Ukraine is slowly mending, but it is evident that the self-consecrated are in the upper ranks of its life. They have taken seats in the Church council, they have seized St. Andrew's Cathedral and are preparing to take other historical shrines of Kyiv into their hands upon a favorable opportunity. In discussions with representatives of the Ukrainian city council, and also with the self-consecrated, it was possible to learn that the council does not want a church schism, and the self-consecrated themselves would leave with the agreement that

a bishop would be appointed to the Kyivan cathedral who was renowned in the greater world for his national feelings, and known for his lengthy work for the good of the Ukrainian Orthodox Church . . . the head of the council of bishops regards his eminence Ilarion, archbishop of Cholm and Pidliassa, as the most qualified for this role, who should be immediately invited to assume the Kyivan throne." Ibid. The Ukrainian word for "self-consecrated" is "самосвяти" (plural, referring to multiple "self-consecrated" clergy), the most common term used to describe the adherents of the 1921 UAOC.

74. Oleksii also proposes transferring Bishop Panteleimon (Rudyk), who was residing in Kyiv at the time, from Kyiv to Poltava.

75. "I convey my most heartfelt thanks to you and the entire holy council of bishops of the holy autocephalous Orthodox Ukrainian Church for the high honor that you have given me, electing me to be archbishop on the altar of the Kyivan throne. I, the unworthy and humble servant of God, have not earned this honor in any way, so I look upon this as that sacrificial obedience that is laid upon me by Almighty God and the holy council of bishops for the organization of the longsuffering throne." Letter from Archbishop Ilarion to Archbishop Oleksii, December 26, 1941, no. 5112, UAA, accession no. 2011-27-1-49.

76. F. Kovalskyi, "До благочинних Волинської єпархії, 'To the Deans of Volyn' Eparchy,' January 9, 1942, no. 42," UAA, accession no. 2011-27-49-1.

77. The election of Archbishop Ilarion to the Kyivan see was a controversial issue among Ukrainian Church leaders and historians. Vlasovs'kyi refers to an essay published in the jubilee book honoring Metropolitan Ilarion in Winnipeg that argues that the Pochaiv Council's invitation for Ilarion to become the archbishop of Kyiv represented the "desire of the Ukrainian populace" and that Ilarion would have been enthroned as Metropolitan of Kyiv and all Ukraine. Vlasovs'kyi states that this argument is a "fantasy," since only an all-Ukrainian council would have the authority to elect and enthrone a metropolitan. Vlasovs'kyi's argument also implies that Ilarion's election would have been detrimental for the Ukrainian Church since the bishops who elected him voluntarily remained within the ranks of the Moscow Patriarchate, which was "opposed to the Ukrainian Church idea." See Vlasovs'kyi, *Нарис історії 4:2*, 212–13, for his assessment of the situation. In a letter written to Vasyl Dubrovsky, dated October 27, 1946, Ilarion asserted that his election as metropolitan of Kyiv was canonical and did not come to pass because of the deliberate interference of Archbishop Policarp (Sikorsky). See Yurii Mytsyk, ed., *Листування Митрополита Іларіона (Огієнка)* [The correspondence of Metropolitan Ilarion (Ohienko)] (Kyiv: Kyivo-Mohylyans'ka academiia, 2009), 207–8. See also Berkhoff, "Was There a Religious Revival?," 541–42.

78. Letter of Archbishop Oleksii (Hromadsky) to Local Clergy, September 1, 1941, UAA, accession no. 2011-27-1-41.

79. "I see it as my responsibility to inform the honorable clergy that this act of Bishop Policarp appears to be a violation of Church rules and will lead to a church schism in Volyn'. . . . Vladyka Dionysii resigned from his position as head of the Orthodox Church, and Volyn' eparchy recognized the Russian Church's jurisdiction over it in 1940. Now his beatitude [Dionysii] is emerging as the leader of the Orthodox Church in the Krakow region, to which we no longer belong. But the supreme Church council among us is the council of the bishops of the Ukrainian Autonomous Orthodox Church. This council no longer has a canonical relationship with Vladyka Dionysii, and therefore the flock of Volyn' cannot receive any Church directives from Warsaw, and equally the vicar bishop of Lutsk (Policarp) cannot represent in his person the entire Volyn' eparchy and unilaterally divide it. Even if His Beatitude Dionysii was our chief hierarch, he would not be able to conduct the division of the eparchy without the council of bishops or the synod. . . . It is necessary to regard the transfer of his grace Bishop Policarp to another church jurisdiction as the relinquishment of his canonical authority for the Lutsk vicariate of the Volyn' eparchy." Ibid.

80. Vlasovs'kyi, *Нарис історії 4:2*, 256–58.

81. Ibid., 256.

82. Archbishop Ilarion (Ohienko), *Слово істини*, nos. 10–11 (August–September 1948), 8. The essay has no title. Ilarion stated that "the consecration of a bishop by priests is 'ecclesial nonsense.'"

83. Ibid., 9–10. Ilarion dismisses the ecclesiology of the 1921 UAOC by suggesting that their leaders promoted *myrianopravnist'*, the rule of the church by the laity, as opposed to sobornopravnist'. He also used the word *narodocezarysmu*, the autocratic rule of the church by the people, to illustrate his belief that the UAOC had removed the hierarchy completely from the church.

84. Ibid. Ilarion explains a proper interpretation of *sobornopravnist'* and implicitly dismisses the legitimacy of the 1921 UAOC in Ohienko, *Ідеологія Української Церкви*, 100–121.

85. Ilarion condemns nationalistic chauvinism, ibid., 131–32.

86. Bohdan Bociurkiw, "Soviet Religious Policy in Ukraine in Historical Perspective," in *Russian Empire: Some Aspects of Tsarist and Soviet Colonial Practices*, ed. Michael S. Pap (Cleveland, OH: Institute for Soviet and East European Studies, John Carroll University and Ukrainian Historical Association, 1985), 103.

87. Ibid.

88. Ibid., 104.

89. Ibid.

90. Letter of Metropolitan Dionysii to Archbishop Oleksii," October 23, 1941, UAA, accession no. 2011-27-6-227.

91. Ibid.

92. Metropolitan Dionysii was consistent in his assertion that Archbishop Oleksii had acted uncanonically, as evidenced by his letter to Archbishop Policarp on November 13, 1941, in which Dionysii asserted that bishops were supposed to attend to pastoral matters only in the eparchies and provinces to which they are assigned. Dionysii depicted Oleksii's decision to return to Moscow as having "ignored canonical order and accordingly sinned against the Church and its people, [and he] must repent and return to the bosom of the Mother Church." UAA, accession no. 2011-27-7-244.

93. Ibid.

94. Vlasovs'kyi, *Нарис історії 4:2*, 214.

95. "To the all-honorable clergy and faithful of all liberated lands of Ukraine (January 29, 1942)," UAA, accession no. 2011-27-105-2023.

96. Vlasovs'kyi explains that Policarp was presenting himself to the proper state official . . . who was Erich Koch's subordinate. On February 25, 1942, Metropolitan Oleksii also presented himself to von Vedelschtedt. Vlasovs'kyi says that the German government recognized the complete freedom of the church, at least at this point in the thorny history of Germany's occupation of Ukraine. See Vlasovs'kyi, *Нарис історії 4:2*, 214.

97. "I call upon the all-honorable clergy and all faithful to execute my directives fully. No one should heed adversarial tempters in the Church, agents having a design to introduce anarchy and discord in our church and community life. . . . In these moments when a bloody battle is being waged between the glorious German army and godless red Moscow on the Eastern fronts, I call upon all clergy and faithful to work peacefully and constructively, and to create normal conditions in the bosom of our holy Church, which needs neither the protection nor the authority of red Moscow. As the administrator, I call upon various destructive agents among the clergy, who have broken away on account of insubordination and the lack of care for the lawful organs of the government, to return to order, reminding them of the parable of the prodigal son." "До всечеснішого духовенства й вірних на всіх визволених землях України" [To the all-honorable clergy and faithful of all liberated lands of Ukraine], January 29, 1942, UAA, accession no. 2011-27-105-2023.

98. Kalkandjieva, *The Russian Orthodox Church*, 126–37.

99. Ibid., 127.

100. Ibid., 129–30.

101. Ibid., 131–32.

102. The texts of the letters from Metropolitan Sergei to the Orthodox flock in Ukraine condemning Policarp and the UAOC are all published in Feodosii (Protsiuk), *Обособленческие движение в Православной Церкви на Украине* [The separation movement in the Orthodox Church in Ukraine] (Moscow: Krutitskoe podvor'e, 2004), 414–25.

103. Vlasovs'kyi, *Нарис історії 4:2*, 216.

104. "In weighing the great tragedy in the epoch of national rebirth of the Ukrainian Orthodox Church in the years 1917–1921, when the Russian episcopate prevented the organization of a Ukrainian Orthodox hierarchy on functional canonical foundations, which led to the consecration of archpriest Vasyl Lypkivs'kyi as the first bishop at the Kyiv Council of 1921 by the hands of presbyters according to the ancient Alexandrian church, prior to the ecumenical councils, but no longer adhered to—considering this, one can understand the great joy of the Ukrainian Orthodox community at the announcement on the historical event of the ordination of Ukrainian bishops in Pinsk by bishops of the Orthodox Autocephalous Church, led by Metropolitan Dionysii." Ibid.

105. Ibid., 218.

106. Ibid.

107. Ibid., quoting Vlasovs'kyi.

108. Ibid., 217.

109. In "Чин приєднання священиків іншої висвяти до УАПЦ 1942" [Rite of return of priests of another ordination to the 1942 UAOC], n.d., UAA, accession no. 2011-27-105-2023.

110. "Від собору єпископів православної церкви на Україні" [From the Council of Bishops of the Holy Orthodox Church in Ukraine], April 30, 1942 (signed by Metropolitan Oleksii), UAA, accession no. 2011-27-6-237.

111. Ibid.

112. Ibid.

113. Архипастирський лист Полікарпа до всечеснішого духовенства і вірних" [Archpastoral letter of Policarp to the all-honorable clergy and faithful], July 1, 1942, UAA, accession no. 2011-27-105-2023.

114. Ibid.

115. Ibid. Later in the letter, Policarp states that reordination is prohibited by the canons of the Church, so ordaining the priests in accordance with the customary practice would be a violation of church order.

116. See Berkhoff, "Was There a Religious Revival?," 553–56, for details on attitudes toward the UAOC in Ukraine.

117. Vlasovs'kyi, *Нарис історії 4:2*, 221.

118. Ibid., 222–23.

119. Ibid., 223.

120. Ibid.

121. "Your report . . . correctly and concisely presents the earlier and contemporary establishment of the Ukrainian Orthodox Autocephalous Church. Very valuable canonical explanations and issues are found in the archpastoral letter of Vladyka [Archbishop]Policarp of July 1. . . . How come I haven't yet received an official report from you of the resolutions of your council of May 17, 1942?" Dionysii merely acknowledged his appointment as locum tenens of the metropolitan see of Kyiv in the letter. Letter from Dionysii to Archbishop Nikanor, no. 916, August 25, 1942, UAA, accession no. 2011-27-7-242a. Dionysii asked the same question in a letter written to Bishop Mstyslav (Skrypnyk), on the same date, UAA, accession no. 2011-27-7-242a.

122. Letter to Archbishop Nikanor, August 25, 1942, UAA, accession no. 2011-27-7-242a.

123. Letter of Metropolitan Dionysii to Archbishop Policarp, August 25, 1942, UAA, accession no. 2011-27-7-242a.

124. The proposed program for the Council of Bishops of the UAOC, which was to be held in Lutsk October 4–8, 1942, can be found in UAA, accession no. 2011-27-27-238 (n.d.). The program was primarily concerned with the usual issues of organizing church life, but also referred to discussion about the convocation of an all-Ukrainian council, a temporary statute for the UAOC, liturgical language, and the problem of the schism in Ukraine.

125. Adapted and abbreviated from Osyp Zinkewich and Oleksander Voronyn, eds., *Мартирологія Українських Церков*, vol. 1, *Українська Православна Церква* [Martyrology of the Ukrainian churches, vol. 1, The Ukrainian Orthodox Church] (Baltimore, MD: Smoloskyp, 1987), 730.

126. See "Урочистий молебен подяки в Берліні" [Solemn prayer service of thanksgiving in Berlin], *Krakivsky visti*, November 15, 1942.

127. This section follows the detailed report by Vitenko titled "Докладна записка священика Олександра Вітенко в справі поєднання автокефальної і автономної Православних Церков в Україні" [Detailed report of priest Oleksander Vitenko on the matter of the unification of the autocephalous and autonomous Orthodox churches in Ukraine] n.d., UAA, accession no. 2011-27-10-1964.

128. Ibid.

129. Ibid.

130. "Пояснення" [Explanation], UAA, accession no. 2011-27-100-1964. This statement was in the records of Metropolitan Ilarion (Ohienko), but it does not address any particular person or audience. The explanation is dated November 27, 1942, at Kremenetz.

131. The addressee of the letter is unknown, as the salutation includes only "ваше преосвященство, преосвященніший владико!" [Your grace, right-reverend master!], dated December 17, 1942. The letter is obviously written to one of the bishops in Oleksii's synod of bishops of the Autonomous Church, since he refers to the UAOC bishops as the bishops of the "Lutsk orientation," and the resolutions of "our" council of bishops. UAA, accession no. 2011-27-100-1964.

132. The disputes among Ukrainians on using Church Slavonic or Ukrainian in the liturgy resulted in new divisions during the war period. See Berkhoff, "Was There a Religious Revival?," 554–57, for an overview of this matter.

133. Ibid.

134. The brief letter includes multiple references to the Orthodox canonical precept of *oikonomia*, which allows the local bishop flexibility in making a canonical decision.

135. Letter of Metropolitan Oleksii to Metropolitan Dionysii, December 15, 1942, UAA, accession no. 2011-27-105-2024.

136. See Berkhoff, "Was There a Religious Revival?," 544–45, on German opposition to the Pochaiv act of union.

137. "Меморандум автономних єпископів-москофілів" [Memorandum of autonomous bishops-Moscowphiles], in Zinkewich and Voronyn, *Мартирологія Українських Церков*, 1:731–33.

138. Ibid., 1:731–32.

139. Ibid., 1:732.

140. Ibid.

141. Лист Єпископа Пантелеймона до благочинних Київської єпархії [Letter of Bishop Panteleimeon to the deans of Kyiv eparchy]. Ibid., 1:734. The only date given is autumn 1942.

142. Лист Митрополита Олексія до своїх єпископів [Letter of Metropolitan Oleksii to his bishops]. Ibid., 1:735.

143. Ibid.

144. "The Ukrainian Orthodox Church during the Time of World War II (1939–1944)," ibid., 1:671.

145. For a complete overview of the brutal German policies toward both Orthodox churches in Ukraine during this period, see Berkhoff, "Was There a Religious Revival?," 538–48.

146. Ibid.

147. "The Church in Ukraine," republished in Zinkewich and Voronyn, *Мартирологія Українських Церков*, 1:745–46.

148. Ibid., 1:745–46. Also see the additional testimonies published in *Мартирологія Українських Церков* attesting to the fact that Germans prevented the synods from holding meetings, and insisted that the statute of the Church must state that the church represents the state, and that no additional bishops may be ordained without the permission of the state (ibid., 1:751–52).

149. Kalkandjieva, *The Russian Orthodox Church*, 119. Also see John Armstrong, *Ukrainian Nationalism*, 3rd ed. (Englewood, CO: Ukrainian Academic Press, 1990), 157–58.

150. Armstrong, *Ukrainian Nationalism*, 158. See Sophia Senyk, "The Orthodox Church in Ukraine in the Twentieth Century," in *The Orthodox Church in Eastern Europe in the Twentieth Century*, ed. Christine Chaillot (Oxford: Peter Lang, 2011), 341.

151. See Feodosii (Protsiuk), *Обособленческие движение*, 476–90.

152. Ibid., 486–88.

153. Ibid., 478.

154. Smyrnov, *Мстислав (Скрипник)*, 116–27.

155. Ibid., 122–23.

156. Ibid., 123.

157. Ibid., 194–95.

158. Berkhoff, "Was There a Religious Revival?," 544.

159. See Bohdan Bociurkiw, "The Ukrainian Autocephalous Orthodox Church in West Germany, 1945–50," in *The Refugee Experience: Ukrainian Displaced Persons after World War II*, ed. Wsewolod Isajiw et al. (Edmonton, AB: Canadian Institute of Ukrainian Studies, 1992), 159–63.

160. "Звернення собору єпископів УАПЦ до Українського народу в 1944 році" [Appeal of the Synod of Bishops of the UAOC to the Ukrainian people in the year 1944], in Zinkewich and Voronyn, *Мартирологія Українських Церков*, 1:765–69. The actual date of the epistle is April 25, 1944. The bishops also severely condemned the aforementioned Metropolitan Nikolai for calling for the eradication of Ukrainian clergy and for disseminating anti-religious propaganda.

161. The anti-Soviet ideology of the UAOC explains the willingness of bishops like Mstyslav to attempt to compromise with the Germans. For example, see Smyrnov's presentation of Mstyslav's correspondence with various Ukrainian political leaders in Smyrnov, *Мстислав (Скрипник)*, 166–69.

162. "Звернення собору єпископів УАПЦ до Українського народу в 1944 році," in Zinkewich and Voronyn, *Мартирологія Українських Церков*, 1:766.

163. A new schism emerged within the ranks of the UAOC when a group of laity and one bishop restored the 1921 UAOC in 1947 in what Ukrainian church historians refer to as the Aschaffenburg schism. For a brief overview of this split within the ranks of the UAOC, see Bociurkiw, "The Ukrainian Autocephalous Orthodox Church in West Germany," 163–65. The Aschaffenburg schism denotes the continued resilience of adherents to the 1921 UAOC among Orthodox Ukrainians.

164. Subtelny, *Ukraine*, 467.

165. Ibid., 468–69. Also see Serhii Plokhy, *The Gates of Europe: A History of Ukraine* (New York: Basic Books, 2015), 272–74.

166. Subtelny, *Ukraine*, 472.

167. Ibid., 473. Subtelny explains the details distinguishing factions of the Ukrainian nationalist units, and also covers the tragic Ukrainian massacre of Poles in Volyn' on 474–75.

168. See Plokhy, *The Gates of Europe*, 265.

169. Harvey Fireside, *Icon and Swastika: The Russian Orthodox Church under Nazi and Soviet Control* (Cambridge, MA: Harvard University Press, 1971), 148–60.

170. Fireside, *Icon and Swastika*, 149, and also Armstrong, *Ukrainian Nationalism*, 149, 154.

171. Fireside, *Icon and Swastika*, 158.

172. Armstrong, *Ukrainian Nationalism*, 152–56.

173. Armstrong suggests that Oleksii signed the act on account of the growing popularity of the autocephalists (ibid., 155), whereas Kalkandjieva states that the Bandera partisans coerced Oleksii into agreement (*The Russian Orthodox Church*, 118). Also see the treatment of this matter in Wassilij Alexeev and Theofanis Stavrou, *The Great Revival: The Russian Church under German Occupation* (Minneapolis, MN: Burgess Publishing, 1976), 176–83. This essay is written as an apology for the autonomist church and the scholarship on the question of German favoritism and autocephalist affiliations with Ukrainian nationalists is quite dated.

174. Ukrainian Orthodox were not alone in greeting Hitler as a liberator; Metropolitan Anastasii (Gribanovskii) of the Russian Orthodox Church outside of Russia also greeted Hitler as the potential liberator of the Russians from Soviet rule—see Dimitry Pospielovsky, *The Orthodox Church in the History of Russia* (Crestwood, NY: St. Vladimir's Seminary Press, 1998), 272.

175. Tymofii Minenko, "Повторювані вигадки затінюють правду" [Duplicated flames obscure the truth], *Herald*, May 21, 1999, 13.

176. Ibid. Minenko caricatures the 1921 line as nationalistic and media-friendly.

177. This protection was not always consistent, especially when one considers the frequent occurrences of attempts to proselytize the Orthodox in Poland, and also Polonize the non-Poles in the Church.

178. Plokhy, *The Gates of Europe*, 274.

179. Ibid.

Notes to Chapter 3

1. See Bohdan Bociurkiw, "The Ukrainian Autocephalous Orthodox Church in West Germany, 1945–50," in *The Refugee Experience: Ukrainian Displaced Persons after World War II*, ed. Wsevolod Isajiw, Yury Boshyk, and Roman Senkus (Edmonton, AB: Canadian Institute of Ukrainian Studies, 1992), 167–69. For details on the post-World War II Ukrainian émigré experience, see the comprehensive treatment of this issue in the essays published in Isajiw et al., *The Refugee Experience*.

2. This brief outline follows Roman Yereniuk, *A Short Historical Outline of the Ukrainian Orthodox Church of Canada (UOCC) on the Occasion of the 90th Anniversary of the Church (1918–2008)* (Winnipeg, MB: Ecclesia, 2008).

3. Ibid., 9.

4. Ibid., 11–12.

5. Yereniuk refers to the lay movement as *naradovtsi*, 12.

6. Ibid., 12–14.

7. Myroslaw Tataryn, "Harvesting Heritage Seeds in Prairie Soil: The Role of *Ukrainskyi holos* in the Formation of the Identity of the Ukrainian Greek Orthodox Church of Canada," *Historical Studies* 71 (2005): 97.

8. Ibid., 16.

9. Ibid., 18–19.

10. Ibid., 20.

11. Oleksander Voronyn, *Історичний шлях УАПЦ* [Historical path of the UAOC] (Kensington, MD: Voskresinnia, 1992), 115.

12. Ibid., 116.

13. Ibid.

14. The most notorious example is of Alexis Toth. For details, see D. Oliver Herbel, *Turning to Tradition: Converts and the Making of an American Orthodox Church* (Oxford: Oxford University Press, 2014), 25–60.

15. Several excerpts from Lypkivs'kyi's letters to Peter Mayevsky illustrate his frustration with Archbishop John, especially letter 17, dated September 7, 1936, in which Metropolitan Vasyl severely criticizes Archbishop John for seeking canonical recognition from the patriarchate of Constantinople. Metropolitan Vasyl' (Lypkivs'kyi), *Листи, 1933–1937* [Letters, 1933–1937] (n.p.: Ukr. Pravoslavne bratstvo im. Mytr. Vasylia Lypkivs'koho, 1980), 39–41.

16. Voronyn, *Історичний шлях*, 121.

17. Lypkivs'kyi's letters also touch upon this sensitive topic: "At Easter time I received a letter from Archbishop Ivan Teodorovych, with a full description of the affair with the 'Zhukovites' [followers of the bishop Zhuk] |. He does not blame himself. He thinks that the real cause of discord lies in the fact that for ages the Ukrainians of Galicia have been divided from Eastern Ukraine, and that the Ukrainians of Galicia have not accepted him as he is from Eastern Ukraine. I think that there is some truth in this matter. But we should make even stronger efforts for unity in order to remove the age-long tragic division of the Ukrainians." From letter 8, dated April 10, 1934, in *Листи*, 21.

18. Paul Yuzyk, *The Ukrainian Greek Orthodox Church of Canada, 1918–1951* (Ottawa, ON: University of Ottawa, 1981), 187–89.

19. Yereniuk, *A Short Historical Outline*, 23.

20. Yuzyk, *The Ukrainian Greek Orthodox Church*, 191. Note that Archbishop Mstyslav did not concelebrate the liturgy, but participated by standing in his *mantia*, a garment worn by bishops and other monastic priests for certain church services. Bishops do not wear the *mantia* during the Divine Liturgy.

21. Ibid.

22. Ibid.

23. Ibid., 23.

24. Yuzyk, *The Ukrainian Greek Orthodox Church*, 192.

25. Yereniuk, *A Short Historical Outline*, 23.

26. Yuzyk, *The Ukrainian Greek Orthodox Church*, 193–94.

27. Ibid., 196–97.

28. Yereniuk, *A Short Historical Outline*, 24.

29. Ibid., 198.

30. Ibid., 199.

31. "I also solemnly declare that I recognize the validity of the hierarchy of the Ukrainian Autocephalous Orthodox Church in the United States of America and Canada, a hierarchy that has renewed the function of episcopal ministry through the act of the first All-Ukrainian Orthodox Church Council in Kyiv, in St. Sophia, in the month of October 1921," from a letter from Bishop Mstyslav to Archbishop John, March 27, 1946, UAA, accession no. 2011-27-92-1835.

32. Letter of Archbishop John, *Dnipro* 30, no. 2 (February 1950): 1–3.

33. Ibid., 2.

34. Letter from Archbishop John to Bishop Platon, December 1948, UAA, accession no. 2011-27-91-1820.

35. Based on a memo from Metropolitan Christopher, August 26, 1949, in UAA, accession no. 2011-27-11-393.

36. Letter from Archbishop John to Metropolitan Christopher, September 9, 1949, UAA, accession no. 2011-27-11-393.

37. As reported by Archbishop John in a letter to Archbishop Ihor (Huba) dated September 1, 1949, UAA, accession no. 211-11-395.

38. Ibid.

39. Ibid.

40. Frank Sysyn notes that this was a Ukrainian-American particularity, since the American Church had more post-World War II immigrants. See Frank Sysyn, "Remarks on the History of Ukrainian Orthodox in Ukraine and North America," *The Ukrainian Weekly*, July 19, 1998, 3.

41. "Соборне послання" [Synodal Epistle], *Церква і народ, Український православний місячник* [Church and People, Ukrainian Orthodox Monthly] (September–October 1950), 2.

42. Ibid.

43. Ibid.

44. "Собор поєднання Українських Православних Церков" [Reunion Council of the Ukrainian Orthodox Churches], *Церква і народ, Український православний місячник* [Church and People, Ukrainian Orthodox Monthly] (September–October, 23.)

45. Ibid., 24–25.

46. The *klobuk* is the monastic head covering worn by monks. It is customary for metropolitans and some patriarchs to wear a white klobuk in the Slavic traditions.

47. "Собор поєднання Українських Православних Церков," 24.

48. Ibid.

49. "О так называемой Украинской Автокефальной Церкви" (On the so-called Ukrainian Autocephalous Orthodox Church], in *Законодательство Русской Православной Церкви заграницей (1921–2007)* [Legislation of the Russian Orthodox Church outside of Russia, 1921–2007], ed. D. P. Anashkin (Moscow: Izdatel'stvo PSTGU, 2013), 127–28. Note that the statement of the ROCOR Synod on the Ukrainian Church was based on a report by Archbishop Antony (Martsenko), who had previously been on the synod of the Autonomous Church in Ukraine.

50. Readers should note the continued existence of the Ukrainian Orthodox Church in America under the jurisdiction of the Ecumenical Patriarchate during this period. Voronyn notes that this church was active in interchurch dialogue, an advantageous position given the patronage of the ecumenical patriarch (see Voronyn, *Історичний шлях*, 121–22).

51. "The consecration of a space beneath the structure of the Memorial Church will take place after the Divine Liturgy, which is to be a manifest sign of our respect for the memory of our relatives and all of those who gave their lives for Christian truth and the will and statehood of the Ukrainian people. The church portion of the celebrations will conclude with a prayer to the all-holy Mother of God and the common singing of 'Beneath Your Compassion,'" in "Комунікат комітету Посвячення Осередку УПЦеркви в Бавнд Брук, Н. Дж" [Communique of the consecration committee of the UO Church Center in Bound Brook, NJ], *Ukrainian Orthodox Word* (UOW), April 1952, 12.

52. "As we see from the project, the Memorial Church in Bound Brook will be not only a beautiful divine temple, before whose altar daily prayers for the souls of our beloved relatives and martyred brothers and sisters will be offered, but also a marvelous example of Ukrainian ecclesial architecture . . . besides this, the Memorial Church in Bound Brook will surely be one of the most precious additions to the spiritual and cultural treasury of the United States of America, which Orthodox Ukrainians offer as expressions of thanksgiving for the liberty of soul and conscience, which they exercise in America." Ibid.

53. "Церква-Пам'ятник" [Memorial Church], UOW (November 1960), 13. The report refers to Shevchenko as "Пророк України" (Prophet of Ukraine) and "Великомученик(а)" (Great Martyr) of the Ukrainian people.

54. Ibid.

55. "Церква-Пам'ятник і рік 1961" [Memorial Church and the year 1961], UOW (January 1961): 10. The author of the article states that the memorial church was built from the fragments of Ukrainian shrines destroyed by the Muscovite hand.

56. Ibid., 10.

57. "Церква-Пам'ятник будується" [Memorial Church under construction], UOW (March 1961): 17.

58. Ibid.

59. Ibid.

60. "The Sunday of June 4 this year [1961] will be for us an authentically great day because on that day we will glorify God for giving us who dwell in foreign lands the reliquary most precious to each Ukrainian heart—fragments from our Ukrainian shrines, which were symbols of the immortal Ukrainian soul. One must understand this gift as the manifestation of God's great mercy, because in the past, many other peoples wandering in exile enriched foreign 'Babylonian waters' with their tears, but rarely has God shown such great kindness to any of these nations as he has shown us, transferring a fragment of the most valuable native thing to dwell in our hearts." Ibid.

61. "Слово Митрополита Іоана під час посвячення Церква-Пам'ятника" [Speech of Metropolitan John at the consecration of the Memorial Church], UOW (November–December 1965), 2.

62. Zinkewich and Voronyn, *Мартирологія Українських Церков*, 1:661.

63. Ibid.

64. Ibid., 1:662.

65. Published in Ukrainian in Zinkewich and Voronyn, *Мартирологія Українських Церков*, 1:662–66.

66. "In the beginning of the 1920s a group of native Ukrainian chauvinists, consisting of a small portion of parish clergy and faithful of the eparchies of our Church in Ukraine, decided to separate from the mother church on account of phyletistic motives. These anti-ecclesial acts found no support in our episcopate, and the clerical leaders of the Russian Orthodox Church placed the proper canonical prohibitions on the schismatics. . . . Then, ignoring this warning and without the blessing of the primate of the Russian Orthodox Church, his holiness Tikhon, patriarch of Moscow and all Rus', the separatists convoked a council in October 1921 called "the All-Ukrainian Council of Clergy and Laity." . . . This pseudo-council proclaimed the existence of the Ukrainian Autocephalous Orthodox Church. The leader of the separatists, Archpriest Vasyl Lypkivs'kyi (deposed at the time), was elected as 'bishop' of the new 'church' by the delegates of the 'council' . . . the ordination itself was

performed by deposed presbyters and laity by the placing of the relics (hands) of the hieromartyr Macarius, metropolitan of Kiev, on Lypkivs'kyi. This blasphemous act was repeated for the next 'ordination' to 'bishop' on archpriest Nestor Sharaivsky (also deposed). The character of these 'ordinations' provided the basis for the assignment of the name 'self-consecrated' to the schismatics among the faithful." Ibid., 1:663–64.

67. Ibid., 1:664.

68. "Is it necessary to remind your holiness that all diaconal and presbyteral 'ordinations' in the UOC-USA, which occurred during the time of its activity, are invalid, while the 'sacred acts' of its clergy are without grace? It must be known to your holiness that for all of the almost fifty-year existence of the UOC-USA, none of the local Orthodox jurisdictions has recognized its canonicity nor has joined it in Eucharistic concelebration. Also, the 'hierarchy' of the UOC-USA has never been a member of the conference of canonical bishops in the USA." Ibid.

69. "Bishop's Sobor," UOW (April 1978), 8.

70. "The Tenth Sobor and a Marginal Note," UOW (July–August 1981), 13.

71. Ibid., 14.

72. Ibid., 25.

73. "Press Review: Patriarch Pimen in New York," UOW (September–October 1982), 8.

74. Ibid.

75. "The Subjugation of the UOC (Kievan Metropolia) to the Moscow Patriarchate 300 Years Ago (Jubilee Note)," UOW (September–October 1986), 3.

76. "Bishop's Sobor," UOW (April 1978), 8.

77. "The Beginning of a New Epoch," UOW (January–February 1987), 12–13.

78. "Archpastoral Easter Letter," UOW (March–April 1987), 2–3.

79. "Our special disdain, however, must be expressed to the Synod of the Ecumenical Patriarchate, which condoned the Patriarchate's trip to the country of tears and sorrow, thus severely damaging the prestige of the Ecumenical Patriarchate." "Archpastoral Nativity Epistle," UOW (January–February 1988), 2.

80. See the "Address of His Beatitude Metropolitan Mstyslav to the Tenth Sobor of the UOC-USA," UOW (July–August 1981), 5–7.

81. "Bishop's Sobor," UOW (April 1978), 9.

82. In all likelihood, the bishops were prohibiting pastors from adopting the service of general confession published by the Orthodox Church in America under the guidance of Father Alexander Schmemann. See Alexander Schmemann, "Confession and Communion," February 16–17, 1972, http://www.schmemann.org/byhim/confessionandcommunion.html (accessed July 23, 2015). Readers should note that the 1978 prohibition of general confession was also a disavowal of the practice permitted by Vasyl Lypkivs'kyi of the 1921 UAOC.

83. "Archpastoral Letter of the Sobor of Bishops of the UAOC on the Occasion of the Inauguration of the Holy Millennium Jubilee Year of the Baptism of Rus'-Ukraine," UOW (July–August 1987), 3.

84. "Archpastoral Letter," UOW (March–April 1988), 3.

85. Ibid., 10, writing on the obligations of the clergy.

86. Ibid.

87. "Resolutions of the Twelfth Sobor of the UOC-USA," UOW (January–February 1989), 6.

88. Semen Sawchuk, *Ідеологічні засади Української греко-православної церкви в Канаді* [Ideological principles of the Ukrainian Greek-Orthodox Church of Canada] (Winnipeg, MB: Ekkleziia, 1975).

89. Ibid., 3–7.

90. Ibid., 5.

91. Ibid., 9–10.

92. Ibid., 11. Sawchuk commented that the Church in Canada did not have the authority to change the calendar, as this was a topic to be submitted to the authority of the global Orthodox Church.

93. Ibid., 14–16.

94. Bishop Wasyly (Fedak), *Keynote Address to the 16th Sobor of the Ukrainian Greek-Orthodox Church of Canada, July 1980* (Winnipeg, MB: Ecclesia, 1982).

95. Ibid., 8.

96. Ibid., 9.

97. Ibid., 13–15.

98. Ibid., 13.

99. "Sobor 2000 Resolutions," *Visnyk*, December 31, 2000.

100. "Nativity Message from His Beatitude Metropolitan Mstyslav," UOW (February–March 1988), 3.

101. Ibid., 14.

102. "Archpastoral Resurrection Epistle Sobor of Bishops of the UAOC," UOW (March–April 1990), 2–3.

103. Ibid., 3.

104. Ibid., 7.

105. Ibid., 3.

106. Ibid., 8–9.

107. Ibid.,

108. "Parma Parish Unveils Millennium Project," UOW (March–April 1988), 17.

109. Ibid.

110. "Millennium Celebration at Greek Orthodox Cathedral, New York City," UOW (May–July 1988), 9.

111. "Patriarchal Millennium Blessing," UOW (August–October 1988), 8.

112. "White House Symposium," UOW (May–July 1988), 19.

113. "President Reagan's Message for Ukrainian Millennium Celebrations," *Ukrainian Weekly*, October 16, 1988, 3.

114. Ibid.

115. "The HOLY CITY for us Orthodox Ukrainians was, is and will remain Kiev—a city, which having been repeatedly plundered for ages, is now enthralled by Moscow. . . . Representing this Jerusalem for us Orthodox Ukrainians outside of our homeland is the Center of St. Andrew the First-Called Apostle, located on what is already referred to as the Ukrainian Brook, nearby the small town of South Bound Brook in New Jersey." "Letter to Leaders," UOW (May–July 1988), 7.

116. Frank Sysyn, "The Third Rebirth of the Ukrainian Autocephalous Orthodox Church and the Religious Situation in Ukraine," in *Religion and Nation in Modern Ukraine*, ed. Serhii Plokhy and Frank E. Sysyn (Edmonton, AB: Canadian Institute of Ukrainian Studies, 2003), 112.

117. "The Protocol of the Extraordinary Sobor of the UGOC in Canada, October 21–22, 1989," (Winnipeg, MB, 1990), 5. In UAA, accession no. 211-27-37-1122.

118. Ibid., 6–7.

119. Ibid., 7.

120. Ibid., 8.

121. Ibid., 3.

122. Published in Ukrainian and English in *Рідна нива, 1991 Український Православний календар-альманах* [Native field, 1991 Ukrainian Orthodox Calendar-Almanac] (Winnipeg, MB: Ecclesia, 1991), 115–19.

123. Ibid., 117–18.

124. Addressed by nos. 3, 4, 6, 8, and 10, ibid., 117–19.

125. "Pre-Sobor Archpastoral Letter of the Sobor of Bishops of the Ukrainian Orthodox Church of Canada," May 13, 1990, UAA, accession no. 2011-27-47-1297.

126. "As we attend the Sobor in Winnipeg, it is necessary for us all to remember that the Sobor takes place through the precept of 'Sobornopravnist.' The essence of Sobornopravnist lies in the fact that decisions at the Sobor are carried out by the Episcopate, clergy, and delegates from the parishes

of our Church, guided by the Holy Spirit. . . . The delegates to the Sobor must be selected from among those faithful whose devotion to the Church serves as an example of a proper and godly life," in ibid.

127. "It must also be understood that the UOCC does not consider herself the "UAOC"; she is the Church of Orthodox Ukrainians of Canada, the majority of whom are born in Canada. Our Church is even governed by a charter which is part of the Canadian legal system. The UAOC, which is now being reborn in Ukraine, is the true, historical Church of the Ukrainian people in Ukraine. We deeply sympathize with our brothers and sisters in Ukraine, with the UAOC, and with the All-Ukrainian Orthodox brotherhood and sisterhood." "The Delegates' Manual of the 18th Sobor of the UGOC in Canada (1990)," in UAA, accession no. 2011-27-47-1297.

128. Letter to O. Krawchenko from St. Sophia, May 2, 2000, UAA, accession no. 2011-27-39-1143.

129. Ibid.

130. Ibid.

131. Resolution no. 2, ibid.

132. "Proposed resolutions to the year 2000 Sobor," n.d., UAA, accession no. 2011-27-39-1143.

133. Ibid.

134. Ibid.

135. Ibid.

136. Ibid.

137. Ibid.

138. "Sobor 2000 Resolutions," *Visnyk*, December 31, 2000.

139. Ibid.

140. "The existence of several Orthodox Churches [in Ukraine] is a reality at the present time. This is not a healthy situation. It is made even worse given the fact that some of these churches do not even come under the jurisdiction of their own prime hierarchs, but rather, submit to that Church which has made a joke of our Church, and desires not to see us free, but slaves, whom she can use to reconstruct a lost empire. We must cast aside such a state of affairs, which is so shameful and dangerous for our nation. . . . And when logic triumphs, turn, as I turned, to His Holiness the Ecumenical Patriarch, asking him to convoke an Ecumenical Council of all the Orthodox Churches in the world. I was not able to achieve this. Other Churches do not hasten to this. . . . There is great need to talk about our canons and about the wrongs inflicted upon our church, and about many other purely Christian issues which [are] of concern to our Church," quoted in "Council of Bishops to the Venerable Clergy and Christ-Loving Faithful of the UOC-USA and in the Diaspora," UOW (April 1995), 13.

141. Ibid.

142. Ibid., 12.

143. Ibid.

144. Letter of Patriarch Alexy to Patriarch Bartholomew (English translation), May 18, 1995, in UAA, accession no. 2011-27-117-2186.

145. Ibid.

146. Response of Patriarch Bartholomew to Patriarch Alexy, July 11, 1995, UAA, accession no. 2011-27-117-2186.

147. The details are explained clearly in "Press Release by the Council of Bishops of the UOC-USA," October 15, 1997, UAA, accession no. 2011-27-117-2185.

148. Ibid.

149. Ibid.

150. Ibid.

151. Ibid.

152. Ibid.

153. Paul Gavrilyuk, "Жажда церковного единства: Международный украинский православный симпозиум в Торонто" [Thirst for church unity: An international Ukrainian Orthodox Symposium in Toronto], Religiia v Ukraïni, May 14, 2014, http://www.religion.in.ua/main/

daycomment/25780-zhazhda-cerkovnogo-edinstva-mezhdunarodnyj-ukrainskij-pravoslavnyj-sim-pozium-v-toronto.html (accessed October 7, 2016); Nicholas Denysenko, "Ukrainian Orthodoxy in Toronto: A Model for Dialogue, a Symbol of Courage," RISU: Religious Information Service of Ukraine, May 17, 2014, http://risu.org.ua/en/index/expert_thought/analytic/56450/ (accessed October 7, 2016).

154. I will treat this event more extensively in chapter 5. See the complete report along with digital images of the original signed agreement at "Decision Reached by Joint Meeting of the Committees," The Ukrainian Orthodox Church of the United States, June 8, 2015, http://uocofusa.org/news_150609_1.html (accessed September 15, 2016).

155. "UOC-MP Hierarchs Concerned about Constantinople's Activity in Ukraine," RISU: Religious Information Service of Ukraine, June 24, 2015, http://risu.org.ua/en/index/all_news/confes-sional/orthodox_relations/60350/ (accessed October 7, 2016).

156. "В УПЦ (МП) прокоментували заяву предстоятеля УПЦ Канади про створення в Україні єдиної помісної церкви" [The UPC (MP) commented on the remarks of the primate of the UOC of Canada on the creation of one local church in Ukraine], RISU: Religious Information Service of Ukraine, August 3, 2013, http://risu.org.ua/ua/index/all_news/confessional/orthodox_rela-tions/60706/ (accessed October 7, 2016).

157. "Митрополит ОЛЕКСАНДР (УПЦ МП)—інтерв'ю 5 каналу" [Metropolitan Oleksander (UOC-MP) – interview with channel 5] 5 Kanal, April 14, 2015, https://youtu.be/RgKU1jJhrks (accessed October 7, 2016).

158. See also Metropolitan Oleksander's assessment of the role of the Ecumenical Patriarchate and the diaspora Ukrainian bishops in "Участь Константинополя у розв'язанні сучасної канонічної кризи у православ'ї в Україні" [Constantinople's participation in the resolution of the contemporary canonical crisis in Orthodoxy in Ukraine], RISU: Religious Information Service of Ukraine, June 16, 2016, http://risu.org.ua/ua/index/studios/materials_conferences/63705/ (accessed October 17, 2016).

Notes to Chapter 4

1. Daniela Kalkandijeva, *The Russian Orthodox Church, 1917–1948: From Decline to Resurrection* (London: Routledge, 2015), 100–113.

2. See Bohdan Bociurkiw, *The Ukrainian Greek Catholic Church and the Soviet State (1939–1950)* (Edmonton, AB: Canadian Institute of Ukrainian Studies, 1996), and Serhii Plokhy, "In the Shadow of Yalta: International Politics and the Soviet Liquidation of the Ukrainian Greek Catholic Church," in *Religion and Nation in Modern Ukraine*, ed. Serhii Plokhy and Frank E. Sysyn (Edmonton, AB: Canadian Institute of Ukrainian Studies, 2003), 58–73.

3. Natalia Shlikhta, "'Ukrainian' as 'Non-Orthodox': How Greek Catholics Were 'Reunited' with the Russian Orthodox Church, 1940s–1960s," trans. Jan Surer, *State, Religion and Church* 2, no. 2 (2015): 77–98; Shlikhta, "'Orthodox' and 'Soviet': The Identity of Soviet Believers (1940s–early 1970s)," trans. Rosie Tweddle, *Forum for Anthropology and Culture* 11 (2015): 140–64; Shlikhta, "'Please Open Our Church . . . in the Name of Historical and Human Value of Socialism': Orthodox Believers' *Letters to Power*, 1960s–Early 1970s," *Textus et Studia* 4, no. 4 (2015): 71–93; Shlikhta, "Portraits of Two Bishops Defending Their Dioceses: A Study of the Orthodox Episcopate in Postwar Soviet Ukraine," *Logos: A Journal of Eastern Christian Studies* 55, nos. 3–4 (2014): 329–58; Shlikhta, "Православні вірні—На захист своїх прав і своєї церкви (на Українських Матеріалах кінця 1940-х–1970-х рр." [Orthodox faithful—in defense of their rights and their church], *Наукові записки* 104 (2010): 34–41; Shlikhta, "Основні форми і методи атеїстичної пропаганди в Українській РСР наприкінці 50-х–на початки 60-х років" [Basic forms and methods of atheistic propaganda in the Ukrainian SSR at the end of the 1950s to the beginning of the 1960s], *Наукові записки* 14 (1999): 80–87.

4. Ihor Mončak, *Florentine Ecumenism in the Kyivan Church: The Theology of Ecumenism Applied to the Individual Church in Kyiv* (Rome: Ukraïnskyi Katolic'kyi Univ. im. sv. Klymenta Papy, 1987).

5. Barbara Skinner, *The Western Front of the Eastern Church: Uniate and Orthodox Conflict in Eighteenth-Century Poland, Ukraine, Belarus, and Russia* (DeKalb: Northern Illinois University Press, 2009), 91.

6. See Cyril Korolevsky, *Metropolitan Andrew (1865–1944)*, trans. Serge Keleher (Lviv: Stauropegion, 1993), 2:504–7.

7. Dimitry Pospielovsky, *The Orthodox Church in the History of Russia* (Crestwood, NY: St. Vladimir's Seminary Press, 1998), 301.

8. "Its first step was Patriarch Alexii's address to the Ukrainian Uniates on the occasion of the victory, which lamented the fact that they were religiously separated from their Orthodox brethren and therefore could not join them in the same churches in a common prayer of thanksgiving to God for the end of the war. After the L'viv Sobor, he issued another address, congratulating the Western Ukrainians on their return to their historical church. The wording of both addresses was such that any member of the Orthodox Church could easily sign it—except for its timing: such congratulations coming on the tail of the NKVD terror sounded like mockery; especially as the message implied the legitimization of the fraudulent 'Sobor.'" Ibid., 301–2.

9. Ibid., 302. Pospielovsky also creates a false equivalence between the UGCC and the Moscow Patriarchate when he implies that the UGCC's union with Rome in the seventeenth century and its repossessing of temples in 1989 were much worse than the role of the Moscow Patriarchate in the pseudo-council of 1946. Sophia Senyk also accuses the UGCC of hypocrisy by referring to the alleged plan of Metropolitan Andrei (Sheptytsky) to forcibly separate the Orthodox in Ukraine from the Russian Church when Austrian victory appeared imminent during World War I. See Senyk, "The Ukrainian Greek Catholic Church Today: Universal Values versus Nationalist Doctrines," *Religion, State and Society* 30, no. 4 (2002): 328–29.

10. Shlikhta, "'Ukrainian' as 'Non-Orthodox,'" 79.

11. Tatiana A. Chumachenko, *Church and State in Soviet Russia: Russian Orthodoxy from World War II to the Krushchev Years*, ed. and trans. Edward Roslof (Armonk, NY: M. E. Sharpe, 2002), 36.

12. Pospielovsky, *The Orthodox Church*, 288.

13. Ibid., 289.

14. Ibid., 292–93.

15. Ibid., 293. Pospielovsky notes the limitations of the thaw, as religious instruction of children was still extremely limited by law.

16. "The encounter with Stalin must have included a foreign policy agenda for the Church, as on May 28 the Patriarch, accompanied by Metropolitan Nikolai, left on an extensive political pilgrimage. They traveled to the Holy Land, to Egypt, where they visited the Patriarch of Alexandria, to Damascus, visiting the Patriarch of Antioch; and then on to England . . . in York Patriarch Alexy publicly attacked the Vatican, very much in line with the latest Soviet foreign policy, declaring the papacy to be the common enemy of both the Orthodox and Anglican Churches. During this 'pilgrimage', Alexei managed to bring back under his omophorion the Russian parishes in Alexandria, Damascus, and London." Ibid., 293–94. Pospielovsky notes that this foreign policy agenda opened the door for Moscow to bring the diaspora churches back under its omophorion.

17. Ibid., 299.

18. Kalkandijeva, *The Russian Orthodox Church*, 218–24.

19. Pospielovsky, *The Orthodox Church*, 299, and Kalkandijeva, *The Russian Orthodox Church*, 226–31.

20. The matter of authority in granting autocephaly is controverted within Orthodoxy. For the most recent literature on this topic, see Maximos (Christopoulos), "The Primacy of the Ecumenical Patriarchate: Developments since the Nineteenth Century," in *Primacy in the Church: The Office of Primate and the Authority of Councils*, ed. John Chryssavgis (Crestwood, NY: St. Vladimir's Seminary Press, 2016), 1:367–84; Moscow Patriarchate, "Position of the Moscow Patriarchate on the Problem of Primacy in the Universal Church," in Chryssavgis, *Primacy*, 1:421–30; and Alexander Rentel, "The Canonical Tradition: Universal Primacy in the Orthodox Church," in Chryssavgis, *Primacy*, 2:555–86.

21. Shlikhta, "Основні форми," 80.

22. Pospielovsky, *The Orthodox Church*, 313–14.

23. Ibid., 313–29. On this topic, also see Zoe Knox, *Russian Society and the Orthodox Church: Religion in Russia after Communism* (New York: Routledge, 2005), 47–57.

24. Shlikhta, "Основні форми," 81.

25. Ibid., 82.

26. Ibid., 83.

27. Hyacinthe Destivelle, *The Moscow Council (1917–1918): The Creation of the Conciliar Institutions of the Russian Orthodox Church*, ed. Michael Plekon and Vitaly Permiakov, trans. by Jerry Ryan, foreword by Metropolitan Hilarion (Alfeyev) (Notre Dame, IN: University of Notre Dame Press, 2015), 158.

28. "In reality, the priest is thus only a hired hand of his parish, subject to the authority of a *starosta*, theoretically elected but actually designated by the local authorities as their official representative." Ibid., 158.

29. Bohdan Bociurkiw, "Religion and Nationalism in Contemporary Ukraine," in *Nationalism in the USSR and Eastern Europe in the Era of Brezhnev and Kosygin*, ed. George W. Simmonds (Detroit, MI: University of Detroit Press, 1977), 82.

30. Bohdan Bociurkiw, "Soviet Religious Policy in Ukraine in Historical Perspective," in *Russian Empire: Some Aspects of Tsarist and Soviet Colonial Practices*, ed. Michael S. Pap (Cleveland, OH: Institute for Soviet and East European Studies, John Carroll University and Ukrainian Historical Association, 1985), 108 (95–111). Also see Bociurkiw, "Religion and Nationalism," 82.

31. Bociurkiw, "Religion and Nationalism," 82–83.

32. "The emphasis was now to be placed primarily on atheist 'conversion' of the flock and the replacement of religious holidays, rites, and ceremonies with Communist substitutes, with the natural attrition of the clergy expected to progressively shrink the churches' institutional base." Bociurkiw, "Soviet Religious Policy," 109. For a comprehensive presentation on the specific strategies of anti-religious propaganda disseminated in Soviet Ukraine after World War II, see Russell P. Moroziuk, "Antireligious Propaganda in Ukraine," in *Russian Empire: Some Aspects of Tsarist and Soviet Colonial Practices*, ed. Michael Pap (Cleveland, OH: Institute for Soviet and East European Studies, John Carroll University and Ukrainian Historical Association, 1985), 113–30. Moroziuk provides an overview of Soviet regulations on the promotion of atheism, and in addition to reviewing the insertion of anti-religious materials in curricula, he also covers national symposia and the promotion of atheism in media and film.

33. Ibid., 110.

34. Ibid.

35. "It is clear that the regime has allowed the Orthodox Church a Ukrainian face in Western Ukraine, in order to win over the suppressed Ukrainian Greek Catholics. For every active member of the clandestine Ukrainian Greek-Catholic Church (UGCC), there are many priests and believers in the official Orthodox Church who would return to the UGCC immediately if the church became legal. For the present this element, as well as the real converts to Orthodoxy, form a strong lobby, which views the proper role of the Orthodox Church as similar to that of the traditionally patriotic and activist UGCC." Frank E. Sysyn, "The Ukrainian Orthodox Question in the USSR," in *Religion and Nation in Modern Ukraine*, ed. Serhii Plokhy and Frank E. Sysyn (Edmonton, AB: Canadian Institute of Ukrainian Studies, 2003), 81.

36. Ibid.

37. Ibid., 81–82.

38. Shlikhta, "'Ukrainian' as 'Non-Orthodox,'" 81.

39. Ibid., 89–91.

40. Ibid., 91.

41. Ibid., 81.

42. Sysyn, "The Ukrainian Orthodox Question," 83–84.

43. "At his election in 1971 Pimen, the new patriarch of Moscow, announced the 'reunion' of Ukrainian Orthodox abroad with his church as a major goal. Indeed, Moscow's recognition of the Russian Orthodox Greek Catholic Metropolia as the Orthodox Church in America in 1970, with the program of gathering all Orthodox believers in the United States and Canada, cannot be seen as

divorced from the Soviet government's and the Moscow Patriarchate's plans to undermine Ukrainian Orthodoxy abroad." Ibid., 85.

44. Staff, "Turning the Pages Back," *The Ukrainian Weekly*, July 14, 1995.

45. Ibid.

46. Letter of Vasyl Romaniuk to Metropolitan Mstyslav, republished in Osyp Zinkewich and Oleksander Voronyn, eds. *Мартирологія Українських Церков*, vol. 1, *Українська Православна Церква* [Martyrology of the Ukrainian Churches, vol. 1, The Ukrainian Orthodox Church] (Baltimore, MD: Smoloskyp, 1987), 867–68. The date of Romaniuk's letter is unclear; the editors speculate that it was written in late 1977 or early 1978.

47. "Turning the Pages Back," *The Ukrainian Weekly*, July 14, 1995.

48. The significance of Black Tuesday will be examined in chapter 5.

49. Shlikhta, "Portraits of Two Bishops," 340–41.

50. Ibid., 340.

51. Ibid., 341–42.

52. Ibid., 342. Shlikhta says that over three thousand signatures were collected in support of Feodosii's petition.

53. Ibid., 357.

54. Shlikhta, "Please Open Our Church," 73–76.

55. Ibid., 82–87.

56. "Свободу совісті гарант" [Freedom of conscience is guaranteed], *Вісті з України* 1045, no. 36, August 31, 1978.

57. Ibid.

58. See Shlikhta, "Portraits of Two Bishops," 335–36.

59. Archbishop Hryhorii, "Боротьба Українського народу проти Унії" [The battle of the Ukrainian nation against the Unia], *Православний вісник* 1 (January 1969): 44–47 (hereafter cited as PV).

60. Ibid., 44.

61. Ibid., 44–45.

62. "In Kyivan Rus'—the common past of the Russian, Belarusian, and Ukrainian nations—our ancestors received the holy Christian faith from the Orthodox East, from Greece. This faith permeated all the corners of the ancient Kyivan regime and created a common Christian culture, literature, art, and book language for all of the nations of the Slavic East. When the era of the Tatar-Mongol horde arrived, the nation of Kyivan Rus' lost its political unity, its territory was divided, but in spite of this its spiritual unity was not lost. It was then united by the holy Orthodox faith, the native Orthodox Church. She was the soul, the center of the uniting strength." Ibid., 45.

63. Ibid., 45. Archbishop Hryhorii does not use the word "Polonization" in this particular paragraph, but his invocation of Orthodox as a *хлопська віра* (a "boy's faith") is a way of using a Polish phrase that caricatures Ukrainians and attempts to demoralize them, to show how adhesion to the Latin faith of Poland would improve them as a nation.

64. Ibid., 46.

65. "The question on the union of Ukraine with Russia was first established by Metropolitan Iov (Boretsky) of Kyiv and Halych, a native of Galicia. This union, even though it did not include the entire Ukrainian nation, was made by the glorious national Ukrainian hero Hetman Bohdan Khmelnitsky, who established the foundation of an indivisible common life of the two fraternal nations though the Pereiaslav treaty." Ibid., 46. Note that Metropolitan Iov was the first bishop consecrated for the Orthodox in Ukraine following the Union of Brest-Litovsk, and he served as the metropolitan of Kyiv from 1620 to 1631. He was canonized as a saint in the UOC-KP in 2008.

66. Ibid.

67. Ibid., 47.

68. Ibid., 48.

69. Filaret (Denysenko), "Слово, виголошине екзархом України, митрополитом Філаретом, у св. Успенському жіночому монастирі м. Мукачева з нагоди 20-річчя возз'єднання

колишніх греко-католиків Закарпаття з Руською Православною Церквою" [The word proclaimed by the exarch of Ukraine, Metropolitan Filaret, in the Holy Dormition womens monastery in the city of Mukachevo, on the occasion of the twentieth anniversary of the reunion of former Greek Catholics of Transcarpathia with the Russian Orthodox Church], PV 9 (September 1969): 291–92.

70. Ibid., 291.

71. Ibid.

72. "Reunion—this is not only a return to the pious faith of fathers and unity with the Orthodox Church. Reunion: this is the triumph of Christian love and peace among the fraternal Slavic nations. The Unia also wrought division, enmity, and hatred. She [Unia] degraded national self-consciousness and was an instrument of the oppression of our nation. Unia was not an act of God. She was an aggressor and served not for the unity of faith, but for the unity of the exterior organization and government of the Roman Church. History has condemned Uniatism as a path to the unification of churches. The eradication of Unia permits the possibility of rebuilding fraternal relations between the Orthodox and Roman Catholic Churches." Ibid., 292.

73. Ibid.

74. "Resolutions of the Holy Synod of the Russian Orthodox Church," PV 7 (July 1971): 2.

75. "Recognize prominent historical events in the life of the Russian Orthodox Church—the return to Orthodoxy in the years 1946–1949 of Greek Catholics from Galicia and Transcarpathia and the annulment of the Brest-Litovsk and Uzhorod Unias." Ibid.

76. Ibid. The same resolution acknowledged the granting of autonomy to the Church in Japan on April 10, 1970, and the recognition of the autonomy of the Church in Finland on April 30, 1957, which was once "a part of the Moscow Patriarchate."

77. Ibid., 2. The resolution adds a recommendation for canonical sanctions to be taken against the leaders of the Russian Orthodox Church outside of Russia.

78. As reported by Bishop Volodymyr (Sabodan) of Chernihiv in "Знаменний ювілей церковної єдності" [Eminent jubilee of church unity], PV 7 (July 1971): 15–16. A hierarchical liturgy is a Divine Liturgy with one or more bishops presiding.

79. Metropolitan Pimen (Izvekov), "Послання місцеблюстителя Московського патріаршого престолу митрополита Крутицького й Коломенського Пимена, преосвященним архіпастирям, кліру й мирянам західноукраїнських єпархій Московського Патріархату в звязку з 25-річчям Львівського Собору" [Epistle of the locum tenens of the Moscow patriarchal throne Metropolitan Pimen of Krutitsky and Kolomensky to the reverend archpastors, clergy, and laity of the western Ukrainian eparchies of the Moscow Patriarchate on the occasion of the twenty-fifth anniversary of the Lʹviv council], PV 7 (July 1971): 9.

80. Ibid.

81. Filaret (Denysenko), "Промова екзарха України, Митрополита Київського і Галицького Філарета на відкритті урочистого акту 15 травня 1971 року" [Speech of the exarch of Ukraine, Metropolitan Filaret of Kyiv and Halych, at the opening of the solemn act of May 15, 1971], PV 7 (July 1971): 10–15.

82. Ibid., 12.

83. Ibid.

84. Ibid.

85. Ibid., 10.

86. Ukrainian Orthodox Church, Moscow Patriarchate. "Двадцятипятиріччя возз'єднання Галицької Греко-Католицької Церкви з Руською Православною Церквою на Львівському Церковному Соборі (1946–1971)" [The twenty-fifth anniversary of the reunion of the Galician Greek-Catholic Church with the Russian Orthodox Church at the Lʹviv Church Council (1946–1971)], PV 8 (August 1971): 13–14.

87. Ibid., 13.

88. Ibid., 14.

89. Nikolai specified sub-Carpathian regional styles of Huculshchyna, Bojkivshchyna, and Lemkivshchyna, ibid.

90. Ibid.

91. "This victory [of the Great Patriotic War] finally overthrew all artificial borders, which contrary to historical justice divided the Ukrainian nation for ages, and permitted us to extend our hands and hearts to the great family of nations of the Soviet Union, to an integral portion of it, our mother—Soviet Ukraine. On these days, all of the nations of our Soviet homeland solemnly commemorated the twenty-sixth anniversary of the victory over fascism." Ibid.

92. "Відповіді митрополита Львівського і тернопільського Николая на запитання кореспондента газети Українські вісті" [Responses of Metropolitan Nikolai of L'viv and Ternopil to the questions of the correspondent of the newspaper *Ukrainian news*], PV 4 (April 1972): 24–25.

93. "The authors of the epistle are attempting to plant the seeds of national enmity between the brotherly nations of the Soviet Union, especially between Ukrainians and Russians. . . . We are not surprised by the opposition to our homeland in the political focus of the epistle, because it is well known that the Ukrainian Catholic Church united itself with Ukrainian nationalistic organizations in the diaspora, and unfortunately, many Uniate clergy actively participate in their activities. But the Ukrainian nation remembers that these same nationalistic organizations wrought terror on Soviet Ukraine liberated from Hitler and his minions, when the '*banderivtsi*' killed their Ukrainian brothers, priests among them." Ibid., 25.

94. Ibid.

95. Metropolitan Nikolai employed the same generalizing language used by other Soviet authorities of the time in speaking of *banderivtsi*. In *The Gates of Europe* (New York: Basic Books, 2015), 280–81, Serhii Plokhy argues that the use of this term is misleading, since not all of the fighters of the Ukrainian Insurgent Army shared Bandera's radical nationalist ideology, while Bandera himself had no control over the forces since he never returned to Ukraine after his imprisonment by the Germans in 1941. John Armstrong suggests that the Bandera groups were responsible for the murder and assassination of the autonomous bishop Emmanuel (Tarnavskii) of Volodymyr-Volynsk in 1943. See *Ukrainian Nationalism*, 3rd ed. (Englewood, CO: Ukrainian Academic Press, 1990), 158–59.

96. Ibid., 26.

97. I. Fedorovych, "Торжество істини і справедливости: До 35-ліття возз'єднання Греко Католицької Церкви Галичини з Руською Православною Церквою" [Triumph of truth and righteousness: Toward the thirty-fifth anniversary of the reunion of the Greek-Catholic Church of Galicia with the Russian Orthodox Church], PV 3 (1981): 27–29.

98. "The terrible time of the Great Patriotic War of the years 1941–1945 arrived. The trials endured by the entire nation revealed the true face of the leadership of the Uniate Greek-Catholic Church in Galicia. It tarnished itself in the eyes of the clerical ranks and the faithful people in its shameful service of the occupiers, betraying the interests of the people and fatherland, taking an active part in attracting young people to a brother-killing war. . . . The Uniate leadership set itself against its flock, becoming co-participants in bloody punishments and terrors. The clerical order and faithful of the Greek-Catholic Church, who suffered from the atrocities of the fascist occupiers . . . could no longer tolerate the disgusting collaboration of the leaders of the Uniate Church with the German invaders; the betrayal of the hierarchs, who blessed the cruelty of the Hitlerites and the band of OUNers." Ibid., 27.

99. Fedorovych's essay includes a long footnote defining the OUN (Organization of Ukrainian Nationalists) as a fascist organization of Western Ukraine that was opposed to the reunion of Western Ukraine with the Soviet Union. For Bociurkiw's explanation of the UGCC favoring the OUN, see *The Ukrainian Greek Catholic Church*, 62–65.

100. Senyk, "The Ukrainian Greek Catholic Church," 326.

101. Bociurkiw, *The Ukrainian Greek-Catholic Church,* 65.

102. Ibid., 65.0

103. Ibid., 29.

104. Ivan Korol, "До 35-Річчя возз'єднання Греко-Католицької Церкви з Руською Православною Церквою (1946–1981)" [Toward the thirty-fifth anniversary of the reunion of the

Greek-Catholic Church of Galicia with the Russian Orthodox Church (1946–1981)], PV 1 (January 1981): 29–31.

105. Pimen (Izvekov), "Послання Святішого Патріарха Пимена голові ради Міністрів ЦРЦР Олексію Миколайовичу Косигіну" [Epistle of His Holiness Patriarch Pimen to the head of the Council of Ministers of the USSR Alexei Kosygin], PV 7 (July 1980): 1–2.

106. Ibid., 1.

107. Ibid.

108. Ibid., 2. Also see Pimen (Iznetsov), "Заява Святішого Патріарха Московського і всієї Русі кореспондетові ТАРС а зв'язку з 35-річчям перемоги над фашистською Німеччиною" [Statement of His Holiness the Patriarch of Moscow and all Russia to the correspondent of TARS on the thirty-fifth anniversary of the victory over fascist Germany], PV 7 (July 1980): 2–3.

109. Ibid., 2.

110. "The churches of our continent, each of which identifies itself as Christian, should unite their efforts with the efforts of all other peacemakers, not to allow the birth of cold, psychological, and other forms of war, but to compel a return to a single, true path—the loosening of international tensions, and a return to the execution of the act of the Helsinki agreement." Ibid.

111. Pimen (Iznetsov), "Послание Святейшего Патриарха Московского и всея Руси Пимена и Священного Синода Русской Православной Церкви преосвященным архипастырям, священному клиру, честному иночеству и всем верным чадам Русской Православной Церкви в связи с 70-летием Великой Октябрьской социалистической революции" [Epistle of His Holiness Patriarch Pimen of Moscow and all Russia and the Holy Synod of the Russian Orthodox Church to the reverend archpastors, the holy clergy, the venerable monastics and all faithful children of the Russian Orthodox Church on the occasion of the seventieth anniversary of the Great October Socialist revolution], Журнал Московской Патриархии 11 (November 1987): 2 (hereafter cited as ZMP).

112. Ibid., 3.

113. Ibid., 3–4.

114. See the lengthy text—ibid., 6.

115. Ibid.

116. Ibid., 6.

117. Ibid., 6–7.

118. Pimen (Izvekov), "Предъюбилейное послание Святейшего Патриарха Московского и всея Руси Пимена и Священного Синода Русской Православной Церкви преосвященным архипастырям, пастырям, честному иночеству и всем верным чадам Русской Православной Церкви, во отечества нашем и за его пределами сущим, к 1000-летию крещение Руси" [Pre-jubilee epistle of His Holiness Patriarch Pimen of Moscow and all Russia and the Holy Synod of the Russian Orthodox Church to the reverend archpastors, the holy clergy, the venerable monastics, and all faithful children of the Russian Orthodox Church in our fatherland and scattered abroad, on the 1000-year anniversary of the baptism of Russia], ZMP 8 (August 1987): 2–6.

119. "The Russian Orthodox Church is always in contact with other religions in the margins of our country, and now we are cooperating with their representatives in working for the strengthening of peace and justice among all peoples." Ibid., 3.

120. "The forthcoming jubilee is a feast also for the children of our church who for various reasons are not to be found at this time within her saving boundaries, and those Old-Believing brothers and sisters who belong to the flocks of other churches who consider their mother to be our Holy Church. Along with them we greet the hierarchs, clergy, and laity of the Russian Orthodox Church outside of Russia, and also the hierarchs, clergy, and laity who are scattered abroad and call themselves the Ukrainian Autocephalous Orthodox Church." Ibid., 4.

121. Ibid.

122. Filaret (Denysenko), "Слово Митрополита Київського і Галицького Філарета перед водосвятним молебнем" [The word of Metropolitan Filaret of Kyiv and Galicia before the prayer service for the blessing of waters], PV 12 (December 1988): 11.

123. Ibid.

124. "The church created beautiful memorials, which enriched Russian culture, they are even now the national pride of our people. When the church uses the word "Russian," she does not have only people of Russian nationality in mind, but also Ukrainians, and Belarusians, because these three peoples came from one common root: Kyivan Rus'. . . . During the difficult years of the Tatar-Mongol yoke, the Church supported the spirit of national unity. She inspired the great prince Dmitry Donskoy and his army at the battle of Kulykovo. . . . She was with the people during the days of the Great Patriotic War. Through all ages, the Church served the moral position of our people." Ibid.

125. See Destivelle, *The Moscow Council*, 157–58.

126. See Shlikhta, "'Orthodox' and 'Soviet,'" 146.

Notes to Chapter 5

1. Frank Sysyn, "The Third Rebirth of the Ukrainian Autocephalous Orthodox Church and the Religious Situation in Ukraine, 1989–1991," in *Religion and Nation in Modern Ukraine*, ed. Serhii Plokhy and Frank E. Sysyn (Edmonton, AB: Canadian Institute of Ukrainian Studies, 2003), 97.

2. Ibid., 99.

3. Ibid.

4. "Patriarch Mstyslav Enthroned," *The Ukrainian Weekly* 47, Sunday, November 25, 1990, 1.

5. See Sysyn's remarks on this matter in "The Third Rebirth," 99.

6. See Natalia Kochan, "'Oh, East Is East and West Is West . . .': The Character of Orthodox-Greek Catholic Discourse in Ukraine and Its Regional Dimensions," in *Eastern Orthodox Encounters of Identity and Otherness: Values, Self-Reflection, Dialogue*, ed. Andrii Krawchuk and Thomas Bremer (New York: Palgrave Macmillan, 2014), 125–40, for a discussion of Western Ukraine as the epicenter for nationalist movements in the UGCC and the non-Muscovite Orthodox churches.

7. Iryna Prelovs'ka, *Джерела з історії Української Автокефальної Православної Церкви (1921–1930)–Української Православної Церкви (1930–1939)* [Sources from the History of the Ukrainian Autocephalous Orthodox Church (1921–1930)—Ukrainian Orthodox Church (1930–1939)] (Kyiv: Inst. Ukraïns'koi Archeohrafiï ta Dzhereloznavstva im. M. S. Hrushevs'koho NAN Ukraïny, 2013).

8. "Announcements from the Patriarchal Chancery," UOW, no. 1 (January–February 1991), 1.

9. "Metropolitan Ioan [Bodnarchuk] expressed his belief that previous Sobors of the UAOC had failed in the completion of a necessary hierarchical construction of the church, and that this Sobor should not make the same mistake. This was a reference to the establishment of a Ukrainian Orthodox Patriarchate, long recognized as a necessity for the church. . . . The historical fact that Ukraine was not an independent nation prohibited action regarding a Patriarchate until now. Realizing that much was changing in the life of the nation, the Sobor of the Ukrainian Orthodox Church proclaimed the establishment of a Patriarchate for the Ukrainian Orthodox Church, which is proper by virtue of its dignity and as a guarantee of its autocephaly and equality among other autocephalous Churches." "And the Gates of the Temple Shall Open: Commentary by a Delegate to the Recent Sobor of the Ukrainian Autocephalous Orthodox Church in Ukraine, Kiev, 5–6 June, 1990," UOW (July–August 1990), 20.

10. "Announcements from the Patriarchal Chancery," UOW, no. 1 (January–February 1991), 1.

11. From "Статут Української Автокефальної Православної Церкви" [Statute of the Ukrainian Autocephalous Orthodox Church], nos. 1.1, 1.2, and 1.6 in UAA, accession no. 2011-101-1975.

12. Ibid., no. 1.7.

13. The statute's language consistently refers to the cooperation of councils with the presiding member of the clergy at each level of church structure. The patriarchal council governs the Church with the patriarch, the eparchial council governs the eparchy with the bishop, and the parish council governs the parish with the pastor. Ibid., no. 1.7.

14. Sysyn, "The Third Rebirth," 101.

15. From the resolutions of the Holy Synod of the Russian Orthodox Church published in PV 1 (1990): 1–2.

16. "This religious organization was not recognized by the Ukrainian Orthodox bishops in occupied Ukraine and was condemned by the Hierarchical Council of the Russian Orthodox Church in March 1942. Bishop Policarp (Sikorsky), as the leader of the so-called Ukrainian Autocephalous Church, and all of her bishops were deposed from sacerdotal orders, and the priests ordained by them were recognized as illegal, and their sacramental acts were without grace. So "metropolitan" Mstyslav Skrypnyk was not in Eucharistic and canonical communion with the Orthodox Churches on account of his uncanonical heritage." Ibid., 1.

17. Ibid., 1.

18. Dimitry Pospielovsky, *The Orthodox Church in the History of Russia* (Crestwood, NY: St. Vladimir's Seminary Press, 1998), 369.

19. See Filaret (Denysenko), "Прес-конференція Блаженнішого Митрополита Київського і всієї України Філарета" [Press conference of His Beatitude Metropolitan Filaret of Kyiv and all Ukraine], published in PV 1 (1991): 1–2.

20. Ibid.

21. Ibid.

22. Ibid., 2.

23. Ibid., 3.

24. Ibid.

25. Ibid.

26. Ukrainian Orthodox Church, Moscow Patriarchate, "Звернення єпископату Української Православної Церкви до Святішого Патріарха Московського і всієї Русі Алексія II та Священного Синоду Руської Православної Церкви" [Appeal of the episcopate of the Ukrainian Orthodox Church to His Holiness Alexy II, patriarch of Moscow and all Russia and the Holy Synod of the Russian Orthodox Church], PV 10 (October 1990): 1.

27. Ibid., 2.

28. Sysyn, "The Third Rebirth," 102.

29. Ibid.

30. Ibid., 118.

31. "Акт об отлучении от церкви монаха Филарета (Денисенко)" [Act of anathematizing the Monk Filaret (Denysenko) from the Church]: ZMP 4 (1997), 19–20.

32. "5-річчя інтронізації Патріарха Димитрія" [The fifth anniversary of the enthronement of Patriarch Dmitry], *Visnyk*, January 15, 1999. Father Jarema's wife also received monastic tonsure, paving the way for his episcopal ordination.

33. Dmitry (Jarema), Ihor (Isichenko), and Evhen Sverstyuk, "Місія поєднання і примирення: Про підготовку об'єднавчого всеукраїнського православного собору" [A mission of unity and reconciliation: On the preparation of a unifying all-Ukrainian Orthodox council], *Наша віра*, nos. 4–5 (March 1994): 1, 3.

34. Ibid., 1.

35. Ibid. See also Taras Kuzio, "In Search of Unity and Autocephaly: Ukraine's Orthodox Churches," *Religion, State and Society* 25, no. 4 (1997): 398–401.

36. Dmitry (Jarema), Ihor (Isichenko), and Sverstyuk, "Місія поєднання і примирення," 3.

37. Ibid.

38. "At the time of my departure from the leadership of the Ukrainian Autocephalous Orthodox Church please remain on this path and do not conduct any councils independently, without the participation of the diaspora portions of our Church. I bless the commemoration of His Beatitude Metropolitan Constantine (after me), the primate of the UAOC in the diaspora and the UOC in the USA, the successor of His Holiness Patriarch Mstyslav . . . I request that the council of Ukrainian Orthodox bishops in the diaspora under the omophorion of his All-Holiness Ecumenical Patriarch Bartholomew to continue working toward the creation of one local Ukrainian Orthodox Church in canonical unity with the ecumenical patriarch." Letter of Patriarch Dmitry (Jarema) to the

Hierarchical Council and Patriarchal Council of the UAOC, December 1, 1999, in UAA, accession no. 2011-27-101-1976.

39. As reported by Archbishop Ihor (Isichenko) in *Офіційна хроніка* 44, no. 2 (2000): n.p.

40. As reported by Archbishop Ihor (Isichenko)in *Офіційна хроніка* 79, no. 4 (2002): n.p.

41. See Sysyn's remarks on the challenge of obtaining recognition within global Orthodoxy in "The Third Rebirth," 109–11.

42. Osyp Zinkewich and Oleksander Voronyn, eds., *Мартирологія Українських Церков*, vol. 1, *Українська Православна Церква* [Martyrology of the Ukrainian Churches, vol. 1: Ukrainian Orthodox Church] (Baltimore: Smoloskyp, 1987), 662–66.

43. Pospielovsky, *The Orthodox Church*, 369. Also see the statute of the UOC-MP and the statute of the Russian Orthodox Church on the UOC, Ukraïns'ka Pravoslavna Tserkva, http://orthodox.org.ua/page/statut-rpts-pro-upts (accessed February 12, 2018).

44. See Ukrainian Orthodox Church, Moscow Patriarchate, "Звернення єпископату," 1–2, for details on the request made by the metropolia along with the rationale for granting the request.

45. Hyacinthe Destivelle, *The Moscow Council (1917–1918): The Creation of the Conciliar Institutions of the Russian Orthodox Church*, ed. Michael Plekon and Vitaly Permiakov, trans. Jerry Ryan, foreword by Metropolitan Hilarion (Alfeyev) (Notre Dame, IN: University of Notre Dame Press, 2015), 117–19, 302–5.

46. Ibid., 193.

47. Ibid., 306.

48. Sysyn, "The Third Rebirth," 106–7.

49. Ibid., 91.

50. See Serhii Plokhy, "Ukrainian Orthodox Autocephaly and Metropolitan Filaret," in *Religion and Nation in Modern Ukraine*, ed. Frank E. Sysyn and Serhii Plokhy (Edmonton, AB: Canadian Institute of Ukrainian Studies, 2003), 128.

51. "Звернення єпископату Української Православної Церкви до Святішого Патріарха Московського і всієї Русі Алексія II та Священного Синоду Руської Православної Церкви" [Appeal of the episcopate of the Ukrainian Orthodox Church to His Holiness Alexy II, patriarch of Moscow and all Russia and the Holy Synod of the Russian Orthodox Church], PV 4 (April 1992): 8–9.

52. Ibid., 8.

53. Ibid., 9.

54. Ibid., 9.

55. Ibid., 9.

56. Note the disparity between this report and the one offered by Pospielovsky, who said that only two of the many eparchial bishops supported autocephaly (Pospielovsky, *The Orthodox Church*, 370).

57. Plokhy, "Ukrainian Orthodox Autocephaly," 129. Also see Pospielovsky, *The Orthodox Church*, 369–70.

58. Plokhy, "Ukrainian Orthodox Autocephaly," 129.

59. Ibid., 130–31.

60. Ibid., 131.

61. Ibid.

62. Ibid.

63. Ibid., 131.

64. Metropolitan Volodymyr (Sabodan), *Доповіді, звернення, промови* [Lectures, correspondence, and speeches] (Kyiv: Fond pam'iati Blazhennishoho Mytropolyta Volodymyra, 2014), 98–102.

65. Ibid., 98.

66. Ibid.

67. Ibid., 98–99.

68. Ibid., 99.

69. Ibid., 102.

70. Plokhy, "Ukrainian Orthodox Autocephaly," 134.

71. On this matter, see Nikolai Mitrokhin, "Aspects of the Religious Situation in Ukraine," *Religion, State and Society* 29, no. 3 (2001): 187.

72. Serhii Plokhy, "Church, State, and Nation in Ukraine," in *Religion and Nation in Modern Ukraine*, ed. Frank E. Sysyn and Serhii Plokhy (Edmonton, AB: Canadian Institute of Ukrainian Studies), 193. Plokhy notes that Moscow patriarch Alexy had supported Ukrainian autocephaly at the 1992 hierarchical synod in Moscow.

73. In his testament, Metropolitan Volodymyr reflected on autocephaly and explained the approach he adopted during his tenure as primate as an attempt to separate the Church from political pressure to obtain official ecclesial independence. In his comments, Metropolitan Volodymyr referred to the perils of both pro-Russian "political Orthodoxy" and Ukrainian nationalism, and stated that the Church must seek and articulate a theological basis for autocephaly (see Metropolitan Volodymyr [Sabodan], *Доповіді, звернення, промови*, 8–12).

74. Pospielovsky, *The Orthodox Church*, 371.

75. Plokhy, "Ukrainian Orthodox Autocephaly," 135.

76. "1. [We resolve to] Unite the Ukrainian Orthodox Church and Ukrainian Autocephalous Orthodox Church into one Ukrainian Orthodox Church—Kyivan Patriarchate. Until the reception of a new statute, the statute of the UAOC will govern the UOC-KP. The signet and stamp of the UOC and UAOC will be used." Published in *Суспільство*, no. 120 (370), June 27, 1992, 6.

77. Ibid., resolutions 5 and 6.

78. *Наша віра* 14 (1992), 2.

79. *Наша віра* 14 (1992), 2.

80. Letter no. 265 from the Ivano-Frankivsk Eparchial Administration to Patriarch Mstyslav and the Holy Synod of the UOC-KP, dated November 17, 1992, and signed by Metropolitan Andrii (Abramchuk) and several priests. In the letter, Metropolitan Andrii appears to be reassuring Mstyslav that the reordinations were in proper order because they occurred before the Russian Church had stripped Metropolitan Filaret of holy orders.

81. *Наша віра* 16 (1992), 1.

82. Dmytro Stepovyk, *Патріарх Мстислав: Життя і архіпастирська діяльність* [Patriarch Mstyslav: Life and Archpastoral Activity] (Kyiv: Mystetstvo, 2007), 320.

83. Kuzio, "In Search of Unity," 398–400.

84. Romaniuk's ascencion through the ranks of the episcopacy to the office of patriarch is notable, as he was another popular member of the lower clergy who eventually assumed the highest office in his church.

85. See a brief synopsis of the history of the cathedral of the Holy Resurrection at Kafedral'nyi sobor na chest' Voskresinnia Khristovoho UPTs, http://sobor.church.ua/istoriya/ (accessed October 10, 2016).

86. See St. Michael monastery website, archangel.kiev.ua (accessed October 10, 2016).

87. Plokhy, 134.

88. See Volodymyr Iatsul'chak, "Про повторні звершення таїнств в Московському патріархаті" [On the repetition of the celebration of sacraments in the Moscow Patriarchate], Ukrainian Orthodox Church, Kyivan Patriarchate, http://archive.cerkva.info/uk/publications/articles/1757-tainstva.html (accessed October 15, 2012). A noteworthy development is the Ukrainian Greek-Catholic Church's (UGCC) official recognition of the validity of the sacraments celebrated in the Kyivan Patriarchate as evidenced by a recent letter from Archbishop Sviatoslav (Shevchuk) (leader of the UGCC) to Patriarch Filaret, November 1, 2012, "Викладено позицію УГКЦ щодо дійсності Таїнства Хрещення в УПЦ КП" [Announcement on the position of the UGCC on the validity of the sacrament of baptism in the UOC-KP], Ukrainian Orthodox Church, Kyivan Patriarchate, https://www.cerkva.info/publications/vykladeno-pozytsiiu-uhkts-shchodo-diisnosti-tainstva-khreshchennia-v-upts-kp (accessed November 5, 2012).

89. See, for example, Filaret (Denysenko), "Patriarch Filaret: Failure to Recognize Autocephaly Not a Big Misfortune," RISU: Religious Information Service of Ukraine, June 13, 2012, http://risu.org.ua/en/index/all_news/confessional/interchurch_relations/48436/ (accessed September 8, 2016).

90. The internal position of the UOC-MP has shifted: see the article "Primate of the UOC: It Is Not Necessary to Rebaptize Schismatics," Kievskaia Rus', September 29, 2010, http://www.kiev-ortho-dox.org/site/churchlife/2331/ (accessed October 10, 2016).

91. See the declarations of the hierarchical synod of the Russian Orthodox Church outside of Russia from Spring 1944, "О так называемой Украинской Автокефальной Церкви" [On the so-called Ukrainian Autocephalous Church], in *Законодательство Русской Православной Церкви заграницей (1921–2007)* [Legislation of the Russian Orthodox Church outside of Russia, 1921–2007], ed. D. P. Anashkin (Moscow: Izdatel'stvo PSTGU, 2013), 127–28.

92. See the long list of bishops who were ordained by Filaret, along with concelebrants: "Щодо ролі патріарха Філарета в архієрейських хіротоніях" [On the role oof Patriarch Filaret in the ordination of bishops] Religiia v Ukraïni, December 8, 2009, http://www.religion.in.ua/main/ofici-yno/2742-shhodo-roli-patriarxa-filareta-v-arxiyerejskix.html (accessed October 10, 2016).

93. See the brief statement published by Filaret (Denysenko), "Незалежній Україні—Незалежну Церкву" [An independent church for an independent Ukraine], Radio Svoboda, August 16, 2011, http://www.radiosvoboda.org/content/article/24298217.html (accessed October 10, 2016).

94. See the KP's official explanation of the violation of this canon in part 7 of its Canonical Status, https://www.cerkva.info/church/vii-zakonnyi-pomisnyi-sobor-upts-1-3-lystopada-1991-r-ta-rozkolnytskyi-tak-zvanyi-kharkivskyi-sobor-27-travnia-1992-r-zakinchennia (accessed February 12, 2018).

95. "On July 9, 1990, Metropolitan Filaret was elected to be the primate of the UOC by the Council of Bishops of the UOC and confirmed in a *tomos* of the patriarch of Moscow. The National Council of the UOC on November 1–3, 1991, confirmed his election, and also rejected all accusations against the primate of the UOC, which at that time were appearing in the mass media." "Патріарх Філарет та незаконне 'позбавлення' його сану" [The Hierarchy of the Kyiv Patriarchate: Patriarch Filaret and His Unlawful 'Defrocking']," https://www.cerkva.info/church/ikh-iierarkhiia-kyivskoho-patriarkhatu-patriarkh-filaret-ta-nezakonne-pozbavlennia-ioho-sanu-zavershennia (accessed September 8, 2016).

96. See ibid for details.

97. Ukrainian Orthodox Church, Kyivan Patriarchate, "Ювілей: Урочиста академія у національному палаці мистецтв Україна" [Jubilee: Solemn academy in the national palace of culture 'Ukraina'], http://cerkva.kiev.ua/news/278.html (accessed February 13, 2018).

98. Ukrainian Orthodox Church, Kyivan Patriarchate, "Вітальна адреса Священного Синоду та Архієрейського Собору Української Православної Церкви Київського Патріархату Святійшому Патріарху Київському і всієї Руси-України ФІЛАРЕТУ з нагоди ювілею 50-ліття служіння на Київській кафедрі" [Address of greetings of the Holy Synod and Bishops' Council of the UOC-KP to His Holiness Patriarch Filaret of Kyiv and all Ukraine on the occasion of the fifty-year jubilee of service on the Kyivan throne], http://vidomosti.kiev.ua/novyny/23-ofitsiini-zakhody/1356-vid-imeni-sviash-chennoho-synodu-ta-arkhiiereiskoho-soboru-mytropolyt-epifanii-vyholosyv-sviatkovu-adresu-pa-triarkhu-filaretu.html (accessed February 13, 2018).

99. Ukrainian Orthodox Church, Kyivan Patriarchate. "Постанови Архієрейського Собору (2016)" [Resolutions of the Bishops' Council], https://www.cerkva.info/church/postanovy-arkhiye-reyskoho-soboru-2016 (accessed February 13, 2018).

100. "Заява Архієрейського Собору" [Statement of the Bishop's Council], https://www.cerkva.info/church/zayava-arkhiyereyskoho-soboru (accessed February 13, 2018).

101. "In our country, one truly Ukrainian Orthodox Church exists—it is the Kyivan Patriarchate, which is the canonical and historical successor of the ancient Orthodox Kyivan Metropolia of the Constantinopolitan Patriarchate, which existed until the year 1686. Also, the Kyivan Patriarchate is the true heir of the Ukrainian Autocephalous Orthodox Church, which existed in Ukraine in diverse forms from 1919–1992, and also [the true heir of] the Ukrainian Orthodox Church, which was subject to the Moscow Patriarchate on account of external necessities, but which confirmed its decision for full autocephaly at its council on November 1–3, 1991. The religious organization that calls itself the "Ukrainian Orthodox Church" is an uncanonical work of the Moscow Patriarchate in Ukraine, the

fruit of the self-styled Kharkiv pseudo-council of 1992 and the 'special services' that organized and conducted it . . . Regarding the status of a patriarchate for the Ukrainian Church, we believe that this status is absolutely fair, historically grounded, and pastorally correct for our local church. . . . However, all things considered, our church is prepared, if necessary, to delay our request for recognition of the dignity of our patriarchate." Ibid.

102. Ibid.

103. Plokhy, "Church, State and Nation in Ukraine," 178.

104. Ibid., 179.

105. Ibid.

106. Ibid.

107. Ibid., 179–80.

108. "The clash on St. Sophia Square ended in tragedy and a resounding scandal that undermined the prestige of the government and of the presidential administration. For the first time in Ukraine, which had attained independence without violence and was justly proud of its tolerant practices, blood had been shed and brute force applied. Metropolitan Filaret and the UOC-KP, on the other hand, could congratulate themselves on a triumph. In a single day, Filaret had been transformed from a figure suspected of arranging the patriarch's murder into a symbol of the national-democratic camp, into the sole individual who could unite the assorted national-democratic forces, which were at odds with one another." Ibid., 180.

109. Ibid.

110. Ibid., 192.

111. For more analysis of the Church's relationship with the state, see Myroslaw Tataryn, "Russia and Ukraine: Two Models of Religious Liberty and Two Models for Orthodoxy," *Religion, State and Society* 29, no. 3 (2001): 163–65.

112. Natalia Kochan asserts that the UOC-KP bases its mission on the fused aspirations of state and ecclesial independence in "'Oh, East Is East,'" 133.

113. See the recent poll taken on Ukraine's trust in world religious leaders, which placed Patriarch Filaret in the lead among them all: "Українці найбільше довіряють патріарху Філарету та Папі Римському" [Ukrainians trust Patriarch Filaret and the Pope of Rome the most] Gazeta.ua, July 3, 2015, http://gazeta.ua/articles/comments-newspaper/_ukrayinci-najbilshe-doviryayut-patriar-hu-filaretu-ta-papi-rimskomu/634968 (accessed October 10, 2016).

114. Adrian Karatnycky, "Religion and the Orange Revolution," RISU: Religious Information Service of Ukraine, December 20, 2004, http://risu.org.ua/en/index/exclusive/kaleidoscope/4152/ (accessed October 10, 2016).

115. See Antoine Arjakovsky, *Conversations with Lubomyr Cardinal Husar: Towards a Post-confessional Christianity* (Lviv: Ukrainian Catholic University Press, 2007), 33–42.

116. Archbishop Ievstratii (Zoria), "Помаранчева революція для церкви стала моментом істини" [The Orange Revolution became a moment of truth for the Church], RISU: Religious Information Service of Ukraine, November 22, 2011, http://risu.org.ua/ua/index/all_news/state/national_religious_question/45578/ (accessed October 10, 2016).

117. Oleh Turii, "Церква і вибори: Уроки 2004 року" [The Church and elections: Lessons from 2004], RISU: Religious Information Service of Ukraine, January 14, 2010, http://risu.org.ua/ua/index/expert_thought/analytic/33861/ (accessed October 17, 2016). See also Nikolai Mitrokhin, "Orthodoxy in Ukrainian Political Life: 2004–2009," *Religion, State & Society* 38, no. 3 (September 2010): 229–51.

118. See Arjakovsky, *Conversations*, 34–35.

119. See Irena Borowik, "Orthodoxy Confronting the Collapse of Communism in Post-Soviet Countries," *Social Compass* 53, no. 2 (2006): 273–74.

120. See Nicholas Denysenko, "Chaos in Ukraine: The Churches and the Search for Leadership," *International Journal for the Study of the Christian Church* 14, no. 3 (2014): 244–47, for a complete analysis of this event.

121. See Cyril Hovorun, "Civil Religion in the Orthodox Milieu," in *Political Theologies in Orthodox Christianity: Common Challenges and Divergent Positions*, ed. Kristina Stoeckl, Ingeborg

Gabriel, and Aristotle Papanikolaou (New York: Bloomsbury, 2017), 257–58. I am grateful to Dr. Hovorun for providing his chapter to me prior to publication.

122. Ibid., 258.

123. See Katja Richters, *The Post-Soviet Russian Orthodox Church: Politics, Culture and Greater Russia* (New York; Routledge, 2013), 36–38; Zoe Knox, "Russian Orthodoxy, Russian Nationalism, and Patriarch Aleksii II," *Nationalities Papers* 33, no. 4 (2005): 534–36, 539–41; Mara Kozelsky, "Religion and the Crisis in Ukraine," *International Journal for the Study of the Christian Church* 14, no. 3 (2014): 224–26; see also Julia Sudo, "Russian Nationalist Orthodox Theology: A New Trend in the Political Life of Russia," *Political Theology* 6, no. 1 (2005): 67–86, for extreme examples of the fusion of nationalism with Orthodox theology. Another important source for this information came from a lecture delivered by Vera Shevzov, "The Concept of 'Russian World': Its Evolution in the Post-Soviet Context," paper presented at the conference "Political Orthodoxy and Totalitarianism in a Post-Communist Era," May 30, 2015, Volos Academy for Theological Studies, Helsinki, Finland.

124. See Aleksandr Verkhovsky, "The Role of the Russian Orthodox Church in Nationalist, Xenophobic and Antiwestern Tendencies in Russia Today: Not Nationalism, but Fundamentalism," *Religion, State and Society* 30, no. 4 (2002): 341–43.

125. See Richters, *The Post-Soviet Russian Orthodox Church*, 118–24; Kozelsky, "Religion and the Crisis in Ukraine," 226–28, and Nicholas Denysenko, "Fractured Orthodoxy in Ukraine and Politics: The Impact of Patriarch Kyrill's 'Russian World,'" *Logos: A Journal of Eastern Christian Studies* 54, nos. 1–2 (2013): 33–68.

126. See Denysenko, "Chaos in Ukraine," 247–50.

127. Viktor Yelensky, "State Program of Celebrations of 1025th Anniversary Is a Humiliation for Millions of Ukrainian Christians and It Further Divides the Country,'" RISU: Religious Information Service of Ukraine, July 26, 2013, http://risu.org.ua/en/index/expert_thought/interview/53128 (March 10, 2014).

128. Ukrainian Orthodox Church, Kyivan Patriarchate. "Київський Патріархат не надавав благословення на твір Акафіст Небесній Сотній" [The Kyivan Patriarchate did not grant a blessing for the work "Akathist to the Heavenly Hundred"], http://www.cerkva.info/uk/news/kyiv/6049.html (accessed September 8, 2016).

129. See Cyril Hovorun, "Christians in Ukraine: Ecumenism in the Trenches," *The Catholic World Report*, March 4, 2014, http://www.catholicworldreport.com/Item/2970/christians_in_ukraine_ecumenism_in_the_trenches.aspx#.UznOwPldWSo (accessed March 31, 2014).

130. My thanks to Nataliya Bezborodova for her insights on these services.

131. Metropolitan Hilarion (Alfeyev), "Actions of the Uniates Have Caused Great Damage Not Only to the Ukraine and Her Citizens, but Also to the Orthodox-Catholic Dialogue," The Russian Orthodox Church: Department for External Church Relations, June 3, 2014, https://mospat.ru/en/2014/06/03/news103524/ (accessed October 10, 2016).

132. Oleh Turii has addressed the issue of conflicts induced by opposing Church identities in the post-Soviet milieu in "Проблема ідентичності в стосунках між церквами-сестрами в сучасній Україні" [The problem of identity in relations between sister churches in contemporary Ukraine] in *"Kościoły siostrzane" w dialogu*, ed. Z. Glaeser (Opole, 2002), 284–98, and "Історичні обставини й тенденції розвитку релігійного життя та міжконфесійних взаємин у сучасній Україні," in *Віра після атеїзму: Релігійне життя в Україні в період демократичних перетворень і державної незалежности*, ed. Miklosh Tomka and Oleh Turii (Lviv: Vid-vo UKU, 2004), 5–45.

133. "Over thirty churches of the Ukrainian Orthodox Church have now been taken over and at least ten are under the threat of attack by schismatics and nationalists, who are trying to depict what is happening as voluntary transition of believers to the so-called Kyiv patriarchate. In actual fact, it was a real bandit, raiding takeover: they hold a meeting of people who are unrelated to the community, then they fake the charter documents with the authorities' assistance, take over the church using nationalist militants, and they throw the church community and the priest out in the street . . . schismatics and their semi-bandit military groups ignore court rulings." "Orthodox Churches under Threat

in Ukraine," RISU: Religious Information Service of Ukraine, January 25, 2016, http://risu.org.ua/en/index/all_news/orthodox/orthodox_world/62270/ (accessed April 19, 2016).

134. See Sophia Senyk, "The Ukrainian Greek Catholic Church Today: Universal Values versus Nationalist Doctrines," *Religion, State and Society* 30, no. 4 (2002): 321–23; 327–28. For a rebuttal of her assertions on nationalism, see Serge Keleher, "Response to Sophia Senyk, 'The Ukrainian Greek Catholic Church Today: Universal Values versus Nationalist Doctrines,'" *Religion, State and Society* 31, no. 3 (2003): 289–306.

135. Arjakovsky, *Conversations*, 34–35. In response to a question about the UGCC's endorsement of Yushchenko in 2004, Husar stated that "we ask clergy not to conduct any propaganda" (34).

136. "With great pain I worry about the situation of Ukraine and ask the Ukrainian people from the holy mountain to support the canonical church, the canonical primate, and canonical synod. We want Ukrainians to support the canonical church. It is necessary for salvation to submit to the canonical church." "Греція: Відомий афонський старець звернувся до Українського народу" [Greece: A renowned Athonite elder appealed to the Ukrainian people], Українська Православна Церква, March 15, 2015, http://news.church.ua/2015/03/15/%EF%BB%BFgreciya-vidomij-afonskij-starec-zvernu-vsya-do-ukrajinskogo-narodu-video/. This news story was accompanied by a video: Fr. Ephraim made this brief statement while standing with Metropolitan Onufry.

137. "УПЦ МП перепросила УПЦ КП за розгром 'козаками' храму в Перевальному" [The UOC MP apologized to the KP on account of the defeat of the "Cossacks" temple in Pereval], LV.ua, June 2, 2014, http://ukr.lb.ua/news/2014/06/02/268563_upts_mp_izvinilas_pered_upts_kp.html (accessed September 9, 2016).

138. "На Рівненщині історична подія: Різні конфесії підписали меморандум про Українську помісну церкву" [A historical event in the Rivne region: Different confessions signed a memorandum on a local Ukrainian Church], Rivne vechirne, November 13, 2014, http://rivnepost.rv.ua/lenta_msgshow.php?id=56002 (accessed September 9, 2016).

139. See "ROC Explained Signing of Rivne Memorandum by Very Strong Political Pressure," RISU: Religious Information Service of Ukraine, November 19, 2014, http://risu.org.ua/en/index/all_news/orthodox/moscow_patriarchy/58257 (accessed September 9, 2016).

140. "Primate of Russian Orthodox Church Arrives in Geneva to Take Part in the Synaxis of Primates of Local Orthodox Churches," The Russian Orthodox Church: Department for External Church Relations, January 22, 2016, https://mospat.ru/en/2016/01/22/news127064/ (accessed September 9, 2016).

141. "His Holiness Patriarch Kirill: Unilateral Recognition of Schism in Ukraine will have Catastrophic Consequences for the Unity of the Orthodox Church," The Russian Orthodox Church: Department for External Church Relations, February 2, 2016, https://mospat.ru/en/2016/02/02/news127695/ (accessed September 9, 2016).

142. "Предстоятель УПЦ разрешил не поминать Патриарха Кирилла" [The primate of the UOC permitted the non-commemoration of Patriarch Kirill], Religiia v Ukraïni, December 29, 2015, http://www.religion.in.ua/news/ukrainian_news/31434-predstoyatel-upc-razreshil-ne-pominat-pa-triarxa-kirilla.html (accessed September 9, 2016).

143. Ukrainian Orthodox Church, Moscow Patriarchate, "Предстоятель УПЦ: Ми молимося за Петра Олексійовича Порошенка як президента нашої держави та брата по вірі" [Primate of the UOC: We pray for Petro Oleksiiovich Poroshenko as the president of our country and brother in the faith], January 29, 2016, http://news.church.ua/2016/01/29/predstoyatel-upc-mi-molimo-sya-za-petra-oleksijovicha-poroshenka-yak-za-prezidenta-nashoji-derzhavi-ta-brata-po-viri-video/ (accessed September 9, 2016).

144. "Bishops of the UOC MP remained seated when President Poroshenko was reading names of heroes of Ukraine," RISU: Religious Information Service of Ukraine, May 8, 2015, http://risu.org.ua/en/index/all_news/community/religion_and_policy/59943 (accessed September 9, 2016). In the Ukrainian version of this brief news article, Bishop Klyment, media officer of the UOC MP, explained that Metropolitan Onufry consistently honors the soldiers who sacrificed their lives for their

country, but remained seated to demonstrate his opposition to the war (http://risu.org.ua/ua/index/
all_news/community/religion_and_policy/59943/).

145. "Глава УПЦ (МП): Мова молитви має бути тільки церковнослов'янська, бо
Українську не всі захочуть служити" [Head of the UOC MP: The language of prayer can only be in
Church Slavonic, because not everyone wishes to serve in Ukrainian], RISU: Religious Information
Service of Ukraine, February 1, 2016, http://risu.org.ua/ua/index/all_news/orthodox/uoc/62354/
(accessed September 9, 2016). See also Borowik, "Orthodoxy," 273–74.

146. See Metropolitan Oleksandr's three-part series, "Ukrainian Orthodoxy: Path to Recovery
of Church Unity, Part II," RISU: Religious Information Service of Ukraine, July 5, 2016, http://risu.org.
ua/en/index/studios/studies_of_religions/63886/ (accessed October 7, 2016).

147. "I affirm that the greatest blame for all this lies on the abovementioned governor. It is in
his will and power to immediately stop the bloodshed and death, but for the sake of his pride he continues to multiply evil. He calls himself a brother to the Ukrainian people, but in fact according to his
deeds, he has really become the new Cain, shedding brotherly blood and entangling the whole world
with lies. His lie is misleading some people, and they think that in fact this ruler protects traditional
spiritual and moral values from the ravages of globalization. But the fruit of his actions, which the
Gospel calls us to evaluate, suggest otherwise." Патріарх Філарет закликав вірних Україн молитися
за справедливий суд над Путіним—"новим Каїном" [Patriarch Filaret called upon the faithful of
Ukraine to pray for a righteous trial of Putin, the "new Cain," RISU: Religious Information Service
of Ukraine, September 5, 2014, http://risu.org.ua/ua/index/all_news/state/national_religious_ques-
tion/57559/ (accessed February 5, 2015).

148. "The sin of corruption is particularly horrible in the current period, when hundreds of
our fellow citizens have sacrificed and are sacrificing their lives for the freedom and independence
of Ukraine, when tens of thousands are living in exile, hundreds of thousands are dwelling in cities
where acts of war are occurring, . . . The one who even in these conditions permits himself to take part
in corruption becomes like Judas Iscariot, because Judas sold the Savior for money, and these betray
their native land and fellow citizens for money and material goods. Their payment will be just as the
one Judas [received]: shame and eternal judgment." in "Звернення Священного Синоду" [Appeal
of the Holy Synod], Ukrainian Orthodox Church, Kyivan Patriarchate, http://www.cerkva.info/uk/
synod/5688-zvernennia-proty-korupcii.html (accessed September 9, 2016). The letter was addressed
the Ukrainian people, signed by Patriarch Filaret on behalf of the UOC KP's Holy Synod, and dated
October 21, 2014.

149. Ibid.

150. Ivan Kapsamun, "Ukraine's Parliament Appeals to Bartholomew: A Historic Step,"
Den'Kyiv.ua, June 22, 2016, http://day.kyiv.ua/en/article/day-after-day/ukraines-parliament-ap-
peals-bartholomew-historic-step (accessed September 9, 2016). The Rada linked the Ukrainian-
language text of the appeal here: http://w1.c1.rada.gov.ua/pls/zweb2/webproc4_1?pf3511=59348.

151. "President: Status of Ukrainian as Only State Language to Be Filled with Real Content,"
President of Ukraine: Petro Poroshenko, September 6, 2016, http://www.president.gov.ua/en/news/
status-ukrayinskoyi-movi-yak-yedinoyi-derzhavnoyi-bude-napov-38093 (accessed September 9,
2016).

152. On this matter, see the excellent analysis by Cyril Hovorun, in Tetyana Kalenychenko,
"Enmity and Hostility Remain Zones of Comfort for Ukrainian Churches," interview with Cyril
Hovorun, RISU: Religious Information Service of Ukraine, January 21, 2016, http://risu.org.ua/en/
index/expert_thought/interview/62242/ (accessed September 9, 2016).

153. For more on this question and its history, see Nicholas Denysenko, "The Appeal of the
Ukrainian Parliament and the Ecumenical Patriarchate," Public Orthodoxy, https://publicorthodoxy.
org/2016/06/20/the-appeal-of-the-ukrainian-parliament-and-the-ecumenical-patriarchate/ (accessed
September 9, 2016).

154. "Акт об'єднання Церков Української Православної Церкви Київського Патріархату
та Української Автокефальної Церкви" [Act of the Union of the Ukrainian Orthodox Church

Kyivan Patriarchate and Ukrainian Autocephalous Orthodox Church], n.d. The supporting documents indicate that a tentative agreement was reached on or around October 19, 1995 (from the personal archive of Mr. Yaroslaw Lozowchuk, used with permission).

155. Memorandum to the Hierarchical Synod of the UOC-KP from Metropolitan Andrii of Halychyna, dated October 19, 1995, bearing the sign and stamp (Lozowchuk archive).

156. According to his official biography, Metropolitan Andrii became the chair of the commission for dialogue into one Ukrainian Orthodox Church. See "Митрополит Галицький, Керуючий Івано-Франківською Єпархією Андрій" [Metropolitan of Galicia and Administrator of the Ivano-Krankivs'k Eparchy Andrii] Ukraïns'ka Avtokefal'na Pravoslavna Tserkva, January 31, 2016, http://church.net.ua/detalno/uapc/mitropolit-galickii-kerujuchii-ivano-frankivskoju-jeparkhijeju-andrii-abramchuk.html (accessed February 12, 2018).

157. Letter of Deans of Ivano-Frankivsk Eparchy of the KP to Metropolitan Filaret, dated August 10, 1995, and containing all signatures (Lozowchuk archive).

158. Ibid.

159. "Журнал засідання No. 2 Архієрейського Собору УАПЦ" [Journal of the second meeting of the Hierarchical Council of the UAOC], August 15, 1996 (Lozowchuk archive).

160. Handwritten report attributed to Metropolitan Andrii, dated June 13, 2001. Contains signatures that bleed off the page (Lozowchuk archive).

161. The joint committee met on June 19, 2001, in Ternopil', and officially informed Patriarch Bartholomew that the two churches were going to seek a way to concelebrate liturgically and outline a path for the creation of a unified Orthodox Church in Ukraine. The report of the joint committee dated June 19, 2001, addressed to Patriarch Bartholomew, was signed by six bishops representing the UAOC and UOC-KP (Lozowchuk archive).

162. Memorandum of Metropolitan Andrii to Metropolitan Mefodii of the UAOC, No. 113, August 17, 2005 (Lozowchuk archive).

163. Letter of the Ivano-Frankivsk Eparchial Council to Metropolitan Mefodii, August 17, 2005 (Lozowchuk archive).

164. Ibid.

165. Letter of the Bishop's Synod of the UAOC to Ecumenical Patriarch Bartholomew, June 26, 2014 (Lozowchuk archive).

166. See the complete report along with digital images of the original signed agreement at Ukrainian Orthodox Church of the USA, "Decision Reached by Joint Meeting of the Committees," June 8, 2015, http://uocofusa.org/news_150609_1.html (accessed September 15, 2016).

167. Ibid.

168. Ibid.

169. "УАПЦ не йде на компроміс з УПЦ КП щодо умов об'єднання" [The UAOC will not compromise with the UOC KP on the conditions of union], RISU: Religious Information Service of Ukraine, July 10, 2015, http://risu.org.ua/ua/index/all_news/confessional/orthodox_relations/60495/ (accessed September 15, 2016).

170. Ukrainian Orthodox Church, Kyivan Patriarchate, "Архієреї УАПЦ відкинули попередні домовленості та компромісні пропозиції і зірвали об'єднання з Київським Патріархатом" [The hierarchs of the UAOC dismissed the previous agreements and compromised propositions and thwarted union with the Kyivan patriarchate], http://www.cerkva.info/uk/publications/articles/7100-zajava.html (accessed September 15, 2016).

171. Ukrainian Orthodox Church, Kyivan Patriarchate, "Журнали засідання Священного Синоду 27 липня 2015 р." [Journals of the meeting of the Holy Synod of July 27, 2015], http://www.cerkva.info/uk/synod/7177-synod-27-07-15.html (accessed September 15, 2016).

172. Ibid.

173. Ibid.

174. Metropolitan Volodymyr (Sabodan), Доповіді, звернення, промови, 118. Metropolitan Volodymyr attributed the pause in dialogue between the churches to problems within the UAOC (ibid., 38).

175. Ibid., 38–39.

176. Ibid.

177. Ibid., 39.

178. "Коментар до рішення Синоду УПЦ про діалог з церквами" [Commentary on the decision of the Synod of the UOC on dialogue with the churches], UNIAN Informatsiine agenstvo, September 11, 2009, http://religions.unian.ua/holidays/264773-komentar-do-rishennya-sinodu-upts-pro-dialog-z-tserkvami.html (accessed September 15, 2016).

179. Metropolitan Volodymyr (Sabodan), *Доповіді, звернення, промови*, 118. Metropolitan Volodymyr called for immediate dialogue with the UOC-KP in his last will and testament, as he anticipated the possibility that the UOC-KP might become a parallel canonical structure in Ukraine (ibid., 6–7).

180. Ukrainian Orthodox Church, Kyivan Patriarchate, "Відбулося робоче засідання Комісії УПЦ для діалогу з УПЦ КП і УАПЦ" [A working meeting of the UOC's commission for dialogue with the UOC KP and UAOC took place], March 26, 2014, http://news.church.ua/2014/03/26/vidbulosya-roboche-zasidannya-komisiji-upc-dlya-dialogu-z-upc-kp-i-uapc/ (accessed September 15, 2016).

181. See "Парад переходів": УПЦ КП і УПЦ (МП) по-різному трактують зміну юрисдикції парафій" [A parade of transfers: UOC KP and UOC MP interpret the change of jurisdiction of parishes differently], Religiia v Ukraïni, http://www.religion.in.ua/news/ukrainian_news/27125-parad-perexodiv-upc-kp-i-upc-mp-po-riznomu-traktuyut-zminu-yurisdikciyi-parafij.html (accessed September 16, 2016).

182. For the future prospects of dialogue among the Orthodox churches in Ukraine, see Lana Samokhvalova, "Московський Патріархат добровільно Україну не 'відпустить'" [The Moscow Patriarchate will not voluntarily "release" Ukraine], interview with Oleksandr Sagan, Ukrinform, December 12, 2015, http://www.ukrinform.ua/rubric-society/1928469-oleksandr-sagan-profesor-religieznavets.html (accessed October 17, 2016).

183. Andriy Chirovsky and Roma Hayda, "Kyivan Church Study Group: An Ecumenical Dialogue Team for Our Times," *The Ukrainian Weekly*, September 12, 2004, http://www.ukrweekly.com/old/archive/2004/370422.shtml (accessed August 4, 2017).

184. For an analysis of Husar's appeal, see Kochan, "'Oh, East Is East,'" 131.

185. For a list of representatives, see Instytut Ekumenichnykh Studii, http://www.ecumenicalstudies.org.ua/ukhat/chleny-ukhat (accessed August 4, 2017). Note that Roman Catholics also participate in the UCAS's activities.

186. For an overview of the purpose of the UCCRO and its agenda of contributing a religious voice to social issues, see Andrii Krawchuk, "Constructing Interreligious Consensus in the Post-Soviet Space: The Ukrainian Council of Churches and Religious Organizations," in *Eastern Orthodox Encounters of Identity and Otherness: Values, Self-Reflection, Dialogue*, ed. Andrii Krawchuk and Thomas Bremer (New York: Palgrave Macmillan, 2014), 273–302.

187. Archbishop Ihor (Isichenko), "Непрочитане послання УАПЦ" [The unread epistle of the UAOC], *Успенська вежа* (December 2014), 3.

188. The surprising proposal of Archbishop Ihor to enter into Eucharistic union with the UGCC appears to symbolize an attempt to create an alliance with the Church in Ukraine in the process of creating an authentic post-Soviet identity that prioritizes education. The twenty-sixth eparchial assembly of Kharkiv-Poltava under Archbishop Ihor's leadership voted in favor of accepting the process of establishing union with the UGCC, for the purpose of one Kyivan Church. See "Харківсько-Полтавська єпархія УАПЦ на чолі з Єпископом Ігорем (Ісіченком) продовжує об'єднавчий процес а УГКЦ" [The Kharkiv-Poltava eparchy of the UAOC with Bishop Ihor (Isichenko) continues the unification process with the UGCC], RISU: Religious Information Service of Ukraine, April 21, 2016, http://risu.org.ua/ua/index/all_news/orthodox/uapc/63151/ (accessed October 21, 2016).

189. Oleksandr (Drabinko), "О войне на Донбассе, автокефалии и заговоре Януковича против Украинской Церкви" [On the war in Donbas, autocephaly and the conspiracy of Ianukovych against the Ukrainian Church], VectorNews, October 6, 2016, http://vnews.

agency/exclusive/43678-o-voyne-na-donbasse-avtokefalii-i-zagovore-Yanukovycha-pro-tiv-ukrainskoy-cerkvi.html (accessed October 14, 2016).

190. Kozelsky, "Religion and the Crisis in Ukraine," 235–36.

Notes to Conclusion

1. Tetyana Kalenychenko, "Enmity and Hostility Remain Zones of Comfort for Ukrainian Churches," interview with Cyril Hovorun, RISU: Religious Information Service of Ukraine, January 21, 2016, http://risu.org.ua/en/index/expert_thought/interview/62242/ (accessed October 14, 2016).

2. "Константинопольський Патріархат в історії України" [The Constantinopolitan Patriarchate in the history of Ukraine]. Complete reports available at "Перспективи єднання українського православ'я та роль Константинополя: Нотатки з конференції," Religiia v Ukraïni, June 10, 2016, http://www.religion.in.ua/main/33115-perspektivi-yednannya-ukrayinskogo-pravo-slavya-ta-rol-konstantinopolya-notatki-z-konferenciyi.html, and "Українське православ'я чекає на активнішу участь Константинополя вирішенні питання розколу в Україн," RISU: Religious Information Service of Ukraine, June 13, 2016, http://risu.org.ua/ua/index/all_news/orthodox/ortho-dox_world/63656/ (accessed October 17, 2016).

3. "Митрополит Олександер (Драбинко): Українська Православна Церква має право на помісний статус" [Metropolitan Oleksandr (Drabinko): The Ukrainian Orthodox Church has a right to local status], Volyns'ka Pravda, http://www.pravda.lutsk.ua/ukr/news/94543/ (accessed October 14, 2016). See also Nikolai Mitrokhin, "Aspects of the Religious Situation in Ukraine," Religion, State and Society 29, no. 3 (2010): 178.

Bibliography

"Акт об отлучении от церкви монаха Филарета (Денисенко)" [Act of anathematizing the monk Filaret (Denysenko) from the Church]. *Журнал московской патриархии* 4 (1997): 19–20.

Alexeev, Wassilij, and Theofanis Stavrou. *The Great Revival: The Russian Church under German Occupation*. Minneapolis, MN: Burgess Publishing, 1976.

Anashkin, D. P., ed. *Законодательство Русской Православной Церкви заграницей (1921–2007)* [Legislation of the Russian Orthodox Church outside of Russia, 1921–2007]. Moscow: Izdatel'stvo PSTGU, 2013.

Applebaum, Anne. *Red Famine: Staline's War on Ukraine. New York: Doubleday, 2017.*

Arjakovsky, Antoine. *Conversations with Lubomyr Cardinal Husar: Towards a Post-confessional Christianity*. Lviv: Ukrainian Catholic University Press, 2007.

———. *Russie, Ukraine: De la guerre à la paix*. Paris: Parole et silence, 2014.

Armstrong, John. *Ukrainian Nationalism*. 3rd edition. Englewood, CO: Ukrainian Academic Press, 1990.

Balashov, Nikolai. *На пути к литургическому возрождению* [On the path of liturgical renewal]. Moscow: Kruglyi stol po religioznomu obrazovaniiu i daikonii, 2001.

Berkhoff, Karel C. "Was There a Religious Revival in Soviet Ukraine under the Nazi Regime?" *The Slavonic and East European Review* 78, no. 3 (2000): 536–67.

"Bishops of the UOC MP remained seated when President Poroshenko was reading names of heroes of Ukraine." RISU: Religious Information Service of Ukraine. May 8, 2015. Accessed September 9, 2016. http://risu.org.ua/en/index/all_news/community/religion_and_policy/59943.

Bociurkiw, Bohdan. "The Autocephalous Church Movement in Ukraine: The Formative Stage (1917–1921)." *The Ukrainian Quarterly* 16, no. 3 (1960): 211–23.

———. "The Orthodox Church and the Soviet Regime in the Ukraine, 1953–1971." *Canadian Slavonic Papers* 14, no. 2 (1972): 191–212.

———. "Religion and Nationalism in Contemporary Ukraine." In *Nationalism in the USSR and Eastern Europe in the Era of Brezhnev and Kosygin*, edited by George W. Simmonds, 81–95. Detroit, MI: University of Detroit Press, 1977.

———. "The Renovationist Church in the Soviet Ukraine, 1922–1939." *The Annals of the Ukrainian Academy of Arts and Sciences* 9, nos. 1–2 (1961): 41–74.

———. "The Russian Orthodox Church in Ukraine: The Exarchate and the Renovationists, and the 'Conciliar-Episcopal' Church, 1920–1939." *Harvard Ukrainian Studies* 26, no. 1 (2002): 63–91.

———. "The Soviet Destruction of the Ukrainian Orthodox Church, 1929–1936." *Journal of Ukrainian Studies* 12, no. 1 (1987): 3–21.

———. "Soviet Religious Policy in Ukraine in Historical Perspective." In *Russian Empire: Some Aspects of Tsarist and Soviet Colonial Practices*, edited by Michael S. Pap, 95–111. Cleveland, OH: Institute for Soviet and East European Studies, John Carroll University and Ukrainian Historical Association, 1985.

———. "The Ukrainian Autocephalous Orthodox Church and Modernization, 1920–1930: A Case Study in Religious Modernization." In *Religion and Modernization in the Soviet Union*, edited by Dennis Dunn, 310–47. Boulder, CO: Westview Press, 1977.

———. "The Ukrainian Autocephalous Orthodox Church in West Germany, 1945–50." In *The Refugee Experience: Ukrainian Displaced Persons after World War II*, edited by Wsevolod Isajiw, Yury Boshyk, and Roman Senkus, 158–81. Edmonton, AB: Canadian Institute of Ukrainian Studies, 1992.

———. *The Ukrainian Greek Catholic Church and the Soviet State, 1939–1950.* Edmonton, AB: Canadian Institute of Ukrainian Studies, 1996.

———. "Ukrainization Movements within the Russian Orthodox Church and the Ukrainian Autocephalous Orthodox Church." *Harvard Ukrainian Studies* 3–4 (1979): 92–111.

Borowik, Irena. "Orthodoxy Confronting the Collapse of Communism in Post-Soviet Countries." *Social Compass* 53, no. 2 (2006): 267–78.

Brusanowski, Paul. "Autocephaly in Ukraine: The Canonical Dimension." In *Churches in the Ukrainian Crisis, ed. Andrii Krawchuk and Thomas Bremer, 47-77. New York: Palgrave MacMillan, 2016.*

Bureha, Volodymyr. "*Нічий Собор*" [No One's Council]. Religiia v Ukraïni. November 25, 2010. Accessed October 8, 2015. http://www.religion.in.ua/main/6987-nichij-sobor.html.

Chumachenko, Tatiana A. *Church and State in Soviet Russia: Russian Orthodoxy from World War II to the Khrushchev Years.* Edited and translated by Edward Roslof. Armonk, NY: M. E. Sharpe, 2002.

Coleman, Heather J. "A Ukrainian Priest's Son Remembers His Father's Life and Ministry." In *Orthodox Christianity in Imperial Russia: A Source Book on Lived Religion*, edited by Heather J. Coleman, 107–30. Bloomington: Indiana University Press, 2014.

Cunningham, James. "Reform Projects of the Russian Orthodox Church at the Beginning of the Twentieth Century." In *The Legacy of St. Vladimir: Byzantium, Russia, America*, edited by John Breck, John Meyendorff, and Eleana Silk, 116–23. Crestwood, NY: St. Vladimir's Seminary Press, 1990.

———. *A Vanquished Hope: The Movement for Church Renewal in Russia, 1905–1906.* Crestwood, NY: St. Vladimir's Seminary Press, 1981.

Demacopoulos, George. "The Popular Reception of the Council of Florence in Constantinople, 1439–1453." *St. Vladimir's Theological Quarterly* 43, no. 1 (1999): 37–53.

Denysenko, Nicholas. "The Appeal of the Ukrainian Parliament and the Ecumenical Patriarchate." Public Orthodoxy. Accessed September 9, 2016. https://publicorthodoxy.org/2016/06/20/the-appeal-of-the-ukrainian-parliament-and-the-ecumenical-patriarchate/.

———. "Chaos in Ukraine: The Churches and the Search for Leadership." *International Journal for the Study of the Christian Church* 14, no. 3 (2014): 242–59.

———. "Fractured Orthodoxy in Ukraine and Politics: The Impact of Patriarch Kyrill's 'Russian World.'" *Logos: A Journal of Eastern Christian Studies* 54, nos. 1–2 (2013): 33–68.

———. "Ukrainian Orthodoxy in Toronto: A Model for Dialogue, a Symbol of Courage." RISU: Religious Information Service of Ukraine. May 17, 2014. Accessed October 7, 2016. http://risu.org.ua/en/index/expert_thought/analytic/56450/.

Destivelle, Hyacinthe. *The Moscow Council (1917–1918): The Creation of the Conciliar Institutions of the Russian Orthodox Church.* Edited by Michael Plekon and Vitaly Permiakov. Translated by Jerry Ryan. Foreword by Metropolitan Hilarion (Alfeyev). Notre Dame, IN: University of Notre Dame Press, 2015.

Dmitry (Jarema), Ihor (Isichenko), and Evhen Sverstyuk. "Місія поєднання і примирення: Про підготовку об'єднавчого всеукраїнського православного собору" [A mission of unity and reconciliation: On the preparation of a unification of the All-Ukrainian Orthodox Council]. *Наша віра*, nos. 4–5 (March 1994): 1, 3.

Evlogy (Georgievsky). *My Life's Journey: The Memoirs of Metropolitan Evlogy.* Compiled by T. I. Manukhina. Translated by Alexander Lisenko. Introduction by Thomas Hopko. Crestwood, NY: St. Vladimir's Seminary Press, 2014.

Fedorovych, I. "Торжество істини і справедливости: До 35-ліття возз'єднання Греко Католицької Церкви Галичини з Руською Православною Церквою" [Triumph of truth and righteousness:

Toward the thirty-fifth anniversary of the reunion of the Greek Catholic Church of Galicia with the Russian Orthodox Church]. *Православний вісник* 3 (1981): 26–29.

Feodosii (Protsiuk). *Обособленческие движение в Православной Церкви на Украине* [The separation movement in the Orthodox Church in Ukraine]. Moscow: Krutitskoe podvor'e, 2004.

Filaret (Denysenko). "Незалежній Україні—Незалежну Церкву" [An independent Church for an independent Ukraine]. Radio Svoboda. August 16, 2011. Accessed October 10, 2016. http://www.radiosvoboda.org/content/article/24298217.html.

———. "Patriarch Filaret: Failure to Recognize Autocephaly Not a Big Misfortune." RISU: Religious Information Service of Ukraine. June 13, 2012. Accessed September 8, 2016. http://risu.org.ua/en/index/all_news/confessional/interchurch_relations/48436/.

———. "Прес-конференція Блаженнішого Митрополита Київського і всієї України Філарета" [Press conference of His Beatitude Metropolitan Filaret of Kyiv and all Ukraine]. *Православний вісник* 1 (1991): 1–4.

———. "Промова екзарха України, Митрополита Київського і Галицького Філарета на відкритті урочистого акту 15 травня 1971 року" [Speech of the exarch of Ukraine, Metropolitan Filaret of Kyiv and Halych, at the opening of the solemn act of May 15, 1971]. *Православний вісник* 7 (July 1971): 10–15.

———. "Слово Митрополита Київського і Галицького Філарета перед водосвятним молебнем" [The word of Metropolitan Filaret of Kyiv and Galicia before the prayer service for the blessing of waters]. *Православний вісник* 12 (December 1988): 11.

———. "Слово, виголошине екзархом України, митрополитом Філаретом, у св. Успенському жіночому монастирі м. Мукачева з нагоди 20-річчя возз'єднання колишніх греко-католиків Закарпаття з Руською Православною Церквою" [The word proclaimed by the exarch of Ukraine, Metropolitan Filaret, in the Holy Dormition women's monastery in the city of Mukachevo, on the occasion of the twentieth anniversary of the reunion of former Greek Catholics of Transcarpathia with the Russian Orthodox Church]. *Православний вісник* 9 (September 1969): 291–92.

Fireside, Harvey. *Icon and Swastika: The Russian Orthodox Church under Nazi and Soviet Control*. Cambridge, MA: Harvard University Press, 1971.

Florovsky, Georges. *Collected Works*. Vol. 4, *Aspects of Church History*. Belmont, MA: Nordland, 1975.

Freeze, Gregory L. "All Power to the Parish? The Problems and Politics of Church Reform in Late Imperial Russia." In *Social Identities in Revolutionary Russia*, edited by Madhavan K. Palat, 174–208. New York: Palgrave, 2001.

———. "Counter-Reformation in Russian Orthodoxy: Popular Response to Religious Innovation, 1922–1925." *Slavic Review* 54, no. 2 (1995): 305–39.

———. "Handmaiden of the State? The Church in Imperial Russia Reconsidered." *Journal of Ecclesiastical History* 36, no. 1 (1985): 82–102.

———. *The Parish Clergy in Nineteenth-Century Russia: Crisis, Reform, Counter-Reform*. Princeton, NJ: Princeton University Press, 1983.

———. "The Stalinist Assault on the Parish, 1929–1941." In *Stalinismus vor dem Zweiten Weltkrieg: Neue Wege der Forschung*, edited by Manfred Hildermeier and Elisabeth Müller-Luckner, 211–34. Munich: Oldenbourg, 1998.

———. "Subversive Atheism: Soviet Antireligious Campaigns and the Religious Revival in Ukraine in the 1920s." In *State Secularism and Lived Religion in Soviet Russia and Ukraine*, edited by Catherine Wanner, 27–62. New York: Oxford University Press, 2012.

———. "Subversive Piety: Religion and the Political Crisis in Late Imperial Russia." *Journal of Modern History* 68, no. 2 (1996): 308–50.

Galadza, Peter. "Eastern Catholic Christianity." In *The Blackwell Companion to Eastern Christianity*, edited by Kenneth Parry, 291–318. Oxford: Wiley-Blackwell, 2010.

———. "Seventeenth-Century Liturgicons of the Kyivan Metropolia and Several Lessons for Today." *St. Vladimir's Theological Quarterly* 56, no. 1 (2012): 73–91.

———. "The Structure of the Eastern Churches: Bonded with Human Blood or Baptismal Water?" *Pro Ecclesia* 17, no. 4 (2008): 373–86.

Gavrilkin, Konstantin. "Russia, Patriarchal Orthodox Church of." In *The Encyclopedia of Eastern Orthodox Christianity*, edited by John McGuckin, 2:498. Oxford: Wiley-Blackwell, 2011.

Gavrilyuk, Paul. *Georges Florovsky and the Russian Religious Renaissance: Changing Paradigms in Historical and Systematic Theology.* Oxford: Oxford University Press, 2014.

———. "Жажда церковного единства: Международный украинский православный симпозиум в Торонто" [Thirst for Church unity: An international Ukrainian Orthodox symposium in Toronto]. Religiia v Ukraïni. May 14, 2014. Accessed October 7, 2016. http://www.religion.in.ua/main/daycomment/25780-zhazhda-cerkovnogo-edinstva-mezhdunarodnyj-ukrainskij-pravoslavnyj-simpozium-v-toronto.html.

Gill, Joseph. *The Council of Florence.* New York: New York University Press, 2011.

Groen, Bert, ed. *Four Hundred Years Union of Brest (1596–1996): A Critical Reevaluation; Acta of the Congress Held at Hernen Castle, the Netherlands, in March 1996.* Leuven: Peeters, 1998.

Gudziak, Borys. *Crisis and Reform: The Kyivan Metropolitanate, the Patriarchate of Constantinople, and the Genesis of the Union of Brest.* Harvard Series in Ukrainian Studies. Cambridge, MA: Harvard University Press for the Harvard Ukrainian Research Institute, 2001.

Herbel, D. Oliver. *Turning to Tradition: Converts and the Making of an American Orthodox Church.* Oxford: Oxford University Press, 2014.

Heyer, Friedrich. *Die Orthodox kirche in der Ukraine von 1917 bis 1945.* Osteuropa und der Deutsche Osten 111. Cologne: Rudolf Müller, 1953.

Himka, John-Paul. "The Greek Catholic Church and Nation-Building in Galicia, 1772–1918." *Harvard Ukrainian Studies* 8, nos. 3–4 (1984): 426–52.

"His Holiness Patriarch Kirill: Unilateral Recognition of Schism in Ukraine Will Have Catastrophic Consequences for the Unity of the Orthodox Church." The Russian Orthodox Church: Department for External Church Relations. February 2, 2016. Accessed September 9, 2016. https://mospat.ru/en/2016/02/02/news127695/.

"Глава УПЦ (МП): Мова молитви має бути тільки церковнослов'янська, бо Українську не всі захочуть служити" [Head of the UOC MP: The language of prayer can only be in Church Slavonic, because not everyone wishes to serve in Ukrainian]. RISU: Religious Information Service of Ukraine. February 1, 2016. Accessed September 9, 2016. http://risu.org.ua/ua/index/all_news/orthodox/uoc/62354/.

Hovorun, Cyril. "Christians in Ukraine: Ecumenism in the Trenches." *The Catholic World Report.* March 4, 2014. Accessed March 31, 2014. http://www.catholicworldreport.com/Item/2970/christians_in_ukraine_ecumenism_in_the_trenches.aspx#.UznOwPldWSo.

———. "Civil Religion in the Orthodox Milieu." In *Political Theologies in Orthodox Christianity: Common Challenges and Divergent Positions*, edited by Kristina Stoeckl, Ingeborg Gabriel, and Aristotle Papanicolaou, 253–64. New York: Bloomsbury, 2017.

"Греція: Відомий афонський старець звернувся до Українського народу" [Greece: A renowned Athonite elder appealed to the Ukrainian people]. Ukraïns'ka Pravoslavna Tserkva. March 15, 2015. Accessed October 20, 2016. http://news.church.ua/2015/03/15/%EF%BB%BFgreciya-vidomij-afonskij-starec-zvernuvsya-do-ukrajinskogo-narodu-video/.

Hryhorii [Zakaliak], Archbishop. "Боротьба Українського народу проти Унії" [The battle of the Ukrainian nation against the Unia]. *Православний вісник* 1 (January 1969): 44–47.

Hryniewicz, Wacław. *The Challenge of Our Hope: Christian Faith in Dialogue.* Cultural Heritage and Contemporary Change Series 4a, Eastern and Central Europe. Polish Philosophical Studies 7. Washington, DC: The Council for Research in Values and Philosophy, 2007.

Husband, William B. "Soviet Atheism and Russian Orthodox Strategies of Resistance, 1917–1932." *Journal of Modern History* 70, no. 1 (1998): 74–107.

Iatsul'chak, Volodymyr. "Про повторні звершення таїнств в Московському патріархаті" [On the repetition of the celebration of sacraments in the Moscow Patriarchate]. March 22, 2012. Accessed February 13, 2018. http://archive.cerkva.info/uk/publications/articles/2256-tainstva.html

Ievsieieva, Tetiana. "Ідеологія і практика православних конфесій України стосовно національного питання у 1920-і рр." [Ideology and practice of Orthodox confessions of Ukraine on the national question in the 1920s]. Accessed October 20, 2016. http://history.org.ua/JournALL/pro/pro_2010_19_2/2.pdf.

———. *Російська православна церква в Україні 1917–1921 рр.: Конфлікт національних ідентичностей у православному полі* [The Russian Orthodox Church in Ukraine 1917–1921: A conflict of national identities in the Orthodox sphere]. Kyiv: Instytut istoriï Ukraïny NAN, 2005.

Ievstratii (Zoria). "Помаранчева революція для церкви стала моментом істини" [The Orange Revolution became a moment of truth for the Church]. RISU: Religious Information Service of Ukraine. November 22, 2011. Accessed October 10, 2016. http://risu.org.ua/ua/index/all_news/state/national_religious_question/45578/.

Ihor (Isichenko). "Непрочитане послання УАПЦ" [The unread epistle of the UAOC]. *Успенська вежа* (December 2014): 3.

Ilarion (Ohienko). *Ідеологія Української Церкви* [Ideology of the Ukrainian Church]. Edited by Mykola Timoshik. Kyiv: Nasha kul'tura i nauka, 2013.

———. *Українська церква: Нариси з історії Української Православної Церкви* [The Ukrainian Church: Outlines from the History of the Ukrainian Orthodox Church]. 2 vols. Edited by Stepan Jarmus. Winnipeg: Konsystoriia UHP Tserkvy v Kanadi, 1982.

Jobert, Ambroise. *De Luther à Mohila: La Pologne dans la crise de la Chrétienté, 1517–1648*. Paris: Institut d'études slaves, 1974.

Kalenychenko, Tetyana. "Enmity and Hostility Remain Zones of Comfort for Ukrainian Churches." Interview with Cyril Hovorun. RISU: Religious Information Service of Ukraine. January 21, 2016. Accessed September 9, 2016. http://risu.org.ua/en/index/expert_thought/interview/62242/.

Kalkandjieva, Daniela. *The Russian Orthodox Church, 1917–1948: From Decline to Resurrection*. London: Routledge, 2015.

Kappeler, Andreas. "*Mazepintsy, Malorossy, Khokhly*: Ukrainians in the Ethnic Hierarchy of the Russian Empire." In *Culture, Nation, and Identity: The Ukrainian-Russian Encounter, 1600–1945*, edited by Andreas Kappeler, Zenon E. Kohut, Frank E. Sysyn, and Mark von Hagen, 162–81. Edmonton, AB: Canadian Institute of Ukrainian Studies, 2003.

Kapsamun, Ivan. "Ukraine's Parliament Appeals to Bartholomew: A Historic Step." Den'Kyiv.ua. June 22, 2016. Accessed September 9, 2016. http://day.kyiv.ua/en/article/day-after-day/ukraines-parliament-appeals-bartholomew-historic-step.

Karatnycky, Adrian. "Religion and the Orange Revolution." RISU: Religious Information Service of Ukraine. December 20, 2004. Accessed October 10, 2016. http://risu.org.ua/en/index/exclusive/kaleidoscope/4152/.

Keleher, Serge. "Response to Sophia Senyk, 'The Ukrainian Greek Catholic Church Today: Universal Values versus Nationalist Doctrines.'" *Religion, State and Society* 31, no. 3 (2003): 289–306.

Kirill (Gundaev). "Проповедь Святейшего Патриарха Кирилла в день памяти преподобного Сергия Радонежского в Троице-Сергиевой лавре" [Sermon of His Holiness Patriarch Kirill on the day commemorating the venerable Sergius of Radonezh in the Trinity-Sergius Lavra]. Russkaia Pravoslavnaia Tserkov': Ofitsial'nyi Sait Moskovskogo Patriarchata. July 18, 2014. Accessed December 8, 2014. http://www.patriarchia.ru/db/text/3692183.html.

Knox, Zoe. "Russian Orthodoxy, Russian Nationalism, and Patriarch Aleksii II." *Nationalities Papers* 33, no. 4 (2005): 533–45.

———. *Russian Society and the Orthodox Church: Religion in Russia after Communism*. New York: Routledge, 2005.

Kochan, Natalia. "'Oh, East Is East and West Is West . . .': The Character of Orthodox-Greek Catholic Discourse in Ukraine and Its Regional Dimensions." In *Eastern Orthodox Encounters of Identity and Otherness: Values, Self-Reflection, Dialogue*, edited by Andrii Krawchuk and Thomas Bremer, 125–40. New York: Palgrave Macmillan, 2014.

Kohut, Zenon. *Making Ukraine: Studies on Political Culture, Historical Narrative, and Identity*. Foreword by Frank Sysyn. Edmonton, AB: Canadian Institute of Ukrainian Studies, 2011.

"Коментар до рішення Синоду УПЦ про діалог з церквами" [Commentary on the decision of the Synod of the UOC on dialogue with the churches], UNIAN Informatsiine agenstvo, September 11, 2009. Accessed September 15, 2016. http://religions.unian.ua/holidays/264773-komentar-do-rishennya-sinodu-upts-pro-dialog-z-tserkvami.html.

Korol, Ivan. "До 35-Річчя возз'єднаня Греко-Католицької Церкви з Руською Православною Церквою (1946–1981)" [Toward the thirty-fifth anniversary of the reunion of the Greek Catholic Church of Galicia with the Russian Orthodox Church (1946–1981)]. *Православний вісник* 1 (January 1981): 29–31.

Korolevsky, Cyril. *Metropolitan Andrew (1865–1944)*. Translated by Serge Keleher. Lviv: Stauropegion, 1993.

Kozelsky, Mara. "Religion and the Crisis in Ukraine." *International Journal for the Study of the Christian Church* 14, no. 3 (2014): 219–41.

Kuzio, Taras. "In Search of Unity and Autocephaly: Ukraine's Orthodox Churches." *Religion, State and Society* 25, no. 4 (1997): 393–415.

Krawchuk, Andrii. "Constructing Interreligious Consensus in the Post-Soviet Space: The Ukrainian Council of Churches and Religious Organizations." in *Eastern Orthodox Encounters of Identity and Otherness: Values, Self-Reflection, Dialogue*, ed. Andrii Krawchuk and Thomas Bremer, 273-302. New York: Palgrave Macmillan, 2014.

Marker, Gary. "Staffing Peter's Church: The Transmigration of Kyivan Clergy in the Early Eighteenth Century." *Kyivs'ka akademiya*, no. 8 (2010): 79–91.

Maximos (Christopoulos). "The Primacy of the Ecumenical Patriarchate: Developments since the Nineteenth Century." In *Primacy in the Church: The Office of Primate and the Authority of Councils*, edited by John Chryssavgis, 1:367–84. Crestwood, NY: St. Vladimir's Seminary Press, 2016.

Meyendorff, Paul. "Ethnophyletism, Autocephaly, and National Churches—A Theological Approach and Ecclesiological Implications." *St. Vladimir's Theological Quarterly* 57, nos. 3-4 (2013): 381–94.

———. "The Liturgical Reforms of Peter Moghila: A New Look." *St. Vladimir's Theological Quarterly* 29, no. 2 (1985): 101–14.

Mitrokhin, Nikolai. "Aspects of the Religious Situation in Ukraine." *Religion, State and Society* 29, no. 3 (2001): 173–96.

———. "Orthodoxy in Ukrainian Political Life: 2004–2009." *Religion, State and Society* 38, no. 3 (September 2010): 229–51.

Mončak, Ihor. *Florentine Ecumenism in the Kyivan Church: The Theology of Ecumenism Applied to the Individual Church of Kyiv*. Rome: Ukraïnskyi Katolic'kyi Univ. im. sv. Klymenta Papy, 1987.

Morosan, Vladimir. *Choral Performance in Pre-Revolutionary Russia*. Russian Music Studies 17. Madison, CT: Musica Russica, 1994

Moroziuk, Russell P. "Antireligious Propaganda in Ukraine." In *Russian Empire: Some Aspects of Tsarist and Soviet Colonial Practices*, edited by Michael Pap, 113–30. Cleveland, OH: Institute for Soviet and East European Studies, John Carroll University and Ukrainian Historical Association, 1985.

Moscow Patriarchate. "Position of the Moscow Patriarchate on the Problem of Primacy in the Universal Church." In *Primacy in the Church: The Office of Primate and the Authority of Councils*, edited by John Chryssavgis, 1:421–30. Crestwood, NY: St. Vladimir's Seminary Press, 2016.

Mulyk-Lutsyk, Iurii. *Історія Української Греко-Православної Церкви в Канаді* [The history of the Ukrainian Greek-Orthodox Church in Canada]. 6 vols. Winnipeg, MB: Vydavnycha cpilka Ekkleziia, 1984–1992.

Mytsyk, Iurii, ed. *Листування Митрополита Іларіона (Огієнка)* [The correspondence of Metropolitan Ilarion (Ohienko)]. Kyiv: Kyivo-Mohylyans'ka academiia, 2006

"На Рівненщині історична подія: Різні конфесії підписали меморандум про Українську помісну церкву; Московський патріархат засудив агресію Росії" [A historical event in the Rivne region: Different confessions signed a memorandum on the Ukrainian Local Church; the Moscow Patriarchate condemned Russian aggression]. RISU: Religious Information Service of Ukraine. November 19, 2014. Accessed October 8, 2015. http://risu.org.ua/ua/index/monitoring/society_digest/58254/.

Oleksandr (Drabinko). "О войне на Донбассе, автокефалии и заговоре Януковича против Украинской Церкви" [On the war in Donbas, autocephaly and the conspiracy of Ianukovych against the Ukrainian Church]. VectorNews. October 6, 2016. Accessed October 14, 2016. http://vnews.agency/exclusive/43678-o-voyne-na-donbasse-avtokefalii-i-zagovore-yanukovicha-protiv-ukrainskoy-cerkvi.html.

———. "Участь Константинопольського Патріархату в процесах улікування церковного розділення в Україні" [Participation of the Constantinopolitan Patriarchates in the processes of healing church divisions in Ukraine]. RISU: Religious Information Service of Ukraine. June 16, 2016. Accessed October 17, 2016. http://risu.org.ua/ua/index/studios/materials_conferences/63705/.

———. "Ukrainian Orthodoxy: Path to Recovery of Church Unity, Part II." RISU: Religious Information Service of Ukraine. July 5, 2016. Accessed October 7, 2016. http://risu.org.ua/en/index/studios/studies_of_religions/63886/.

"Orthodox Churches under Threat in Ukraine." RISU: Religious Information Service of Ukraine. January 25, 2016. Accessed April 19, 2016. http://risu.org.ua/en/index/all_news/orthodox/orthodox_world/62270/.

"'Парад переходів': УПЦ КП і УПЦ (МП) по-різному трактують зміну юрисдикції парафій" [A parade of transfers: UOC KP and UOC MP interpret the change of jurisdiction of parishes differently]. Religiia v Україні. October 10, 2014. Accessed September 16, 2016. https://www.religion.in.ua/news/vazhlivo/27125-parad-perexodiv-upc-kp-i-upc-mp-po-riznomu-traktuyut-zminu-yurisdikciyi-parafij.html.

Partykevich, Andre. *Between Kyiv and Constantinople: Oleksander Lototsky and the Quest for Ukrainian Autocephaly*. Edmonton, AB: Church Studies Program, Canadian Institute of Ukrainian Studies, 1998.

"Patriarch Mstyslav Enthroned." *The Ukrainian Weekly* 47, November 25, 1990.

"Патріарх Філарет закликав вірних Україн молитися за справедливий суд над Путіним—'новим Каїном'" [Patriarch Filaret called upon the faithful of Ukraine to pray for a righteous trial of Putin, the "new Cain"]. RISU: Religious Information Service of Ukraine. September 5, 2014. Accessed February 5, 2015. http://risu.org.ua/ua/index/all_news/state/national_religious_question/57559/.

Payne, Daniel. "Nationalism and the Local Church: The Source of Ecclesiastical Conflict in the Orthodox Commonwealth." *Nationalities Papers* 35, no. 5 (2007): 831–52.

Pew Research Center. "Religious Belief and National Belonging in Central and Eastern Europe." http://www.pewforum.org/2017/05/10/religious-belief-and-national-belonging-in-central-and-eastern-europe. Accessed September 25, 2017.

Pimen (Izvekov). "Послание Святейшего Патриарха Московского и всея Руси Пимена и Священного Синода Русской Православной Церкви Преосвященным архипастырям, священному клиру, честному иночеству и всем верным чадам Русской Православной Церкви в связи с 70-летием Великой Октябрьской социалистической революции" [Epistle of His Holiness Patriarch Pimen of Moscow and all Russia and the Holy Synod of the Russian Orthodox Church to the reverend archpastors, the holy clergy, the venerable monastics and all faithful children of the Russian Orthodox Church on the occasion of the seventieth anniversary of the Great October Socialist Revolution]. *Журнал Московской Патриархии* 11 (November 1987): 2–7.

———. "Послання місцеблюстителя Московського Патріаршого престолу митрополита Крутицького й Коломенського Пимена, преосвященним архіпастирям, кліру й мирянам західноукраїнських єпархій Московського Патріархату в звязку з 25-річчям Львівського Собору" [Epistle of the locum tenens of the Moscow patriarchal throne Metropolitan Pimen of Krutitsky and Kolomensky to the reverend archpastors, clergy, and laity of the western Ukrainian eparchies of the Moscow Patriarchate on the occasion of the twenty-fifth anniversary of the Lviv Council]. *Православний вісник* 7 (July 1971): 9.

———. "Послання Святішого Патріарха Пимена голові ради міністрів ЦРЦР Олексію Миколайовичу Косигіну" [Epistle of His Holiness Patriarch Pimen to the head of the Council of Ministers of the USSR Alexei Kosygin]. *Православний вісник* 7 (July 1980): 1–2.

———. "Предъюбилейное послание Святейшего Патриарха Московского и всея Руси Пимена и Священного Синода Русской Православной Церкви преосвященным архипастырям, пастырям, честному иночеству и всем верным чадам Русской Православной Церкви, во отечества нашем и за его пределами сущим, к 1000-летию крещение Руси" [Prejubilee epistle of His Holiness Patriarch Pimen of Moscow and all Russia and the Holy Synod of the Russian Orthodox Church to the reverend archpastors, the holy clergy, the venerable monastics, and all faithful children of the Russian Orthodox Church in our fatherland and scattered abroad, on the 1000-year anniversary of the baptism of Russia]. *Журнал Московской Патриархии* 8 (August 1987): 2–6.

———. "Заява Святішого Патріарха Московського і всієї Русі кореспондетові ТАРС із зв'язку з 35-річчям перемоги над фашистською Німеччиною" [Statement of His Holiness the Patriarch of Moscow and all Russia to the correspondent of TARS on the thirty-fifth anniversary of the victory over fascist Germany]. *Православний вісник* 7 (July 1980): 2–3.

Plokhy, Serhii. "Church, State, and Nation in Ukraine." In Plokhy and Sysyn, *Religion and Nation*, 179–86.

———. *The Gates of Europe: A History of Ukraine*. New York: Basic Books, 2015.

———. "In the Shadow of Yalta: International Politics and the Soviet Liquidation of the Ukrainian Greek Catholic Church." In Plokhy and Sysyn, *Religion and Nation*, 58–73.

———. "Ukrainian Orthodox Autocephaly and Metropolitan Filaret." In Plokhy and Sysyn, *Religion and Nation*, 128–35.

Plokhy, Serhii, and Frank Sysyn, eds. *Religion and Nation in Modern Ukraine*. Edmonton, AB: Canadian Institute of Ukrainian Studies, 2003.

Popivchak, Ronald. "The Life and Times of Peter Mohyla, Metropolitan of Kiev." *Logos: A Journal of Eastern Christian Studies* 43–45 (2004): 339–59.

Pospielovsky, Dimitry. *The Orthodox Church in the History of Russia*. Crestwood, NY: St. Vladimir's Seminary Press, 1998.

"Предстоятель УПЦ разрешил не поминать Патриарха Кирилла" [The primate of the UOC permitted the non-commemoration of Patriarch Kirill]. Religiia v Ukraïni. December 29, 2015. Accessed September 9, 2016. http://www.religion.in.ua/news/ukrainian_news/31434-predstoyatel-upc-razreshil-ne-pominat-patriarxa-kirilla.html.

Prelovs'ka, Iryna. *Джерела з Історії Української Автокефальної Православної Церкви (1921–1930)–Української Православної Церкви (1930–1939)* [Sources from the history of the Ukrainian Autocephalous Orthodox Church (1921–1930)—Ukrainian Orthodox Church (1930–1939)]. Kyiv: Inst. Ukraïns'koi Archeohrafiï ta Dzhereloznavstva im. M. S. Hrushevs'koho NAN Ukraïny, 2013.

"Primate of Russian Orthodox Church Arrives in Geneva to Take Part in the Synaxis of Primates of Local Orthodox Churches." The Russian Orthodox Church: Department for External Church Relations. January 22, 2016. Accessed September 9, 2016. https://mospat.ru/en/2016/01/22/news127064/.

"Primate of the UOC: It Is Not Necessary to Rebaptize Schismatics." Kievskaia Rus'. September 29, 2010. Accessed October 10, 2016. http://www.kiev-orthodox.org/site/churchlife/2331/.

Rentel, Alexander. "The Canonical Tradition: Universal Primacy in the Orthodox Church." In *Primacy in the Church: The Office of Primate and the Authority of Councils*, edited by John Chryssavgis, 2:555–86. Crestwood, NY: St. Vladimir's Seminary Press, 2016.

Richters, Katja. *The Post-Soviet Russian Orthodox Church: Politics, Culture and Greater Russia*. New York: Routledge, 2013.

"ROC Explained Signing of Rivne Memorandum by Very Strong Political Pressure." RISU: Religious Information Service of Ukraine. November 19, 2014. Accessed September 9, 2016. http://risu.org.ua/en/index/all_news/orthodox/moscow_patriarchy/58257.

Roberti, Jean-Claude. *Les Uniates*. Paris: Cerf, 1992.

Roslof, Edward. *Red Priests: Renovationism, Russian Orthodoxy, and Revolution, 1905–1946*. Bloomington: Indiana University Press, 2002.

Sagan, Oleksandr. *Вселенське Православ'я: Суть, історія, сучасний стан* [Ecumenical Orthodoxy: Existence, history, contemporary status]. Kyiv: Svit znan', 2004.

Samokhvalova, Lana. "Московський Патріархат добровільно Україну не 'відпустить'" [The Moscow Patriarchate will not voluntarily "release" Ukraine]. Interview with Oleksandr Sagan. Ukrinform. December 12, 2015. Accessed October 17, 2016. http://www.ukrinform.ua/rubric-society/1928469-oleksandr-sagan-profesor-religieznavets.html.

Saunders, David. *The Ukrainian Impact on Russian Culture: 1750–1850*. Edmonton, AB: Canadian Institute of Ukrainian Studies Press, 1985.

Sawchuk, Semen. *Ідеологічні засади Української греко-православної церкви в Канаді* [Ideological Principles of the Ukrainian Greek-Orthodox Church of Canada]. Winnipeg: Ekkleziia, 1975.

Schmemann, Alexander. "Confession and Communion." February 16–17, 1972. Accessed July 23, 2015. http://www.schmemann.org/byhim/confessionandcommunion.html.

Senyk, Sophia. *History of the Church in Ukraine*. Vol. 1, *To the End of the Thirteenth Century*. Orientalia Christiana analecta 243. Rome: Pontificio Instituto orientale, 1993.

———. *History of the Church in Ukraine*. Vol. 2, *1300 to the Union of Brest*. Orientalia Christiana analecta 289. Rome: Pontificio Instituto orientale, 2011.

———. "The Orthodox Church in Ukraine in the Twentieth Century." In *The Orthodox Church in Eastern Europe in the Twentieth Century*, edited by Christine Chaillot, 323–53. Oxford: Peter Lang, 2011.

———. "The Ukrainian Greek Catholic Church Today: Universal Values versus Nationalist Doctrines." *Religion, State and Society* 30, no. 4 (2002): 317–32.

Ševčenko, Ihor. "The Many Worlds of Peter Mohyla." *Harvard Ukrainian Studies* 8, nos. 1–2 (1984): 9–40.

———. *Ukraine between East and West: Essays on Cultural History to the Eighteenth Century*. 2nd edition. Foreword by Frank Sysyn. Edmonton, AB: Canadian Institute of Ukrainian Studies, 2009.

Shevzov, Vera. *Russian Orthodoxy on the Eve of Revolution*. New York: Oxford University Press, 2004.

———. "The Russian Tradition." In *The Orthodox Christian World*, edited by Augustine Casiday, 15–40. New York: Routledge, 2012.

Shlikhta, Natalia. "'Orthodox' and 'Soviet': The Identity of Soviet Believers (1940s–early 1970s)." *Forum for Anthropology and Culture*, no. 11 (2015): 140–64.

———. "Основні форми і методи атеїстичної пропаганди в Українській РСР наприкінці 50-х–на початки 60-х років" [Basic forms and methods of atheistic propaganda in the Ukrainian SSR at the end of the 1950s to the beginning of the 1960s]. *Наукові записки* 14 (1999): 80–87.

———. "'Please Open Our Church . . . in the Name of Historical and Human Value of Socialism': Orthodox Believers' Letters to Power, 1960s–Early 1970s." *Textus et Studia* 4, no. 4 (2015): 71–93.

———. "Portraits of Two Bishops Defending Their Dioceses: A Study of the Orthodox Episcopate in Postwar Soviet Ukraine." *Logos* 55, nos. 3–4 (2014): 329–58.

———. "Православні вірні—На захист своїх прав і своєї церкви (на Українських матеріалах кінця 1940х–1970-х pp.)" [Orthodox faithful—in defense of their rights and their church]. *Наукові записки* 104 (2010): 34–41.

———. "'Ukrainian' as 'Non-Orthodox': How Greek Catholics Were 'Reunited' with the Russian Orthodox Church, 1940s–1960s." Jan Surer, trans. *State, Religion and Church* 2, no. 2 (2015): 77–98

Skinner, Barbara. *The Western Front of the Eastern Church: Uniate and Orthodox Conflict in Eighteenth-Century Poland, Ukraine, Belarus, and Russia*. DeKalb: Northern Illinois University Press, 2009.

Smolii, V.A. and P.S. Sokhan', eds. *Другий Всеукраїнський Православний Церковний Собор УАПЦ, 17-30 жовтня 1927 року: Документи і матеріали* [The second All-Ukrainian Orthodox Church Sobor, October 17-30, 1927: Documents and materials]. Kyiv: Instytut Ukraïns'koï arkheohrafiï, Instytut istoriï Ukraïny, 2007.

Smyrnov, A. I. *Мстислав (Скрипник): Громадсько-політичний і церковний діяч, 1930-1944)* [Mstyslav (Skrypnyk): Community-political and Church Activist (1930-1944)]. 2nd edition. Kyiv: Smoloskyp, 2009.

Sokhan', P. S., Serhii Plokhii, and L. V. Iakovlieva, eds. *Перший Всеукраїнський Православний Церковний Собор УАПЦ, 14-30 жовтня 1921 року* [The first All-Ukrainian Orthodox Church Council of the UAOC, 14-30 October 1921]. Kyiv: NAN Ukraïn, In-t Ukr. arkheografiï ta dzheroloznavstva im. M. S. Hrushevs'koho, 1999.

Starodub, Andryi. *Всеукраїнський Православний Церковний Собор 1918 року: Огляд джерел* [The All-Ukrainian Orthodox Church Council in 1918: An examination of sources]. Kyiv: NAN Ukraïn, In-t Ukr. arkheografiï ta dzheroloznavstva im. M. S. Hrushevs'koho, 2010.

Stepovyk, Dmytro. *Патріарх Мстислав: Життя і архипастирська діяльність* [Patriarch Mstyslav: Life and Archpastoral Activity]. Kyiv: Mystetsvo, 2007.

Stone, Andrew Blane. "Overcoming Peasant Backwardness: The Khrushchev Antireligious Campaign and the Rural Soviet Union." *Russian Review* 67, no. 2 (2008): 296-320.

Subtelny, Orest. *Ukraine: A History*. 3rd edition. Toronto, ON: University of Toronto Press, 2000.

Sudo, Julia. "Russian Nationalist Orthodox Theology: A New Trend in the Political Life of Russia." *Political Theology* 6, no. 1 (2005): 67-86.

Sysyn, Frank E. "The Formation of Modern Ukrainian Religious Culture: The Sixteenth and Seventeenth Centuries." In Plokhy and Sysyn, *Religion and Nation*, 1-22.

———. "Remarks on the History of Ukrainian Orthodox in Ukraine and North America." *The Ukrainian Weekly*, July 19, 1998, 3.

———. "The Third Rebirth of the Ukrainian Autocephalous Orthodox Church and the Religious Situation in Ukraine, 1989-1991." In Plokhy and Sysyn, *Religion and Nation*, 88-119.

———. "The Ukrainian Orthodox Question in the USSR." In Plokhy and Sysyn, *Religion and Nation*, 74-87.

Tataryn, Myroslaw. "Harvesting Heritage Seeds in Prairie Soil: The Role of *Ukrainskyi holos* in the Formation of the Identity of the Ukrainian Greek Orthodox Church of Canada." *Historical Studies* 71 (2005): 94-109.

———. "Russia and Ukraine: Two Models of Religious Liberty and Two Models for Orthodoxy." *Religion, State and Society* 29, no. 3 (2001): 155-72.

Tikhon (Belavin). *Патріархъ Тихонъ объ автокефаліи полской церкви Православный Русскій календарь на годъ 1925* [Patriarch Tikhon on the autocephaly of the Polish Church, Russian Orthodox Calendar for the Year 1925], 78-80. N.p.: Senator U. Lazho, 1924.

Tonoyan, Lydia S., and Daniel P. Payne. "The Visit of Patriarch Kirill to Ukraine in 2009 and Its Significance in Ukraine's Political and Religious Life." *Religion, State and Society* 38, no. 3 (2010): 253-64.

Tsurikov, Vladimir, ed. *Metropolitan Antonii (Khrapovitskii): Archpastor of the Russian Diaspora*. Readings in Russian Religious Culture 5. Jordanville, NY: Foundation of Russian History, 2014.

Turii, Oleh. "Die katholischen Kirchen und die ökumenischen Beziehungen in der Ukraine." *Ost-West: Europäische Perspektiwen* 2 (2001): 95-106.

———. "Die Union von Brest 1595/96: Entstehung und historische Hintergründe." *Glaube in der 2. Welt: Zeitschrift für Religionsfreiheit und Menschenrechte* 4 (1977): 12-16.

———. "Історичні обставини й тенденції розвитку релігійного життя та міжконфесійних взаємин у сучасній Україні" [Historical circumstances and tendencies of development of religious life and inter-confessional relations in modern Ukraine]. In *Віра після атеїзму: Релігійне життя в Україні в період демократичних перетворень і державної незалежности*, edited by Miklosh Tomka and Oleh Turii, 5–45. Lviv: Vid-vo UKU, 2004.

———. "Проблема ідентичності в стосунках між церквами-сестрами в сучасній Україні" [The problem of identity in relations between sister churches in contemporary Ukraine]. In *"Kościoły siostrzane" w dialogu*, edited by Z. Glaeser, 284–98. Opole, 2002.

———. "Традиційні церкви в незалежній Україні: Проблема ідентичности" [Traditional churches in independent Ukraine: problems of identity]. *Ї: Незалежний культурологічний часопис* 22 (2001): 115–32.

———. "Церква і вибори: Уроки 2004 року" [The church and elections: Lessons from 2004]. RISU: Religious Information Service of Ukraine. January 14, 2010. Accessed October 18, 2016. http://risu.org.ua/ua/index/expert_thought/analytic/33861/.

Ukrainian Autocephalous Orthodox Church, Kharkiv Eparchy. "Рішення Священного Синоду Української Греко-Католицької Церкви" [The decision of the Holy Synod of the Ukrainian Greek-Catholic Church]. September 18, 2015. Accessed October 8, 2015. http://uapc.org.ua/rishennya-svyaschennoho-synodu-ukrajinskoji-hreko-katolytskoji-tserkvy/.

Ukrainian Orthodox Church, Kyivan Patriarchate. "Архієреї УАПЦ відкинули попередні домовленості та компромісні пропозиції і зірвали об'єднання з Київським Патріархатом" [The hierarchs of the UAOC dismissed the previous agreements and compromised propositions and thwarted union with the Kyivan Patriarchate]. July 9, 2015. Accessed September 15, 2016. https://www.cerkva.info/publications/arkhiierei-uapts-vidkynuly-poperedni-domovlenosti-ta-kompromisni-propozytsii-i-zirvaly-obiednannia-z-kyivskym-patriarkhatom.

———. "Ювілей: Урочиста академія у національному палаці мистецтв Україна" [Jubilee: Solemn academy in the national palace of culture "Ukraina"]. May 12, 2016. Accessed October 10, 2016. http://cerkva.kiev.ua/news/278.html

———. "Київський Патріархат не надавав благословення на твір Акафіст Небесній Сотній" [The Kyivan Patriarchate did not grant a blessing for the work "Akathist to the Heavenly Hundred"]. December 23, 2014. Accessed September 8, 2016. http://archive.cerkva.info/uk/news/kyiv/6049-zajava-pro-akafist.html.

———. "Постанови Архієрейського Собору (2016)" [Resolutions of the Bishops' Council]. May 13, 2016. Accessed February 13, 2018. https://www.cerkva.info/church/arkhiiereiskyi-sobor-kyivskoho-patriarkhatu-2016.

———. "Відбулося робоче засідання Комісії УПЦ для діалогу з УПЦ КП і УАПЦ" [A working meeting of the UOC's commission for dialogue with the UOC KP and UAOC took place]. March 26, 2014. Accessed September 15, 2016. http://news.church.ua/2014/03/26/vidbulosya-roboche-zasidannya-komisiji-upc-dlya-dialogu-z-upc-kp-i-uapc/.

———. "Вітальна адреса *Священного Синоду та Архієрейського Собору Української Православної Церкви Київського Патріархату Святійшому Патріарху Київському і всієї Руси-України Філарету з нагоди ювілею 50-ліття служіння на Київській кафедрі*" [Address of greetings of the Holy Synod and Hierarchical Council of the UOC-KP to His Holiness Patriarch Filaret of Kyiv and all Ukraine on the occasion of the fifty-year jubilee of service on the Kyivan throne]. May 14, 2016. Accessed October 10, 2016. http://vidomosti.kiev.ua/novyny/23-ofitsiini-zakhody/1356-vid-imeni-sviashchenno-ho-synodu-ta-arkhiiereiskoho-soboru-mytropolyt-epifanii-vyholosyv-sviatkovu-adre-su-patriarkhu-filaretu.html.

———. "Викладено позицію УГКЦ щодо дійсності Таїнства Хрещення в УПЦ КП" [Announcement on the position of the UGCC on the validity of the Sacrament of Baptism in the UOC-KP], November 2, 2012. Accessed November 5, 2012. https://www.cerkva.info/publications/vykladeno-pozytsiiu-uhkts-shchodo-diisnosti-tainstva-khreshchennia-v-upts-kp.

———. "Заява Архієрейського Собору" [Statement of the Bishops' Council], May 13, 2016. Accessed February 13, 2018. https://www.cerkva.info/church/zayava-arkhiyereyskoho-soboru.

———. "Журнали засідання Священного Синоду 27 липня 2015 р." [Journals of the meeting of the Holy Synod of July 27, 2015]. July 27, 2015. Accessed September 15, 2016. https://www.cerkva.info/church/zhurnaly-zasidannia-sviashchennoho-synodu-27-lypnia-2015-r.

———. "Звернення Священного Синоду" [Appeal of the Holy Synod]. October 22, 2014. Accessed September 9, 2016. https://www.cerkva.info/church/zvernennia-sviashchennoho-synodu-22-10-2014.

Ukrainian Orthodox Church, Moscow Patriarchate. "Двадцятип'ятиріччя возз'єднання Галицької Греко-Католицької Церкви з Руською Православною Церквою на Львівському Церковному Соборі (1946–1971)" [The twenty-fifth anniversary of the reunion of the Galician Greek-Catholic Church with the Russian Orthodox Church at the L'viv Church Council (1946–1971)]. *Православний вісник* 8 (August 1971): 13–15.

———. "Предстоятель УПЦ: Ми молимося за Петра Олексійовича Порошенка як президента нашої держави та брата по вірі" [Primate of the UOC: We pray for Peter Oleksiyovych Poroshenko as the president of our country and brother in the faith]. January 29, 2016. Accessed September 9, 2016. http://news.church.ua/2016/01/29/predstoyatel-upc-mi-molimosya-za-petra-oleksijovicha-poroshenka-yak-za-prezidenta-nashoji-derzhavi-ta-brata-po-viri-video/.

———. "В УПЦ (МП) прокоментували заяву предстоятеля УПЦ Канади про створення в Україні єдиної помісної церкви" [The UPC (MP) commented on the remarks of the primate of the UOC of Canada on the creation of one local church in Ukraine]. RISU: Religious Information Service of Ukraine. August 3, 2013. Accessed October 7, 2016. http://risu.org.ua/ua/index/all_news/confessional/orthodox_relations/60706/.

———. "Звернення єпископату Української Православної Церкви до Святішого Патріарха Московського і всієї Русі Алексія II та Священного Синоду Руської Православної Церкви" [Appeal of the episcopate of the Ukrainian Orthodox Church to His Holiness Alexy II, patriarch of Moscow and all Russia and the Holy Synod of the Russian Orthodox Church]. *Православний вісник* 4 (April 1992): 8–9.

———. "Звернення єпископату Української Православної Церкви до Святішого Патріарха Московського і всієї Русі Алексія II та Священного Синоду Руської Православної Церкви" [Appeal of the episcopate of the Ukrainian Orthodox Church to His Holiness Alexy II, patriarch of Moscow and all Russia and the Holy Synod of the Russian Orthodox Church]. *Православний вісник* 10 (October 1990): 1–2.

Ukrainian Orthodox Church of Canada. *Ювілейна книга на пошану Митрополита Іларіона* [Jubilee book in honor of Metropolitan Hilarion). Winnipeg, MB: Trident Press, 1958.

Ukrainian Orthodox Church of the USA. "Decision Reached by Joint Meeting of the Committees." June 8, 2015. Accessed September 15, 2016. http://uocofusa.org/news_150609_1.html.

Ul'ianovs'kyi, Vasyl'. *Церква в Українській державі 1917–1920 рр.* [The church in the Ukrainian republic in the years 1917–1920]. Kyiv: Lybid', 1997.

"УАПЦ не йде на компроміс з УПЦ КП щодо умов об'єднання" [The UAOC will not compromise with the UOC KP on the conditions of union]. RISU: Religious Information Service of Ukraine, July 10, 2015. Accessed September 15, 2016. http://risu.org.ua/ua/index/all_news/confessional/orthodox_relations/60495/.

"UOC-MP Hierarchs Concerned about Constantinople's Activity in Ukraine." RISU: Religious Information Service of Ukraine. June 24, 2015. Accessed October 7, 2016. http://risu.org.ua/en/index/all_news/confessional/orthodox_relations/60350/.

"УПЦ МП перепросила УПЦ КП за розгром 'козаками' храму в Перевальному" [The UOC MP apologized to the UOC KP on account of the defeat of the "Cossacks" temple in Pereval]. LV.ua. June 2, 2014. Accessed September 9, 2016. http://ukr.lb.ua/news/2014/06/02/268563_upts_mp_izvinilas_pered_upts_kp.html.

Vasyl' (Lypkivs'kyi). *Історія Української Православної Церкви*. Vol. 7, *Відродження Української Церкви* [History of the Ukrainian Orthodox Church. Vol. 7, Rebirth of the Ukrainian Church]. Winnipeg, MB: Fund of Ivan Hryshshuk, 1961.

——. *Листи, 1933–1937* [Letters, 1933–1937]. N.p.: Ukr. Pravoslavne bratstvo im. Mytr. Vasylia Lypkivs'koho, 1980.

——. *Проповіді на неділі й свята, слово Христове до Українського народу* [Sermons on Sundays and holy days, the word of Christ to the Ukrainian people]. New York: Ukr. Pravoslavne bratstvo im. Mytr. Vasylia Lypkivs'koho, 1988.

Verkhovsky, Aleksandr. "The Role of the Russian Orthodox Church in Nationalist, Xenophobic and Antiwestern Tendencies in Russia Today: Not Nationalism, but Fundamentalism." *Religion, State and Society* 30, no. 4 (2002): 333–45.

Vetochnikov, Konstantinos. "La 'concession' de la metropole de Kiev au patriarche de Moscou en 1686: Analyse canonique." Paper presented at the Twenty-Third International Congress of Byzantine Studies, Belgrade, August 22–27, 2016.

"Відповіді митрополита Львівського і тернопільського Николая на запитання кореспондента газети Українські вісті" [Responses of Metropolitan Nikolai of L'viv and Ternopil to the questions of the correspondent of the newspaper *Ukrainian news*]. *Православний вісник* 4 (April 1972): 24–26.

Vlasovs'kyi, Ivan. *Нарис історії Української Православної Церкви* [Outline History of the Ukrainian Orthodox Church]. Vol. 4. 2nd edition. New York: Ukrainian Autocephalous Orthodox Church, 1990.

——. *Outline History of the Ukrainian Orthodox Church*. Vol. 1, *The Baptism of Ukraine to the Union of Berestye (988–1596)*. New York: Ukrainian Orthodox Church of the USA, 1956.

——. *Outline History of the Ukrainian Orthodox Church*. Vol. 2, *XVII Century*. Edited by Ivan Korowytsky. Translated by Mykola Haydak and Frank Estocin. New York: Ukrainian Orthodox Church of the USA, 1979.

Volodymyr (Sabodan). *Доповіді, звернення, промови* [Lectures, correspondence, and speeches]. Kyiv: Fond pam'iati Blazhennishoho Mytropolyta Volodymyra, 2014.

Voronyn, Oleksander. *Історичний шлях УАПЦ* [Historical path of the UAOC]. Kensington, MD: Voskresinnia, 1992.

Ware, Kallitos. "'Neither Jew nor Greek': Catholicity and Ethnicity." *St. Vladimir's Theological Quarterly* 57, nos. 3–4 (2013): 235–46.

Wasyly (Fedak). *Keynote Address to the 16th Sobor of the Ukrainian Greek-Orthodox Church of Canada, July 1980*. Winnipeg, MB: Ecclesia, 1982.

Wawrzonek, Michał. *Religion and Politics in Ukraine: The Orthodox and Greek Catholic Churches as Elements of Ukraine's Political System*. Newcastle, UK: Cambridge Scholars Publishing, 2014.

"Харківсько-Полтавська єпархія УАПЦ на чолі з Єпископом Ігорем (Ісіченком) продовжує об'єднавчий процес а УГКЦ" [The Kharkiv-Poltava eparchy of the UAOC with Bishop Ihor (Isichenko) continues the unification process with the UGCC]. Accessed October 21, 2016. RISU: Religious Information Service of Ukraine, April 21, 2016, http://risu.org.ua/ua/index/all_news/orthodox/uapc/63151/.

Yelensky, Viktor. "State Program of Celebrations of 1025th Anniversary Is a Humiliation for Millions of Ukrainian Christians and It Further Divides the Country." RISU: Religious Information Service of Ukraine. July 26, 2013. Accessed October 8, 2015. http://risu.org.ua/en/index/expert_thought/interview/53128.

Yereniuk, Roman. *A Short Historical Outline of the Ukrainian Orthodox Church of Canada (UOCC) on the Occasion of the 90th Anniversary of the Church (1918–2008)*. Winnipeg, MB: Ecclesia, 2008.

Yuzyk, Paul. *The Ukrainian Greek Orthodox Church of Canada, 1918–1951*. Ottawa, ON: University of Ottawa, 1981.

Zhivov, Victor. "Архиерейское обещание: Эволюция текста в России XV–XVIII веков и проблемы церковной истории" [Hierarchical promise: The evolution of the text in Russia in the fifteenth to seventeenth centuries and problems of church history]. In *Православное учение о церковных таинствах*. Vol. 2, *Евхаристия: Богословие священство* [Orthodox teaching on church sacraments: Eucharist, theology, priesthood] edited by Mikhail Zheltov, 365–86. Moscow: Sinodal'naia bibleisko-bogoslovskaia komissiia, 2009.

————. "The Question of Ecclesiastical Jurisdiction in Russian-Ukrainian Relations (Seventeenth and Early Eighteenth Centuries)." In *Culture, Nation, and Identity: The Ukrainian-Russian Encounter, 1600–1945*, edited by Andreas Kappeler, Zenon E. Kohut, Frank E. Sysyn, and Mark von Hagen, 1–18. Edmonton, AB: Canadian Institute of Ukrainian Studies, 2003.

Zinchenko, Arsen. *Визволитися вірою: Життя і діяння митрополита Василя Липківського* [Deliverance through faith: The life and activity of Metropolitan Vasyl Lypkivs'kyi]. Kyiv: Dnipro Publishing, 1997.

Zinkewich, Osyp, and Oleksander Voronyn, eds. *Мартирологія Українських Церков*. Vol. 1, *Українська Православна Церква* [Martyrology of the Ukrainian Churches. Vol. 1, The Ukrainian Orthodox Church]. Baltimore, MD: Smoloskyp, 1987.

Index

Unia, 146; and life in Soviet Ukraine, 150; and Metropolitan Oleksii, 91; and Moscow Patriarchate (MP), 135–136, 157–158; and Mstyslav's health, 164–165; and National Ukrainian Millennium Committee, 121; and 1942 UAOC, 179; and 1946 L'viv council, 158, 218; and ordination rites, 80, 101; and Orthodox patriarchate in Kyiv, 164; and Patriarch Pimen, 156; and Patriarch Tikhon, 60; and peoples of Kyivan Rus', 145; of Poland, 49, 59–70, 83, 91; and reception of 1921 UAOC clergy, 81; and relationship with state, 90–91, 153; and Renovationist Church, 53; and rite of bishop's consecration, 43–45; and rite of episcopal consecration, 101; and Roman Catholic Church, 157; Rus' Orthodox Church, 147; and Slavic nations, 146; Slavic Orthodox churches, 66; Soviet persecution of, 148, 159; and Soviet state's absence, 53, 55; and Soviet Union, 152–153, 157; and synods of bishops, 43, 60; and teaching of Alexander Schmemann, 116; and tsarism, 51; and Ukrainian Churches, 3, 5, 40, 47, 48, 49, 51, 52, 53–54, 59, 60, 64, 70–83, 90–94, 120, 124, 161–170, 207, 209–210; and Uniatism, 149–150; and unity of Kyiv and Moscow, 158; in the West, 92. *See also* autocephaly; Orthodox Church in America (OCA); Poland, Church in; Russian Orthodox Church; Ukrainian Autocephalous Orthodox Church (UAOC); Ukrainian Orthodox Churches

Orthodox Church in America (OCA), 112, 128, 138, 148

Parfenii (Levitsky), (Archbishop), 28–29
Petliura, Symon, 22, 23
Pimen, Patriarch, 21, 103, 110–112, 115, 119, 127, 130. *See also* Moscow Patriarchate (MP)
Platon (Rozhdestvenskii), (Metropolitan), 20
Platon, Bishop, 99, 101
Pochaiv Unification Council (1942), 59, 70–76, 77, 82, 83–87
Poland: autocephalous churches in, 222; and Church in Poland, 66, 67, 68, 75; as a communist state, 91; Galicia as part of, 59, 94; and Greek-Catholic Church, 59–60, 136; and Ivan (Ohienko), 66; and Metropolitan Dionysii (Valedynsky), 60, 61, 62, 64, 65, 83, 89; and Moscow Patriarchate (MP), 60, 64; multinational church of, 61, 65; and Orthodox Church, 5, 9, 49, 59–69;

Orthodox populations of, 59–60, 66, 68, 136; and religious identity, 157; and rule of Ukraine, 89, 146; and Russian influence in Church, 62, 65; synod of bishops in, 60–61, 62; *tomos* of autocephaly for, 65, 66–69; and Ukrainization, 92; and World War II deaths, 94

Poland, Church in: and apostolic succession, 103; and autocephaly, 66–69, 76, 92, 111, 120, 138, 153; and election of metropolitan of Kyiv, 72; and Kyivan Metropolia, 67, 68; and Metropolitan Dionysii (Valedynsky), 66, 70, 72, 73, 79, 82, 111; and Moscow Patriarchate (MP), 66, 67, 92, 138, 142, 157; and 1924 *tomos* of autocephaly, 128, 129, 217; and 1942 UAOC, 79, 83and Orthodox Ukrainians, 60, 65, 67; and Patriarch Tikhon, 66; and Pochaiv meetings, 73; and Ukrainian Autocephalous Orthodox Church (UAOC), 67, 70, 76; and Ukrainian identity, 141; and Volyn' eparchy, 69, 71

Poroshenko, Petro, 4, 198
Prelovs'ka, Iryna, 8
Putin, Vladimir, 190, 195, 220

Reagan, Ronald, 121–122
religion: and atheism, 156; and Catholicism, 3, 6, 95–96, 97, 136–138; and church renewal, 7, 8, 15, 16, 17, 47; and church's local dimension, 36; and democratic political theology, 9–10; and Greek translations of Gospels, 36; and Islam, 3, 208; and Judaism, 3, 94, 208; and liberation theology, 38; and limits of episcopal power, 26; and modern nation-state, 5; and monothelitism, 39; and Moscow Patriarchate (MP), 192; and Mother of God, 106; and national consciousness, 37; and Nicene Creed, 179; and Orthodox Christianity, 3–4, 5, 95–96; and political theologies, 10, 51, 54–55, 59, 106–109, 118, 133, 159; and Presbyterians, 95; and Protestantism, 3, 74, 121; and public religious identities, 8–9, 10–11, 13, 19, 24, 26, 46, 51, 54–55, 105, 184, 195, 197; and rebirth, 38, 79; and religious freedom, 106, 109, 118, 122, 133, 138, 139, 142, 143, 155, 159; and religious pluralism, 3, 13, 109, 204; and role of laity, 7, 23, 74; and Roman Catholics, 96, 97; and sacraments, 38, 42, 75, 80, 103, 115, 139, 191, 196; and saints, 25, 170; and secularism, 28; and Ukrainian periodicals, 66, 145–147; and Uniatism, 136,

145, 147, 149, 150, 152, 165, 191, 192. *See also* identity

Romaniuk, Vasyl, 142–143, 162

Russia: and annexation of Crimea, 219; and annexation of Kyiv, 13; autocephalous churches in, 222; and bishops' role, 28, 40, 55; and church as state's organ, 28; and church renewal, 7, 17, 54; and church structure, 210–211; and commitment to Soviet Union, 125; and Cossack rebellions, 6; and council of 1917, 55; and creation of Ukrainian Church, 16–17; and Empress Catherine II, 6; and federation with Ukraine, 22; former empire of, 16, 17, 53; Georgia in, 29; and Greek translations of Gospels, 36; imperial past of, 50; and Ivan Mazepa, 21–22, 65; and Kyivan Rus', 146; and Moscow, 9, 27, 33, 37, 39, 41, 49, 53, 55, 68, 72, 118, 129, 152, 163, 164, 170; and Moscow Council of 1917–18, 7, 17–19, 24, 32; and Moscow Patriarchate (MP), 3, 7, 130, 174, 185, 193, 210, 213; and Orthodox Church, 3, 7, 17, 41, 53; Orthodox eparchies of, 28; and Peter I's Spiritual Regulation, 17, 210; political turmoil in, 7, 16, 17, 18, 54; and recreation of patriarchate, 210; and reunification with Ukraine, 89; and Russian World strategy, 187; and Russification, 6–7; and tsars, 6, 7, 21, 37–38, 54, 210, 217; and Ukraine, 144, 145–146, 197, 198–199, 217; and World War II deaths, 94. *See also* nationalism; Putin, Vladimir; Russian Orthodox Church; Soviet Union (USSR)

Russian Orthodox Church: and anniversary of October Revolution, 154; and autocephaly, 171–172, 186; autocracy of, 125; and baptism of Rus', 154; Bishops' Council of, 3; and Byzantine Orthodoxy, 210; and Canon 10 of Oct. Council, 41; and Church in Poland, 66; and church renewal, 17, 52, 210; and conflict with Ukrainian Church, 42, 168; and ecclesial legitimacy, 42; and Ecumenical Patriarchate (EP), 106; laity's involvement in, 17; and Maidan crisis, 191–193; and Metropolitan Filaret (Denysenko), 110, 154–155; and millennium celebration, 154; and Moscow Patriarchate (MP), 17, 42, 110, 142, 149; and nationalism, 166; outside of Russia, 104, 142, 148, 154; and Patriarch Tikhon, 18, 153; peacemaking goal of, 154; and socialism, 153; in Ukraine, 36, 65; and Ukrainian autocephalists as illegitimate, 111;

and Ukrainians, 6, 17, 30, 41, 95–96, 97, 128; and unity of Kyiv and Moscow, 152; and USSR, 152–153

Saint Andrew's Cathedral, 27, 79

Saint Andrew's Memorial Church, 105, 106, 107–109, 115, 162, 219

Saint Nicholas Cathedral, 25, 27, 107

Saint Sophia's Cathedral, 21, 24, 25, 33, 107, 163, 179

Serbia, 3, 5, 13, 66, 198

Sergei, Metropolitan, 70, 218

Shevchenko, Taras, 6–7, 37, 107

Shlikhta, Natalia, 10

Skrypnyk, Stepan, 57, 64, 88

Slovakia, 66

sobornopravnist' (governance by council): and American church, 103; and Archbishop Ilarion (Ohienko), 74; and Bishop-Elect Ilarion, 63; and Canadian church, 103, 117, 118, 124, 125; and ecclesiology, 214–215; and identity, 54; and Metropolitan Ilarion (Ohienko), 100; promotion of, 56; restoration of, 125; and rite of bishop's consecration, 45; and Ukrainian church, 28, 42, 45–47, 48, 50, 51, 56, 93, 103, 104, 162, 164; and Western democratic values, 6, 130

Sokolowsky, Ksenofont, 39–40

Sophronius, 38–39

Soviet Union (USSR): and annexation of West Ukraine, 136, 156; and anniversary of October Revolution, 153–154; anti-religious policy of, 55, 75, 77, 89, 92, 135, 139–140, 142, 143–144, 155–156, 159; and autocephaly, 54, 55, 66, 72, 74, 82; Bolsheviks of, 7, 24, 41, 53, 70, 71, 77, 79, 82, 89, 106, 218; and Church in Poland, 66; and church unity, 10; Cold War environment in, 153; collapse of, 122, 132, 133, 143, 163, 186, 207; and control of Ukrainian church property, 35; and creation of Ukrainian Church, 54; and defeat of Nazi Germany, 135, 146, 152, 153, 156, 218; and demands of freedom for churches, 121; and deposition of Archbishop Policarp, 73; and Ecumenical Patriarchate (EP), 114; and Galicia, 146; German invasion of, 75; and independent republics, 186; KGB of, 91; and Khrushchev, 94, 139; and Kyivan Rus', 152; and liquidation of Greek-Catholic Church, 10, 69; and liquidation of UAOC, 43, 50–53, 56–57; and Metropolitan Sergei (Stragorodsky), 91; and millennium